# WHATEVER HAPPENED TO THE ISLAMISTS?

OLIVIER ROY
AMEL BOUBEKEUR

(*Editors*)

# Whatever Happened to the Islamists?

*Salafis, Heavy Metal Muslims
and the Lure of Consumerist Islam*

Columbia University Press
New York

Columbia University Press
*Publishers Since 1893*
New York
cup.columbia.edu
© Olivier Roy, Amel Boubekeur, 2012
All rights reserved

Library of Congress Cataloging-in-Publication Data

Whatever happened to the Islamists? : Salafis, heavy metal Muslims and
the lure of consumerist Islam / Olivier Roy, Amel Boubekeur (editors).
    p. cm.
Includes bibliographical references and index.
ISBN 978-0-231-15426-0 (alk. paper)
ISBN 978-0-231-80115-7 (e-book)
1. Islam and politics. 2. Salafiyah. 3. Islam and secularism.
I. Roy, Olivier. II. Boubekeur, Amel.

BP173.7.W43 2012
320.55'7—dc23

2012003970

∞

Columbia University Press books are printed on permanent and durable
acid-free paper. This book is printed on paper with recycled content.
Printed in India

c 10 9 8 7 6 5 4 3 2 1

# CONTENTS

# ABOUT THE CONTRIBUTORS

**MOHAMED MOSAAD ABDEL AZIZ** teaches religion at the Department of Comparative Cultural Studies, Northern Arizona University. His research focuses on new trends within the Muslim Brotherhood in Egypt, such as blogging. He is also a PhD candidate at the Department of Religious Studies, Emory University. His dissertation is entitled 'A New Theoretical Approach to Islamism: The Muslim Brotherhood Group in Egypt'.

**AMEL BOUBEKEUR** is a research fellow at the Ecole des Hautes Etudes en Sciences Sociales and the Ecole Normale Supérieure in Paris, a research associate at the Maghreb Center in Washington, DC and at the Centre Jacques Berque in Rabat. Her research focuses on European Islam and Maghreb politics. Previously she has been an associate scholar at the Carnegie Middle East Center in Beirut and the head of the Islam and Europe Programme at the Centre for European Policy Studies in Brussels. She is the author of *Civil resistance and changing politics in post-uprisings North Africa (Forthcoming, 2012), European Islam: Challenges for Public Policy and Society* (CEPS, 2007) and *Le Voile de la Mariée: Jeunes Musulmanes, Voile et Projet Matrimonial en France* (L'Harmattan, 2004).

**VALENTINA FRATE** is a PhD student in sociology at the EHESS in Paris. She has undertaken field research in Egypt with the support of the former director of the CEDEJ in Cairo, Alain Roussillon. Since 2009 she has been working for a European project called *Europublicislam*.

**MARTIJN DE KONING** is a postdoctoral fellow at Radboud University on the 'Salafism: Production, Distribution, Consumption and Transformation of a Transnational Ideology in the Middle East and Europe' project, funded by the NWO. He focuses on the demand side of religious knowledge by exploring how young Muslims actively engage with the writings of major religious leaders of the different Salafi currents in the Middle East and their representatives in the Netherlands.

**MARK LEVINE** is professor of Modern Middle Eastern history at UC Irvine and a distinguished visiting professor at the CMES, Lund University Sweden. His books include *Heavy Metal Islam: Rock, Resistance, and the Struggle for the Soul of Islam* (Random House, 2009), *Impossible Peace: Israel/Palestine Since 1989* (Zed Books, 2009), *Why They Don't Hate Us: Lifting the Veil on the Axis of Evil* (Oneworld, 2005), and *Overthrowing Geography: Jaffa, Tel Aviv and the Struggle for Palestine, 1880–1948* (UC Press, 2005), as well as several forthcoming volumes for UC Press. He is a columnist for al-Jazeera International.

**JEAN MARCOU** is a professor at the Grenoble Institute of Political Studies, France. He was previously a senior researcher at the French Institute of Anatolian Studies in Istanbul (*IFEA—Institut Français d'Etudes Anatoliennes—Turkey*) where he managed the Observatory of the Turkish Political Life (Observatoire de la Vie Politique Turque—*OVIPOT*). He was also the director of the French Section of the Faculty of Economics and Political Science of the University of Cairo (Egypt) from 2000 to 2006. His main fields of research address Turkish political life (such as constitutions, elections and political parties) and the evolution of the balance of powers in the Middle East (Turkish foreign policy especially).

**ROEL MEIJER** teaches Middle Eastern history at Radboud University in Nijmegen and is senior researcher, at the Institute of International Relations, Clingendael. He wrote his PhD on Egyptian intellectuals, *The Quest for Modernity: Secular Liberal and Left-wing Political Thought in Egypt, 1945–1958* (Routledge, 2002). He is editor of six anthologies, among them *Cosmopolitanism, Identity and Authenticity in the Middle East* (Routledge, 1999), *Alienation or Integration of Arab Youth: Arab Youth between the Family, the State and the Street* (Routledge, 2000), and the latest, *Global Salafism: Islam's New*

*Religious Movement* (Hurst, 2009) and *The Muslim Brotherhood in Europe: Burdens of the Past, Challenges of the Future* (Hurst, 2012). He is currently writing a book about religious and national identity in Saudi Arabia.

**OLIVIER ROY** is one of the most distinguished analysts of and commentators on political Islam in the Muslim Middle East and Central Asia and on comparative religions. He is professor at the European at the European University Institute in Florence and author of several highly acclaimed books, including *The Politics of Chaos in the Middle East, Globalised Islam*, and *Holy Ignorance*, all of which are published by Hurst.

**PATRICIA SLOANE-WHITE** is an assistant professor of anthropology at the University of Delaware. Her research concerns Islamic capitalists and the Islamic workplace. She was recently awarded a senior research Fulbright fellowship to study the Islamic economy in Malaysia. The author of *Islam, Modernity and Entrepreneurship among the Malays* (Palgrave Macmillan, 1999), she has published numerous articles on middle-class culture and piety and the urban work lives of Malaysian Muslims.

**FREDERIC VOLPI** is a senior lecturer at St Andrews University. Dr Volpi's research focuses on the interaction between Islamism, democratization and civility. He has investigated the construction of political Islam in pseudo-democratic contexts in North Africa (Algeria and Morocco) and its implications for European foreign and multicultural policy. He is the author of *Political Islam Observed: Disciplinary Perspectives* (Hurst, 2010), *Political Islam: A Critical Reader*, editor (Routledge, 2010), *Democratization in the Muslim World: Changing Patterns of Authority and Power*, editor with F. Cavatorta (Routledge, 2007), *Transnational Islam and Regional Security: Cooperation and Diversity between Europe and North Africa*, editor (Routledge, 2006), and *Islam and Democracy: The Failure of Dialogue in Algeria* (Pluto Press, 2003).

# INTRODUCTION

# WHATEVER HAPPENED TO THE ISLAMISTS OR ... POLITICAL ISLAM ITSELF?

*Amel Boubekeur and Olivier Roy*

'Islamism' or 'political Islam',[1] the political, cultural and religious projects that emerged in the 1930s and made a breakthrough in the late 70s and 80s with the Iranian Islamic Revolution, the Afghan Mujahidin movement, the surge of Hizbullah in Lebanon, Hamas in Palestine and FIS in Algeria,[2] were initially perceived to be driven only by authoritarian, angry, and fundamentalist-inspired religious radicals determined to ensure the destruction of modernity, capitalism and Western society and culture.[3] From the 1990s onwards some scholars insisted on the shift of many Islamist movements towards a kind of 'Islamic democracy' supporting coalitions and pluralistic elections, while Western public opinion was still identifying political Islam as a modern form of fascism and Nazism,[4] or with any kind of radical violence expressed by Muslim militants, thus blurring the lines between actors as various as the Muslim Brothers, the Taliban and al-Qaeda. But fixing Islamists either as a spontaneous illustration of Muslim politics in the context of a nascent identitarian Muslim Democracy or as totalitarian conquerors only ignores the depth of changes that these actors as well as Muslim civil societies have been experiencing over the

1

last decade in their use of political Islam. The Islamist electoral victories that have followed the 2011 uprisings in North Africa and the Middle East have shown us how political Islam can be mobilized in different ways. On the part of Tunisian and Egyptian civil societies, voting for Islamist parties was, in a post-authoritarian context, motivated more by a hope to see the fulfillment of promises of moral politics, the fighting of corruption, economic redistribution, reconciliation and social justice, rather than by an adhesion to discourses on Shari'a and the need for creating new Islamic institutions. On the ruling elite's side, favoring the victory of non-challenging Islamist parties, like the pro-monarchy Justice and Development Party in Morocco, has been a way to organize political transitions without losing control. As for Islamists themselves, when they (latterly) joined the demonstrations against the regimes all over the Arab world, they were careful not to restrict their revolutionary narratives to just their vision of political Islam. They understood that they should not prioritise their affiliation to a specific party or only be in sympathy with their usual followers in order to gain legitimacy. By inscribing their actions in the global reformist promises of Arab revolutions they have been able to play down their inability to launch the proper Islamic revolution they have been talking about for ages. But in doing so, they have also de facto contributed to the disembedding of political Islam from simple oppositional strategies, a situation that is bringing them new challenges. Those who have accessed power have not yet fundamentally challenged previous governance practices nor invented new Islamic ways to govern. With the rising visibility of new competitive forms of political Islam, such as newly politicized salafi or a conservative youth who have come back to Islam and do not want to be linked with any partisan structure, we are now seeing unprecedented levels of complexity and pluralization of the field of political Islam, which may multiply generational and internal structural conflicts that Islamists will have more and more problems in managing.

Beyond the usual interpretations of political Islam as being limited to traditional Islamist discourses, this volume focuses on the ideological and cultural transformations this ideology has been through these past ten years and how new forms of political Islam are entering ordinary Muslims' everyday lives.

How do we then evaluate the modern trajectory of Islamism and the changing nature of Islamist movements across the Muslim world? What has happened to the Islamists who have held such a prominent place in the religious and political arena in the Muslim world for almost a century?

While the title of this book is 'Whatever Happened to the Islamists?' it is perhaps more accurate to think of this compilation as an assessment of the ways in which the ideology of political Islam, like all other ideologies, has gradually evolved over time towards more modern social, cultural, economic and institutional ways of using Islam politically. The authors look beyond traditional Islamist movements, and examine how individuals are now using the ideology and codes created by early Islamists to mobilize, organize and make sense of the world around them. The new forms of networks and partnerships that are emerging between politicized Islamic actors are examined, and some conclusions about the future direction of Islamism as a historical and political project are drawn out.

*Definition of Terms: Islamism, Neo-fundamentalism
and Post-Islamism*

Scholars have long been preoccupied with describing the phenomenon of political Islam, and have employed a variety of terms and labels to create a theoretical framework for categorizing Islamist movements. This panoply of terminology includes: 'fundamentalism', 'radical Islam', 'militant Islam', 'political Islam'[6] and 'Islamism'. Academics have also tried to capture the changing nature of Islamism as a political ideology by using a host of additional qualifying labels, such as 'neo', 'post', 'failure', and 'decline'. It is therefore important to begin with a basic definition of terms: What do we mean when we refer to 'Islamism', 'neo-fundamentalism' and 'post-Islamism'? Until recently, 'Islamism' mainly referred to the ideology that employs Islam as a tool for political action. Islamism claims to recreate a true Islamic society, not simply by imposing the Shari'a, but also by establishing an Islamic state through political means.[7] Traditionally, Islamism's core aims were the imposition of a new moral code upon civil society and the inversion of the equilibrium of the political forces. 'Islamists' are those who view

Islam not merely as a religion, but also as a complete system with a set of cultural codes, legal structures, economic arrangements and political ideologies that should be integrated into all aspects of society. For the Islamists, the Islamic State should attempt to recreate the 'golden age' of the first decades of Islam by uniting the ummah and superseding tribal, ethnic and national divides. Islamism is a historical phenomenon which emerged in the late nineteenth century as a result of the influential religio-political writings of Jamal al-Din al-Afghani (1839–1897), Muhammad Abduh (1849–1905), Rashid Rida (1865–1935), Sayyid Qutb (1906–1966), and Hasan al-Banna (1906–1949), who established the influential Society of Muslim Brothers in Egypt in 1928.[8] Originally a movement consisting largely of Arab reformist intellectuals, Islamism focused upon utilizing Islam to confront Western economic and political domination and on overcoming the decline of colonized Islamic societies. Later, Islamism was conceived of as an alternative to other ideologies that had developed in the Arab world, such as pan-Arab nationalism.[9] Islamism experienced an upsurge in the early 1970s as a language of self-assertion to mobilize those largely middle class citizens who felt marginalized by the dominant economic, political or cultural processes in their societies.[10] This second generation of post-colonial Islamist activists conceived of Islamism in a more overt political competition forming political parties and sought to participate in national electoral politics. Yet, Islamist movements also met severe repression from Arab regimes bent on retaining their political power during the 1970s, 1980s and 1990s. Arab leaders developed myriad tools for eliminating, co-opting and neutralizing the Islamist opposition.[11]

By the mid-1990s it became clear that Islamists were not succeeding in their attempt to establish a revolutionary Islamic polity and economy. In addition to being forced to cope with various forms of systematic repression, Islamist movements also had difficulty maintaining their ideological and political appeal in the changing globalized world. For a lot of Muslim citizens the idea of the creation of an Islamic state was no longer an option. As new generations of Muslims began experiencing a de-territorialization of Islam[12]—with Islam becoming more disconnected from a specific historical and geographical context—they reinvented Islamist ideology and adapted historical Islamist codes and traditions to fit their new settings. Some turned to new religious revivalist paths, such as 'neo-fundamentalism'.[13] Neo-fundamentalists do not identify with any particular nation state and are transnational and global in nature, using the notion of the ummah. Neo-fundamentalism is less concerned with purely political issues targeted by Islamists, and rather focused on the spirituality of individual believers. One particularly influential group within this category of neo-fundamentalism are the Salafis, those who are inspired by the exemplary models of the first generations of pious ancestors who succeeded the Prophet in the early Islamic period, as opposed to the Islamist ideals developed in the early twentieth century.[14] Modern Salafis criticize Islamist movements for utilizing Western political tools[15] and trying to reform Islam in line with Western modernity. They consider the majority of the political concessions and evolutions on the question of identity that the Islamists have undertaken, to be unacceptable alterations of the tradition of the Prophet.[16]

In addition to 'neo-fundamentalism', a new category has recently emerged in scholarship, that of 'post-Islamism'.[17] Throughout the 1990s old Islamist revolutionaries renounced earlier radical ideas and departed from their sometimes violent methods, lamenting the danger of the idea of the religious state to both religion and the state and developing a more pluralistic vision for their Islamic projects. Islamism shifted towards practical and ideological compromises vis-à-vis politics.[18] The emergence in the mid-1990s of al-Wasat party in Egypt as an alternative to both militant Islamists and the Muslim Brothers or the pluralism of Islamic parties in Turkey (the split of the Refah Party between the Sa'adat Party and Justice and Development Party) signaled the rise of 'post-Islamism'. A 'post-Islamist' society is one in which the Islamist parenthesis has profoundly altered relationships between Islam and politics, but did not lead to a renewed call for an Islamic State.[19] Whereas Islamism marks the over-politicization of religion, post-Islamism seeks new autonomous spaces and means of expression beneath party politics.[20]

While this narrative posits a gradual transition from Islamism to options of neo-fundamentalism or post-Islamism, it also represents an attempt to capture the changing dynamics of Islamist movements across time. The use of the terms 'neo' and 'post' are not meant to imply the abrupt end of an ideology or a complete rupture with the past.[21] A host of observers have pointed out that, especially given the Islamists' limited opportunity to exercise political power in the face of authoritarian and despotic regimes, it may be premature to write the obituary of Islamism and declare the beginning of a post-Islamist period.[22] Indeed, Islamist activists are not monolithic, and Islamist movements are dynamic and constantly evolving, engaged in a continuous process of redefining themselves over time. Islamist actors are agents of their societies and cultures, and as culture is not a set of static codes but a series of flexible and evolving processes, Islamists are continually shaping their politics in order to help define their own realities.[23]

It is the contention of this book that the boundaries between Islamism and post-Islamism are fluid and interconnected, bound by deep historical continuities and not by sharp ruptures. The evolution and future of Islamism must be conceived of as in continuity with Islamist tradition, rather than as a break from its historical antecedents. The use of the terms 'Islamism' and 'post-Islamism' is meant to serve primarily as an academic and theoretical tool, in order to signal change and difference. Though the chapters in this volume make it clear that there have been significant shifts in the strategies, outlooks and tactics used by Islamist groups, it is not to say that the advent of post-Islamism represents the definitive historical end of Islamism. As the initial energy and appeal of the oppositional and revolutionary Islamist project has faded, the new generation of Muslim activists is reinventing and experimenting with new forms of activism, mobilization and organizational structures. The emergence of the new discourses that are explored in this book was not only born out of the early historical Islamist experience but also draws heavily upon its codes as well as other political cultures.

## Identifying New Channels for the Political Mobilization of Islam

The world has undergone a multitude of profound global shifts since the institutional politicization of Islamist movements in the

1970s and onwards—changes which have pushed and pulled Islamist movements in different directions. The crisis of the nation-state as well as the transformation of traditional forms of authoritarian governance in the globalized era have challenged traditional conceptions of political identity and citizenship that Islamists have built and had an important impact on how religious arguments are politically mobilized.[24]

The challenge for current scholarship is thus to identify how today's Muslims, Islamists included, are responding to these immense global changes, using Islam to empower themselves in new ways, and according twenty-first century globalized and cosmopolitan politics with religious belief. Identifying new channels for the political mobilization of Islam, putting the emphasis upon the ways in which new cultural forms and social structures are impacting and influencing the way that politically-engaged Muslims are utilizing the language and codes of Islamism, forming new networks of mutual support or utilizing new modes of communication is the purpose of this book. Today political Islam is penetrating new public spaces and new individual figures are creating new political Islamic imaginaries.[25] How are we to explain the multitude of new actors using Islam to empower themselves, from Turkish Islamist entrepreneurs to young Muslim activists who attend Islamic pop concerts? Through empirical research and direct fieldwork, the authors of this volume examine the historical continuities between these new actors and the older usual forms of political Islam, charting the Islamists' path of evolution through the present. The changes in modes of religiously inspired political activism and participation that are examined in the chapters that follow can broadly be outlined in the following set of categories:

a) An Activist Culture of Consumption: The Islamic Use of New Media and Arts.

Whereas traditional Islamists relied heavily upon the ideas and writings of prominent historical religious thinkers—as well as traditional modes of preaching as tools for mobilization—modern Islamic actors are increasingly utilizing alternative modes of cultural production and communication, including various forms of new visual media and arts to build their political corpus such as the internet, satellite television, CDs and DVDs, illustrated books and pamphlets. They are producing new forms of consumer culture in order to spread their message and mobilize supporters who are consuming these Islamic cultural products with greater frequency. New media technologies, such as the internet and text messaging used, for example, to organize demonstrations, hold the benefit of being more difficult for governments to censor, and therefore present Islamists with the opportunity to distribute their message on a wider national and transnational stage. Young members of the Egyptian branch of the Muslim Brotherhood have begun to wage a new form of struggle that they term an 'e-jihad'. The Brotherhood has somewhat playfully adapted the Qur'anic concept of jihad (struggle), or the religious duty of all Muslims to struggle in the way of God and struggle to improve society, by calling on its followers to join a host of Islamic e-mail lists and visit Islamic websites in a virtual or e-jihad,[26] encouraging people to sign petitions for Islamic social causes online, or posting blog posts about relevant topics of Islamic culture and politics.

Developing Qur'anic software that can be downloaded onto mobile telephones and laptops, or marketing Qur'anic lectures on websites, audiocassettes, CDs and DVDs, certainly help "modern" Islamists to challenge traditional religious authority structures. For the consumers, watching the Egyptian televangelist preacher Amr Khaled on his satellite-broadcasted television program, or listening to the sermons of religious imams on an iPod or portable CD player represents a way to maintain their Islamic religiosity, while also continuing to watch television, use the nternet, listen to music and watch Islamic soap-operas.

This new Islamic culture of consumption rooted largely in secular codes based on the aesthetic norms of the West—on Western liberalism and competition—is bypassing traditional political issues.[27] This renewal is taking place outside the traditional codes of Islamism from the 1970s and 1980s, which were based on austerity, strict control over the body and adherence to an aesthetic of purity rooted heavily in halting the consumption of cultural products and opposition to Western culture (i.e. the rejection of certain styles of singing, writing, and artistic production seen as gratuitous and un-Islamic). Pious Muslims are rejecting the highly conservative, anti-consumer ethos associated with this form of Islamism, and instead are now embracing and trying to re-introduce an Islamic ethos into the various forms of leisure that they once shunned, including music, concerts, television, and the cinema. The old idea of the Islamist protest of cultural consumption has been replaced by pious artists who promote religious diversity as well as a commitment to the free market, consumerism and individualism in order to get empowered.

The prototypes for this new landscape of simultaneously religious and secular forms of activism are singing imams armed with both guitars and the Qur'an who have performed in French national tours;[28] Islamic hip-hop artists who rap about both spiritual and political topics;[29] Moroccan Muslim heavy metal artists who perform at large outdoor concerts and sing about issues of global concern to Muslims, such as war and peace, oppression and the lack of freedom of expression;[30] and veiled Egyptian actresses and entertainers who have repented from their previous "unislamic" careers and returned to the Egyptian artistic scene by promoting Islamic movies and television shows.[31] More than ever, new Muslim cultural actors are trying to attain a more prominent place on the global stage by creating an Islamic culture that presents itself as cool, fashionable (i.e. modern) and competitive, producing a range of specific products that have contributed to the creation of a 'cool Islam', including: Islamic streetwear, Islamic soft drinks, Muslim pop idols and even Muslim comedians.

The evolution from classical Islamism to incorporating these new forms of Islamic culture and artistic empowering mobilization is an important indicator of the recent transformation of politically engaged Muslims. They are participating in cultural production that is leaving behind traditional forms of Islamist activism representing the choice of an individual consumer.

## b) Erasing Hierarchical Structures and Islamizing businesses

Today's politically-engaged Islamic actors can no longer be considered members of religious groups in the traditional sense, as described by post-Weberian church-sect typology. Armed with various forms of new media and new cultural tools, Islamist movements are re-inventing new modes of religious belief and abandoning the traditional structures of religious hierarchy. Traditional modes of religious organization have given way to new understandings and frameworks that challenge existing social controls and accommodate self-political autonomy. Modern Islamist movements are engaged in a process of desinstitutionalization, creating decentralized networks that employ new organizational structures. The branches of the Muslim Brotherhood in Europe and the Arab world, for example, have significantly altered their original organizational posture since the 1970s and 1980s. Some form of the Brotherhood's hierarchical structure remains—the movement still organizes weekly meetings, collects monthly financial contributions and maintains formal regional chapters. However, it is rapidly becoming more decentralized: de facto members are increasingly acting as individuals, rather than taking instructions from a central decision-making authority. Individual members are opening their own social and cultural business units, such as publishing houses, multimedia companies, human rights organizations, law firms, research centers, schools and charity organizations without doing so under the name of a party.

Outside of the traditional Islamist matrices, non-classical political figures such as Islamic entrepreneurs are trying to create an 'Islamic economy' driven by 'Islamic corporations'. For example, young Malaysian company directors are trying to 'rebrand' old forms of political Islam into a global corporate force by integrating it into their businesses. Malaysia's pious Muslims are now becoming prominent businessmen by integrating traditional Qur'anic concepts into their corporate culture. Not only are these actors employing fully Shari'a compliant financing into their businesses, but they are also integrating the concept of *shura*, by promoting regular mutual consultations and discussions between employees, and *zakat*, by engaging in Islamic philanthropy, charity and corporate giving into their business models.[32]

c) The Changing Nature of Political Involvement: Do Islamists Still Want to Create an Islamic State and why Salafi are getting repoliticized?

Today's Islamist movements are also focusing more explicitly upon cultural and social goals. Some have even abandoned the goal of a radical transformation of the political system and the overtaking of the state. Yet while their goals are often more limited in scope, these mobilized Muslims should not be viewed as apolitical or as abandoning their political goals altogether. They have altered the early priorities of political Islam and, in many cases, now legitimize state authority for pragmatic reasons, but they still challenge the state and seek to engage in politics and overcome sources of oppression in new ways. They accept elections, not just to win, but also as a way to manage a diverse political scene and they accept coalition governments with secular forces. For example, after an extended Islamic religious revival took hold in West Africa in the 1970s—a resurgence which ultimately envisioned the creation of an Islamic state—a significant change occurred in the 1990s, and the leaders of many West African Islamic movements no longer seek involvement in politics in the traditional sense; they now participate in political activities outside of party politics. While these movements continue to oppose government policy, they have also realized that they need the state support, and they therefore respect the rules laid out by the existing political system.[33]

While traditional Islamists tend to be portrayed as explicitly political in their outlook, Salafi movements have often been seen as cultural movements without a clear political program, but even that categorization is beginning to change. 'Traditional' Wahhabi movements were not involved in political negotiations with states, and some claimed to be movements of piety rather than movements with a political aim. Yet, modern Dutch Salafi movements in Amsterdam, for example, have started engaging in politics in new ways, adjusting their language and strategies in a way that accommodates Dutch secular society. Since the 1990s and with increasing speed post-9/11, the different branches of Salafism in the Netherlands have become increasingly engaged in the Dutch political scene, attempting to influence the power structures in society by collective action. While the Dutch Salafi organizations do not tend to participate in public political demonstrations, they have engaged in the politics of 'resistance' and 'distinction', trying to transform the oppressive structures of society and build up their position as the only legitimate representatives of Islam in the Netherlands.[34] The repoliticization of Salafi groups in Egypt and Tunisia through their involvement in post-revolutionary electoral processes also provides us with an opportunity to understand how political Islam can be displayed differently according to new political environments. The role of violence in contemporary Islamist movements has also evolved significantly from the groups who garnered international attention for their use of assassinations, bombings, and armed military struggle. As the political goals of Islamist movements have shifted, and the demographic profile of their followers has changed, with the rise of a modern professional class that is influenced by a more cultural form of Islam than preoccupied with ideological goals, their relationship to violence has evolved in turn. Some movements, like the Egyptian branch of the Muslim Brotherhood, have rejected violence entirely, adopted a new discourse of pluralism, tolerance, cooperation and co-existence, and now participate in political party-politics. Still other movements, like the Syrian branch of the Muslim Brotherhood and the Egyptian Gama'at al-Islamiyya legitimized and advocated the use of violence in the past, but have now changed course, revising their past outlooks by ejecting violence and accepting revisionism, tolerance and moderation.[35]

## Islamism in a Globalized World: A New Part of the Global Political Culture

The process through which the traditional Islamist movements have transitioned to today's post-Islamist forms of political Islam has been non-linear. As politically-engaged Muslims connect with the problems of identity in a constantly changing world, they have adapted the Islamic codes and social and cultural practices of political elders to fit the modern era. The changes recently experienced by Islamists are indeed directly linked to the way globalization has challenged traditional political boundaries.[36] Their participation in cosmopolitan societies has shifted their traditional Islamic/Western divides, pushed individuals' interpretations of political Islam ahead and forced them to redraw the traditional forms of their organizations.[37] The globalization of political Islam and its divorce from any particular culture[38] has created transnational politically active Muslim identities which made it possible to say that Islamism has now become a fixed part of the global political culture and history.

Today's Islamists are clearly drawing from a globalized political patrimony and its notions of democracy, competitiveness, solidarity and equity in order to redefine what modern political Islam should be. Thus, today's Islamists reveal that ideologies, as constructed sets of meanings and interpretations that provide us with a program for social and political action,[39] are constantly being transformed and never die. In this way, Islamism has followed the path of other global ideologies that have adapted across time, such as communism or socialism. The recent events in the Middle East have already shown how Islamists are adjusting to political changes, that they are witnessing as opposed to shaping. These movements have been triggered by a younger post-Islamist generation which has used micro-politics via Facebook and social networking, not to talk about the Islamic State but to join global discourses on freedom and pluralist societies. In the face of failed party politics in the Arab world and post-September 11 fears in the West, Muslims activists who want to put forward Islam as a political marker will be forced to continue to devise new forms of social, cultural and political networks, and to develop new tools to mobilize and attract followers who are seeking what a modern Islamic political identity could be. How Islamists will adapt to continuing changes in the global landscape is the primary question for the scholarship on Islamism to address in the future.

# PART I

# WHAT HAVE OLD ISLAMIST
# IDEAS BECOME?

# 1

# IS 'ISLAMISM' A NEO-ORIENTALIST PLOT?

*Olivier Roy*

The term 'Islamism' was coined in the late 1970s by French political scientists researching the sudden rise of religious Muslim political movements, whose acme was the Iranian Islamic revolution of 1979. I must confess that I don't know who used it first. I personally borrowed it from Jean-François Clément, who pointed out to me the conspicuous use of the adjective 'Islami' by militants wishing to oppose the ideal Islamic polity to the existing Muslim society; that is, the term Muslim was used to describe a cultural and sociological affiliation to Islam, and Islami a militant commitment to turn such a Muslim society into a real Islamic one. For instance, in his book *Islamic Law and Its Introduction*, Abul A'la al-Maududi asserts that a society should not only be Muslim by 'culture', but should also be Islamic by implementing the *Shari'a* as the exclusive source of all institutional and legal systems. Maududi failed to differentiate between the two terms; he believed that ultimately a good Muslim could only support an Islamic policy. However, the emphasis he placed on defining an authentic Muslim political system; his use of the term 'Islamic ideology' (an obvious neologism); his call for an Islamic constitution; and establishing Jama'at-i Islami as a political organization, are all clear indications that, although he was careful to refer to a more traditional conception of politics among Muslim clerics (for instance the centrality of Caliphate), Maududi was thinking within the framework of the modern state: he rarely bothered to extensively quote the vast classical literature dwelling on the relations between Islam and politics. Most Islamist thinkers tend to ignore the centuries-old *ulama*'s legal and political schools of thought: starting with a reference to the first Islamic community at the time of the Prophet, the Islamists deliberately positioned their 'fundamentalism' (back to the fundamentals, that is the Qur'an and the Sunnah) as a way to break away from traditions (Maududi for instance ignored the real historical caliphates, such as the Ottoman empire, in favor of an abstract model). This 'ideologization' of Islam is also apparent in Hasan al-Banna's thought and among his followers. Neologisms like *mafkura* (ideology), *hakimiyya* (sovereignty) and, for the most radical, a 'revolution' (*sawra, inqelab*) found their way in to their frameworks. This chapter will not repeat the litany of what makes Islamism new (in short: taking modern society as a complex and differentiated entity; stressing the need to address specific social categories: '*mustazafin*' or deprived people, women, students; addressing the issue of economy, social justice, constitution, beyond the issue of a strict implementation of *Shari'a*). One must not take this to mean that traditional Muslim scholars dismissed social justice, rather they perceived such acts to be a matter of personal good practice through *zakat* and *sadaqa* as opposed to a 'state' responsibility, beyond the issue of the personal righteousness of the ruler.

Hence my definition of Islamism as the recasting of Islam into a political ideology with the aim of transforming the society through the state made sense. Nevertheless many critiques have been raised against such a use of the concept of Islamism,[1] which could be summarized as follows. Firstly the concept of Islamism artificially isolates some patterns of religious-political behaviors from a continuum both in terms of chronology and of attitudes towards religion; it constructs these patterns as a relatively autonomous sphere of political action, while in fact continuity with previous schools of thought, overlapping with more traditional forms of religiosity, irrelevance of the distinction between political action and personal devotion from the point of view of the actors, tend to void 'Islamism' of its heuristic dimension. Secondly constructing 'Islamism' around the notion of the state implies a Western perception of political action and ignores precisely the specificity of the relationship between Islam and politics.

Starting from these premises the debate on Islamism tended to become a debate on the role of social scientists, as if they were trying to conceptually harness the movements of identity-protest from Muslim societies and to provide intellectual tools to Western governments in order to curb these movements. Scholarship turned into expertise is often seen, in the post-colonial quarters of academia, as becoming a neo-orientalist tool of control which does not interact with the 'real' Muslim world.

Such criticisms point to various important issues. The issue of the relationship between political scientists and governments in the West will not be explored here. Rather, the focus will be on the relevance of the concept of Islamism with the 'reality' (an ugly notion, apparently, in social sciences). First I should say that I do accept a part of these criticisms. Indeed the concept of 'Islamism' does isolate some patterns of religious and political activism; and it is true that 'Islamism' is not the whole story. An Islamist may also be a devout believer indulging in personal and private religious practices. Islamist movements may (like the Refah Party in Turkey) or may not (as with the Muslim Brothers) primarily be a political party; within them is an important dimension of 'religious community' which cannot be ignored in favor of their exclusive political dimension. The concept of Islamism certainly stresses a process of re-Islamization of the society from above, but this does not mean that we ignore grass-roots and societal re-Islamization (or more exactly the fact that the religious markers and narratives become explicit and more visible in the public sphere, independently of the program and action of Islamist parties). 'Islamism', in my eyes, is only Islamism: an inquiry into how local actors recast contemporary movements of political protests within a new religious narrative. What I was describing was not an 'essence'—a kind of well-defined political category—but a process of politicization taking shape in a given context. The use of a practical concept to understand the specificity of a given political momentum does not suppose the perennial existence of a new category of political actors and political thought that could stand alone. Nobody can be born an Islamist, or live and die as an Islamist (except in jail). It is a term that defines a specific set of political and ideological patterns, a political practice in a specific historical context. In the contemporary historical context there is a centrality of the state, whether it has been borrowed or is the embodiment of a nation, whether or not it is legitimate, or congruent with local traditions. Even the Taliban adhere to the state. The political scene and landscape in which the Islamists deploy their activism is shaped by the state, and they must deal with the issue, regardless of whether it is a Western concept.

I have never used the term 'Islamism' to imply an equivalent for any form of politicization of Islam, and if I have authored a book entitled *The Failure of Political Islam*, it is mostly because my French publisher considered that at that time (1992) the term Islamism was not familiar enough to the public. But Islam has always been politicized. Reference to Islam in the political field is absolutely not a trademark of Islamism. I have always defined Islamism as a more precise and narrow phenomena: the explicit recasting of Islam as a political ideology (which once again does not mean that Islam ceased to be also a path for personal salvation for the Islamists) and a stress on the need to control and build an 'Islamic state'. Neo-fundamentalists, from Salafis to Taliban, have also had an impact on, and an interest in politics, as well as the jihadists going to Bosnia or Afghanistan. But they are not Islamist: they stress either *Shari'a* or the virtual *umma*. To merge under the term of 'Islamism' with any kind of contemporary Muslim militancy is nonsensical (but it is the way in which the contemporary media use this term). There is a thread connecting the Muslim Brothers, the Iranian Islamic revolution, Hamas, Hizbullah and the former Refah Party, which does not connect them to al-Qaeda or the Taliban, in terms of objectives, constituency, territorialization, conceptualization and political practices. Thus Islamism is the specific form of Islamic militancy that has engulfed the Middle East from the early 1970s. Once again there are other threads and continuities that link the Islamist movements to other forms of militancy: some of the radical Egyptian militants (or *'takfiri'*) who claimed affiliation to Sayyid Qutb split from the Muslim Brothers (as did Ayman al-Zawahiri); 'Abdullah 'Azzam, the founder of the Jihadi movement in support of the Afghan Mujahidin, was also a former Muslim Brother. Hence the choice of defining 'Islamists' by privileging some specific patterns (centrality of the state; building a grass-roots political movement, if not a party; setting up front organizations and specific branches aimed at specific audiences; considering different strategies inside a given and territorial political landscape, from armed struggle to elections and political alliances) is precisely that: these criteria allow us to have a more open and differentiated approach towards Islamic militancy. It is not just Western governments that need a more sophisticated approach to the Muslim world political landscape (it is worth noting that more often than not they simply refuse to adopt a more sophisticated approach, because it would undermine their political agenda, as is clear in the concept of the 'War on Terror'). The oxymoron on which the critics of (neo-) Orientalism build their argument is the following: they criticize the supposed neo-Orientalists either for providing a false description of Muslim societies, or for providing intelligence tools to Western governments, which means relevant analyses of the society. Each criticism might be valid, but they cannot be held together: for instance, when the American Association of Anthropologists forbade its members to brief American militaries going to Afghanistan, it supposes that anthropologists have something relevant to say, not that they are 'neo-orientalists' distorting facts to fit with the imperialist ego of the West. Conversely, if social scientists are no more than neo-Orientalists, why are they worried about tipping off the US Defense Department if it will just hasten the defeat of the US troops on the ground? I am in fact convinced that a more sophisticated approach is beneficial for most of the protagonists. It is also needed by the local actors: to blend together criticism of Israel and indiscriminate terrorism, as do many media and politicians, does not help the Palestinian people. To provide the media with a potentially more nuanced presentation of actors in the Muslim world also helps Western public opinion to gain a more accurate impression. But the social scientist should know that he or she will not dissipate the ideological mist of prejudices that characterizes public debate by 'telling the truth'; in fact his or her conceptualization is part of a more complex interactive picture where the social scientist is also an actor, an observer and a partisan.

Clearly, forging the notion of Islamism is a conceptual choice which could be justified only because of its heuristic consequences, not as a way to 'essentialize' any party. Because the concept has a history, the actors it describes also have a history: they are shaped by the events and by their own political activism. The present Turkish Prime Minister Recep Tayyip Erdogan no doubt was an Islamist when he was a young militant of the Refah Party, but his decision to build the AK Party on a different basis was not just tactical, it was because his own political practice convinced him of two things. First there was no way to impose an Islamic state on Turkey (at least without a civil war), secondly the fact that secular Kemalism was running out of steam opened the door for a new kind of political party: parliamentarian in politics, liberal in economy, conservative in terms of culture and values; in short, his model was something between the right wing of a German Christian democrat party and the American Christian right. Questioning sincerity and double speak will not suffice: sincerity is not a concept of political science. There is a given society, in this case a Turkish society that has internalized political secularism, a given political structure (the weight of the army) and a given strategic context (candidacy to the European Union). This means that Islamist political practices could be shaped under very different contexts: controlled democracy as in Turkey, repression as in Egypt and Tunisia, civil war as in Algeria, limited parliamentary participation as in Jordan and Kuwait, success of the revolution as in Iran. However, mainstream Islamists from various routes arrived at the same conclusion: the blueprint of an Islamic state is not viable; instead alliances, compromises and democratization are essential. Of course some quarters did not buy this opening: the dedicated Iranian Islamists and fringes of the Egyptian Muslim Brothers, for instance. But a consequence of that historicization is that the new generations of 'angry Muslims' do not take the same path: when they join an Islamist movement, it is not to fuel a revolution. The radicals among the new generation jump directly to the global jihad, which contributes to disconnect Islamism with radicalization, and to push 'old' Islamists to stress first either democracy or implementation of the *Shari'a*. Hence the concept we helped to forge is put into question by the very changes of the political landscape in the Middle East, not by a retrospective reconsideration of our previous analysis. Islamism is associated with generational phenomena.

The second argument (Islamism is constructed on the Western premise of state supremacy) stresses the imposition of Western conceptual categories in branding as Islamists many Muslim militants who have a more complex agenda, which cannot be exhausted through this use of Western categories: the term Islamism cannot grasp the authenticity of Islamic activism because it casts it into a very Western problematic, that of (but not limited to), the state, democracy and civil society.[2] This is a recurrent theme in the criticism of 'neo-Orientalism' by scholars of cultural and postcolonial studies.[3]

The problem is there: if the conceptualization by Western scholars of the protest movements waged by the 'Other' is irrelevant, alienating and aiming at depriving the 'Other' of his or her authenticity; that is, if it is the continuation of a colonial approach by other means (neo-Orientalism), then how are the political practices of the actors to be defined? This question is often left unanswered: the protest of the 'Others' is hypostasized as a sort of moral category, because they fight against imperialism, they cannot be 'deconstructed' by sociology and political science; the righteousness of the 'Other's' struggle makes him immune to categorization. The debate between the deconstructionism of academic discourses and a militant debate on right and wrong is in constant flux.[4] The Western scholar cannot speak for the 'Other', the (true) subaltern cannot speak (as Gayatri Spivak said), and the Muslim intellectual who uses the concepts of the West is driven by false consciousness. So no assessment is possible. Hence the heavy trend of the postcolonial studies to concentrate on internally deconstructing discourses—but what about the field? The hyper intellectualist deconstructionist approach is often coupled with an emotional political militancy of support for the identity-protest movements stemming from the Muslim societies. The disconnect between an abstract inward-looking scholarly analysis and vocal militant activism is striking and explains largely the tensions and splits dominating the field of Middle East Studies.

But the argument that the oppressed 'Others' are deprived of their authenticity by Western scholars who impose on them a ready-made grid of analysis, simply ignores the fact that the 'Other' does speak and write. There is a huge intellectual production by Islamist militants and thinkers. We can read Hasan al-Banna, Maududi and Khomeini; their (and others') writing are widely distributed and debated. As noted elsewhere in this chapter, they also use terms like 'state' 'constitution' and 'revolution', and also borrow Western political categories (state, party, militancy and economics). The state is being taken seriously and becomes the real stake in a strategy of empowerment. Any social scientist who goes to the field knows how local militants not only have read their own political literature, but also know about the scholar's own writing, listen to his interviews.

Some militants have previously been members of leftist movements, and many others did interact (to collaborate or to confront) with leftist movements that explicitly use a 'Western' conceptual matrix (that of Marxism). Globalization is not an empty term. When debating with Islamist militants during my numerous trips to the Middle East, I have never been confronted with a critique of my concept of Islamism (it is only among academic circles in the West that this critique arises). On the contrary, my interlocutors were quite happy to see that the 'newness' or modernity of their movements, both in terms of ideas and of sociological background, are acknowledged, which raises another question: what if the 'Western scholars', instead of denying the authenticity of the protest religious movements, were in fact helping these movements to present a more acceptable, if not pleasant, face to the Western public opinion? What if complacency would be more at stake than neo-Orientalist arrogance and contempt? Such an accusation is recurrent among Western Islamophobes who deny the newness of Islamism because they consider that the real issue is Islam per se. To sum up, the scholar of Islamism comes under attack on his left by progressive 'Saidian' critics (disciples of the late Edward Said), who consider him as a post colonial neo-Orientalist, full of contempt for the 'Other', and on the other hand by culturalist right-wingers who see him as a fellow traveler of radical Islam.

What many Islamists did not buy in my book *The Failure of Political Islam* was not my definition of Islamism, but the very notion of failure. As an Iranian mullah, professor at the Mufid university in

Qom, told me publicly in 1994 during a lecture there: 'Why do you speak of failure? We won!' From my meetings with PAS people in Malaysia to militants in London, the main critique about my book was that it defines the concept of a 'true Islamic state' as contradictory. But other militants came to the same conclusions through their own political trajectory, as did many cadres of the AK Party in Turkey. In a word, the 'Failure of Political Islam' has been as much part of the debate inside Islamism as part of a neo-orientalist construct of political Islam.

Although it is true that 'Islamists' cannot be reduced to Islamism (as any militant cannot be reduced to the ideology he supports at a given time), this concept is largely shared by the militants. This mirror-effect between the political scientist and the political activist is not surprising: both are part of an interactive game. The Islamist is not locked in his bubble of authenticity: he seeks also to convince, to eventually find an acceptable compromise with the West and to be recognized. Islamists do not follow an agenda definitively incompatible with Western categories of political science, even if their own self, their background, their trajectory, and their future, cannot be reduced to an abstract concept. But this is true for any militant anywhere.

The refusal to share common political categories with Western observers is not to be found among Islamists, but is more apparent in other radical groups, such as Salafis and jihadists. The problem is that the term 'Islamism' is now used by the media to designate any association between Islam and violence. That is another predicament of research in social science: a term is coined precisely to take distance from representations shared with public opinion, politicians, media and even some scholars: 'Islamism' is thus used to introduce some distance, when the 'political scientist' used to give interviews to journalists, hearings or memos for politicians, stressing that the general term which was in use (fundamentalism) was used to designate heterogeneous movements. But it worked too well in a sense; in few years, the term Islamism was used with the same meaning than fundamentalism: a justification of political violence through religion. There is a definite gap of meaning between the use of a term in social science and the migration of this term into the public debate. Social scientists do not own the terms they coined and cannot erect borders between their researchers and politics (and if they do it, they are the first to cross these borders). Let the debate continue.

2

# THE PROBLEM OF THE POLITICAL
# IN ISLAMIST MOVEMENTS

*Roel Meijer*

The major paradox of Islamism[1] is that it is a modern phenomenon
that emerged as a reaction to Western penetration of the Islamic
world. Previously politics and religion were perhaps loosely
related in theory but separated in practice.[2] In many ways classical
Islam was apolitical and the *ulama* tended to shy away from rulers,
who in most cases were thugs.[3] Although the *ulama* won the battle
with the Abbasid caliphs (750–1258) over the monopoly to interpret
Islamic law, they never succeeded in establishing their authority
over the ruler, with the result that a split occurred between the
ruler, who dominated politics, and the *ulama*, who acquired religious authority and held sway over the text. Classical political
theory recognized this division of labor, laying down the necessity
of obeying the ruler (*wali al-amr*). This is a minimalist doctrine.
According to Islamic law obedience to the ruler is mandatory, even
if he is unjust and incompetent, and revolt is rejected unless he
actively works against Islam. Modern totalizing claims to provide
a worldview and a complete social, economic and political system
embodied in an 'Islamic state' should be regarded as a reaction to
Western colonial rule. They are a response to condescension
towards conquered peoples whose 'backwardness' was not

27

ascribed to socio-economic circumstances or a power struggle, but to their deficient civilization, associated with their corresponding inferior religion; in this case Islam. The major problem with this counter-claim was that at the time Islam-inspired movements generally rejected politics (as a form of negotiation and compromise, and a means to reach certain delimited goals) and deeply feared its mechanisms as a source of corruption of authenticity and religious purity. The result has been a deep, but for a long time hidden, crisis; Islamic movements claim to be all things at once while not having the political instruments (which they had never developed) to deliver. Whereas in theory Islamism promises a perfect society and is able to mobilize people on the basis of its slogan, 'Islam is the solution' (*al-islam huwa al-hall*), in practice it suffers from the weakness of populism and its simple solutions to complex problems, which are believed to be located in the personality of the ruler, the morality of the believers and adherence to God's rule. In his famous book *The Failure of Political Islam*, Olivier Roy argued almost twenty years ago that Islamism's problem is the limitation of politics to virtue and piety.[4] All the rest is 'sin, plot or illusion'.[5] Concentrating on values instead of politics, Islamism ignores the need for a political program, open debate, and the value of checks and balances in curtailing power and the flexibility to produce a stable political practice.[6] Its basic flaw is to prefer purity and utopia above concrete results.

Modern Islamic movements have been engaged in three archetypical strategies to reach their goals of acquiring power and establishing an Islamic state. The first strategy concentrated on preaching (*da'wa*) as a means of peacefully spreading the call and convincing Muslims to lead the correct life of the *Sunna*, the example of the Prophet Muhammad. In its more activist version under the guise of 'commanding good and forbidding wrong', or *hisba*, this approach can adopt a violent form of coercion.[7] The political assumption of *da'wa* is that once Muslims lead a pious life a virtuous Muslim society will appear and political power will automatically follow without leaders having to dirty their hands. One finds the most extreme, apolitical version of this strategy in countries which did not experience colonialism and where political doctrine still goes back to classical tradition. In Saudi Arabia, for instance, the doctrine of obedience to the ruler has been promoted by Wahhabism/Salafism, leading to a more classical division of labor between the *ulama*, who gained control over society, while the ruler, the family of Sa'ud, acquired a monopoly over politics, the economy and foreign policy.[8] In this arrangement, the *ulama* actively discourage any political debate as deviant, leading to an internal division (*fitna*) which might undermine the power of the political and religious authorities. On the other extreme, modern Islamic political activism uses force and wages jihad[9] in order to capture the state and impose an Islamic society from above. In Egypt, the best example was the Jihad Organisation, which was involved in the assassination of President Sadat in 1981. In establishing the Islamic state in this manner, activist consciousness remains pure; their hands unsullied and their belief in their righteousness intact. The problem with these two strategies is that they are political in the sense that they seek power and transform society while at the same time the political dimension of the action is denied. Moreover, the stress on religious purity, the religious sanction of jihad, and the rejection of politics, as well as the tendency to view the political adversary as deviating (*inharif*) from the straight path rather than having a different opinion, an equally valid interpretation of the Islamic law, or representing other interests, stimulates the use of violence. The third and least popular option, which has only recently developed, is to recognize the limitations of *da'wa*, reject the severe liabilities of violence (jihad), and embrace politics (*hizbiyya*)[10] as a means to reform society and power relations while recognizing the existing order. As is the case with *da'wa*, the acceptance of *hizbiyya* means adopting the long term view.[11] But it also means that leaders have to become more savvy and interested in the world; willing to become immersed in topics that do not immediately touch upon religion, or even recognize that religion has its limitations and can be seen as an inspiration rather than a model. The process of accepting politics as intrinsically valid and a separate sphere is a tortuous road. The repressive nature of authoritarian regimes in the Middle East has not been helpful, but, paradoxically, it has in a way strengthened this trend. While on the one hand, regimes make it extremely difficult to become democratic in a non-democratic context, on the other hand movements have adopted democratic claims in order to oppose these states in a universal idiom and formulate their claim in the form of civil rights. At the same time, however, the unstable context also demands that these movements remain flexible, moving between the three archetypical strategies of *da'wa*, *hizbiyya* and *jihad*, or combining them (sometimes by promoting jihad outside its borders, as in Iraq and Palestine, taking part in elections, while building up a civil society by means of *da'wa*). This flexibility, often regarded as ambiguity, has laid them open to the accusation of opportunism or even duplicity. Such ambiguity is increased by the often opaque internal struggles between the different Islamic movements or different currents within movements. Recently, the clash over doctrine and strategy has been represented by the reformist Muslim Brotherhood on the one hand and the apolitical, quietist Salafism—both in its peaceful and in its jihadi apolitical forms—on the other. If in the former *hizbiyya* has become accepted, in the latter it is rejected as a form of unbelief (*kufr*).

This chapter will address the emergence of modern Islamic political thought by first looking back at the origins and nature of Islamism as it emerged as a *da'wa* organization and its subsequent development of the Jihadi trend. It will than analyze the two currents in the 1960s that tried to resolve its ambiguity by either taking the route of jihad or concentrating on *da'wa*. The second section will analyze the outcome of their debate and their attitude towards violence by using the examples of the Egyptian al-Jama'a al-Islamiyya, the Saudi Jihadi ideologue Yusuf al-'Uyairi (also known as 'Ayiri), the Iraqi Association of Muslim Scholars, and finally the Egyptian and Syrian Muslim Brotherhood. Moreover, this chapter will illustrate that Salafism, as promoted by Saudi Arabia, is the least likely solution as it tries to smother all forms of politics in an attempt to re-assert the authority of the *ulama* and stifle critique of the monarchy. My argument is that during the past twenty-five years major changes have occurred within the Islamic movement; the writings underpinning both trends have become much more sophisticated. Their development is dictated by their interpretation of 'reality'. Much can be learnt from their definition of reality. Is it evil and must it be changed, or does it contain the seeds of mutual understanding and acceptance? And what is the relationship between sacred texts and reality?

## The Advantages and Drawbacks of Ambiguity

One of the major problems of political Islam is that when it arose as a movement and an ideology with the establishment of the Muslim Brotherhood in 1928 in Egypt, it was forced to make exaggerated claims in opposition to Western political, economic and cultural colonial dominance. At the same time, it had to engage with the secular nationalist concept of religion of the Wafd Party, which in its attempt to mobilize Copts, relegated it to the private sphere as expressed in the slogan 'everyone his religion and the nation for everyone'. As part of the process of turning Islam into an ideology, the Brotherhood claimed to represent a comprehensive all-inclusive religious 'system' (*nizam*), laying claim in the words of its leader Hasan al-Banna (1906–49) to be everything from 'a Salafiyya message, a Sunni way, a Sufi truth, a political organization, an athletic group a cultural-educational union, an economic company, and a social idea'.[12] It enshrined political ambiguity by proclaiming the Qur'an, with its limited political directions, to be the constitution, while violence was sanctioned in the form of jihad. Hasan al-Banna rejected politics (*hizbiyya*) because it meant in his words to become involved with 'notables and names' and 'parties and societies'.[13]

Despite the fact that the Brotherhood emerged as an organization that was primarily directed towards *da'wa* and the spreading of the true call under the assumption that the problems of the Muslim world derived from the deviation from the straight path, it in fact quickly became involved in the political intrigues of the monarchy. The monarchy realized its potential as a counterweight to its nationalist opponents after the Brotherhood gained nationwide popularity due to its campaign to support the Palestinian uprising in 1936.[14] In the end, however, the connection with the monarchy and the conservative minority parties did not work out well for the Brotherhood. The Brotherhood's massive growth of adherents turned it into a political force in itself, while the discovery by the police of its paramilitary 'battalions', which were mobilized during the Arab-Israeli war in 1948, made the monarchy realize that the Brotherhood was a dangerous ally. The Brotherhood was disbanded in 1948. The subsequent assassination of Prime Minister Nuqrashi by the Secret Apparatus and the reprisal of killing Hasan al-Banna by the secret police concluded the first phase of its experiment in the political arena.[15] Its subsequent re-emergence in 1951 ended even more disastrously after the failure of the assassination attempt on Nasser in 1954. The military cracked down on the Muslim Brotherhood, hanged several of its leaders and sent its members to detention camps, from where they only emerged in the 1970s. Because of its armed wing, the Secret Apparatus (*al-jihaz al-sirri*), the new military regime could easily justify the repression of the Brotherhood by condemning it as a terrorist organization.[16]

This trajectory was not inevitable and universal and was specifically related to the Egyptian mother organization of the movement. How other branches developed depended on local circumstances. In Syria, where a branch of the Brotherhood had been founded in 1940s, the Brotherhood actively took part in politics and ran for elections between 1945 and 1963, even offering ministers in several cabinets.[17] Despite the participation of the Syrian Brotherhood in parliamentary politics, it did not result in a theoretical underpinning of democracy, which, like in Egypt, was feeble anyway and was interrupted by military putsches. In Jordan, the Brotherhood enhanced its reputation as an ambivalent force when it supported King Hussein against the pan-Arab movement in the 1950s.[18] It benefited hugely from this deal, and until the liberalization in 1989, the Brotherhood was able to gain access through its alliance with King Hussein to crucial sectors of society, as education and welfare organizations. Being registered as a NGO meant it was never allowed to act as a political force and elaborate its political ideas.[19] In Palestine the Brotherhood played a similarly ambivalent role, and was even supported by the Israelis against the PLO on the assumption that it was non-political and based on personal salvation.[20]

Besides the adverse circumstances in many of these countries, internal obstacles also hampered the development of a political theory and program (*barnamaj*). Opening a debate on political strategies and concepts always contained the threat of internal strife (*fitna*)[21] which might challenge the authority of the leaders and endanger unity. To prevent this, appointments to such organs as the Maktab al-Irshad—the Brotherhood's politburo—were made by the leader himself, or by co-optation. Reflecting the highly authoritarian nature of politics at the time, the political culture of the Brotherhood was based on the principle of 'obedience' (*ta'a*) and 'listening' (*sam'*), which would not be challenged until the 1980s.[22] The authoritarian terms of obedience and listening are Qur'anic, and are also much in evidence in Salafism where they are used to legitimize the total adherence to the opinion of the *ulama*.

## Repression and the Deepening of Da'wa and Jihad as Strategy and Ideology

In the 1960s and 1970s the ambivalence towards politics was resolved in two directions, neither of them conducive to the emergence of political theory and practice. The first was the revolutionary route of Sayyid Qutb (1906–66), the second the 'moderate' official response of the Muslim Brotherhood.

Sayyid Qutb's total war on the military regime in Egypt as a means to end the ambiguity of the Brotherhood under Hasan al-Banna, led to the complete suppression of politics and the opening of the floodgates to violence. Although highly activist, paradoxically his project for the liberation from political secular tyranny of the authoritarian state and its totalitarian nature (*shumuliyya*) was directed by another total subjection, to that of the sovereignty of God (*hakimiyya*). Paradoxically, in this totalitarian form of Islamism, human freedom is gained by total submission to God:[23]

This religion is really a universal declaration of the freedom of man from servitude to other men and from servitude to his own desires, which is also a form of servitude; it is a declaration that sovereignty (*hakimiyya*) belongs to God alone and He is the lord of all the worlds.[24]

Qutb refused to address the specific issue of divergent interpretations, individual differences and the possibility of dissension and internal debate, i.e. the opening up to politics, already feared under the monarchy by the Brotherhood. Instead, he strove for unity and mobilization of the believers by a vanguard (*tali'a*) for the jihad against the ruling regimes which were regarded as pre-Islamic (*jahiliyya*) and therefore based on unbelief (*kufr*). Discipline and obedience in the revolt against the *taghut* (idol) are put by Qutb at the service of self-sacrifice and martyrdom and regarded as the only means of becoming a true Muslim. Ironically, with the introduction of excommunication (*takfir*) as a political instrument Sayyid

Qutb set the scene for individual megalomaniacs, leading to what he wanted to avoid: internal strife (*fitna*) and an endless sectarian circle of condemnation of those who do not approve of one's own doctrine (always regarded as universal), thus further Islamizing and colonizing the field of politics. If the goal was still to establish an Islamic state, the emphasis shifted towards action and jihad as a purifying act of washing away the sin of politics.[25]

The answer the Brotherhood formulated in response to Qutb at the time was equally unhelpful in developing new political theories. By falling back on the old concept of *da'wa* Qutb's concept of *takfir* was not criticized in political terms but in theological ones. The argument was that it was impermissible for one Muslim to judge another Muslim and condemn him unless this done along very strict lines. Strategically, Hasan al-Hudaybi's *Preachers, Not Judges* (*Du'a, la quda*) is typical of the Brotherhood's withdrawal to its most inconspicuous minimalist tactical position under threat of annihilation of the authoritarian state.[26] Besides condemning the concepts of *jahiliyya* and *takfir*, its tactic, later evolved by the subsequent General Guide 'Umar Tilmisani (1973–1986), was to create a Muslim society rather than a state, in the expectation that in due time the state would automatically fall into the lap of the community if a majority of Muslims lived piously. It was assumed that the *Shari'a*—left undefined—contained all the answers to contemporary problems and following it would eliminate the necessity of politics. This position was equally apolitical, for it was still based on the utopian idea that if all Muslims were virtuous, politics and the necessity of solving conflicts would become redundant. It also did not solve the issue of ambiguity, as the Brotherhood still strove for power, acted politically by creating an Islamized parallel civil society and a state within a state, while at the same time denying they had any political ambitions. This of course was not only the fault of the Brotherhood but of the political system as a whole. President Sadat had released the Brotherhood from prison at the beginning of the 1970s on the condition that it did not mingle in politics.

In the 1960s and 1970s both tendencies evolved further and deepened. Many members of the Brotherhood fled to Saudi Arabia, where the authoritarian and apolitical tendencies were further underpinned and enhanced. Neither the apolitical Salafism of the religious establishment of the Saudi grand mufti Bin Baz and the main *hadith* specialist Nasir al-Din al-Albani, nor the activism of Juhayman al-'Utaybi was conducive to the development of a truly political Islam.[27] In Saudi Arabia itself the mixture of the activism of the Brotherhood and Salafism would lead to a new hybrid propounded by such thinkers as Muhammad Surur Zain al-'Abdin and 'Abd al-Khaliq 'Abd al-Rahman. Both studied at the Islamic University in Medina, the centre of the transnational expansion of Salafism (80 per cent of its students were foreigners), became critical of the Brotherhood for its lack of religious depth and tried to combine the dogmatism of Salafism with the activism of the Brotherhood. They had special influence on the Saudi Sahwa as a political Salafi movement that in the 1990s would criticize the monarchy and demand reforms after the Saudi monarchy had allowed American troops to be stationed on 'Holy soil'. Other forms of Salafism would also evolve. In Jordan, the apolitical Salafi movement would emerge as a new protest movement, as the Muslim Brotherhood had been co-opted by King Hussein in his struggle against Nasserism and pan-Arabism.[28] In Afghanistan the jihadi trend would have its field day and blossom into a variety of spectacular forms developed by 'Abdallah 'Azzam, 'Abd al-Qadir bin 'Abd al-'Aziz, bin Laden and others, like Yusuf al-'Uyairi. Repressed in its political expression, outraged by moral corruption and Western interference in the Middle East, their hope for liberation lay in striving for a total destruction of the enemy. Martyrdom, still in its infancy in Qutb's works and imagination, would become central to their arguments.

Three approaches to violence have evolved since the 1980s. The first, influenced by Qutb, is to spread the call by intimidation and non-direct opposition against the ruler, exemplified by the practice of violent *hisba* in breaking up festivals, burning video shops, and intimidating opponents, and ending in jihad against the ruler. The second is to unleash global jihad and jihadism as a permanent revolution. And the third is to use jihad as a means of national resistance against foreign occupation. All three reject politics (*hizbiyya*), but they differ in their methods between low level warfare, global jihad, and violence in the service of national resistance. The basic difference between these currents and their tactics is reflected in their interpretation of reality.

## Al-Jama'a al-Islamiyya's Tactic of Low Intensity Warfare

Most academic works concentrate on the Jihad Group and jihad against the far enemy.[29] In the Egyptian context, the Jama'a al-Islamiyya was much more important and developed a much more specific form of violence.[30] The Jama'a al-Islamiyya is a generic term used in the mid-1970s for apolitical pious university societies that spread the call and organized services for its members while promoting pious Islamism. During the 1970s they gradually became politicized, radicalizing as soon as the Left was crushed and the regime was caught between its contradictory policy of playing the Islamic card and becoming dependent on the United States and making peace with Israel.[31] The Jama'a rejected the Brotherhood's deal with the state of limiting its activities to *da'wa* as too soft and law-abiding.[32] Instead, it found in the principle of 'commanding right and forbidding wrong' (*al-amr bi-l-ma'ruf wa-l-nahy 'an al-munkar*), or *hisba*, a potent repertoire of contention to justify the use of violence as a flexible and multi-faceted political tool to intimidate its opponents, maintain control and discipline over its following, as well as provoke the state by increasingly taking over more public space and whittling down its authority.[33]

Of the three means of forbidding wrong by the heart (*bi-l-qalb*), by the tongue (*bi-l-lisan*) and by the hand (*bi-l-yad*), (that is, 'change the wrong-doing with violent force' [*manhaj al-taghyir al-munkar bi-quwa*]), clearly the last became the most important.[34] At the end of the 1970s and 1980s, the Jama'a would become notorious for its intimidation of students and Egyptian citizens. The Jama'a's lawyer and a former prominent leader, Muntasar al-Zayyat (born 1956), describes in his memoirs how as a young zealot in the 1970s he smashed liquor stores belonging to Christian Coptic minority in Aswan, the town where he was brought up.[35] Universities were terrorized by the Jama'a, who broke up cultural festivals, prevented singing, forbade mingling of sexes and enforced a religious code of chastity.[36] As the acceptance of violence expanded at the end of the 1970s, the Jama'a started to train with weapons in the hills of Asyut in Upper Egypt, eventually merging with the Jihad Organization in 1980 and embracing jihad as a means of ending the *jahiliyya* state.[37] They found its justification in 'Abd al-Salam Faraj's tract, *The Hidden Duty*[38] and in Qutb's *Milestones*, both famous for metaphorical descriptions of reality.

How politically underdeveloped the Jama'a in fact was, became clear during the assassination of president Sadat in 1981. The only aim of Khalid al-Islambuli, the assassin of Sadat, was to remove the corrupt tyrant (*taghut*), missing the opportunity to wipe out the political elite at the bandstand during the commemoration of the October War in 1981.[39] The botched revolt in Asyut two days later was an isolated revolutionary spark that was quickly stamped out by the state. All the other attempts to take over crucial centers of power, such as the television station, were abandoned for lack of preparation. In the end, the attack was typical of late nineteenth-century European 'anarchism of the deed', which was meant to set an example, betting on a spontaneous uprising, without really making a political analysis of the overwhelming odds they faced in the power of the state and drawing up a strategy to overcome them.[40]

Inevitably the spectacular assassination of Sadat was followed by a deep gloom in prison where hundreds of members of the Islamist movement and innocent youth were thrown together. What saved the movement and its apolitical line of commanding right and forbidding wrong was the systematic torture of its members.[41] In order to prevent their previous mistake, the writings of the second half of the 1980s were highly political, providing historical analyses of the plight of Islam which explained in concrete terms their methods of operandi,[42] giving detailed analyses of the political system in Egypt,[43] as well as emphasizing the inevitability of the confrontation with the state,[44] while appealing to the public against the repression of the state.[45] The difference with the tracts of the previous period is that all of them dealt with 'reality' and especially with 'means of changing reality'.[46] None of them presented a political theory, besides how to 'make' a revolution by means of jihad. At the same time cadre training and more ideological indoctrination seems also to have evolved, making the Jama'a into a tighter organization. An interesting insight into this period is given by

Khalid al-Birri (born 1972), who describes how he in his youth in the 1980s applied the intimidation tactics in his secondary school and neighborhood.[47] At the same time the Jama'a was able to penetrate the marginal neighborhoods of Cairo, like Imbaba, Ayn Shams and Bulaq Dakrur.[48]

Even with their more sophisticated political analysis, the second generation leaders did not realize that the provocative nature of commanding good and forbidding wrong (hisba) together with their highly aggressive pamphlets constituted a standing provocation to the authorities and would ultimately lead to another confrontation with the state. From 1987 onwards clashes with the state increased until 1990, when a violent continuous low intensity war broke out after the state assassinated the Jama'a's spokesman and in retaliation the speaker of parliament was assassinated. In the end, violence, which cost 1,500 people their lives, and from 1992 was also aimed at tourists, alienated the Egyptian public from the Jama'a.

It took another seven years before the Jama'a was soundly defeated militarily. The interesting aspect of its defeat was not that it had happened—never in question—but that its leadership subsequently reversed its ideas. Suing for peace, they completely revised their ideas on the use of violence. The first sign of 'revisionism' (muraja'at), as it was called, occurred during a trial in Aswan in 1996, when a member of the Jama'a read a letter in which he condemned violence. It was addressed to the Egyptian people and 'the elite of this noble population'. It especially condemned internal strife (fitna), the classic rejection of violence and revolt against the ruler. It was also thoroughly nationalist, in the sense that it deplored the weakening of Egypt, once a powerful nation, now being humiliated by its enemies, Israel and the United States, which were taking advantage of the internal turmoil.[49] The Initiative to End Violence, as the whole campaign was called, was interrupted by the Luxor massacre in November 1997, but was continued in 2001. In January 2002 the Jama'a issued four tracts in which they explained the ideological reasons for the 'revisionism' concerning violence.[50] Subsequently, they would issue another two tracts, one denouncing violence in Saudi Arabia[51] and another further expounding on their ideas.[52]

Revisionism makes a strong case against the use of violence and the dangers of extremism (*ghuluw*), and pronounces itself in favor of tolerance and moderation. The dichotomous worldview of the Charter of an eternal struggle between the West and Islam is still there.[53] However, the reasons for going astray are that violence and jihad have become goals in themselves.[54] According to the authors, the Jama'a had lost sight of the principles and general goals of Islam. Jihad can only have meaning when it is used for the general good. The solution the Jama'a seeks is still geared to leading man to be virtuous and man's ultimate goal is 'submission to his God' (*ta'bid al-nas li-rabbihim*).[55] There are, however, important differences with the earlier tracts from the 1980s in their focus on the relationship with politics. They warn the Islamic movement that knowledge of religious texts is not enough; it must be combined with knowledge of 'reality' (*waqi'*). A crucial remark that highlights their heightened realism is that 'profound knowledge of the *hari'a*, as well as a penetrating sense of reality and a deep understanding of politics are necessary tools for tackling this subject'. Continuing the argument, they state that 'otherwise, people will destroy themselves, spill blood and lose their homeland without justification and without serving the common good and attaining their goal'.[56] To end the preponderance of text over reality, Islam is no longer portrayed in the Qutbian sense as a complete (*kamil*), total (*shamil*) and conclusive (*khatim*) program (*manhaj*) that solves all problems as soon as the *Shari'a* is implemented. Likewise, the idea that the Jama'a itself has a monopoly of truth is relinquished. Rather, life is now acknowledged to be complex and the sources of Islam must be interpreted and debated in order to adjust them according to differences in place and time in which Muslims live.[57] For the same reason history is re-evaluated. Historical experience is now regarded as a source of wisdom,[58] and the West is no longer just rejected but is also regarded as a source of inspiration as long as it does not contradict Islam. Nor should all the ills of the Middle East be blamed on the West.[59] All those previous methods used to combat the state and impose its will on the population have been constricted by a series of conditions. For instance, the use of *takfir*, the excommunication of a ruler, a state or an individual, is forbidden.[60] Jihad must be based on consensus of the *umma*, permission to exert it must be acquired through permission of the *ulama* and can only be executed by the state.[61]

Despite these major steps forward to liberating Islam from the total subjection to the text, and the rejection of violence in principle and practice (it cannot be used against the interests of the *umma*), the 'Initiative to End Violence' still suffers from some of the previous flaws. While it opens up the space for the political, it does not include its own autonomous rules. For instance, in a revealing answer to a question about the role of parliament, the authors stated that they regarded it as 'only one of the many means of spreading the call (*da'wa*)'.[62] From this remark and others, it is clear that politics still only functions as a instrument to establish Islam as a moral code. In this sense a major opportunity to clear the way for transforming *hisba* into a principle of civic responsibility and as a means of checking the power of the state was missed.[63]

### Yusuf al-'Uyairi and the Permanent Salafi Jihadi Tevolution

Yusuf al-'Uyairi, as the first leader of al-Qaeda on the Arabian Peninsula, is probably one of the most well-known of the second generation ideologues and fighters. His extensive writings inform us of the importance and function of violence and how it relates to politics and political theory.[64] Remarkably, 80 per cent of his work deals with an analysis of the political situation, i.e. 'reality', the rest with the legitimation of violence. His activism is geared towards changing reality (*taghyir al-waqi'*)—which is totally rejected—and much of his work, which typically can only be found on the internet,[65] deals with reality and ways to revolutionize society in different countries of the Muslim world: Saudi Arabia,[66] Afghanistan,[67] Chechnya,[68] Philippines,[69] and Iraq.[70] His minute analysis of the 'on-the-ground' situation in these countries and the economic and political relations with the Middle East and especially Saudi Arabia with the United States, gives his work a highly realistic quality. His analysis suggests that it is not religion as such that is the reason for rejecting the West. Rather, the manipulation of the region by the West and especially the United States for its own interests is the reason for revolt against the prevailing system.[71] Using modern terms such as 'imperialism' (*isti'mar*) 'Uyairi regards these international relations as deeply flawed. Any persons or institutions co-operating with the West are therefore rejected, whether they are rulers, *ulama*, or Westernized 'intellectuals'. Despite the political character of 'Uyairi's work, his writings are essentially non-political in the sense that they are harnessed to a strategy, like that of Sayyid Qutb, or even the Muslim Brotherhood in the past, which utterly rejects politics as a pragmatic way to solve problems. Although he is highly flexible in his ideas about how to combat the enemy and is even tolerant in his religious estimation of many of the movements he analyses—not rejecting them because they do not completely adhere to Salafism, such as the Taliban[72]—his whole work is steeped in a deep moralism and abhorrence of corruption and tarnishment of the self by a pragmatism that could lead to compromise (*tahadun*), co-operation (*ta'awun*) and co-existence (*ta'ayush*); that is the political.[73] He draws his ultimate conclusion from this stance: rather than compromise one's principles and religion—one's very reason to exist as man—and engage in negotiations with the adversary, one is admonished to fight him until victory and the establishment of God's rule on earth or find a glorious death as a martyr and win paradise. In this respect 'Uyairi repeats the fallacy of some currents of 'political' Islam that purity instead of the corruption (*fasad*) of politics is the highest goal.[74]

The reason for this uncompromising attitude is 'Uyairi's adherence to a metaphorical overarching master narrative of the clash of civilizations between the West and Islam as a zero-sum game. In this apocalyptic vision of the world, there is no compromise because the West that is bent on destroying the Muslim world, not just by economic and political domination, but also on account of its cultural war on Islam. The result will be the loss of Muslims of their humanity and their 'bestialization'.[75] As in Qutb's view, the world is divided in dichotomous forces of evil and good in which there are no shades of grey. And as everyone who does not support the forces of good belongs to the opposite side, a continuous war should be waged not against the West alone, but against all Muslims who are connected with the West and are regarded as *kuffar*. Unlike Qutb, however, 'Uyairi crushes the political not on the anvil of *hakimiyya* or on the practice of commanding good and forbidding bad (*hisba*), as in the case of the Jama'a, but on that of Jihadism, which has become a culture in itself, demanding submission to its totalitarian intellectual, physical and moral demands. The victorious sect (*al-ta'ifa al-mansura*), a crucial doctrine in Salafism,[76] is regarded as the vanguard of the jihadist project and has privileged access to knowledge because its members are at the forefront of the civilizational battle.[77]

'Uyairi's writings are perhaps the best illustration of the creative flight jihadist literature has taken since the 1970s, as well as the political dead end this current has worked itself into. While it struggles to come to grips with reality and is capable of defining and analyzing the sources of political inequality and repression and corruption, and has been clever in mobilizing resistance and appealing to the imagination of the people due to the deplorable state of affairs in the Middle East finds itself in, its Manichean concept of the world as a permanent struggle between good and bad prevents it from coming to terms with reality and coming up with a political program and stating its goals other than to establish a virtuous society. 'Uyairi's revolution failed in Saudi Arabia after the first explosions on 12 May 2003. The state easily isolated its members and hunted them down during the following years and Yusuf al-'Uyairi became one of the first victims when he was killed on 29 May 2003.[78]

### The Iraqi Association of Muslim Scholars and Islamo-nationalist Resistance

As 'Uyairi had predicted at the end of his life, it is in Iraq that the full potential of jihad would be fulfilled, but this would not adopt the transnational form he had hoped.[79] In Iraq the ideologies of resistance and jihad developed by Hamas, bin Laden or 'Uyairi, came together and could be readily used by the opponents of the American invasion. The Association of Muslim Scholars (AMS, or in Arabic *Hay'at 'Ulama al-Muslimin*) would use and pick from them as it felt fit. The difference with the other currents was that the AMS tried to focus, control and direct violence for its own localized goals. The AMS was established as a nation-wide organization of Sunni religious scholars of all directions. The major political breakthrough of the AMS occurred during the first crisis in Fallujah in April 2004 when it openly supported the resistance.[80]

The AMS is a typical Islamo-nationalist movement that legitimates the violent struggle for liberation in nationalist and religious terms, and does not primarily—like Sayyid Qutb or Yusuf al-'Uyairi—cast the struggle between the Middle East and the West as an eternal, global struggle of Islam against the West. Framed in the nationalist terminology, the AMS leader Harith al-Dhari stated, 'we as Iraqis limit ourselves to defending our country and we know what the interests of this country are'.[81] A transnational terrorist organization like al-Qaeda in Mesopotamia is rejected not only for its indiscriminate killing of Iraqi citizens, especially Shi'is, but also for the fact that Abu Mus'ab al-Zarqawi was a 'non-Iraqi and a foreigner' and has 'other goals than the national resistance'.[82]

The AMS also gratefully used the advantages of ambiguity so typical of the earlier Islamist movement to hide behind. For instance, it regarded itself as standing above the political parties and claimed unassailability as 'a religious authority on Islamic law' (*marja'iyya diniyya wa shar'iyya*).[83] The AMS, according to one of its spokesmen, is 'not a political party, nor a movement', rather it 'contains political parties' and leaves room for 'a diversity of opinions'.[84] On the other hand, it is clear that the AMS strove for political power and was dictatorial in its single-minded pursuit to be regarded as the sole representative of the Sunni Arabs, as is apparent in the expression that it is the 'national and religious duty of the *ulama* [to] lead the people on the right path'.[85] That this also meant that the AMS endorsed, if not actively supported, the use of violence against the US was clear when it stated that it regarded itself as 'spiritually' (*ruhan*) close to the resistance.[86] However, the most important non-political method the AMS became famous for was the boycott, a practice it has adopted from another nationalist-religious movement, Hamas. With tremendous consequences for the Sunni community in Iraq the AMS led the boycott of the 'political process' from 2003 to the summer of 2005. As a result, the Sunnis did not participate in the general elections of December 2004 and belatedly participated in the negotiations for the constitution in summer 2005 and were encouraged to fight in the resistance.[87]

The best insight into the AMS's justification of resistance, and indirectly of violence and the political boycott, is provided by the writings of Muhammad 'Ayyash al-Kubaysi, its chief ideologue.[88]

Four topics stand out which demonstrate the special ideological mix of internal, nationalist and Salafi elements (and even Ba'thist and pan-Arab, not mentioned here) in the ideology of the AMS. First, the ideological legitimation of resistance was initially primarily couched in a non-Islamic discourse of international law. In a debate on a television program on Al-Jazeera, just after the fall of Fallujah in November 2004, when the whole of Anbar province was in uprising and it was clear that the resistance was there to stay, Kubaysi stated that each nation, whether they were Vietnamese or Arab, non-Muslim or Muslim, had the right to armed resistance against the forceful occupation of its country. As it was a natural human right (*haqq al-insan*) it was not necessary to call for jihad or issue a *fatwa* to sanction it.[89] The AMS preferred the term resistance (*muqawama*) to that of jihad.[90]

However, despite this effort to coach the insurgency in nationalist/religious terms, along the lines of Hamas, it is clear that the AMS adopted large chunks of Salafi Jihadism as developed by, among others, bin Laden and 'Uyairi. This is especially apparent in Kubaysi's vehement condemnation of moderate *ulama*, who oppose armed resistance, as hypocrites (*munafiqun*), one of the prominent themes of the Jihadi Salafi writings. In response to the Iraqi Islamic Party, which had participated in the political process, 'Abd al-Salam al-Kubaysi asserts that this is not the time for mutual leniency (*tasamuh*), and flexibility (*lin*). As the American invasion is a direct attack on the Islamic *umma* by the unbelievers there is only room for armed resistance, and all Muslims should subordinate their life to the waging of jihad.[91] Resistance, he stated, has become an individual duty (*fardh 'ayn*) that can only be ignored at the risk of denying the unity of God, *tawhid*.[92]

Third, while the AMS adopted an uncompromising stand on the predominance of resistance, it tried to make a distinction between legitimate Sunni resistance against the American occupation and the indiscriminate terrorism of Zarqawi, whose actions were increasingly directed against Shi'i Iraqis who were regarded as 'collaborators'. The official position of the AMS was that both Iraqi civilians and military, even those of the National Guard, who were mostly Shiites, belong to this category.[93] In numerous communiqués the AMS condemned terrorist attacks against 'innocent people' (*abriya'*).[94] However, Kubaysi did make a case for 'martyrdom operations', as long as they were in the service of national liberation. These martyrs were regarded as courageous and faced death with equanimity and strong faith (*'aqida wadiha*) for a noble goal (*hadaf nabil*).[95]

Fourth, the AMS succeeded in organizing an uncompromising boycott of all political institutions because they were established with the aim of bringing the Shi'a to power. The AMS did not reject democracy outright, but stated that 'true democracy is impossible under an occupation'.[96] The angle the AMS chose to frame this ideological point was to accuse the Americans of deliberately instigating sectarian strife (*al-fitna al-ta'ifiyya*).[97] Kubaysi was convinced that the American aim was to convince the Shi'is that they were an oppressed sect (*al-ta'ifa al-mazluma*).[98] In line with its counter-frame that Iraq was a united nation, the AMS cleverly used the insurgency in Fallujah in 2004 to propagate its Arab and Islamic program of unity between Shi'is and Sunnis. In order to win over Muqtada al-Sadr, who at the time was a potential ally of the AMS, its ideologues repeatedly asserted that the martyrdom of Imam Husayn at Kerbala was now an example for all who defended Islam against the invasion of unbelievers. According to Muhammad 'Ayyash al-Kubaysi, Imam Husayn had established a school of martyrdom (*madrasa al-Husayn al-ishtishhadiyya*) that was an example for Sunnis and Shi'is together.[99]

The AMS is typical of resistance movements in the Middle East and the ways they could draw on a huge reservoir of violent rhetoric to justify a totally negative attitude towards politics and what in Iraq was called the 'political process', which was supported by the Iraqi Islamic Party, a branch of the Muslim Brotherhood, which accepted *hizbiyya*.[100] Even if this process was fatally mismanaged by the Americans and discriminatory to the Sunnis, it is clear that the fundamentally 'apolitical' stance of the AMS damaged the chances of the Sunni community to salvage some of their power and influence. In the end, the ambiguity of the AMS towards violence against Shi'is, would damage its relations with Shi'i organizations that supported resistance against the United States. Only a spark was needed to unleash the Shi'i forces against the Sunni community in Baghdad to punish them for their ambiguous attitude towards politics and religious condescension towards Shi'is, whose increased power the AMS was unwilling to countenance. When that spark came with the bombing of the Askari shrine in February 2006, this studied ambivalence backfired and Sunni neighborhoods were cleansed of any inhabitants.

### The Egyptian Muslim Brotherhood and the Acceptance of Hizbiyya

The alternative to this ambiguity—openly rejecting violence, unconditionally embracing democracy and the rule of law—occurred in the 1980s. The tone of this development had already been set when the former general guide Hasan al-Hudaybi condemned the concepts of *takfir* and *hakimiyya* in the 1960s. This attitude was initially reflected in the traditional stance of the Brotherhood towards President Mubarak when he came to power in 1981. It accepted a ruler along the lines of *wali al-amr*, even if he is a tyrant, as long as he maintained the minimum of Islamic principles as the 'imam of necessity' (*imam al-darura*).[101]

The major breakthrough occurred when during the 1980s the room for the establishment of political parties and holding elections expanded, despite the fact that the establishment of parties on the basis of religion was banned by the 1976 Parties' Law. What made this possible was the emergence of the second generation of the members of the Brotherhood as a professional middle class. At a meeting in 1983 in Cairo, Tilmisani argued that becoming a party had several advantages: the Brotherhood would no longer be a secret organization, it could acquire experience in the political process, and it would finally have direct access to ministers and officials.[102] Once it had decided to take part in parliamentary elections, the Brotherhood formed alliances with other parties in 1984 and 1987, and after having boycotted the elections in 1990 and 2000, it won a spectacular eighty-eight seats in 2005.[103] All analysts agree that since then the Brotherhood has obtained an excellent reputation in parliament, showing political skills and discussing issues that were of broader concern of the people than only the implementation of the *Shari'a*, such as unemployment, inflation, corruption, debts, privatization.[104] Part of this success must be explained by the growing experience the younger generation of the Brotherhood acquired in the professional syndicates, winning the elections of the Medical Syndicate in 1984, of the Engineer's Syndicate in 1986, and the Pharmacists' Syndicate in 1988. From there they reached out to other social classes in society. The new generation also maintained close contacts with the student movement and the campuses,[105] subsequently winning the majority of seats in the student unions of Cairo, Alexandria and Zaqaziq, Mansura and at al-Azhar universities in the second half of the 1980s.

Ideologically, the new trend was supported by an increasing number of internal publications that gradually opened the road to a parliamentary system (*hizbiyya*). In 1984 the Brotherhood drafted a manifesto which banned all restrictions on political parties, organizations or political gatherings that intend to express the views of a particular group as regards a particular issue.[106] In 1987 it recognized the Christian Coptic minority as full citizens,[107] and in 1994 it issued statements on women's rights and party pluralism. In their *Shura and Party Pluralism in Muslim Society*, of the same year, it stated that the Qur'an stipulated 'that the *umma* is the source of all powers'.[108] It furthermore called for a legislature with oversight functions and binding decisions. A year later it published the *Statement on Democracy*, re-confirming the equal rights of non-Muslims (Copts), the sovereignty of the people, stating that 'people have the right to invent different systems, formulas, and techniques that suit their conditions, which definitely vary according to time, place and living conditions', and rejecting violence.[109] However, during the repression of the second generation leaders in 1995 and their imprisonment until 2000 the Brotherhood lapsed into the old style rhetoric of its older generation of general guides, Mustafa Mashhur (1996–2002) and Ma'mun al-Hudaybi (2002–2004), but after their release it picked up its earlier liberal trend. When the last of the old guard had died in 2004, the Brotherhood announced under its new Guide Muhammad 'Akif, it would do something about the internal democracy, limiting the number of years of a general guide and deputy guides were elected among the younger group.[110] Finally, in a press conference on 3 March 2004 the General Guide declared a 'Muslim Brotherhood reform initiative'.[111] This initiative called for reforms in politics, judiciary, economics and education, and confirmed its earlier position regarding universal suffrage, freedom of personal conviction and expression of opinion, freedom of political parties and organizations, the army's dissociation from politics and limited powers of the President.[112] A written constitution and the separation of powers, with an independent judiciary, the repeal of the emergency laws, and activating parliament's oversight role, had by that time become part of its standard program.[113]

The ambiguity of the Muslim Brotherhood was not totally dispelled in this period. The election slogan of 1987, 'Islam is the solution', which had irritated the government when it was used during the Brotherhood's relief program after the earthquake, was retained in the elections of 2005.[114] In its thorough study of the reform of the Brotherhood, the Carnegie Endowment concludes that if it has made important strides in political liberalization, its sacrosanct concept of religious point of reference or source (*marja'iyya*), forms a limit to going the full length of giving politics its own space and becoming a political party instead of a religious movement.[115] A further reason for concern was its opposition to artistic and philosophical freedom in the form *hisba*, commanding the good and forbidding the bad, for which the Jama'a became infamous.[116] This is no small matter when it comes to violence, as is demonstrated by the condoning by the Brotherhood leader Muhammad al-Ghazzali of the assassination in 1992 of the fiercely anti-Islamist publicist Faraj Fawda. Although the Brotherhood accepts the parliamentary system, its conservative cultural and philosophical and potentially repressive measures, can restrict the freedom of speech and stimulate the use of violence against individuals.[117]

## 'Quietist' Salafism: Piety and the Denial of Politics

The development of ideas within the Muslim Brotherhood has been vehemently opposed by the Islamic movement and not just the Egyptian state. The extent of opposition to the tendency to accept politics is exemplified by transnational, quietist Salafism, which is perhaps one of the fastest growing Islamic movements at the moment.[118] In its opposition to these new trends Salafism[119] can be compared with the counter-reformation of the Roman Catholic Church against Protestantism (although, ironically, Salafism resembles early Protestantism in many respects),[120] as a struggle that is waged in the name of the Oneness of God (*tawhid*). Its authority is typically based on the claim to have access to the Truth (regarded as transparent) and therefore to have superior knowledge ('*ilm*) of the sources of the Islam (Qur'an and *hadith*), which raises the Salafis to the status of the saved sect (*al-firqa al-najiya*). Individual salvation, purity in doctrine, rather than political mobilization is the crucial issue. As a typical throwback to an earlier period, their opponents are not condemned for their political ideas as such but are attacked as religious deviants (*munharifun*). Against them is launched the whole range of theological weapons Salafism can muster: by incorporating non-Islamic terms and concepts the opponents are accused of committing innovation (*bid'a*); by giving their political leaders authority they are accused of worshipping humans, an infringement of the doctrine of the Oneness of God (*tawhid*) and committing the major sin of giving God associates (*shirk*);[121] and by giving priority to activism instead of piety they are called *harakis* (activists), a curse in Salafi anti-political parlance.[122] Although quietist Salafism is careful not to excommunicate its opponents (*takfir*), they are vilified, their reputation smeared and their followers ostracized, with the implication that their souls hang in the balance and they are on the brink of becoming unbelievers (*kuffar*).

If in other movements a greater openness and debate is discernable, in Salafism discourse is controlled and directed solely to the text that allows only for one interpretation. Because knowledge can only be reached after a long study of the text, in practice the *ulama* control the access to Truth. The normal believer is discouraged or even forbidden to think outside the restricted parameters laid down by the *ulama*, let alone engage in an open debate with 'others', allow self-reflection (other than in religious terms), or question the authority of the religious establishment. The pronouncement that 'questioning is in principle forbidden and is not allowed except when it is necessary'[123] is perhaps one of the most revealing remarks made by Sheikh Rabi' Hadi ('Hadee') al-Madkhali, one of the major sheikhs of the older generation (b. 1931).[124] And although the appeal of Salafism is ascribed to its non-hierarchical nature—as everyone has access to the sources—in practice an inner circle of mostly Saudi *ulama*, who are appointed to a hierarchy of different official Saudi religious institutions,[125] determine doctrine and practice. The struggle, therefore, is for authority and most of the internal struggle is waged by denying other Salafi *ulama*, but especially non-Salafi *ulama*, and above all non-*ulama*—often the case of the Muslim Brotherhood that is led by laymen—their religious authority and by implication the right to have a (political) following.

Needless to say, in the political context of the Middle East, or even Europe with its emphasis on integration, this non-political, quietist attitude of Salafism is highly political.[126] But Salafism is not simply political by recognizing the state in practice, this recognition is also theoretically grounded in the principle of *wali al-amr*, the doctrine of unconditional obedience to the ruler, who can only be opposed when he actively undermines Islam.[127] The other principle defending the status quo is that of the rejection of politics as a threat to the unity of the *umma* because it leads to dissension and division (*fitna*). To Salafism the only accepted form of politics is to give discrete advice (*nasiha*), which is always done away from the public eye and is never published.[128] Unsurprisingly, much of the critique of Salafism by its opponents, including Jihadi Salafism, is aimed at undermining the credibility of the *ulama* as stooges of the state.

Quietist, conservative Salafism has adopted two ways to steer the debate away from politics and the role of its *ulama* in condoning the iniquity of the prevailing political system in the Middle East. One is to emphasis a correct daily demeanor that is focused on piety and accepts the status quo. Whereas Jihadi Salafism concentrates on the struggle (jihad) and activism as self-fulfillment (even if it means martyrdom), and the Brotherhood focuses increasingly on practical politics as a means to achieve its goals, 'apolitical' Salafism emphasizes correct behavior and a positive attitude based on civilized norms (*akhlaq*) as its main task, next to propagating the right creed and promoting the right *manhaj*, or practice. In its view, living according to *akhlaq*, in fact following the Sunna of the Prophet, is a sign of belonging to the chosen sect.[129] Extremism (*ghuluw*), together with dissension (*fitna*),[130] its dangerous twin brother, are regarded as enticements of the devil. This means that the individual should defend his own honor, respect those of others, maintain social stability, and above all pursue 'moderation of emotions'. Uncontrolled feelings, such as passions (*ahwa'*), hatred (*aghrad*), resentment (*ahqad*),[131] are believed to lead to extremism (*ghuluw*) or fanaticism (*ta'assub*). Instead, such qualities as endurance (*sabr*), wisdom (*hikma*), friendliness (*rifq*),[132] truthfulness/correctness (*sidq*), and brotherhood (*ukhuwa*)[133] among Muslims, are promoted. The correct practice (*manhaj*) is based on *wasatiyya*, which means following the straight path (*sirat al-mustaqim*) that keeps the believer in the middle of the road and prevents him from falling in the pitfalls of excess (*ifrat*) and severity (*tashaddud*) on the one hand and negligence (*tafrit*) on the other, while applauding generosity (*samaha*), enhancing facilitation (*taysir*) and condemning destruction (*halak*), obstinacy (*tanatta'*) and transgression (*tajawuz*) in deeds and sayings.[134] That the positive attitudes mentioned above are equated with the right creed (*'aqida*), is clear from the accusation that those who oppose Salafism, 'the overwhelming majority of the Muslims', are called 'the people of innovation and passions' (*ahl al-bid'a wa-l-ahwa'*).[135]

From this Salafi terminology and mentality it seems that we are back at Olivier Roy's critique of moralism in his *The Failure of Political Islam*, in which virtue is everything and all the rest is 'sin, plot or illusion'. But it would be a mistake to underestimate the tenacity and pluck of quietist Salafism; it is a highly sophisticated, battle-hardened movement that has been locked into a fierce struggle with its adversaries, especially political Islam since the 1970s,[136] and has developed a highly polemical discourse, called 'muscular' by some.[137] In practice this discourse is a reflection of Salafism's capacity to use Islam's historically-grown ambiguous relations with the state to its utmost.[138] Its power is based on its excellent relations with the authoritarian state from which it obtains privileges in the form of finance and the freedom to build mosques and religious institutes in exchange for attacking their common enemies—especially political Islam—and exerting a pervasive influence on the population. However, it has obtained the largest following when it is led by those who manage to keep their independence from the state (there is always the danger that its opponents accuse the *ulama* of *shirk* for aligning themselves too strongly with the state and infringing upon *tawhid*, the exclusive submission to God), at least publicly, as was the case in Yemen under Muqbil bin Hadi al-Wadi'i.[139] This combination of fighting political battles in the name of pure religion reached its most obvious form in its attack on 'extremism' (*ghuluw*) later conveniently presented as the Saudi 'War on Terrorism'. By some regarded as a recent policy that dates from 9/11 and especially 2003, when Saudi Arabia came under attack from al-Qaeda on the Arabian Peninsula,[140] (led by among others Yusuf al-'Uyairi) it dates back to the split with the Muslim Brotherhood in the 1980s and 1990s, and even earlier.[141] Much of the debate also concerns the relationship with reality, which is the red thread through most modern Islamic political thought. Whereas critics of Salafism, such as 'Abd al-Khaliq 'Abd al-Rahman, accuse the Salafi sheikhs in Saudi Arabia of having lost contact with reality, they deny that reality should be the main focus of religion.[142]

It is illuminating to delve deeper into this anti-terrorism campaign not only to show how Salafism works, but also to give an insight into the sharp divisions that are opening up between Salafism and the Muslim Brotherhood as a result of the greater involvement of the latter in politics. A variety of adversaries are targeted by quietist Salafism in this campaign, each for different reasons. Favorite targets are the founder of the Muslim Brotherhood, Hasan al-Banna (d. 1949) (who is accused of being totally ignorant of Islam, and being a political activist before a religious purifier), Sayyid Qutb[143] (for being the founder of Jihadism and corrupting Salafism), and above all the two 'hybrids' between the Brotherhood and Salafism, Muhammad Surur Zayn 'Abidin[144] and 'Abd al-Rahman 'Abd al-Khaliq,[145] or more recently Abu Hasan al-Ma'rib[146] (these last three for being the closest to Salafism and diluting Salafism in Brotherhood activism). Not incidentally all these adversaries are Egyptians (except for Muhammad Surur, who is Syrian), although the Egyptian 'hybrids' have left their homeland long ago under Nasser. They studied at Medina Islamic University in the 1960s and there mixed the doctrinaire Salafism with Brotherhood activism. All are in the end thrown together as sources of terrorism and their genealogy is traced further back to the first century *hijra* and the *khawarij*, a radical sect that is vilified by Salafis because it assassinated the third rightly guided caliph 'Uthman, and therefore are called neo-*khawarij*. They are condemned for being political activists and typically are defined as 'people of passions, innovation and partisanship/divisions' (*ahl al-ahwa' wa-l-bid'a wa-l-tahazzub*).[147]

If unity (*wahda*) and the Muslim community as a unified whole is represented by Salafism as upholders of the Truth and defenders of the *umma*, its opponents are regarded as the opposite. Even their names, according to Salafis, give them away as deviants promoting division (*fitna*), and endless variations on the terms for group (*jama'a, firqa*) are used to disqualify them. The fact that they train followers as cadres (*kawadir*)[148] in itself is regarded as leading to division, their flexibility in accepting divisions on creed and *manhaj* confirms their misjudged tolerance,[149] while a host of further accusations, such as promoting leadership,[150] trying to mobilize the population, disrespect for Saudi Arabia,[151] or support of Saddam Hussein against Saudi Arabia in 1990–1,[152] and above all the acceptance of *hizbiyya* (partyism) and *tahazzub* (partisanship), as well as other modern notions such as pluralism[153] and equal rights for Christian Copts[154] means that they belong to the 'sects of destruction' (*al-firaq al-hilak*) and are held directly responsible for terrorism.[155]

### The Pluralist Breakthrough? The Case of the Syrian Muslim Brotherhood

Despite this strong counter-current, some branches of the Muslim Brotherhood have continued on the road the Egyptian branch pioneered. The Syrian Muslim Brotherhood, led by 'Ali Sadr al-Din al-Bayanuni, who lives in exile in London, has adopted a more profound reformist program than its Egyptian sister organization. Like its Egyptian branch, the Syrian Brotherhood had clashed with the state and had lost out. Unlike the Egyptian branch, however, whose members were in prison when Sayyid Qutb launched his ideas, the Syrian branch was illegal but active and was taken over by a radical wing at the end of the 1970s that led to a clash with the state almost ending in the fall of the Syrian Ba'th regime.[156] The Syrians are therefore more comparable to the Egyptian al-Jama'a al-Islamiyya. This also applies to the revision of their previous ideas on violence. Having started to come to terms with their past in the 1980s,[157] the major public breakthrough occurred in 2000 when The Syrian Muslim Brotherhood issued a critical overview of its own history and its violent past.[158] In an interview in 2002, Bayanuni, who had been involved in the violent clash with the regime as Deputy-General Guide from 1977 to 1982, stressed the necessity of revisionism (*muraja'at*) as a principle: 'it is continuous and permanent; we are constantly revising our life'.[159] It was followed in August 2002 with the presentation of *The Noble National Charter*[160] and the organization of a national conference in London, in which Nasserists, Ba'thists, communists and independent Islamists participated. Finally, in 2004, it published an extensive document of more than a hundred pages, *The Political Project for the Syrian Future*,[161] in which it spelled out its revisionist views, not only rejecting violence and accepting democracy but also embracing a fundamentally new concept of Islamic politics and a thoroughly revised worldview based on a humanist foundation in which the Qutbian *hakimiyya* (sovereignty of God), the Salafi *tawhid* (Oneness of God), and even the Ikhwani *marja'iyya* (sources of Islam) are replaced by the centrality of mankind *insan* (humanity) as the point of reference. The basis of the reform program of the Syrian Brotherhood is the acceptance of the idea of pluralism (*ta'addudiyya*).

Not surprisingly, the basic difference with the other currents is reflected in its approach to 'reality' (*waqi'*). Whereas in Salafism, and especially Jihadi Salafism, reality is regarded as a source of evil and corruption and a thinker like 'Uyairi tries to impose his will on reality and manipulate it in the service of a permanent revolution, or in the Egyptian Brotherhood's case reality is approached with ambivalence, in the writings of the Syrian MB reality is regarded as a fact of life and is accepted as a source of inspiration for reform. Although it is true that it regards Syrian 'reality' as stagnant (*rukud*), dominated by repression (*qahr*) and injustice (*zulm*),[162] it is not rejected because it does not conform to the holy texts of the Qur'an and *hadith*. The Syrian Muslim Brotherhood (MB) accepts reality as a much broader 'social reality' (*al-waqi' al-ijtima'i*), which is anchored in history 'in all its forms, ideational, cultural, behavioral', including its 'customs and tradition'.[163] The Syrian Brotherhood's concept of reality is therefore inclusive and recognizes the importance of the 'Islamic social heritage' (*turath islami ijtima'i*) as the cultural heritage of the past fourteen hundred years, which forms the 'material

ground' on which 'civilizational projects' are based.[164] The consequences of this historical relativism is not only applied to Syrian
past but also to the Brotherhood's own past and the recognition that
it does not embody the truth (*haqq*) but is fallible.[165] The same 'realistic' method is applied to the West. The Brotherhood recommends
its members not to reject the West as the 'Other (*akhar*); rather they
are encouraged to critically evaluate the West, differentiate between
institutions and individuals and accept the positive aspects of its
culture—not just its technology—as part of 'living reality' (*al-hayat
al-waqi'iyya*). Amongst the positive achievements of the West are
international norms of justice, human rights and the concept of good
governance, which should be embraced as universal values and part
of the 'accomplishments of human civilization'.[166]

Recognizing the historical past and present 'social' reality, the
Syrian MB accepts the existence of diversity (*tanawwu'*) as represented in individual forms of interpretation and viewpoints. Diversity is regarded as a universal phenomenon, not an aberration: 'It
is the true reality of every human community'.[167] The Brotherhood
regards it as the only way to preserve the unity of the nation.[168] As
Islam recognizes the difference of tribes and nations, it calls for
mutual understanding (*ta'aruf*) and promotes a 'positive constructive dialogue' (*al-hiwar al-ijabi al-banna'*) that will lead to the respect
and recognition of the Other (*i''tiraf bi-l-akhar*).[169] Having rejected
the claim to truth (*haqq*), so common in political Islam or Salafism,
the emphasis is on mutuality as a 'method of debate' (*manhaj al-
hiwar*).[170] Force is rejected because: 'in this age, with its enormous
range of freedom, it is no longer possible to impose principles
(*aqa'id*), methods (*madhahib*), ideas (*afkar*) or systems (*anzima*) from
above'. Even the *Shari'a* cannot be imposed by force, and fighting
by the sword is only used in self-defense and never as means to
spread the faith.[171] But there are even more important reasons why
the *Shari'a* cannot be imposed. As the Brotherhood recognizes that
the *Shari'a* only provides general guidelines/goals (*al-maqasid al-
'amma*), 'every generation is allowed to choose the form that is in
accordance with *its reality* and to realize *its goals*'.[172] In fact, history
went awry when *ijtihad* (individual interpretation) was no longer
applied and the 'gap between interpretative of the Islamic law and
reality became enormous'.[173] The Brotherhood creates an autono-

mous space for politics by recognizing that the texts (Qur'an and the Sunna) in themselves are holy, but that interpretation 'is not holy and is subject to revisionism and debate'.[174] Moreover, in contrast to Qutb, the Brotherhood embraces the liberating capacity of human reason: 'Islam has given mankind rationality (*'aql*) and a will (*irada*) that forbids him to let his freedom be confiscated in the name of an interest or rule of some people over others *whatever pretext* [including Islam]'.[175]

Politically this view of human life as a historical project, located in a specific time and space, is reflected in the acceptance of pluralism (*ta'addudiyya*). If the *marja'iyya* (religious reference point and source) in the programs of the Egyptian Brotherhood is a barrier for the full autonomy of the political, in the Syrian Brotherhood it has become the basis of and coincides with pluralism and political autonomy.[176] Having accepted the plurality of political parties, each with their own political program and civil society, the concept of the change of power (*tadawiliyya*), it also recognizes the ascension to power of different methods of politics (*manahij*) and different programs (*baramij*), opinions and interpretations, becomes essence of the *marja'iyya*.[177] Even if it states that these should be 'within the confines of the general religious principles of the *umma*' (*fi itar al-marja'iyya al-'amma li-l-umma*), it leaves no room for control over this process.[178] Furthermore, the addition of such vague concepts such as *marja'iyya* 'civilization' (*marja'iyya hadariyya*) immediately relativizes it and regards it not in rigid legal terms but as a flexible, historically, contingent identity (*huwiya dhatiyya*).[179] Moreover, the concept is broadened by accepting universal non-Muslim successes in the field of human rights and basic freedoms, and the notion that 'we strive to benefit from the experiences of the international community'.[180] Finally, even if the *Shari'a* is accepted as the juridical framework, it is mostly regarded in general terms as promoting justice (*'adl*), equality (*musawa'*) and mutual responsibility (*takaful*).[181] The central concept in the political philosophy of the Syrian Brotherhood is citizenship (*muwatina*), which in modern times has replaced the concept of the protected religious minorities (*dhimmis*) and guarantees complete equality in rights and duties, which must be laid down in the constitution.[182] Another part of the *marja'iyya* and citizenship is the sanctity of contracts.

The modern state is a 'contractual state' (*dawla ta'aqudiyya*), which 'is based on the free choice that is the expression of the will of the people'.[183] Given the increasing rift between Salafism and the Brotherhood, it was not surprising that revisionism (*muraja'at*) was immediately and vehemently attacked by a Salafi ideologue as Abu Basir al-Tartusi.[184]

*Conclusion*

Islamic political thought has come a long way during the past quarter of a century. By both trying to justify and reject violence and embracing democracy it has become much more sophisticated than the original Muslim Brotherhood of Hasan al-Banna, Sayyid Qutb, or the simple tracts of the Egyptian groups which caught international attention in the 1970s.[185] Even compared to the Gudrun Krämer's analysis of the movement in the mid-1990s, political thinking has deepened and broadened and has become more complex. In particular the struggle between Salafism and the Brotherhood has given it an extra dimension. It seems safe to say that on the whole political consciousness of the Islamist movement has grown, as is apparent from its concern with 'reality', which includes the interests of its following, the preservation of the organization, the complexity of the struggle with the state and the keen awareness that violence is a dead-end that will end in destruction not only of the own organization but also of the prospects of Islam as a whole. The emphasis with at least its more perceptive leaders and thinkers has moved on to civil rights and the development of Islamic concepts of citizenship and an interest in constitutional reform and the restriction of political power instead of expanding it in the name of God. The rise of this new attitude is not an accident; it is linked to the emergence of a professional class that emphasizes an Islamic identity, has acquired vested interests and has become part of a new middle class that entertains new ambitions and new ways of attaining these ambitions. As these ambitions have become more clearly defined, the ideas and methods of the struggle have become more focused and realistic. At the same time, it is clear that this trend has not succeeded and is heavily contested. A strong imaginative jihadist (youth) culture has emerged that has given violence a new impulse. As is apparent, not all Brotherhood-inspired movements have laid down their weapons. National-religious resistance in Palestine still uses the religious rhetoric of jihad, but this serves a specific goal of liberation and national and international mobilization has become less of a goal in itself and has less of a utopian dimension, as is the case of Jihadi Salafism.

The overall picture now seems to be a triangular struggle between Jihadi Salafism of Osama bin Laden, Yusuf al-'Uyairi and others on one angle, the different Muslim Brotherhood branches on the other, and purist, quietist Salafism on the third. The differences are reflected in the way the currents analyze reality and the discourse and terminology they have developed in analyzing it or rejecting it. Although there are mixtures and 'hybrids', as we have seen with the Association of Muslim Scholars in Iraq, which mixed Jihadi Salafism with nationalism and pragmatism, or the Salafi purist and Brotherhood activist combination in Muhammad Surur and 'Abd al-Khaliq, on the whole the relations are clear. During the past three decades the professionals of the Brotherhood have developed a whole new inclusionary discourse on 'reality' that includes terms like humanity (*insan*), culture (*hadara*), heritage (*turath*) and modernism (*hadatha*). Within this discourse terms have evolved connoting mutuality (typically a sixth or eighth form in Arabic), like tolerance (*tasamuh*), co-operation (*ta'awun*), co-existence (*ta'ayush*), mutual understanding (*tafahum*), respect (*ihtiram*), mutual recognition (*i'tiraf*); or political terms that reflect flexibility, like multi-party system (*hizbiyya*) democracy (*dimuqratiya*) and freedom (*hurriya*). In the end 'positive' political/cultural connotations, like pluralism (*ta'addudiyya*), progress (*taqaddum*), and even previous traditional theological terms as reform (*islah*) and renewal (*tajdid*) are accepted and given a new content. This trend has infiltrated the writings of previous jihadi or more radical activist groups, such as the Jama'a al-Islamiyya and other violent groups that recently have renounced violence, which show how strong this trend has become and the extent to which violence has been discredited.

In contrast, Jihadi Salafism revolves around unbridgeable dichotomy. Reality is primarily regarded as negative and the world is seen as a clash of civilizations, a zero-sum game. Progress is regarded not as the political manipulation of reality but as its destruction in order to install a new order. This is expressed in the adoption of rigid exclusionary theological terms which draw clear borders between the saved and the damned. Its discourse revolves around a strict definition of creed (*'aqida*) and principles (*mabadi'*) which lead to a certain method and tools (*manhaj*) to distance one-self from the evil and show loyalty (*wala' wa-l-bara'*), and to imple-ment (*tatbiq*) the method (*manhaj*) by means of jihad. It is a top-down deductive method and its success depends on discipline and bravery of the *mujahid* rather than the flexibility and wit of the lawyer or the creativity of the social movement. It is the violence of the person who has made himself believe that he has nothing to lose, rather than the member of the middle class who has property and children to protect. This has not been a continuous process, but is a combination of the revival of the Qutbian trend, the closed worldview of Salafism, and the disastrous policy of the West in the Middle East and the Muslim world. Whereas it seemed that during the past two and a half decades, with the defeat of the Muslim Brotherhood in Syria in the 1980s, the Groupe Islamique Armé (GIA) in Algeria and al-Jama'a al-Islamiyya in Egypt in the 1990s, violence was discredited as a theoretical and practical dead end, after 9/11 and especially after the US invasion of Afghanistan and Iraq, jihadism has been given a new life-lease, on the ground in Iraq, and especially in the imagination of young people by means of the internet. Although with the defeat of al-Qaeda in Iraq the trend now seems to be moving again in the direction of the coun-tervailing trends, this battle is by no means over. The most impor-tant question is, what next? As the authoritarian regimes in the Middle East hardly seem inclined to budge and are unwilling to liberalize their political system sufficiently to further stimulate the democratic tendencies in the Brotherhood movements, having thoroughly defeated the violent trend in Syria, Saudi Arabia, Egypt, Algeria, Morocco. Instead, they seem to invest heavily in quietist Salafism, or other forms of quietist and pious Islam, as a means to combat the canalization of political demands by the mid-dle classes. This will have far-reaching consequences. In ideological and practical politics the continuation of authoritarian regimes means that ideological ambiguity and practicing politics 'by other means', i.e. religion, will continue. Although violence has become impossible and counter-productive and thinkers along democratic lines have become important, one wonders how strong this trend can become if the avenues of expression of these trends are limited. A big question is the role Salafism will play in this battle of the minds and canalization of grievances. Will the pious, quietist, conservative trend, directly or indirectly supported by authoritarian states, prevail, or will the hybrid forms with a greater activist orientation become more prominent? Will Jihadi Salafism die out or revive again? One point, however, is certain: insight into the development of these trends and the transformations in their mutual relations is important for European policy towards states in the Middle East, Muslim populations in the region and Muslims in Europe, as so many of these trends are also present on European soil. Simply denying that Islam is dynamic and therefore should not be condemned as a whole—as some politicians and academics in the Netherlands insist it should—is not only not an option but is also counter-productive, for it drives many Muslims into the arms of the most intolerant trends.

# 3

# TURKEY

## BETWEEN POST-ISLAMISM AND POST-KEMALISM

*Jean Marcou*[1]

The establishment of true democracy in Turkey has for long been held back by what Nilüfer Göle calls 'the vicious circle of Turkish politics'.[1] In every period of democratic progress there has been a revival of religious values. The repeated military interventions seen during the second half of the twentieth century all sought—despite variations in context and in methods—to check this development in one way or another. This is because, for the army and the elites holding the commanding positions in the state, secularism has always been the ultimate objective. Secularism does not only mean separation of religion and state, it embodies an ideal of modernization of society from the top down, which was the founding principle of the Republic in 1923. But since the establishment of multi-party democracy after the Second World War, the governing secularist elites have often realized that universal suffrage could mean submission to the people's values, especially their religious values. For that reason, while agreeing to democratization they have never given up a right to watch over the operation of the system, so as to invoke a right of intervention when necessary.[2]

Since 2002 there has been a new cycle with the coming to power of the AKP,[3] a party that emerged from the Islamist movement but no longer defines itself as Islamist. This party's political success, and especially its electoral success, seems to be breaking the vicious circle of controlled democracy just mentioned. The present chapter analyses the origins of this post-Islamist phenomenon[4] and its gradual conquest of the main centers of power, and then examines the implications of the current political changes in Turkey.

## From Islamism to Post-Islamism: The Three Ages of Turkish Islamism

The AKP victory in 2002, involving a spectacular defeat of the traditional parties, was also the outcome of a spectacular change in Turkish Islamism.

### The First AKP Victory, November 2002

What happened in Turkey on 3 November 2002 was a historic event, in many ways recalling the blows inflicted on the political and military establishment by Adnan Menderes in 1950 and by Turgut Özal in 1983. With 34.22 per cent of votes cast the AKP, a new party just emerging from Islamism, won 363 of the 550 seats in the Turkish Grand National Assembly. Thus it not only had a comfortable absolute majority, it was only four members short of the enhanced majority required for revising the Constitution and for electing the President of the Republic in the first round of voting.

While the AKP's success had been expected, having been forecast in opinion polls, the scale of it caused surprise, for nobody had forecast such a rout of the other Turkish political formations, especially the parties of the outgoing government coalition (the DSP,[5] MHP[6] and ANAP). In fact, besides the AKP only the CHP,[7] the People's Republican Party founded by Mustafa Kemal, which obtained 19 per cent of the vote and won 163 seats, was now represented in the Grand National Assembly. The other political parties, whether of the centre right (like the DYP[8] and the ANAP), of the left (like the DSP) or of the far right (like the MHP), failed to reach the threshold of 10 per cent of votes cast needed to have representation in the parliament.

Even though this event was immediately identified by commentators as the latest twist in the long story of relations between Islam and the reforming secularist state in Turkey, soundings of public opinion showed that the main reason for the AKP's great success was based on the difficult economic situation and the social crisis that Turkey had been going through for several years. But while the economic situation and the consequent social problems were the voters' main preoccupation in the 2002 parliamentary elections, that does not mean that the elections had no political significance. In fact the massive switching of votes to the AKP, by voters of all sympathies, showed the Turkish electorate's distrust of the parties of the system, which were blamed for the political impasse into which Turkey was plunged. Tired of the impotence and demagogy of the traditional parties, Turkish voters preferred to turn—as Rus-‚en Çakır told us—to 'men with hearts and convictions'.[9] However, those men would not have been able to win if they had not managed to carry through a profound change within themselves, in many ways resembling a real cultural revolution.

The Metamorphoses of Turkish Islamism

At the very moment when they had just won their victory, paradoxically the Islamists vanished from Turkey's political landscape. In the 2002 elections the only political formation calling itself truly Islamist—Necmettin Erbakan's Saadet Partisi[10]—won only a meager share of votes (2.5 per cent), too small for it to have any representation in parliament. For its part the sweepingly victorious AKP, which came from the same stable as the Saadet Partisi, now rejected the label of 'Islamist' and called itself a 'conservative democratic' party. To understand this, it is essential to look back at the growth of the Refah Partisi in the 1990s.

Refah was originally the heir to the political parties created by Necmettin Erbakan, whose experiences from the late 1960s onwards constituted what we have termed the 'first age of political Islam in Turkey'.[11] This party's increase in strength reached a peak between 1994 and 1997. After taking control of the biggest cities in the country in the local elections of 1994, and emerging as the leading party in the parliamentary elections of 1995, in 1996 Refah saw its leader, Necmettin Erbakan, appointed Prime Minister. However, the situation then was not like that in 2002, because unlike the

AKP later, Refah did not have a parliamentary majority. Erbakan in fact headed a coalition government where he had to come to terms on essential matters with Tansu Çiller's DYP. So he was never able to carry out properly the policy he desired. And above all, on 28 February 1997, the Islamist leader was hit by a severe order from the National Security Council (NSC),[12] calling on him to respect secularism and the fundamental principles of the Republic. This event, recalled today as the 'post-modern coup d'état', was the starting signal for a series of maneuvers by the army which, by provoking the dislocation of the governing coalition, eventually brought about Erbakan's resignation in June 1997. In effect the political-military establishment, without any need for direct military intervention, succeeded in halting the first experiment at Islamist government. This setback was followed, in January 1998, by the dissolution of Refah by the Constitutional Court, another traditional defender of the secular state. Even though another party was set up to replace it, the Fazilet Partisi,[13] the Islamists' spirit seemed to have been broken for a time by this blow. There followed an electoral defeat in the 1999 parliamentary elections, and then internal divisions and the problems caused by successive bans on holding public office imposed on the main leaders. So ended the second age of Turkish Islamism, the age of militant Islamism.

However, this political adversity turned out to be an opportunity for revival, leading to the creation of the AKP. Some Islamists engaged in critical reflection, based on their experience in government, which emphasized the need to get away from the position of an anti-system protest force so as to join positively in the major political debates in Turkish society: on democratization, human rights, the position of women, the application for membership of the European Union, etc. This orientation towards a new beginning, led by Recep Tayyip Erdoğan and Abdullah Gül, was opposed by the barons of Turkish Islamism gathered around Necmettin Erbakan, especially at Fazilet's first and only congress.

That congress was a true turning point. The modernists under Recep Tayyip Erdoğan resisted the party leadership and for the first time challenged the monolithic line that had prevailed until then in all the previous Turkish Islamist formations. After this development and the dissolution of Fazilet in 2001, two parties emerged to claim that party's heritage: on one side the Saadet Partisi, which Necmettin Erbakan's supporters joined, on the other the more moderate AKP, headed by Recep Tayyip Erdoğan and Abdullah Gül.

From its foundation the AKP displayed a determination to appeal to activists and personalities from other political groups or from civil society. This new trend was amplified during the 2002 election campaign by a clearly visible change in behavior. On a number of the problems facing society the post-Islamists of the AKP, giving up ideological slogans, embarked on dialogue and advocated a search for consensus. In an economic and social context in which the parties of the system were completely discredited, and many voters saw their traditional certainties shaken, this strategy allowed the AKP to widen the traditional electoral support base of the Turkish Islamist movement, and this made it possible for the party to achieve its best ever score and gain an absolute majority in parliament.

### The Secularist Establishment and the 'AKP Phenomenon'

No real partisan political opposition to this new phenomenon took shape during the 2002–07 parliament. However, following the 2002 elections the Kemalist party, the CHP, had a card to play, as it was the only opposition party represented in parliament, and could use its historic name to exploit the discontent and disappointment that the AKP—like any party in power—was likely to arouse. But over five years the CHP and other parties of the system—especially those of the centre right, the DYP and ANAP—all failed to work out a strategy for return to power.

This situation showed how Turkey's political class and traditional elites were incapable of talking to the people, having been so used to speaking on its behalf for so many years. Far from facing the reality of the 'AKP phenomenon', those political leaders tended to underestimate it, even to despise it. This attitude had all the arrogance of educated classes looking down on those they see as political upstarts. Many experienced political leaders in 2002 thought that the AKP, a 'catch-all' party, would split and that its leaders, in view of the difficult economic and social situation, would not last more than a few months in charge of the government.[14] Hence they confined themselves to opposing the new government, constantly accusing it of having a 'hidden agenda' to re-Islamize society from below.

As the traditional parties' capacity for response was feeble, it was above all state institutions, controlled by the army, that took responsibility for the secularist counter-attack. Confrontation between a government dynamic impelled by the AKP and state power in the hands of the political-military establishment steadily developed during the 2002–07 parliament. Alongside the army and the judicial hierarchy (particularly the Constitutional Court, the Court of Appeal and the Council of State), the Presidency of the Republic, since 1999 in the hands of a former judge of the Constitutional Court, Necdet Sezer, was at the heart of the resistance network, notably blocking the enactment of suspect government reforms and controlling appointments to senior state positions. In October 2003, at the National Day ceremonies, the Presidency set itself up very symbolically as a bastion of republican secularism, by refusing to invite AKP ministers' wives who wore the *hijab*. The YÖK[15]—the effective national directorate of the universities, controlling rectors' appointments and teaching programs—proved to be another particularly active supporter of the secularist camp.

There were a number of difficulties and contradictions in the counter-attack, however. Between 2002 and 2004 in particular, a considerable number of AKP reforms—demilitarization of civilian public institutions, progress on the rule of law, minority rights, decentralization, etc.—were directly linked to Turkey's application to join the EU. This meant that in opposing the AKP, the secularist camp often found itself in opposition to Europe. At first bothered by this contradiction, some '*laikçi*'[16] gradually came to turn it to their account, seeing Europe as a 'threat' to the secular Republic.

At the same time the questions of the attitude to adopt towards the AKP government and the application for EU membership aroused divisions, and even plans for a coup d'état, within the army itself. But with a moderate character like General Hilmi Özkök as Chief of General Staff from 2002 to 2006, it was possible to keep relations between the government and the army calm. All things considered, even though the experiment started by the AKP victory was able to run its course in this first parliament, it can be suggested that a logic of bipolar confrontation was established at that time, to be revealed and expressed in an especially significant way during 2007, when presidential and parliamentary elections were held.

## The Presidential Crisis and the Parliamentary Elections of 2007

From the end of 2006 there was increasing tension at the highest levels of the state, between the AKP government and the institutions that particularly represented Kemalist orthodoxy. It was not so much the parliamentary elections, scheduled for November 2007, as the presidential election that caused this state of tension and led, in April and May 2007, to a serious crisis, resulting in the parliamentary elections being brought forward to July.

### Presidential Election Issues; Growing Tension at the Top (End of 2006–Beginning of 2007)

In Turkey, which has since the 1950s been under a simple parliamentary regime where the prime minister governs with the support of a majority, the President is above all a referee, a guarantor of the Republic's founding principles.[17] However, the 1982 Constitution, drawn up after the 1980 coup d'état, added to the president's prerogatives,[18] giving him, notably, the important power of appointment to senior state posts and the possibility of blocking enactment of laws considered dangerous to the Republic, by a sort of suspensory veto. Ahmet Necdet Sezer, elected in 1999 and known for his Kemalist ideas,[19] often came into conflict with the government between 2002 and 2007, making use of the powers just mentioned. Hence, during the 2002–7 parliament, the presidency of the Republic became for secularists a final line of defense against a majority party in control not only of the government and parliament but also of 70 per cent of Turkey's municipal authorities (including most of the big cities). This presidential role of containment was strengthened by the fact that, from 2001, the National Security Council's powers were greatly reduced, and it officially no longer had any more than consultative power. But as well as this political and constitutional contest there was a symbolic one: preserving the Çankaya[20] from the 'ultimate affront' to that sanctuary of the secular Republic—the possible election of an AKP president with a wife wearing the *hijab*!

And as President Sezer approached the end of his term of office, initially scheduled for 16 May 2007, it seemed likely that Recep Tayyip Erdoğan could succeed him. The president was then still elected by the Grand National Assembly, the single-chamber parliament where the AKP had since 2002 had a large majority. The approaching presidential contest thus became a cause of heightened rivalry between the government in power and the state power wielded by the establishment.

So the latter, from the autumn of 2006, set about persuading the Prime Minister not to stand for the presidency. This task was undertaken first of all by the army and its new Chief of General Staff, General Yaşar Büyükanıt. Far from being what is called in France a *'grande muette'*,[21] the army in Turkey thus became 'the big talker', never ceasing to express its views on both national and international affairs in the months before the presidential elections. Its untimely declarations were in reality all aimed at spreading the message that, despite recent demilitarization reforms, the army was still a political actor that could not be bypassed. On 12 April 2007, some days before the deadline for registration of candidates for the presidential election, General Büyükanıt even held a press conference where he set out a profile for the new president, emphasizing that the person chosen must be committed to secularism, 'in acts and not only in appearance'.

At the same time the YÖK made its views known equally clearly. Speaking during a general conference of rectors on 5 April 2007, its chairman, Erdoğan Teziç,[22] caused surprise by calling for the election to the presidency of the Republic of a neutral person committed to secularism and 'modern science'. Erdoğan Teziç went further and, speaking as a constitutional expert, spoke of the conditions attached to the election of the next president of the republic. He explained that for this election there must be, in the first round, a quorum equal to two thirds of members of parliament, 367 out of 550 in all (though the letter of the Constitution does not stipulate anything like this),[23] and he warned Recep Tayyip Erdoğan of the risk of a boycott of the vote by opposition deputies if he dared to stand for election. The TÜSIAD,[24] the leading Westernized employers' organization, did not hesitate to join the campaign also, though in a less categorical way, and called on the Prime Minister not to stand, about ten days before the presidential election.[25]

The mobilization of secularist forces reached a peak, from mid-April 2007, with the holding of Republican *'miting's*[26] for the defense of secularism[27] in the major cities. Through these gatherings the secularist camp aimed to back up an argument it had been developing since the onset of the crisis: that the parliament elected in 2002, which because of the voting system represented only 55 per cent of the Turkish voters, lacked legitimacy for electing a president to serve for the next seven years.[28]

## Presidential Election Boycotted and Annulled (April 2007)

This institutional and popular show of force did not make the AKP give way, and eventually it presented Abdullah Gül as candidate for the Presidency of the Republic, on 25 April 2007. This unexpected development, far from calming the fears aroused by the possibility of Erdoğan standing, heightened them. Indeed the AKP government's foreign minister, one of the party's founders, whose wife Hayrünnisa wore the *hijab* like Recep Tayyip Erdoğan's wife,[29] was no more acceptable to the secularists as a candidate.

So Abdullah Gül's candidacy sealed the presidential crisis, and the Kemalist party carried out its threat of a boycott, made in the wake of the YÖK chairman's statements. On 27 April 2007 the opposition deputies, mainly of the CHP, refused to take part in the first round of the presidential election and applied to the Constitutional Court for annulment of the vote. A few days later, on 1 May 2007, the Court, considering that 367 deputies were needed not only for election of the President (as Article 102 of the Constitution said) but also for the vote to take place (which was more debatable), granted the application. This decision, which made it impossible to continue with a presidential election by the outgoing parliament, effectively caused the parliamentary elections to be brought forward.

But this still-born presidential election was notable, above all, for the famous 'e-memorandum' in which the army, in the evening of the day of the first round of voting (27 April 2007), recalled on its website its determination to see that the Republic's founding principles were respected, also emphasizing the 'worrying' development of practices contrary to secularism. This 'e-memorandum', which some called an 'e-coup d'état', brought an immediate and very sharp reaction from the government, reminding the army of its duty towards the Constitution. Never had a civilian government spoken in that way to the military authorities. This incident illustrated the extreme tension that was to dominate the staging of the parliamentary elections, now brought forward to 22 July 2007.

## July 2007: The AKP's Second Victory

Following the elections on that day the AKP, with 46.4 per cent of votes cast, had well exceeded its 2002 score (34.3 per cent), while its main adversary the CHP (allied to the DSP) only just retained its share of votes (with 20.79 per cent compared with 19.4 per cent), and the nationalist MHP (with 14.25 per cent, compared with 8.3 per cent in 2002) was the only other party to get past the threshold of 10 per cent needed for representation in parliament; the Kurds of the DTP[30] won twenty seats through the arrangements for independent candidates. How to explain this unanswerable AKP victory?

The first explanation probably lies in the AKP's skill in playing the game of parliamentary democracy and positioning itself as a party of government. In a very significant way the AKP's campaign called on Turkish voters to vote as in a referendum both for the Prime Minister's concrete achievements and for his re-election. Rather than enter into the logic of the conflict started by the still-born April presidential election, Recep Tayyip Erdoğan preferred to move out of the crisis from the top, running a real campaign for general elections. It is indeed striking how the majority party, far from taking up the challenge of the ideological debate as it had done throughout the presidential crisis, ended up distancing itself from the quarrel between *'laikçi'* and *'dinci'*.[31] By deferring consideration of latent conflicts such as the one concerning the ban on the *hijab* at universities, by reassuring business circles, and by setting out to win over neglected minorities and communities (especially the Armenians, Kurds and Alevis), Recep Tayyip Erdoğan plainly set out to broaden his electoral base. Meanwhile his main adversaries concentrated above all on crystallizing an ideological conflict with secularism or nationalism.

The second explanation for the AKP victory is less tactical and more fundamental; it relates to the party's ability to rise to the challenges of contemporary Turkey and talk to the people. For the AKP's victory was not so much a victory of Islamism over secularism, it was above all the victory of a popular movement that represented the changes in Turkey during the last decade. While the party retained influence in traditional rural areas, it had influence above all among the newly urbanized working classes, which had tasted a better life and now wanted to see their situation and the setting of their lives improved.

As in 2002, in the last resort economic and social concerns were those that most motivated Turkish voters. This shows that the conflict that we have just described at length was also a social confrontation between, on the one hand, a secularized elite which had for long had a monopoly of the main loci of power in the state and the major means of production, and, on the other side, new social groups still influenced by religious values and traditions, but now on the way up the social ladder. Recep Tayyip Erdoğan—who, we should recall, comes from that social background—responded to these groups' aspirations by his economic achievements between 2002 and 2007.

## The Second AKP Parliament

After the AKP victory in the parliamentary elections, Abdullah Gül was elected President of the Republic by parliament at the end of August 2007; while the CHP vainly persisted with its attitude, the other opposition parties newly elected (the MHP, DSP and DTP) decided not to boycott the vote. Taking over the presidency set the seal on an altered political balance favoring the AKP, which was shown first in a reopening of the constitutional question.

### The Constitutional Question Reopened

The 1982 Constitution had always been contested in Turkey since it came into force, and on the eve of the AKP's accession to power

71

in 2002 there was even a relative political consensus around the idea of constitutional reform.[32] However, to avoid fuelling suspicions that it had a hidden agenda, the AKP government carefully avoided raising the constitutional question during the first parliament it controlled (2002–07), and worked above all on securing the adoption, by measures to harmonies legislation, of reforms required for the opening of negotiations for EU membership; those negotiations started in October 2005.

It should be obvious that the 2007 elections reopened the debate on the continued existence of a Constitution that had emerged from the coup d'état of 1980; for the main obstacles to an AKP member standing for the presidency were the Constitutional Court and the institutions (such as the YÖK) and the standards set up as safeguards by the 1982 Constitution. In October the government secured passage of a constitutional revision responding to the presidential crisis of April-May 2007.[33] But most important, at the same time it set about the framing of a new Constitution, called a 'civilian Constitution'. In the AKP's view the 2007 crisis had clearly shown that the state power was using devices in the 1982 Constitution to block the way for the projects of a government chosen by universal suffrage. This meant that the eventual demilitarization of the Turkish political system involved elaboration of a new Constitution.

However, the proposal for a 'civilian Constitution' was to prolong indefinitely the political polarization caused by the 2007 elections. By reopening debates on secularism, it revived during 2008 the conflicts between the government and the Kemalist state institutions defending the system. It was not so much the army, now weakened, as the judicial hierarchy that confronted the AKP when it embarked on reforms. In June 2008 its constitutional amendment lifting the ban on wearing the *hijab* was annulled by the Constitutional Court, and before that court the Prosecutor General of the Appeal Court brought an action for the dissolution of the AKP; this, however, ended with financial penalties only.

Although the majority party overcame this new crisis, it delayed the party's project for a 'civilian Constitution'. But finally, in 2010, while it was heading for the end of its second parliament, the government decided to carry through a constitutional revision aimed at curbing its principal adversary, the judicial hierarchy. This reform restructured the Constitutional Court and the Supreme Board of Judges and Prosecutors, lifted the immunity granted to the authors of the 1980 coup d'état, and set out a series of varied measures like the creation of a post of ombudsman. This initiative seemed to involve some risk for the AKP, after its only partial success in the local elections of March 2009 and signs of the wear and tear of holding power, indicated particularly by some AKP reforms getting bogged down, such as the 'democratic opening' intended as a political answer to the Kurdish question. The constitutional revision was finally adopted by a referendum which was held, symbolically, on 12 September 2010.[34] Recep Tayyip Erdogan's party secured a 58 per cent 'Yes' vote, much higher than had been forecast by polls, showing once again its skill at running an election campaign, during which it had succeeded in showing itself as the party of change even after eight years in government. In addition, by winning its sixth victory since 2002[35] in a popular vote, the AKP reinforced the myth of its invincibility and showed that the process it had begun when assuming power was far from slowing down. The Kemalists of the CHP, vanguard of the campaign for a 'No' vote, were not able—even though they were in the midst of a revival after a new leader, Kemal Kılıçdaroğlu, had taken over—to carry conviction as a democratic alternative in this constitutional debate, in which they found it difficult to avoid being seen as defenders of the 1982 Constitution. Once again, the AKP managed to get a very wide spectrum of votes on its side, notably from people who, without totally agreeing with the party, sought above all to show their desire for the complete disappearance of a constitutional text derived from a military coup d'état.

*The Army Cut Down to Size*

While this revision of the Constitution was more modest than the project for a civilian Constitution—which was in any case expected to be on the agenda again in the campaign for the next parliamentary elections—that is no reason to overlook the spectacular changes that have occurred since 2007 regarding the position and the political role of the army.

Contrary to a commonly-held idea, the special presence of the army in Turkey's political system was not the result of permanent military influence in public affairs since the founding of the Republic. The army's contemporary political role was forged above all through the successive interventions which, in the second half of the twentieth century, enabled it to move in force into the whole Turkish system.[36] The 1982 Constitution was the culmination of a process that made the army a real political body, with a right to intervene in the major loci of power, usually not subject to common legal process, and enjoying an organic autonomy allowing it to co-opt its own chiefs. It is this system that seems to have been definitively dismantled since 2007. From being a dominant actor in the Turkish political system, the army is in fact turning into a more and more dominated actor.

This process was made possible by the combined actions of the courts and the media. In retrospect one may consider that it was already starting at the end of the preceding parliament. In 2005–06, in the Şemdinli affair,[37] a prosecutor dared to make investigations in circles close to the general staff. In 2007, in the affair of Admiral Örnek's notebooks, the weekly *Nokta* published the former Turkish navy chief's diaries describing two preparations for a coup d'état in 2004. But in the former case the magistrate entrusted with the case was finally taken off it, and in the latter, the magazine was purely and simply closed down. Since then that situation has become unthinkable.

Since 2007, in fact, the press and the courts have revealed a series of military plots or activities on the fringe of the law by the army. The exposure of the emblematic 'Ergenekon' network, a nationalist organization implicated in numerous destabilization operations, with ramifications in the army, the press and the universities, was followed by non-stop revelation of military plots or secret criminal activity: the Cage plan,[38] the 'plan of action against reaction',[39] the Balyoz plan,[40] etc. The *Taraf*[41] daily played a central role; it originated most of the revelations, which constantly cast suspicions on the army, showing how it assumed it could act illegally with impunity.[42] At the same time some ordinary magistrates, when handling these cases, did not hesitate to act against military personnel of whatever rank—unlike the judicial hierarchy which had, in the past, more often covered up these activities. In 2008 retired generals were charged and imprisoned, but 2009 saw this happen to serving senior officers, and in 2010 it was seen that no military authority, of whatever rank, was immune from a summons or a humiliating arrest and the consequences that followed.

This policy of putting the military hierarchy in its place was also expressed by major reforms and transfers. In June-July 2009, in the wake of the revelation of the 'plan of action against reaction', the government passed a law reforming military justice. It authorized civilian courts to try military personnel in peacetime for conspiracy against the government, acts prejudicial to national security, organized crime or violation of the Constitution, and also gave civilian courts competence to try civilians in peacetime for offences that had previously come under the military penal code. This law was annulled by the Constitutional Court in January 2010, but that did not affect the competence that civilian courts had acquired concretely, since the start of the 'Ergenekon' affair, to prosecute military personnel. Lastly, in July-August 2010 the government, for the first time, challenged the appointments and promotions that the Supreme Military Council[43] made each year, by refusing to promote military personnel facing legal proceedings and, as a sequel, blocking for five days the appointment of the new Chief of General Staff who had been put forward. This event seemed to experts a decisive step forward towards total demilitarization of the Turkish political system.

*The AKP and Contemporary Changes in the Turkish Political System*

Other changes, important for the evolution of political power relations, are in progress, as well as those affecting the judicial system and the army. Since 2007 in particular, the government, well in control of the top levels of the civil service, has taken control of the YÖK and the university hierarchy more generally, which had for long been a centre of opposition to it. As for the media, the supremacy of the Doğan group,[44] another focus of opposition to the government's actions, is being challenged by the gradual disintegration of the group, by the rising power of pro-government media, and by the success of press organs of a new type, like the *Zaman*[45] and *Taraf* dailies.

These alterations in balance within the apparatus of the state and the media would not be a cause for concern if the media had not appeared, in the last few years, as the only institution capable of counterbalancing an all-powerful government. The CHP, even though it was confirmed in 2007 as the main opposition force, is finding it difficult to become a credible party of government. It represents the elites and a portion of the middle classes, and struggles to attract support from the popular masses. Its initiatives to win the votes of women wearing the *hijab* (after previously opposing the constitutional revision to lift the ban on the *hijab* at the universities) and its criticisms of the army (after frequently working to thwart demilitarization reforms) have often led to its message being ignored since the start of the present parliament. The CHP is permanently caught between its aspiration to be a European social democratic party, on the one hand, and its attachment to the security system inherited from Kemalism, on the other. Hence it is struggling to get into the post-Kemalist era. However, the enthronement of the CHP's new leader, Kemal Kılıçdaroğlu, in May 2010, after the scandal that brought down the immovable Deniz Baykal, has given new hope to the secularist camp. Many prominent personalities who had left the party have returned to it, and Kemal Kılıçdaroğlu, presented by his supporters as the Gandhi of Turkish politics, centers his language mainly on the satisfaction of social needs and the struggle against corruption. This new Kemalist leader, who originates from Tunceli, could also regain the Alevi vote, which has been tending to turn away from the party in recent years. But the CHP will have a hard task to get beyond the 30 per cent share of the vote that it needs if it is to rival Recep Tayyip Erdoğan's party.

This weakness of the parliamentary opposition arouses fears of too much concentration of power. It is significant that in the language of the secularist opposition, the allegation of a 'hidden agenda'—seeking to show that there was an Islamist plot lurking behind the AKP government's actions—has been replaced by the theory of a 'civilian coup d'état', arousing fears of a dictatorship of the majority. Public opinion, without going so far as to share that analysis, is nonetheless wondering about the ongoing alteration in balance. Notably, Hanefi Avci's work describing the infiltration of the police by Fethullah Gülen religious organization was one of the best-sellers of the summer of 2010.[46]

The AKP for its part is following, more than ever, a pragmatic strategy playing on several of its facets. Recep Tayyip Erdoğan's party is a political force contesting the army's hold over the system; it also repudiates the taboos of Turkish history, recognizes Turkey's diversity of identity and religion, and presents itself as the herald of the rule of law and democracy. It emerged from the Islamist movement, and it readily praises, when necessary, some moral rigidity or a patriarchal idea of the family, while regularly making ambiguous statements about alcohol consumption, polygamy or homosexuality. But as a party of government, defender of the Turkish state, it returns when necessary to nationalist language to oppose Kurdish demands or refuse recognition of the Armenian genocide.

In addition there has been, since the beginning of the second AKP-controlled parliament, a very clear change in Turkish foreign policy,[47] now following the theories of the new foreign minister, Ahmet Davutoğlu. Turkey, which refused to vote for the latest set of sanctions against Iran in June 2010, and whose relations with Israel have continued to worsen, has revived its links with its Arab-Muslim environment. This good neighbor strategy, which some called 'neo-Ottomanist', is shown—besides the policy orientations adopted—by the quality of the personal relations AKP leaders have established with their Muslim neighbors; they do not look down on those neighbors as their secularist predecessors did. In addition, although the Turkish leaders officially deny any hegemonic intentions, their country's new political and economic influence concentrates the attention of the peoples of the region because of the model that it presents in many respects. Turkish television soap operas are watched by millions of Arab viewers, who admire a country where a political party that emerged from the Islamist movement has become the driving force for political change.

It is too soon to say whether these changes will lead to a deepening of democracy or to the coming of an AKP state to replace the previous Kemalist state. However, it is important to note that the changes that have occurred in Turkey during the second AKP-controlled parliament have been the fruit of social and political dynamics proper to Turkey, rather than initiatives linked to Turkey's EU application. Since 2007 the European Commission has constantly reproached the Turkish government for its delay in making the reforms it must carry out to be admitted to the EU. And yet, paradoxically, with the reduced role of the army, the weakening of the judicial hierarchy, and the challenging of several taboos on which the Kemalist state has lived for a long time, Turkey has never changed so much as in the last few years.

4

# THE NEW TREND OF THE MUSLIM
# BROTHERHOOD IN EGYPT

*Mohamed Mosaad Abdel Aziz*

*Background*

To understand the present or future of the Muslim Brotherhood
Group (MBG), Islamism must first be traced and defined. In this
chapter Islamism does not refer specifically to 'political' Islam,[1] but
rather to a more extensive 'modern' Islam. Thus Islamism is
defined as a modern discourse of Islam. It is a discourse whose
object is a reified, though always changing, form of Islam. Three
modern constructions helped to reify Islam and create its modern
discourse: Orientalism culturally, capitalism economically, and the
nation-state project politically. The continuous changes of these
constructions are echoed by ongoing changes in the discourse of
Islamism. Therefore, the landscape of Islamism, as well as the
courses of Islamic movements, has been shaped through cultural
discourses of Orientalism, post-colonialism, or the War on Terrorism; economic institutions of state corporatism, private capitalism,
or economic globalism; and the political structures of nationalist or
neo-liberal states.

There is an ever-growing list of researchers whose work focuses
on Islamic movements. In an old, but not dated, piece, Eric Davis
summarizes their approaches in two models: ideational and socio-

logical. The first views those movements in terms of the development of Islamic thought while the second pays more attention to the social bases and recruitment patterns.[2] Davis asserts that although the sociological model has the privilege of socially contextualizing the Islamic movements, it views the ideology in terms of crude materialism or psycho-social needs.[3] Besides, it fails to 'provide an historical context within which to situate the growth and development of Islamic radicalism'.[4] He suggests a structural model, which is 'centered on the concepts of accumulation, legitimation and authenticity'.[5] His main argument is that 'the increasing contradiction between differential accumulation and decreasing legitimacy (because of state's failure) produces a crisis of authenticity'.[6] In this crisis of authenticity, Davis roots Islamic fundamentalism.

While trying to tie the socioeconomic and cultural factors together, Davis, much like many writers who obsessively question Islamists' faithfulness to 'democracy', frames his work as political competition between two independent political actors; namely Islamists and the state.

Here Davis offers a straightforward Marxist perspective, where Islamists belong to a specific class that is marginalized from state institutions and do not own the economic means of production. In spite of Davis' argument, Ziad Munson writes that the deprivation, anomie, strain and class arguments all fail according to the empirical evidence. To make his point, Munson offers four tables that cover the period from 1930 to 1950 which illustrate how the high days of the Muslim Brotherhood coincided with lower urbanization rate, low representation of the assumed marginalized traditional class in the ranks of the MBG, lower population growth, lower GDP and GNP, and higher equitable distribution of income in society.[7] If the extent of the economic activities of MBG members and institutions in Egypt over the last thirty years is taken into account, the 'control of economic resources' argument could not prevail.[8]

One wonders, however, why it should be a problem, crisis or failure of some sort that is always expected to lie behind the emergence of Islamism. Bryan Turner, for instance, begins his article, 'Class, Generation and Islamism', by writing, 'Political Islam or Islamism is the consequence of social frustrations, articulated around the social divisions of class and generation that followed from the economic crises of the global neoliberal experiments of the 1970s and 1980s'.[9] Islamism is usually portrayed as an aberrant Islam that is either an unexpected or unfortunate mistake in the normal course of history. Michaelle Browers, however, contends that 'there is no "Islam" that can be held apart from "Islamism". Islam contains both more and less ideological expressions and the aim of studies of political ideologies should be to understand those Islamic elements that manifest themselves *as* political ideologies'.[10]

This problem of singling out political Islam from Islam repeats itself when the term 'activism' is used, as a purposeful social action, to define Islamism. Asef Bayat accepts the argument that the term 'political Islam' is simply irrelevant. 'Islamic activism' is a term that 'lacks specificity to point to the recent upsurge of action'. He proposes that activism means 'extra-ordinary, extra-usual practices which aim, collectively or individually, institutionally or informally, to cause social change'.[11] Bayat's 'extra-ordinary' reflects the awkwardness of drawing a line between religious activity and religious activism. Besides these links there is a third difficult line Islamists must extend between the religious and the non-religious in their action. What makes a grocery store Islamic in the sense that its owner calls it 'Supermarket Islamco'? There is one answer to the three difficult questions and it is not ethnographically convenient. What makes Islam Islamism, activity activism, and a mundane action religious is only the intention of the social actor. Can we define a social phenomenon and research it when it is marked by such an elusive essence?

My proposal is not to isolate Islamism, but rather to reconnect it. To isolate Islamism is to isolate and define a specific ideology, distinct social actors, whom we call Islamists, and distinct activities, which we recognize as activism. In *Putting Islam to Work*, Gregory Starrett argues that the modern Egyptian government's moral legitimacy is based on its claim of responsibility for the protection of the Islamic heritage and for the provision of trustworthy religious guidance to young people; it is an embrace between political authority and religious legitimacy, a modernizing project that does not break with traditional religious authority. Islamists, in Starrett's view, are not the prime movers of Islamism, that is politicized Islam, but its end result. Starrett's thesis is that the government had politicized Islam through mass education policies, a strategy which is Islamizing the society and creating a need for a specific form of Islam.[12]

This understanding of the formation of the modern nation state in Egypt should be complemented by the thesis proposed in *Defining Islam for the Egyptian State* by Jakob Skovgaard-Petersen. Petersen argues that state muftis have been striving to Islamize, that is to re-conquer lost territory and incorporate it in an Islamic field of meaning, be that in the field of economics, public morality or elsewhere.[13] Skovgaard-Petersen has placed their significant role in the context of the institutionalization of the modern Egyptian state. In his view, it is that 'entirely new forms of Islam sprang up with the nation state'.[14]

Islamism, therefore, cannot be singled out as a separate ideology, political agenda, or activism of a specific political group that could be called Islamists. Islamism is a modern discourse of Islam that has developed through the foundation and changes of the modern nation-state. The state here should not be used synonymously with the government. The state is the globally embedded, locally extending, modern association of institutions and processes which reflects the interests, conflicts and tensions of different social groups in Egypt, as well as a number of social discourses and the unfolding of capitalism. It is through this state that the core knowledge of Islamism, its system of power, and its subjectivities have been produced and changed.

## Consolidated State/Consolidated Islamism

Most researchers trace Islamism back to 1928, when Hasan al-Banna (1906–1949) founded the MBG. They root it in the breakdown of the last Islamic Caliphate in 1924. In these writings, if the downfall of the pan-Islamic state was the political reason, it was the religio-political ideas of al-Afghani (1838–1897) and Muhammad Abduh (1865–1905) that inspired al-Banna and his movement intellectually. This fanciful narrative is supported by texts, many of which come from the writings of MBG members and leaders themselves. But it simply ignores the history of the modern Egyptian nation state.

In Egypt in the early nineteenth century, a medieval state, ruled by a foreign, tax collecting, military elite, subordinated, at least nominally, to a pan-Islamic caliphate whose Sultan resided in Istanbul, was converted by a persistent and at first decisive Ottoman governor, Mehmet Ali Pasha (1769–1849), into a consolidated modern nation state. The newly emerging state had its own mighty army, to which the Egyptians were drafted by the late 1820s.

The Pasha Mehmet Ali supported his agricultural reforms, launched an industrial revolution and founded schools of engineering, medicine, midwifery, languages, administration and arts and crafts. Bureaucracy was extended to administer and regulate all these state operations. Finally, by threatening the Ottomans, he forced them to reach an agreement with him, recognizing the hereditary rule of his family and clearer borders to his country.

Thus it is not only the birth and consolidation of a nation state, but also an extensive politicization of a society and its internal relationships. All social operations, from agriculture to industrial production, internal and external trade, education, health services, transportation, marriage, and jurisdiction have become bureaucratically administered by a hegemonic central state. The political, which was once specific, militarily and necessary only in inter-state relationships, has now absorbed all sorts of social, economic, cultural and religious authorities and has blended with a consolidated nation-state to produce bureaucratic procedures such as registries for births, deaths and marriages, laws, vaccination charts, pedagogical curricula, official religious holidays, etc. A discursive tradition whose tremendous power was diffuse, and only locally negotiated or bargained, and which was certainly frightening to any future centralized state, had to be tamed and controlled. It is this centralization of the state and its evolving political economy that demanded a modern, objectified Islam which could be rationally regulated and applied to the newly-emerging public spheres.

One important feature of this nation state is that it was, following the European model, created in continuous relation with the West. Mehmet Ali Pasha, who had seen himself as a Muslim ruler gaining advantages from Western science and technologies, especially regarding his military force, was succeeded by Khedives, whose Western raising and education made them want their country to embrace Western civilization. Proudly, Khedive Isma'il announced: 'My country is no longer in Africa; we are now a part of Europe'.[15]

In addition to the political, economic and social organization of society, Islam was also being reproduced in Europe. A scholarship of Orientalism was developing, which, in the words of Edward Said, had the 'triumphant technique for taking the immense fecundity of the Orient and making it systematically, even alphabetically, knowable by Western laymen'.[16] A modern reified and systematically classified form of Islam was unfolding, creating with it a set of questions which both Orientalists and Muslims would answer. It was this systematization of Islam, joined by the creation of specific modern spheres of, for instance, the economy, the polity, the family, etc., which made it possible for statesmen, scholars, academicians, teachers, social activists and a new strand of socio-political religious activists (who would later come to be known as Islamists) to talk about 'Islam' and economy, politics, family, women, human rights, social justice.

That was not the only relationship between Islam and the West. Politically, the creation of the state was preceded by the French invasion; the virtual independence was achieved in contestation with Europe; and the successors of the Pasha had to submit to the will of Europe and later to British occupation. Economically, the increasing debts to Western banks, the Dual Control, a board of British and French commissioners who were granted the authority to control the Egyptian State budget, and more importantly, the economy that was increasingly bound to a Global market made Egyptians feel that foreign political oppression was augmented by economic exploitation. If we add an arrogant discourse of Orientalism that claimed Western superiority, we can understand why the heart of modern Islam was reactionary resistance and a call to independence. 'Islam is the Way', the 'Islamic Alternative', or the more intellectual 'Islamization of Knowledge' are post-colonialist manifestations of this Islam.

With its celebration of medieval Islamic civilization and its continuous call for a Caliphate, many scholars regard Islamism as inherently alien, if not hostile, to both nationalism and the nation state. Let us examine this thesis from a sociological angle: the formation of the elite. Mehmet Ali's monopoly over land was later dismantled by his successors. Egyptians bought land and created new estates, forming an agricultural aristocracy with descendants of Turkish and Circassian origin. The army gave another route to Egyptians to be a part of the elite, a move intentionally designed by Khedive Said to guarantee the loyalty of village headmen. Others made their way through education to be state officials. Scholars, like Muhammad Abduh and intellectuals, like Lutfi al-Sayyid, were also a part of this elite. The common denominator of all these groups was their peasant background.[17] Arthur Goldschmidt pointed to the fact that: 'The rudimentary journals, schools, parliaments, and law courts combined to nurture a new class of educated Egyptians whose occupations demanded an articulate response to what was happening in their country'.[18]

It was hardly possible to separate Islamism from nationalism at this time, and probably up to the 1952 Revolution. Unlike in Syria, where nationalism was born against an Ottoman Islamic Caliphate, in Egypt Turkey was a possible ally or a helpless one at worst. The enemy was the British occupation, against which nationalism, Islamism and the state were fighting together. This Islamism-Nationalism-State unity is a fundamental, though frequently forgotten, fact that has shaped the socio-political reality of Egypt from the emergence of the modern Egyptian nation state until the present.

This history is essential to understand that the discourse of the MBG is divorced neither from nationalism nor from state ideology. It explains the harmony between MBG and King Farouq in the early years of the Group, the support of Sadat for the Group's activities and the continuous toleration of a considerable presence of the Group during Mubarak's years. Because it is the King or the President, not the Parliament, who heads all state institutions, and because it was state, not private, capitalism that animated the economic life of the country, the state represented a wide variety of ideologies. This is true when the state was claimed to be a liberal monarch, when it was a one-party socialist republic, or when it turned to a multi-party system. In short, the adoption of Islamism by the State is not merely tactical; it is strategic. The State has always maintained the duties of propagating a correct modern

interpretation of Islam, protecting an Islamic identity and representing, or sometimes defending, Islam internationally.

## Dissociated State/Dissociated Islamism

### Economic Liberalization

By the end of 1960s the Egyptian State was challenged politically,
ideologically and economically. Sinai had fallen under Israeli occupation; Arab Nationalism was recognized by the masses as an
unfounded romantic project; and socialist policies resulted in a
huge and crippled public sector. Through the reign of Sadat during
the 1970s the country witnessed a dramatic change. Politically, a
fast and limited victory over Israel in 1973 was quickly followed by
a peace process and a sudden shift to the Western Camp. Ideologically, the state gradually adopted liberal democracy and turned
into a multi-party political system. Economically, private capitalism was introduced and officially promoted.

A shy turn to private capitalism in the 1970s was boosted in 1981
with the New Company Law, which 'provided a straightforward
way for enterprises to be established with national capital'.[19] A new
private sector shortly unfolded, with an increasing rate of private
industrial projects. The state has gone further in privatizing the
public sector, including two of its four banks. This turn was accompanied socially by a flourishing consumerist culture that had arisen
and these politico-economic changes had repercussions for Islamism and the MBG.

### The Challenge

In the interviews I conducted during 2003 with MBG activists and
ex-activists, most of the interviewees expressed deep frustration
with their Group. They criticized their Group on both theoretical
and practical levels. Theoretically, they resented the adherence of
the MBG to an old fashioned, dated, rigid, shallow and monoto-
nous ideology. The Group, in their opinion, was becoming isolated
from the surrounding world. A doctor informant called it 'autism',
for they fight wars and solve problems that only exist in their
imagination. What MBG has to do is engage in everyday reality

and develop a pluralistic discourse that offers a range of views without attaching themselves to only one perspective.

Practically, they no longer admired the 'Islamic' social, educational and business projects of the 1980s and early 1990s. They emphasized their shallowness and pretension, in terms of claiming Islamic authenticity. Above all, they stressed two shortcomings which they considered dangerous. First, they were not professional projects; business and brotherhood are combined, resulting in failure in both aspects. Second, and more importantly, they were politicized; even an 'Islamic' grocery store was presented as an Islamic alternative to what the state offers. The relief work after the Cairo earthquake of 1992 was frequently cited as an obvious example. They complained that the social work, which had to come, in their opinion, before any political work, had been hindered by political activism. Most of them perceived the idea of standing for parliamentary elections as mere nonsense. Winning the elections is simply impossible and only creates animosity with the state. Some of them proposed that those who are interested in practicing politics should be allowed to do it away from the Group and its organization.

Interestingly, in my interviews the failure of the state was considered secondary in significance, if at all, to the challenges of 'globalization'. The aspects of global challenges, according to them, are many. Politically, a hegemonic US with an army that is deployed in the heart of the Islamic and Arab World is a risk to the future of Arabs and Muslims. Many of them highlighted the economic challenges, seeing little chance for Arabs and Muslims to compete in a global market. They cited many examples from their own work and economic activities. They also added the scientific and technological challenges. They bitterly criticized the reality in the country and the lost chances of the past. Besides, they are not very comfortable with all the socio-cultural effects of globalization.

Though they sometimes use globalization and a hegemonic US interchangeably, they do not identify globalization with the 'West'. Moreover, they never demonize globalization. In fact, they frequently celebrate its good aspects. For instance, they always mention the increased connectivity and their continuous communication with a global society as an unprecedented advantage for Islamic activism. National governments cannot restrict their influence and activities. They also retold stories of successful communication with other foreign groups through the internet. More importantly, they embark on global social discourses to shape their agenda. They rationalize their demands on the bases of human rights, women's rights, religious freedom, citizenship, environmentalism, pluralism, cultural diversity, etc. Moreover, they join global social movements and situate themselves appropriately within their frameworks of action. Davis' argument of authenticity is certainly dated; the pendulum is swinging back to openness, not authenticity.

Against Davis' thesis, once again, my interviewees re-legitimized the state. A radical transformation of the political system is not thought of as far as social, economic and cultural reform is concerned. The state that used to be recognized by Islamists as a mere agent of the West is seen now as a national defender against American hegemony. They cited a number of examples, such as the support of the government for their demonstrations against the Iraq War, and the *fatwa* issued by Sheikh al-Azhar that jihad became an individual responsibility for Muslims after the Americans had invaded Iraq. These responses came from people who had been detained, and sometimes tortured, by the state. On the other hand, they are not happy with the state policies. They see the state as less important than before. In a global political context, the state has less to do. Therefore, they not only re-legitimize the State, but also decentralize it.

## The Change of Discourse Knowledge

Postmodernists, such as Foucault and Lyotard, attack any notion that there might be a meta-language, meta-narrative, or meta-theory through which all things can be connected, represented or explained. Truth, an Enlightenment value, is also rejected. Truth refers to order, rules and values; it depends on logic, rationality and reason—all of which are questioned by the postmodernists.[20] In the interviews this author carried out, there was a recurring sense of a disintegrated meta-narrative of Islamism. Problems are given particular reasons which do not fit into a comprehensive conception of Islam. In contrast, core knowledge of the newer discourse of Islam is a concept of openness. It is mentioned numerous times during each interview and looks like the identifying feature of newer

Islamists. Besides, it is usually presented in contrast to 'closedness', which is attributed to the past of Islamism. A typical comment might be: 'We are not as closed as we were in the 1970s; we are now open; male and female employees work together in the same workplace, and we cover cinema and arts in our publications'.

Besides, they are eager to join global social movements; and they always celebrate this kind of activity as an indication of their success: that is, their 'openness'. More importantly, they are not only reframing their discourses, but also metamorphosing them in order to neatly fit into global social discourses of human rights, women's rights and environmental rights. These are not the kind of discourses of 'Islam and human rights', where Islam is displayed as the religion of human rights; they are universal human rights discourses in which local issues are embedded. Moreover, they try to stretch the scope of their interest to accommodate a multitude of alternatives. On the *Islam On Line* website, one of the most successful websites founded by activists coming from the MBG,[21] for instance, there is a page for science and health. This page links to nine others. Not only is the scope of interest stretched, but the views presented are also intentionally multiplied. A number of different and contradictory views are supplied and offered simultaneously. The editors I met said that both they and their readers like to have many alternative views exposed. However one must question how a certain 'choice of view' or practice as mundane as choices has come to be considered as Islamic.

Two aspects, however, are considered, for a choice to be Islamic. First, it has to be useful; second, it should not be legally prohibited. The question is not what God wants us to do, believing that doing it is a guarantee of a happy life and eternal Heaven. The point is what could be useful now and the question is: does God mind it at all? The entire Islamic system, which was once consolidated by previous versions of Islamism, is reduced into mere redundant, flexible and extremely negotiable borders.

However, it should be acknowledged that the meta-narrative has never disappeared. Occasionally it arises in interviews, articles, books and speeches. The interviewee who discusses openness and global social activism, suddenly switches to recite how Islam will finally overcome the global powers of evil and erect its just Caliphate. The second concept that makes up the core knowledge of newer Islamism is resistance. This is not just a trace of the past, but it is also rooted in the present, in the same way that openness is. The miserable politico-economic situation nationally, the American invasion and occupation of Iraq, the bombing of Lebanon, and the unsolvable Palestinian question are all realistic reasons for the continuation of this concept.

The newer resistance is qualitatively different. A doctoral student of philosophy told me that it is not a problem to comply with reality as long as one keeps rejecting it in the heart. This privatization of resistance, where the battlefield is the psyche, is one among other interesting aspects of the newer resistance. Resistance is not a continuous project; Islamists conduct some of it, some of the time. It is a place to be visited, not a home to be dwelt in. One recites the meta-narrative to know that ultimately—that is, in the very distant future—Islam will win; resistance is symbolic. Bauman writes:

> ...the age of ideology may not be yet over, its agony may yet prove not to be terminal, but most certainly its present condition has changed beyond recognition the likeness it bore since the inception of modernity. An ideology without a project—some project which by being a project and a plan for action spells out a future different from the present—is an oxymoron, a contradiction in terms.[22]

In this sense, you can be a student at the American University in Cairo, regularly paying the tuition and receiving the liberal education, but, still, you boycott Coca Cola. I asked my interlocutor why he boycotts Coca Cola, when it is produced in Egypt by an Egyptian company. He said it does not matter; it gives the public a collective chance to resist, and sends the right message to the Americans. The meta-narrative as an ideology loses its project. Its monument is out there, but very empty.

## The Change of Structure

Like the MBG meta-narrative, the MBG's hierarchical organization does exist. Weekly meetings, monthly financial contributions, as well as all the geographical and action chapters are still there. Like the MBG meta-narrative, however, this structure is being emptied of its content and gradually decentralized. A structure through which daily instructions that must be blindly obeyed, instructions that tell members what kind of sports they should practice, what kind of schools they should attend, and whether the spouse they have chosen is the right one certainly does not exist anymore. The collective project has fragmented into a plethora of individual projects which have absorbed all the energy of the old structure. Moreover, a new structure has emerged from the old one.

The stagnation of the movement, the rigidity of its regulations, and the ambiguity of its vision pushed the initiative and active core of members of the MBG to the margins. At the margins of the Group, not outside it, those active members persistently created their own social or business projects. They relied on the resources of the MBG to build up their new careers. New social, cultural and business units, such as publishing houses, multimedia companies, human rights organizations, law firms, polyclinics, advertisement agencies, research centers, schools, charity organizations, orphanages and others, evolved. These are not the institutions of the 1970s and 1980s, which were founded by the MBG as part of Islamizing society and providing an Islamic alternative. These are individual projects that belong to MBG members. The founders, nonetheless, would rely on their Group affiliation to raise capital, recruit employees and create markets.

These newly emerging units became gradually independent. They are well-established enough in the socio-economic market that they rely less on their previous affiliation. Parallel to this, they network with each other. A multimedia company will print its packages at a printing shop owned by a brother and advertise its products through an agency belonging to another brother. Moreover, such a company will find agents and distributors nationwide who are or were MBG members. The more each unit does its social, cultural, or economic work, the more the network gets established and extended and the more these units depend on the network, not the Group. Money, workers, activism, research, contracts, information, activists, and new knowledge flow through this newly-emerging network. Besides, this network is embedded in a similar and more extensive global network of business and activism. The multimedia company can create projects that are financed by workers in the rich Gulf countries, manufactured in Egypt with technical support from North America finally to be distributed worldwide.

The dynamism of this new structure is high, but it is economically regulated. MBG hierarchy, once again, is still there; a nice place to frequent once a week, during the weekly meeting, and to support by paying the modest monthly fee.

New protocols and ethics maintain this network that weaves business and activism. First of all, competitive politics is strictly prohibited. The same multimedia company will, for instance, produce CDs of the *fiqh* lessons of Sheikh Qaradawi, but not his political ones. An orthopedist will allow one or two religious pictures to be hung in his clinic, but not the MBG calendar. MBG members are welcome to work in these units, but they are not allowed to conduct their MBG meetings or exchange MBG leaflets in the workplace. Professionalism is the key word of this network. Workers are hired, contracts are signed, and relations are extended according to professional standards. If the printing shop asks for higher prices, or provides lower quality, it will not be contracted. If the most pious person does not have the right academic qualifications, he will not find a place in this network. Someone's position inside the MBG hierarchy, or outside it, if he has already quit, should ideally have nothing to do with his/her position within the network, or its units. Salaries, prices, project management, promotions and other everyday conduct are regulated by professional and market ethics.

Brotherhood is appreciated, but consciously and continuously quarantined so that it does not disturb work relationships. In some cases, MBG members filed cases against other members because they did not honor their contracts. This behavior is always understood, if not appreciated. Twenty years ago, MBG leadership would typically intervene to solve personal and business conflicts. Now, it is not even invited. Brotherhood should support, not spoil, business; a statement one will hear repeatedly, usually followed by 'business is business', in English.

Some interviewees suggested that the hierarchy itself should marketize its operations. After transforming MBG internal relations within the new network into economic ones, they want to extend this transformation to the MBG hierarchy itself. The best speaker, not the most pious or the highest in the hierarchy, should be the imam of Friday prayer. Besides, he must get paid for his work. Volunteerism is appreciated, but it should not be the rule. If brotherhood and business must be clearly separated, business and mission are frequently fused. In short, business is the mission for those running it. This is not an excuse offered by businessmen. On the contrary, a number of businessmen, whom I interviewed, had feelings of guilt that business does not leave any time for *da'wa*. However, their brothers and sisters always emphasize that for them business is the mission. All they are required to do is to make their businesses successful. Even within the traditional hierarchy, an absence from a weekly meeting or neglect to attend public activities is highly tolerated, if not sometimes encouraged. The new network is open to the public. Not every worker in this business unit or that social organization is necessarily an MBG member, or ex-member, an Islamist or even an observant Muslim. Nor is every unit linked only to similar units. Because the network is rooted in the open market, it must be open to everyone. The network is actively weaving interrelationships with different social, cultural, economic, and political bodies and includes people of all walks of life.

An Islamic discourse of openness produces this network as much as it is reproduced by it. It has an internal economic logic that regulates its dynamics on the bases of profit and loss, demand and supply, high mobility, initiative and creativity, and produces a number of concepts and ethics that carve out the new discourse. Amongst those I interviewed, for instance, about the Israeli Palestinian conflict and the position the MBG should take regarding Peace Process, there was a consensus that peace is the only way to solve the Palestinian issue. The majority of them, however, would call it the only possible, practical or globally accepted solution. That does not reflect old-fashioned resistance that leads people to fight as soon as fighting is possible. That only reflects an active logic of bargaining and compromise that paves the way to more real change.

As one might expect, this discourse, by mediating power, advantages some people while marginalizing others. The nature of the newly-created units, the accepted inter-relationships among them, the character of the subjectivity that is produced by such a discourse, the questions that may be raised, and those that may not be thought of, as well as the issues that are raised and those that are downplayed, if they exist at all, are all shaped by this neo-liberal discourse. Bauman chose the metaphor 'consumer co-operative' to capture the nature of post-modern cultural labor. He wrote:

Things that happen inside the ideal consumer co-operative are [like culture] neither managed nor random; uncoordinated moves meet each other and become tied up in various parts of the overall setting, only to cut themselves free again from all previously bound knots. Spontaneity here does not exclude, but, on the contrary, demands an organized and purposeful action, yet such action is not meant to tame, but to invigorate spontaneity of initiative.[23]

Likewise, the freedom and spontaneity of action in the neo-liberal network is organized and regulated. After all, the network of openness is not open to everyone.

An Azharite scholar who gives *fatwas* substantiated by texts and quotations collected from traditional writings is not welcome unless he dresses, speaks, rephrases his *fatwa*, and transmits it differently. A pious preacher will have no audience interested in his speeches until he becomes a TV star. An editor of Arabic educational CDs was promoted because he speaks fair English, has friends overseas, and posts video clips on the net, which he films with his digital camera; all these qualifications are irrelevant to his work. An Upper Egyptian columnist complained to me that he is neglected by his superiors and colleagues because he does not appear 'bourgeois' enough for their new taste. There is no specific elite that conspires to produce this discourse, weave this network or marginalize some people. Power is embedded in the network itself; different individuals willingly modify themselves to fit into its influential sites.

## Consumption as Activism

In his classical work *Postmodernism or the Cultural Logic of Late Capitalism*, Fredric Jameson views late capitalism as involving a prodigious expansion of capital into hitherto un-commodified areas. He fuses the two Marxist structures of economy and culture because the economy has conquered culture in order for everything to become culture. Jameson writes that images, styles, and representations are not the promotional accessories to economic products; they are the products themselves; culture is 'commodified'.[24] According to Jameson, the economic urgency of producing fresh waves of increasingly novel-seeming goods assigns an increasingly essential structural function and position to aesthetic innovation and experimentation. Post-modernist culture, being commodified, is judged in terms of what gives immediate pleasure and makes money.[25]

Mike Featherstone in his book *Consumer Culture and Postmodernism* tries to see not only the commodification of culture, but also the cultural aspect of the economy:

To use the term 'consumer culture' is to emphasize that the world of goods and their principles of structuration are central to the understanding of contemporary society. This involves a dual focus: firstly, on the cultural dimension of economy, the symbolization and use of material goods as 'communicators' not just utilities; and secondly, on the economy of cultural goods, the market principles of supply, demand, capital accumulation, competition and monopolization which operate *within* the sphere of lifestyles, cultural goods and commodities.[26]

Therefore the cultural aspect and the meaning of consuming specific goods must be afforded as much attention as we accord to the production and consumption of cultural symbols in our inquiry of the new Islamic discourse. The consumption of specific CDs, websites, head scarves, Qur'an software downloaded on mobile phones, laptops, blue jeans, casual shirts, or audiocassettes of the British Muslim singer Sami Yusuf, is an indication of being a new Islamist: a religious bourgeois. Classes of the past were determined by the ownership of the means of production. Classes of today are determined by consumption. Halbwachs stresses that 'our use of time in consumption practices conforms to our class habitus and therefore conveys an accurate idea of our class status'.[27] Hebdige also stated that consumer identities and lifestyles constitute social types and categories that may be used in a more positive way by sociologists so as to develop a 'sociology of aspiration'.[28]

Different activities are conducted to consume the cultural signs casually attached to them. Signing petitions online, blogging, waging e-jihad, joining the anti-debauchery party, or volunteering in anti-nudity brigades, are means to be open and neo-Islamist. It is not a problem that petitions online are, in the best case, read only by their signatories; blogs have so far been recycling tired discourses and liberal rhetoric; e-jihad most often means joining a handful of Islamic e-mail lists; the objective of anti-debauchery brigades is to resist the persistent desire to masturbate; or calling on women to don the *hijab* is the mission of the brigades, for the real point is the cultural sign of being open, and probably resistant too. Signs and commodities, as cultural theorists have emphasized, are dissociated. When a member of the anti-debauchery party declares that he will be the first martyr in this party, it means that he will not submit to his desire to masturbate. Civil jihad, which was celebrated for a while, during the summer of 2003, before it was forgotten, like other successive waves of fashion, could mean founding a non-governmental organization, chatting with some North Americans curious about Islam, paying charity, writing and publishing an article, or simply improving one's career. It does not matter; it all depends on the consumer and which commodity she or he wants to attach to this consumed sign. Civil jihad is neither real nor false; it is hyper-real, as Baudrillard would have put it. Civil, the secular European concept, comes next to jihad, the Islamic concept, in complete harmony, for the combined term refers to neither civil nor jihad. It is a simulacrum: a copy of a copy, where there is no original; it is a pastiche that means to surprise the nostalgic consumer and satisfy his or her yearning for the new. It could turn into resistance and produce 'DoS/denial of service', 'hacktivism', automated 'e-mail bombs' and 'e-Guerillas'; and/or it could lend to openness and become dialogue and global cooperation. Consumers demand choice, which must always be available. For this to happen, the consumer must not finally choose any one of them. The point is not to choose and commit to that choice; the point is to experience and explore various options.

## Differentiated State/Differentiated Islamism

### The State Divided

Frequently, economic liberalization, an ambiguous concept, is meant to indicate the liberation of economic actors from the influence of political actors. That was definitely not the case in Egypt, if it was ever elsewhere. Eberhard Kienle, for instance, wrote that, 'it has been argued convincingly that President Sadat sought to create a new class of entrepreneurs able to enrich themselves, yet dependent on the state and thus forming a constituency for his regime to rely on'.[29] There has been no independent new economic power that could challenge the state. The 'new' power was manufactured and regulated within the state apparatus. In *State and Public Policies in Egypt since Sadat*, Nazih Ayubi wrote about the composition of this new class: 'The social base for this change in orientation was a realignment of classes that brought to the fore an alliance between elements from the pre-revolutionary semi-aristocracy, the state bourgeoisie of the sixties, and the commercial/financial cliques of the infitah era'.[30]

Ayubi, however, does not naïvely take this alliance as a homogeneous structure. He clearly points to the internal contradictions and writes:

It should also be clear that the commercial bourgeoisie has already started to acquire a life of its own. Although the state machine is amenable to the interests of the newly-emerged class conglomeration of infitah, it does strive to play the role of the arbiter between the various fractions of the evolving bourgeoisie, and even to maintain a certain degree of 'relative autonomy' vis-à-vis the conflicting class interests in the society.[31]

Ayubi follows this analysis by stating that 'political power in Egypt is still basically in the hands of the state bourgeoisie'.[32] Ayubi's analysis is thoughtful and insightful, but there are three problems with it. First, the 'state' is used awkwardly, for it denotes competing sectors and their arbiter. Secondly, it portrays a struggle, or a balance of power between what he calls the 'commercial bourgeoisie' and the 'state bourgeoisie'. The state bourgeoisie is a unified sector that, although in alliance with the commercial bourgeoisie, has enough autonomy to seek the interests of the other social classes. Third, in his analysis, the commercial bourgeoisie is fragmented into fractions. This analysis is critiqued further on in this chapter; James Mayfield's theories will first be explored.

In his work *Local Government in Egypt*, Mayfield pointed to the difficulty of reforming what he called a mixed economy. He identified three sources of tension and resistance inside the governmental bureaucracy to the neo-liberal reforms. First, there are the high-ranking civil servants who have occupied comfortable positions in the management of the state sector and para-public enterprises, and who are now worried about privatization, restructuring, or liquidation of the public portfolio. Second, there are the private suppliers of the state-owned enterprises and the government, as well as everybody benefiting from rent-seeking situations derived from excessive regulations and who now dread the elimination of the lucrative field of public contracts and other artificial uncompetitive situations. Third, the public sector employees, who number almost six million, also worry about these changes that are always accompanied by both high unemployment rates and an inadequate social security system.[33] Mayfield draws a picture of a central neo-liberal government whose policies are resisted by a peripheral governmental alliance. In Mayfield's bipolar situation we find, using Ayubi's categories, specific state bourgeoisie and specific commercial bourgeoisie in alliance.

To shed more light on Mayfield's alliance and to bring forth an essential element which he and many other researchers forget, we must refer to Robert Springborg's *Mubarak's Egypt: Fragmentation of the Political Order*, in which he highlights the competition between President Mubarak and the Minister of Defense Abu Ghazala (1982–1989). Abu Ghazala, who was also the Deputy Prime Minister, extended the operations of the Army beyond the military limits. Springborg wrote:

The patronage network that he has established in the military and that tails off into the public and private sectors, for example, makes it very difficult for anyone to undermine his authority. Presumably it would require a much broader move against elements of the *infitah* bourgeoisie to ensnare Abu Ghazala, but the continued strength of that group/class and the military and of the alliance between them militates against such a move.[34]

This passage shows that besides high- and low-rank state bourgeoisie and their crony private suppliers who make up the bulk of the *infitah* bourgeoisie, there is also the Army and its extensive network.

Mayfield's bipolar situation is correct, but it is not a central—peripheral opposition. Nor is it a state bourgeoisie versus commercial bourgeoisie power competition. What obtains in Egypt now, what the state has become, is two clearly distinguished politico-socio-economic networks. Each of these networks is based on a different economy, ideology, and set of state institutions. There is a well-established network that includes the traditional political elite, the bureaucrats, whether high or low ranking, the lucky private suppliers who have been enjoying the public contracts in situations Mayfield correctly described as uncompetitive and who benefited from *infitah* policies to develop their activities, and the army. There is also a new network of commercial bourgeoisie who have benefited from the economic reform policies of Mubarak, new state bourgeoisie that is bitterly competing for sites of power and influence inside the regime, and all those social groups who are engaged in activities rooted in the new economy.

The Group Divided

Like the State, the MBG has also divided into two conflicting and communicating structures. This is not a generational conflict, old guard versus new guard conflict, or even a self-explanatory difference in attitudes, as shallow assessments have characterized it.[35] Those are two structures that are rooted in two different economies and produce two different discourses.

On 30 July 2007 'Isam al-'Iryan, the famous member of the Political Bureau of MBG, published an article on the MBG official website commenting on the Turkish elections and the victory of the Justice and Development Party, which has strong Islamic roots. Al-'Iryan was responding to a question that had been obsessively raised by the MBG: could what happened in Turkey happen again in Egypt? In his answer, he listed the lessons that could be concluded from the Turkish experience. He emphasized that Islam and democracy can get along in complete harmony and that for an Islamic party to make it to power it has to be open to all national social groups and ideologies and invite everyone to come along and participate in fighting corruption and autocracy. He also emphasized the necessity of encouraging openness to the West and making the Muslims participate in building a global human civilization.[36]

Three days later, on 2 August 2007 Gum'a Amin published a counter-article on the same website, signed with his title: a member of the Guidance Office of MBG. His article was titled 'The Turkish Question and Clarifying the Concepts'. In his article, he briefly congratulated the Turkish Party and then made a clear statement that such an experience would not be repeated by the MBG. His point was that although the Islamic Turks had made it to power, they had to stop being Islamic to do so. The MBG's objective, according to him, is not to be in power; the objective is to Islamize the society. The West will tolerate Erdogan because he is no longer really an Islamic politician; the West will not tolerate the MBG because the Group will always hold fast to Islamic principles.[37] Here, we find two contradictory points of view' a common occurrence whenever an MBG leader is invited to comment on an event or to respond to a question about their agenda.

## Sluggish Neo-liberalism

The pace of neo-liberal progression, whether in the state or the MBG, is now slowing down. The authors of *A Political Economy of the Middle East* showed the notorious and adverse results of liberating the economy:

Although the Washington Consensus view hoped that macro-stability and deregulation would stimulate export-led growth, in fact Egyptian growth was largely driven by investment in inventories and by public investment in huge infrastructural projects, such as the New Valley and Toshka Irrigation projects (ERF 2004). Second, the growth of exports—particularly job-creating manufactured exports—was unimpressive. Indeed, by one conventional measure, the Egyptian economy's integration with the global economy *declined* during the 1990s: Exports as a percentage of GDP fell from 46.6% in 1980 to 31.2% in 1990 and 24.6% in 2000. Merchandise exports as a percentage of GDP fell from 8.1% to 4.7% from 1990 to 2000.[38]

The startling figures show that though there has been an increase in industrialization, the manufactured products had to be consumed in the local market. That fails the simple rule of capitalism: accumulation or crisis.

On the landscape of the MBG, the neo-liberal discourse had too many problems to continue its progress. The management of two inherently contradictory concepts was not always successful. Besides, the promise of the openness discourse could not be possible with wars in Iraq and Afghanistan, provocative statements and comics in Europe, the banning of the *hijab* in France, double standard nuclear policies when it comes to Iran, and more. Leaving political crises aside, the very people who are engaged in the new economy have discovered how difficult, if possible at all, it is to compete globally. This is a setback for a discourse whose beginning was a global framing of both the challenge and the solution. Moreover, the more this discourse opens up, the less it could claim an Islamic identity. What makes an Islamic discourse Islamic if—like socialist, nationalist, Marxist and secular liberal discourses—it reduces its agenda to fighting autocracy and corruption? What makes an Islamic discourse Islamic if—like global discourses of human rights, environmental rights, women's rights, and so on—it calls for a peaceful and happy global society?

This point concerning authenticity brings us to the recently released MBG draft of a political party platform. Many observers, researchers, and MBG bloggers expressed their shock at the conservative nature of the draft. Two specific issues were highlighted: that a woman or a non-Muslim cannot be the President; and a council of religious scholars has to be formed to examine the conformity of government decisions and laws to the *Shari'a* (Islamic law). Given the open and fierce opposition of MBG bloggers to the document, one may assume that it was authored and approved by a small group of high-ranking members to be imposed on the bases of the MBG. However, that was not actually the case. Before its release, the document had gained the acceptance of the majority of MBG members. In fact, there were many voices that protested the too progressive nature of the document, fearing that this could threaten its Islamic nature.

The above incident is not difficult to explain. It is only the unfounded research, writings and media celebration of the neo-liberal Islamic voices and their potential for changing the MBG that make an incident like this difficult to explain. Marc Lynch, whom the draft convinced to travel all the way from Washington to Cairo and meet with the General Guide and a group of the MBG bloggers wrote enthusiastically, 'These online discussions are a manifestation of a new trend among young Muslim Brothers and a dynamic new force inside the organization'.[39] Many newspapers, including *Al-Masri Al-Yawm* and *Al-Dustur*, covered the MBG bloggers frequently and at length. TV satellite channels, from *Al-Arabiya* to

*Al-Jazeera*, among others, have interviewed 'Isam al-'Iryan and 'Abdil Mun'im Abu al-Futuh, featuring them as the liberal, reform voices coming from the heart of MBG leadership. Those voices are appealing to the media, but that does not give them any undue weight inside the hierarchy of the Organization. The neo-liberal discourse, as previously noted in this chapter, is rooted in a network of business and activism, not in the old hierarchy of the MBG. The more people are active and centralized in the new network, the less significance they have in the old hierarchy, for their positions have long been replaced by others, whose beliefs, views and projects are harmonious and well-fitted in this specific structure.

When it comes today to the official structure of the MBG, those who have influence are the ones marginalized in the neo-liberal network. It is those members, not the neo-liberal 'reformers', and certainly not the 150 webloggers, who are responsible for getting eighty-eight MBG members into Parliament. It is those tens or hundreds of thousands of MBG members, whom the neo-liberal discourse had ignored; never attended to their Islamic sensibilities; could not fulfill any of their ambitious promises; and did not tolerate in its network, who make today, not a specific rigid leadership, but the substance and hierarchy of a growing MBG organization. Commenting on the controversy and protest that the Draft had faced, the General Secretary of the MBG said clearly and simply:

We do not bargain on principles. We cannot abandon our principles, for if we abandoned them we would no longer be Muslim Brothers. And Muslim Brothers will be but Muslim Brothers! We listen to everyone, even the secularists. However, abandoning Šarī'a, or bargaining on principles, is rejected.[40]

If we now visit the state, we find its forgotten network returning with insistence and impetus. Egypt has been witnessing a series of workers, and civil servants' protests, sit-ins and strikes. Those who always celebrate the liberal triumph, whether they are journalists or researchers, are accustomed to framing their triumphs marches to liberal democracy. The fact, however, is that it is a march against liberal economic policies. What those protesters demand is a movement back to a socialist welfare state. What they demand is not democracy, but free health service, free education for their children, a cessation of the privatization policy that makes them lose their jobs, and an increase in their monthly stipends. Other groups of the old network are neither silent nor devoid of power. Most important of all these groups is the army. This army, which has long been engaged in the political life of the Egyptian State, is certainly not watching the changes in the state or among Islamists without interest.

## A Future of Differentiation

Internal state conflicts and struggles are shaping the political future of Egypt. It is hard to predict how this situation will resolve, and it is beyond the objective of this chapter to investigate it further. The significance of Egypt in American politics is a determining factor in this struggle. Both new state bourgeoisie and the army have mutual interests with the United States. However, the once powerful American pressure to democratize the Middle East was soon aborted. The interests of the United States, and the significance of Egypt in its politics, are security and military, not economic. The army that saved the Egyptian economy once in 1991 by participating in the first Gulf War and consequently removing the heavy military debt resumes its central position in political life. Regardless of who will be the next president, a question that obsesses national and foreign analysts, both of these two state networks will have their place in the future. A differentiation of the state's functions will result in re-distribution of both responsibilities and rights among the two differentiated networks.

MBG leadership clearly knows that it is not its time now to make it to power. Internal MBG conflicts are likely to be muffled. A real chance to take over power, or at least to engage seriously in a fair political competition, would reveal such conflicts and contradictions. It is unlikely that this chance will exist in the near future. Besides, the energy of change has already been channeled into a neo-liberal network of business and activism, easing any possible internal tension. For the traditional organization, it will be a step away from oppressive military rule. Liberal voices like those of al-'Iryan or Abu al-Futuh, who still cling to their positions in the traditional hierarchy, have neither a view that could still hold as distinguishably Islamic, nor strong influence among the Group's cadres. The MBG has already started a new phase through drafting its political party platform. If given official permission to form a political party, the MBG will found a party that is aimed to function as a conservative Islamic opposition party, which works through negotiations and compromises with the state. Researchers who wonder whether the MBG will be democratic once it is in power are wasting their time. The MBG will neither reach power nor turn democratic in the liberal sense that those researchers have in mind.

# PART II

# NEW ISLAMIST LANDSCAPES

5

# REINVENTING POLITICAL ISLAM

## THE DISENGAGEMENT OF EUROPEAN ISLAMISTS

*Amel Boubekeur*

Discussing the Islamist phenomenon in a European context is problematic and may even be considered historically and geographi-
cally nonsensical. Islamist thought[1] emerged in the Muslim world
in the early twentieth century and was marked by the profound
changes that took place in these societies. However, the waves of
immigrants and influences that have passed between the Muslim
world[2] and the West since the late 1970s can help us to measure the
impact of Islamist thought in contemporary Europe.

The history of the emergence of a European Islamist-inspired
activism is not linear but dynamic. It was established through the
contributions of different generations of exiled Islamist activists
from the Muslim world who established themselves in Europe, and
then by their 'successors', young Muslim activists born in Europe
who have reappropriated Islamist codes in their European context.
Although Islamism in the West should be understood in light of its
history in the Muslim world, it should also, and perhaps more
importantly, be contextualized through the specific relations that
European Muslim minorities have with European states.[3] These
European parameters will transform the original Islamist identity

imported from the Muslim world into a new identity. Therefore describing today's younger generation of Muslim activists that have the defense of Islam at the center of their reasons for mobilization as Islamists will no longer be accurate. However the historical impact of the installation of Islamism and its codes in the West in the construction of these European Muslim activists' identities cannot be overlooked.[4] For that reason I will use the term 'Islamism' or 'Islamist' when discussing the historical ideology that has stemmed from the Muslim world, and 'political Islam' and 'Muslim activists' when exploring new generations' use of Islamism.

In order to understand the role of the legacy of Islamist codes on the paths taken by young European activists, the process of 're-Islamization' needs to be explored. In Europe, re-Islamization is not Islamism in itself; it is the process of reappropriation of an Islamic[5] heritage, often transmitted through Islamist channels. It aims to restore the committed religious sentiment of Muslim youth. Re-Islamization should not be confused with parents, originally from Muslim countries, transmitting a religious identity to their children. On the contrary, it emphasizes a voluntary Islamic religiosity, which is accompanied by a feeling of belonging to a particular group, that of the successors of Islamism.[6] This chapter seeks to understand how, after a period where young people become adapted to an Islamist ideology imported from the Muslim world, i.e. re-Islamization, they have reappropriated these codes for themselves according to their daily realities in the West and invented new forms of political Islam.

This chapter will explore the process of re-Islamization over the period from the 1980s to the present day, but will not be concerned with the evolution of groups subject to processes of radicalization leading to terrorist violence. Although occasionally re-Islamization leads some to engage in violent action, the frame of action of these violent groups is no longer Islamism as they refer to a different political tradition that is linked to jihadism. Similarly, 'neo-fundamentalist' groups such as Salafi Wahhabis will not be explored.[7] While Islamists and their heritors seek to have their values recognized as majority values through their actions of social aid, predication and their reclamation of cultural and political rights, neo-fundamentalists do not want to overcome others' beliefs and are happy to live in isolation from society. The vast majority of them do not take part in charitable activities or in political demonstrations relating to the defense of Muslim interests and are not involved in processes of political or identity negotiation with states and civil society as they reject the use of secularized politics.

Finally, it is important, when analyzing the contemporary transformations of Islamism, to be careful of the use of the concept of 'restoration'. Indeed the idea of restoration is already inherent to the own discourse of Islamists who like to present themselves as reformers of alienating traditions. In the huge literature concerning Islamist movements they are indeed always shown as breakers of old institutionalized or social forms of Islamic identities. However, it is also important to understand that, even if they perceive themselves as everlasting revolutionaries and Islamism as a constantly fresh ideology, Islamists may become institutionalized actors, having their de facto political generation fixed in history, and thus leaving room for new generations of activists.

So what are the analytical categories that can explain the link between the early Islamist ideology and the use of it by European re-Islamized activists who are trying to invent new forms of political Islam? A first option is one of the post-Islamist scholarly currents.[8] It demonstrates that 'new' actors are in the process of emerging, consummating their definitive break with Islamist ideology following its political failure in Muslim countries. Islamism is thus seen to be a revolution that has been more or less aborted, leaving no other choices for its former adepts than the path of withdrawal with either the neo-fundamentalist option, a position resembling a minoritarian retrograde resistance, that of terrorist violence, or dispersal in the public space using new secular and depoliticized forms of Islamic identity. In discussing how Islamists were disturbed by the failure of their great initial Project, it is important to note that today it is not only a process of external constraint (like the failure of Islamism to overcome the Muslim world's political systems) which guides the emergence of new types of Islamic militancy, but also an internal phenomenon of an activist fatigue among Islamists who are disengaging from Islamist codes that are no longer relevant. The external failure of the Islamist revolution in establishing an Islamic state should not occult the way in which Islamism became an institution that internally impinged on its own activists. When a revolutionary ideology becomes the rule, it leads to an ideological fatigue on the part of the activists who see that the notion that had initially appealed to them disappears; it is diluted in the contestation of the traditional rules of their environment and the capability to create new codes.

The future of Islamism is always analyzed in terms of new emergent political traditions which will replace it (qualified by the words: failure, decline, post-, neo-). Instead of conceiving of Islamism simply in terms of rupture, the term will be analyzed in this chapter through its possible continuity with the phenomenon of disengagement. When it emerged, Islamism was analyzed as a break from the tradition of political systems of the Muslim world, and with the ancient cultures. However, this Islamist culture was created suddenly; all it did was adapt a pre-existing Muslim identity to the political and social context of the time. Today we must revert to this configuration to comprehend the contemporary transformations of Islamism in the West and elsewhere. The use of Islam as a political resource dominating all other available resources has not disappeared. Today it is the idea of the reinvention of the self as a committed Muslim that is at stake, in reaction to the stigmatizing effect of the oppositional and aggressive Islamist modes of action. It is not only a matter of taking a reflexive position in view of the social and political failure that Islamism experienced, but it is also, internally, the routinization, the massification and the extension of Islamist codes outside the activist group that made them lose their capacity of transformation of the world. The successors of contemporary Islamism have the same feeling of uneasiness towards it as the Islamists themselves had towards the traditions of the Muslim world. Islamism is transformed into a tradition; a heritage in relation to which one must take a position in order to reinvent a universe of meaning for committed Muslims in Europe.

How do groups such as Muslims in the West committed to the question of Islam reconstruct themselves in the wake of the emergence of individualist values and activist paths, and the plurality of meanings given to Islamic actions? How do they adapt to the 'domination of the [Islamist] reference'[9] when it comes to the creation of Islamic political identities? How do they adapt to the domination of the Islamist reference which forces each committed Muslim, possessor of the inheritance of certain codes used by Islamism, to identify himself as an Islamist?

## *The Islamist Inspired Re-Islamization of European Muslims*

In the European context, the group that can be meaningfully qualified as Islamist is that of the activists and thinkers originally from the Arab world (particularly Egypt, Algeria, Tunisia, Morocco, Jordan, Syria and Lebanon), who opposed their regimes and sought exile in Europe in the 1970s and the early 1980s. It also includes post-graduate students, imams, professors of Islamic science, orators and leaders of various Islamic associations. From the early 1980s these actors took responsibility for the re-Islamization of young Muslims born in Europe by offering them religious studies classes and organizing conferences and apprenticeship of the religious practice in the mosques but also by creating young Muslim associations for cultural and political education activities.

The immigrant parents who lacked experience of intellectualized or politicized forms of Islam,[10] found their practices of religious transmission challenged by these upcoming figures. Their children perceived the 'traditional' Islam taught by their parents as the embodiment of corrupt cultural traditions, thus rejecting this notion in favor of the 'original' Islam—the only one capable of bringing them salvation. Part of this young activist group was directly re-Islamized by contact with Islamists through conferences, meetings, literature and new codes that they spread. Presenting their codes as the Islamic orthodoxy and not as a specific political ideology, the influence of the exiled Islamists was much larger than the regular circle of activists they may have recreated. It reached an even greater number of young Muslims who were not in direct contact with them and who just sought to better understand their faith or their identity as teenagers.[11]

It should be mentioned that during the 1980s the majority of immigrants' children were not receptive to the use of religion as a political resource, instead they preferred to invest their time in anti-racist movements.[12] At the same time, the exiled Islamists thought of their presence in the West as temporary, aiming at preparing their return to their countries of origin once Arab regimes had been overthrown and an Islamic state had been established. However at the end of the 1980s, and the early 1990s, the convergence of disappointment with the movements founded on the ethnicity of young Muslims born in Europe and the realization of the impossibility of return for the exiled Islamists, changed the situation. The need for exiled Islamists to answer the quotidian questions of young Muslim Europeans concerning a religion that they knew little about favored the repositioning of their activities in Europe and rendered obsolete their political ideals directed towards Muslim countries. For the children of immigrants who engaged in the *'deen'* (used here in the sense of voluntarist religion), Islam would no longer be lived through ethnic belonging but would become committed and engaged, giving a religious dimension to identity search and to their dominated social position, such as that at the end of the 1980s in Europe, when young Muslims were extremely affected by racism, cultural and social exclusion and unemployment.

The driving idea of Islamist re-Islamization at the end of the 1980s and the beginning of the 1990s was that of the liberation from and rupture in the traditional religious identity of the parents. Their depoliticized religiosity was seen to be unable to face State political discrimination towards Muslims and responsible for their low social status. Young re-Islamized Muslims also considered this immigrant parental Islam as made invisible in the European white secular public space. The Islamist re-Islamization gave them great revolutionary goals to overcome this marginalization, which will be explored in the following sections.

Introducing Islam in the Public Sphere

Re-Islamization as a visible and clearly activist phenomenon expressed the need among those who adopted it to make Islam a public element. First Islam needs to be taken out of its 'religion of immigrants' package. While parents used to think of themselves as just 'temporary visitors', who cannot have visible and public demands based on their minority religion, children label themselves as full European citizens and asked for a full recognition of their Islamic identity in the public sphere. Daring to assume one's religious practice in the public sphere, by wearing the veil, head-scarf or having a beard, in reclaiming an assiduous practice of fasting or prayer in High Schools, for example, contained a dimen-sion of revolutionary transgression of the previous public and private boundaries which governed Islam in Europe. Islamic prin-ciples had to be at the center of the public space, to come out of their minoritarian position and to become majoritarian. The recon-sideration of the place of women also participated significantly in the desire to transform Islam as a visible and engaged political identity.[13] The participation of women was clearly valued within Muslim youth associations. Even if re-Islamized young women were sometimes relegated to the preparation of sandwiches at the organization of Islamist conferences, Islamist re-Islamization brought an alternative vision of the place of women in Islam. Thus female preachers, public speakers and women knowledgeable in religion emerged within mosques, associations and Institutes of Islamic Studies, and challenged the traditional household feminine figures of mothers from the Maghreb, Turkey, Pakistani or sub-Saharan Africa, which belongs only to the private sphere.[14] Women were urged to follow the example not of their mothers, but of the wives and female companions of the Prophet, in participating politically as they did in the early years of Islam, in the establish-ment of an Islamic society. For young women born in Europe, the wearing of the veil was considered in the 1990s as the fulfillment of emancipation from alienating traditional roles through authen-tic Islam. This new form of political Islam allowed women to escape from the solidification of their role in the private space by making the veil public at schools and universities, in 'visible' jobs, on the street and sport centers. Places where their mothers' veils never went.

## Returning to a Pure Islamic Culture and Norms

Young people born in Europe were affected by the way their coun-tries had delegitimized the culture of their parents as an archaic immigrant culture incompatible with Western standards. This cul-ture was often presented at school or in the media as being backwards, unrefined and the product of an unproductive third world. As a means of challenging this refusal of their parents' culture, much of this re-Islamized youth explained that 'cultural traditions and not Islam' were the cause of the backwardness that Muslims suffered from. As a response to this 'backwardness' an obsession of reacquiring a pure Islamic culture, that of the time of glorious Islam, emerged. The reinvention of culture on Islamic foundations was to allow for the reactivation of a new dignity because it conformed to religious norms. This culture was to distance itself from everything that had been deprecated in the West or rendered myth, such as the culture of the suburbs or delinquents, or the use of dialect by parents, to be replaced by the re-Islamized with a fascination for classical Arabic, the language of the Qur'an. They were also to distance themselves from the 'nice' docile political norms of their parents ('do not steal, do not lie and respect other people'), which had only served to consolidate their dominated position in European societies. The precedence of the Islamic norm was intended to be first and foremost inspired by the *Sunna*, Prophetic tradition, but in reality it allowed a group that was in the process of constructing itself to invent its own social practices. Re-Islamicized youths were further attached to these norms because they were not present in the religiosity of their parents, which reinforced the feeling of living an authentic Islam, in rupture. This feeling of belonging to a collective life that was both activist and voluntary was also materialized by the sharing of Islamist intellectual references such as Sayyid Qutb, Hasan al-Banna and Yusuf al-Qaradawi.[15] There was, on the part of those of the same generation with similar life experiences (children of immigrants seeking new forms of powerful Islam), a sort of self-confirmation that these were the true references of the group. This does not necessarily mean that this culture reinforced their individual religious practices at an individual level, but it materialized a collective Islamic identity that was established through the pertinence of new norms. These norms are visible in the way in which the relationships of 'Islamic' couples have been reinvented[16] or the way eating habits have been complicated, by listing and memorizing the gelatins and food additives which have pork in them. In everyday life, thank you was not 'that's really nice of you' but *barakallahu fik* or *jazakallahu khair* (May God reward you with goodness). Joy or enthusiasm were not demonstrated by 'that's so cool', but rather by saying *mashallah* (what Allah has willed) or *subhanallah* (Glory be to God). Group reunions cannot begin without introducing the name of God with a *bismillahi ar-rahman ar-rahim* (in the name of God, the most Gracious the most Merciful). Music and arts were also regulated by turning them towards God and performing Islamic reminders through Islamic plays or Islamic songs (*nasheed*).[17] This culture was opposed to the 'futility' of the West, as well as to parents and young non-observant 'assimilated' Muslims. It strengthened faith and materialized an activist lifestyle where the group must take care not to be sullied by its environment.

## Militancy and Politicization

Both the political meaning and the framework of militancy involved in re-Islamization were profoundly marked by relation to the group. The essential element was solidarity among the members of this tight-knit group, all persecuted (by parents, the school system) for their Islamic authenticity. The fraternity that was born of this experience had the effect of putting the common good of committed Muslims at the head of the list of political aims of the group. Defending 'brothers' and 'sisters', had to take priority over personal interest, and for those most engaged, to lead to the sacrifice of personal life. Marriage within the group was strongly encouraged. Very strict discipline, along with homogenization of certain forms of participation aimed to allow each member of the group to be stronger to confront the exterior, the feeling of allegiance being cultivated by each member. The political identity had to be alternative, whilst simultaneously proclaiming equal treatment.

The associations of young Muslims have taken up a position in the secular European political game (in calling for electoral participation, and the respect for the Republic), but in line with the political logic of religious citizenship.[18] Praying in front of a town hall and proclaiming the glory of God was not a means of establishing an Islamist caliphate in a given town, but instead a way of informing the mayor that the discriminatory policy in the attribution of land for the construction of mosques would cost him dearly in votes. This is a new and true Islam for these young people, which allows an investment in citizenship and democratic participation. The discourses of those who spoke publically of re-Islamization distinguished themselves from the purely theological discourse of the 'ancients' in emphasizing the solutions that Islam can bring to social problems. They therefore appropriated the European political codes from the point of view of Islam, and over-invested in the conciliation of European and Muslim identities. The idea was to set themselves apart from their immigrant parents, for whom abandoning their nationality for a European nationality meant renouncing Islam. It was necessary to oppose the idea that integration through a group—that of politically committed Muslims—prevented them from being good citizens. Organizations such as associations and committee meetings, which were to be adopted by the majority of the associations of re-Islamized youth, are the signs of a need both to come together as a closed group and to act according to European methods, which correspond to their experience. The *deen camp* (the Islamic holiday 'faith camp') is typical of this attempt to construct European and Islamic militancy. Between a nature trail and a game of football attendees would get up at five o'clock to recite the *ma'thurat* (religious incantations) and *al wasayal 'achar* (the ten recommendations) of Hasan al-Banna. The *tarbiyya Islamiyya* (Islamic development) was not military training but was accompanied, for these teenagers, by a session of push-ups after morning prayer. The activists in contact with older Islamists, as well as engaged Muslims who were re-Islamized 'from afar' developed the feeling of being part of an elite chosen by God to further the cause of Islam. With constancy and discipline, Islam would be welcomed into each house, thanks to the will of God on one hand and to the constitution of the Islamic elite that would occupy key posts in European societies on the other. The sacred was at the centre of their political beliefs, along with the desire to take their place as Islamic powerful interlocutors toward the State on the question of social problems and integration.

Checking Social and Economic Domination

The re-Islamized youth in the West inherited a general disqualification of the figure of the immigrant. This happened via the State and its institutions (immigrant parents often not having the right to vote) and European societies (that see them as strange foreigners). Their Islamist-inspired true Islam, through the promise of social promotion that follows Islamic investment (if you are a good committed Muslim you will succeed), had to erase these elements of stigmatization. It was thus very important for re-Islamized youth to perfectly master the native language of the country in which they lived and to pay attention to their physical appearance, especially through the classical beard-suit-tie combination for the men. Simultaneously appropriating and Islamizing the signs of Western domination represented the promise of greater influence and a position of leadership, leading to progress and modernity. In this line of thought, the re-Islamized youth came to consider science and education as the means to major success. Firstly, they had to be knowledgeable in religious science. This was in order to ensure a privileged place within the group, based on discussions full of Islamic arguments (each discussion, as profane as it might be, would be illustrated by the recital of a Qur'anic verse, or the sayings of the Prophet, the *hadiths*) and in order to legitimize their personal decisions (for instance, wearing the veil or marrying someone not chosen by the family) despite the opposition of their parents to this new arrogant Islamic identity. Note that the majority of the re-Islamized and the activists in the associations were autodidacts using (often Islamist) readings; few of them went on to pursue a purely theological education. Secondly the profane sciences at university would allow for new sources of power. They were very impressed by the level of education of the Islamists exiled in Europe, which reversed the negative image that the majority of their workers' parents had. Thus the profane sciences had mainly an external objective in academic success which was to represent, through the emergence of a new generation of powerful and educated Muslim activists, the means of overthrowing the arrogant domination of the West which denied the glorious past of the Muslim world and above all its possible renaissance.

## The Activist Fatigue and the Disengagement of the Re-Islamized

The enthusiasm created during the 1990s by the promises of revolutionary change associated with re-Islamization largely dissipated over the 2000s. These promises of the liberation of tradition were largely replaced by a new form of alienation from the codes of Islamism, which, initially dynamic, became authoritarian and left young activists fatigued by so much rigor and tension. Moreover, the adoption of these codes failed to valorize Islam as a solution to the problems of the marginalization of Muslims in the public space. On the contrary, there is now a greater stigma attached to the reinforcement of the image of committed Muslim activists as a sectarian and dubious group.[19] For these activists spirituality has suffered from the mechanical adoption of Islamist norms, and the codes of re-Islamization have in turn become restrictive traditions.

After nearly twenty years of re-Islamization the results are deceiving. That is, growing stigmatization, and even the exclusion of visible signs of belonging to Islam in the public sphere, catastrophic family situations with parents and children more estranged by the 'true Islam' than reconciled, and disqualification of the goal of political influence and claims to equal treatment based on Islamic arguments, which are now qualified as communitarian. The re-Islamized have also aged; the modes of predication relayed by then teenagers based on opposition (to parents, to general society) are no longer effective. They are disappointed by the leaders they chose as role models and who failed in the objectives they set themselves—the Islamization of society, political influence over European and Muslim states, failure of claims in terms of social and cultural rights such as the wearing of the veil, and the fight against Islamophobia. The re-Islamized activists thus increasingly believe that they participated in the superficial scene setting of an Islamic modernity that systematically used Islam as a means of distinction for the group, without considering the efficiency of these methods at an individual level. Has Islamist re-Islamization become 'a justification for modernity without itself actually becoming modern'?[20]

In a context such as this, many activists distance themselves and disengage from an identity inherited from Islamism. Since the early 2000s the committed Muslims are rethinking their links to the structures that re-Islamized them (associations, leaders, speakers, mosques, Institutes of Islamic studies and peer groups more generally). For most of them, it is not a matter of rupture but of repositioning oneself with regards to the codes and rules of re-Islamization. The reasons for disengagement are those of a rising unease linked with the disidentification with Islamism in the absence of gratification or the weight of a group that no longer confers a common well-being.

It is evident that the phenomena of 'notabilization'[21] of a certain number of Islamist elites, especially through the institutionalization of their relation to the state, led to the weakening of the promise of a collective well-being, a common fight that Muslim activists could only win collectively. In reality only a minority has managed to transform the resource of political Islam into personal profit. In fact, belonging to the group, either real for the volunteers and activists, or symbolic among those re-Islamized 'from afar' and adopted visible Islamic behaviors, was costly for most members. Refusal of French or German nationalities, marriages within the group that fall apart when the group is over, loss of employment, scams and financial abuse of solidarity, are some cases where re-Islamized and former Islamists have had to pay the price of belonging to their specific group. The idealistic new Islamic community that should have strengthened its members for their belonging to it, in reality made them weaker.

Finally, we have witnessed, particularly since 11 September 2001, a massification of public Islamic codes such as the massive adoption of the headscarf among young women, which deprives them of their previous revolutionary and Islamist character. First and foremost for public opinion, Islam has become an object of public debate, thus dispossessing the Islamists and their re-Islamized activists of the meaning they have attributed to their actions.[22]

*Escaping the Oppositional Islamist Perspective*

Just as they had rejected an authoritarian definition of their identity by the tradition of the parents, the state or the public sphere, historical Islamist activists and re-Islamized European Muslims are increasingly rejecting the static image of Islamism as a tradition. However, this activist fatigue which can lead to disaffiliation of members from the Islamist-inspired associations of re-Islamization, doesn't necessarily lead to a total rupture with the idea of still using forms of political Islam as their main identity resource. However, the forms of their Islam-based political and social participation will no longer be rethought through the group imperatives but instead in light of their personal desires.

The re-Islamized have changed their conception of power. They no longer consider that a political use of Islam should be done with an oppositional Islamist minority perspective. The more they have interacted with other forces and other actors in the processes of social and political domination (such as the media, the European states institutions, the other non-Islamic activists), the more they have understood that the techniques of the appropriation of power should be attempted neither in opposition nor in resistance, but in negotiation. The position of the secular Western dominant actors versus the religious dominated Muslim victims[23] instituted by the historical Islamist codes is thus profoundly destabilized. The idea that their Islamic identity should be based upon a resistance to the imposition of cultural norms by the West is deeply questioned.[24] Re-Islamized actors are developing more efficient modes of negotiation and inclusion of their Islamic references in the global public space. And it works. For example, it is evidenced in how, since the early 2000s, Islam has influenced the redefinition of certain concepts belonging to the Western political tradition, such as that of secularism, having the secular actors themselves use Islamic arguments in order to define the behavior that Muslims should have in the public space (what the Qur'an does or does not state about the veil for example in order to convince young girls to take it off).[25] In this instance Muslims may choose to position themselves at the centre of the system that dominates them in order to make structural changes from within, not by rejecting this system, but instead merely by taking part in the debates.[26]

They still argue for better representation in the public space. However, it is no longer based on the desire to construct alternative mediums, like relying only on Islamist newspapers or websites, but on enlarging their network, their audience and their influence in non-Muslim circles. The principle predicators can now write for major daily newspapers and the old Islamist-inspired websites regularly interview non-religious actors from the public space on questions not necessarily linked to Islam. What matters is a visibility of Islam that is not constructed by signs of opposition but by indicators of legitimacy from the majority non-Muslim population standards. If it is a matter of talking about the question of Islam in Europe, the preference would be for talk shows, on national television channels rather than in communitarian religious chats. The profile of the Islamic activists is also renewing itself. Henceforth they refuse to position themselves as sub-actors in the Islamic category and abandon an Islamic counter-space that stigmatizes them. A headscard-wearing Danish woman, who saw herself (after the scandal around the caricatures of the Prophet) made the host of a televised debate program, refused to see her headscarf as the reason for her appointment and spoke instead of her competencies. No longer claiming membership to a specific group of activists also allows, paradoxically, for the transformation of politicized Islam into a personal resource, in the objective of an individual career.

The Islamist re-Islamization in the West has failed to perpetuate itself as such. However, its codes are at the foundation of a whole imaginary, from the appearance of specific actors and at the origin of debates that have profoundly altered the way in which the question of Islam is addressed today. How does this heritage transform itself? In what way do the former categories of action and participation proposed by re-Islamization reconstitute themselves in the daily lives of committed Muslims?

The re-Islamized, now tired of speaking through the rigor of the traditional categories of re-Islamization, are currently reforming them. These reconversions are the expression of new personal desires that correspond to their change of status in European society as they are now older and more socially stable with a different religiosity and other activist concerns. They also have to adapt to the changes in the political framework within which European Islam has evolved and which increasingly stigmatize claims for a committed Islam. Thus they maintain a complex relationship with the codes of re-Islamization, between repulsion and a desire for demarcation. They do not completely do away with these codes, out of tenderness or nostalgia, or out of the obligation to assume a past they are unable to undo, or even out of the lack of a better option; their re-Islamized practices are thus today still unstable and not yet formalized.

What committed Islamic actors seek today is personal development and the ability to act autonomously. At stake for them is the need to replace the stigmatized and disqualified image of visibly engaged Muslims in the secular public space, particularly via investment in culture and economics, rather than an obsession with revolutionary and oppositional Islamist politics. It will also be a matter of eliminating the oppositional logic of confinement in the activist Islamist counter-space which was imposed by the division of the Islamist world between the true believers and the 'others'. They will attempt to maintain an undemanding, non-oppositional identity for Muslims engaged in the public sphere. There is a clear desire to reposition themselves in relation to the criticisms leveled at Islamism as an ideology that is out of touch with the world, too severe, without personal liberty for activists, and always in tension and opposition. There is also a real sense of anticipation around the prospect of increased in terms of their legitimacy in speaking publicly with regard to their changing political environment. They move from being the intermediaries capable of representing the underprivileged Muslim youth to no longer wanting to be assimilated to them. The example of the 2005 riots in French suburbs and the incapacity of the re-Islamized activists to control them is a good illustration of their normalization.[27]

Rather than party and state politics, it is the question of ethics that may repair the present problematic tone of Islamist re-Islamization. Indeed, oppositional politics was until recently the only avenue open to re-Islamized activists to express themselves and promote their 'true' Islam. Today the disillusions of their previous commitment introduce two new fields of implication: culture and economics. They already existed during re-Islamization but were only pretexts for consolidating the existence of the group, denying the personal pleasure of the auditor or the individual career of the artist. For example, the Islamic songs, *nasheeds*, were only on topics such as the suffering of Muslim children in Bosnia, or the plays displayed in the form of sermons about the 'brothers who stray from the *deen*'. Today these categories defined by the exiled Islamists' experience are progressively falling apart. The profile of the new politically engaged Muslims has been pluralized beyond the activist careers proposed by re-Islamization. It is possible to be a very traditional imam and sing a *nasheed* in a rhythm and blues style.

The notoriety given by these kinds of visible and secularized activities tends even to replace the religious and political historical legitimacy that early Islamists were using to consolidate their authority over European Muslims. Indeed, in order to guarantee the loyalty of their followers, the new forms of political Islam have to offer them something more concrete than idealistic notions of a (hypothetical) Islamic revolution. This is more of a consumer relationship that has been established between the promoters of new forms of political Islam and the rest of the committed Muslims, through their concrete production of goods such as (but not limited to), books, cassettes, disks, plays, Islamic goods, cloths, food and financial services. This new way of promoting Islam overthrows the hierarchical frameworks that the former Islamist militancy instituted. In order to present oneself as a genuine Islamic public figure, one must emphasize one's own individual testimony rather than the doctrine of a particular organization. It is the degree of self-confidence and persuasion of the leader that will motivate and confirm the commitment of the adepts. Thus far this chapter has analyzed the renewal of the Islamist figure of the *murshid*,[28] at the general or national level, through the local figure of the coach. The guide is an immobile figure whose adepts wait patiently for the arrival of the Islamic state. The coach, on the other hand, encourages the personal development of his adepts via their engagement in micro-projects. Today one can claim the heritage of Tariq Ramadan without being a close activist in the same way that one can make Islamic clothing, music, sketches, policy, economics, and sacred things, without being limited by any kind of organization.

## *The New Mediums of Political Islam: Competitiveness, Culture, Economics and Ethics*

In the new forms of political Islam, the values of market and competition are replacing those of self-denial and amateurish charity for the former activist.[29] Henceforth the production of a CD of spiritual songs, the commercialization of an Islamic soda, or the latest publication on the situation of Muslims must meet the standards of the global market. This desire amongst committed Muslims to be competitive actors is visible in the construction of an Islamic ethic of 'work well done', of the image of the Prophet as a great merchant, or of wealth valued by God. The profile of the former activist, the eternal student who must search for science 'even if as far away as China' (according to one of the sayings of the Prophet), is replaced by the professional who is responsible for presenting Islam as a competitive faith. A sign of the times is the tendency of young Muslims to pursue studies in finance, rather than the natural or human sciences that were favored by their re-Islamized elders. To ensure the defense of Islam, money seems now more efficient than philosophical debates on what an Islamic society looks like. The means of action of Islamic projects have thus been profoundly destabilized. The homework help that was once organized by re-Islamized students for the children of the mosque has now been replaced by day-long seminars on the promotion of academic success by consultants in Islamic finance, or by Islamic rappers who come to schools to organize writing seminars or anti-drug talks. The alms of the believers, once collected within local networks, can now be given via telephone companies who offer to transfer part of the money from monthly consumption to Islamic NGOs. Following the riots in 2005 in France, the Islamic Development Bank wanted to finance the entrepreneurial projects of the economically excluded 'young Muslims from the suburbs', thus contesting the monopoly of the World Islamic League, who were behind the construction of numerous mosques in Europe in the 1990s. The means of publicizing speeches on what Islam should be have also changed dramatically. To announce an Islamic event (a conference, a demonstration or to share writings) a list of emails and SMS alerts has replaced the traditional word of mouth system, which was only possible by physically going to the association, the mosque or being in regular contact with other members. Those who initiated these changes no longer wanted to be numbed by group actions. They are not organic leaders of the group but rather individual actors who wanted to move from a community of brothers that was weighty and stigmatized, to a community of partners that is dynamic and profitable. Thus, young Muslim associations now propose seminars in speed reading, time management and how to present oneself in a job interview.

The discourse of these new Islamic figures is no longer exclusively based on the question of religion but aims to normalize political Islam as an ethical ideology that can be shared by anyone. This is an ethical and consensual spirituality that is now offered, and will undo the categorization of Islam, as an incompatible imported identity. 'Islamness' has become diffused; one no longer needs to be part of a restricted group of activists to have an ethical-Islamic reference, within which many different types of projects with very different types of partners can be initiated. There is a need to secularize the way in which the problems of Muslims are addressed, notably via ethics. Basing themselves on the question of common values, they may reach non-re-Islamized or disengaged Muslims, or even non-Muslims. The ideal of these new figures is not to give highly coded conferences to small groups of adepts but rather to construct a discourse that rises beyond the community. They now address their message of Muslims engaged on different subjects to a variety of audiences. Their target can no longer be read in relation to class, age, or religious affiliation.

Thus the traditional causes of re-Islamization, such as the wearing of the veil or the occupation of Palestine, are no longer only shared amongst re-Islamized activists, but may also be defended in partnership with anti-globalization groups, or even homosexuals who are concerned about minority rights. If the post-colonial question, for example, is increasingly important in their discourse it is because they, along with many other movements in Europe today, are engaged in contesting the monopoly of a white, Judeo-Christian and hegemonic European male identity. This is indicative of the secularization of their political Islamic identity thanks to the interaction with other non-Muslim actors. For example, we might also see the leader of an association closed to the ideology of the Muslim Brotherhood move from the management of an Islamic bookshop called *Tawhid* (the Oneness of God) to the organization of philosophic discussion groups with academics, in a center renamed for Malcolm X. Malek Bennabi[30] is no longer read as an Islamic thinker but as one of the authors of 'colonizabilty'. These causes evidently remain political, but they are less related to questions of religion than to a common ethic of respect for minority peoples and their histories. Their request for recognition of the contribution of foreigners to Europe is also a sign of their reconciliation with their parents and of the possibility for them to rediscover their plural selves beyond the codes taught by the re-Islamizing Islamist group. These are new ways of approaching political engagement through new partnerships and identifications, in which Islam remains an important element but is no longer exclusive or particularistic.

Two different dynamics must be retained in this renewal of the soul of committed Islam: the secularization and realignment of supports with a globalized culture and the repoliticization (and not depoliticization) of their claims in new and different forms. The understanding of political power and of the means of changing society has also changed. Actors of these new forms of political Islam, because they are at the center of the modern world—but in an alternative way—have the opportunity to reinforce para-political power which allows them 'to change the world without taking the power'.[31] Ethics are henceforth the social links that Islamism can no longer be. As a general framework for these post-Islamist transformations, ethics allow for a justification of Islamic re-engagement, in giving activists different and individual reasons to believe and independence in the choice of support for their actions. Despite the diversification of reasons for continuing to situate one's engagement in relation to Islam, these reasons become coherent in an ethical-Islamic whole that allows for a consensual engagement in terms of a common struggle for the best possible world to be built.

## *When Political Islam Becomes No More Than One Political Tradition Available Among Others*

Proposing the concept of Islamism as a political tradition that is fixed in history which can then be transformed has allowed us to avoid two possible traps. The first would be to consider both Islamism and re-Islamization, the inheritor of its codes, as a permanent revolution from which its adepts cannot extract themselves. Although they are group phenomena, Islamism and re-Islamization never led to consensus on the definition of the means of action amongst their members and different generations of activists. Their world of meaning was always reworked by the adepts themselves, according to time and place; either for external reasons (the necessity of readapting to the social and political realities of the moment), or for internal reasons (individual disenchantment of the activists and the reconstruction of the sense of belonging to the group). Moreover, the new political militancy paths now chosen by actors who have been through a process of re-Islamization, show us that the codes of Islamism no longer belong just to the Islamists themselves. Having these codes normalized in the public sphere, Islamism and re-Islamization are no longer the obligatory passage for those who wish to use Islam to support its political demands and mobilizations. They represent a historical marking; a fluid resource that very different actors can use.

The second pitfall would have been the presentation of the weakening of Islamist structures, their 'decline', their 'failure', or their 'afterwards', as a total rupture with what occurred before. We cannot guarantee that people who turned their back on Islamists also turn their back on political Islam. Therefore it is not because Islamism as a political ideology may be defeated or outdated that committed Muslims are inventing new political practices or return to mimicking the secularized forms of political modernity against which Islamism was conceived. They may use some elements promoted by Islamism and mix it with other political traditions. The disinstitutionalization of Islamism does not mean the disappearance of political Islam.

When it implanted itself in Europe, Islamism was already an uprooted movement (from the Muslim world). Its specificity is thus to have been transformed itself into a political tradition, despite its desire to impose new codes and revolutionary practice. Islamism must be conceived of in its continuity rather than via the idea that it constitutes a break with other political traditions (on the contrary it always strongly relied on the symbols of other traditions itself) and that post-Islamism would thus represent a total rupture. Today the Islamist codes are historically relativized, which allows the actors concerned with the question of political Islam to adopt a position of renewal. Furthermore, in becoming a tradition, Islamism has allowed re-Islamized European Muslims to learn how to manage changes in their evolving identities by no longer expressing these changes via conflict or opposition.

When political Islam is analyzed, the reference to Islamist codes is omnipresent and now represents a common language, as much for non-activist Muslims as for the media and the state. However these codes cannot be considered a timeless framework given that the actors using them already regard it as no more than one political tradition among others.

6

# POLITICAL ISLAM IN WEST AFRICA FROM THE 1980s TO THE PRESENT

*Muriel Gomez-Perez*

The Islamic revival which began at the end of the 1970s, and which intensified over the next two decades in francophone West Africa, can only be understood if it is first placed within a larger historical context—one that encompasses the 1940s, 1950s and 1960s. Indeed, it was during this earlier period that young West Africans decided to create associations, having returned from Arabic studies in Egypt, Algeria or Tunisia, or from a pilgrimage to Mecca, or business activities in the Arabian Peninsula. Thus, beginning in the mid-1940s, graduates from al-Azhar in Cairo founded the *Subbanu al-Muslimin* association in Bamako. In 1953 several young Arabic-speaking residents of Dakar, drawn from leading Marabout families, founded the Union Culturelle Musulmane [Muslim Cultural Union] (UCM). Also in Dakar, francophone Muslim students created the Association Musulmane des Étudiants d'Afrique Noire [Muslim Association of Black African Students] (AMEAN) in 1954. These new Muslim organizations had multiple goals, including the planning of conferences and debates to promote a return to the Qur'an and the Sunna, as well as a deeper knowledge of the fundamental principles of Islam. They also sought to open modernized Arabic schools with new courses (such as arithmetic, history and Arabic grammar), and using new pedagogical methods (class levels, programs, schedules, workbooks, tables, textbooks) in order to allow Muslims of all ages to understand passages from the Qur'an without recourse to an intermediary, rather than simply memorizing them. With these objectives, these young Muslims positioned themselves as guides and as the vanguards of change, referring to themselves using the Arabic terms Salafi (Companions of the Prophet and the 'Rightly Guided' First Four Caliphs), or Wahhabi, or using the description 'crossed arms'.[1] They cast themselves in opposition to two other prominent actors. On the one hand, they criticized the practitioners of traditional Islam for their superstitious beliefs, their limited knowledge of the Qur'an, their dependent links with their followers or students (*tullab*), and their collusion with the French colonial administration. On the other hand, this same administration was criticized for trying to close Islamic schools and to limit, if not eliminate, any relations between sub-Saharan Muslims and the Arab-Muslim world. The confrontation tended to become starker at the end of the 1950s with the rise of nationalism, the movement against the Algerian War, and the campaign against the 1958 referendum and the Balkanization of Africa. Instead, the new Muslim associations favored immediate independence. This campaign was launched by the UCM at its federal congress (22–25 December 1957), where there was participation by representatives from the regions of Upper Volta, French Sudan, Guinea and Côte d'Ivoire.

The victory of the 'yes' side in the referendum and the successive declarations of independence in 1960 brought an end to the dynamic activities of these groups of young Muslims for a period of about twenty years. Indeed, these young independent states, with their large Muslim majorities, were guided by the principle of secularism in their constitutions and were occasionally influenced by catholic advisors (Upper Volta). These states largely followed a proactive Islamic policy: organizing pilgrimages to Mecca; structuring the training of Arabic teachers in colleges and secondary schools; controlling the distribution of scholarships to students wishing to study at Arab universities; initiating diplomatic relations with Arab nations; and controlling and structuring religious life by creating Islamic associations[2] designed to protect the existing social and religious order. The specific objectives of these associations were to bring together all variants of Islam within each country and to serve as the transmission mechanism for what the state wanted Islam to be. They were also intended as an interface between the Arab-Muslim world and the authorities in order to obtain important subsidies from Arab countries and to gain Islamic legitimacy, both internationally and within each country. Following this logic, the young Muslims of the 1940s and 1950s were pushed aside in favor of other Muslims, sometimes drawn from the Brotherhoods (Senegal). But the most important criterion for inclusion was a readiness to openly collaborate with the newly-independent states.

Beginning at the end of the 1970s, following events in the Arab-Muslim world, a religious revival emerged, notably Senegal and then in Mali, extending to Burkina Faso, Niger, and Côte d'Ivoire beginning in the early 1990s. Numerous Islamic associations were created, whose leaders and activists demanded a central place for Islam in political and social life. First of all, this chapter will study how this religious revival manifested itself and evolved. Should it be seen as a sign of the radicalization of Islam in francophone West Africa or of the influence of the global context where Islam was suddenly taking on a prominent place in politics and international relations? Or should this hyper-religiosity be seen as the result of internal changes within the societies under study? Secondly, the main themes developed by the different movements and personalities which entered the public sphere will be analyzed. This will allow for a portrayal of how these Islamic movements were simultaneously both local and global in nature and how they represented a break with previous generations insofar as they cast themselves in a leadership role. They nevertheless occasionally collaborated with their elders on certain issues such as the moral regulation of society. Finally, this chapter will reflect on the profound significance of these changes, showing how the relationship between religion and society evolved to the point that it has become possible to speak in terms of a new religious culture which led to the emergence of a 'religious public sphere' and opened the possibility of a 'civil religion'.

## Towards a More Visible and Media-Savvy Islam

Beginning in the late 1970s, and especially during the mid-1980s, the religious climate in several countries changed with the proliferation of mosques, of *madaris* and of neighborhood Islamic associations. In Côte d'Ivoire, the Association des Élèves et Étudiants Musulmans de Côte d'Ivoire [Côte d'Ivoire Muslim Students' Association] was created in 1979; the Muslim community of the Riviera in 1982; in Senegal, Jamaatou Ibadou Rahmane (JIR) was created in 1978; the Association des Étudiants Musulmans de l'Université de Dakar [Association of Muslim Students of the University of Dakar] (AEMUD) in 1984; and the Organisation pour l'Action Islamique [Organization for Islamic Action] (OAI) and Jamra in 1985. Night classes in Arabic were established and achieved success in places like Bamako. Islamic newspapers (*Études Islamiques* in July 1979; *Djamra* in 1983; *Wal Fadjri* in January 1984; *Le Musulman* in 1983; *L'Étudiant musulman* in 1989 in Senegal; and *Iqra* in 1989 in Niger) and Islamic radio programs[3] appeared on the scene. In this regard, the case of Mali was very innovative since the *ulama* showed a particular interest for radio, going so far as to offer their know-how to the programs. It should also be noted that there was a great increase in the number of public meetings, speeches, and bookstores.[4] This vitality of Islam was also evident within the Brotherhoods with the creation of *dahiras* in Senegal. Also, the 'fight for the construction of a mosque on campus was the centerpiece of this strategy for asserting a religious presence on the university scene',[5] and '[a]ll of these developments point to the possibility that the climate had evolved even if the latter cannot rightly be described as a revolutionary'.[6] That is, as Coulon states:

Islam was no longer an activity for the old; I would go so far as to say that it is becoming an activity for the young in opposition to the gerontocratic powers. It serves to criticize the establishment. It acts as a vehicle for, and method of discovery of, the right to expression for young people. The Islamic leadership is being transformed by it, for this new elite seeks to distinguish itself from the older Muslim leaders and its members hope to act as community leaders. (…) These new clerics, whom I call litterati, believing they have more knowledge than the older generation, freely denounce the less orthodox practices of their elders and the latter's compromises with the powers that be.[7]

Islamic space grew larger during the 1990s, a sign of Islam's greater visibility. Numerous new mosques were built, especially in residential areas, and participation in the pilgrimage to Mecca increased among the young. The *madaris* were so successful that in Mali they were integrated into the state-sponsored public education system and in Côte d'Ivoire, following some Muslims who asked that their *madaris* also be integrated into the national education system. Women and youth exhibited an increased desire to display their Muslim identity, a phenomenon also evident on university campuses, in the workplace, in hotels and within government agencies, with a special focus on dress codes (loose-fitting clothing, head scarves to cover the hair, neck and shoulders) and codes of behavior (greetings, ways of speaking and looking that give external signals of one's affiliation with a particular branch of Islam and humility among women).[8] The number of Islamic associations exploded in certain countries like Niger[9] and Côte d'Ivoire[10] and their growth continued in other countries (in the 1990s the Association des Élèves et Étudiants Musulmans du Burkina [Burkina Muslim Pupils' and Students' Association] and the Centre d'Études, de Recherches et de Formation Islamique [Centre for Islamic Studies, Research and Training] in Burkina Faso). An Islamic newspaper, *Plume libre*, appeared in Côte d'Ivoire in 1992 and *an-Nasr* in January 2004 in Burkina Faso. But most of the Islamic newspapers that were in printed in the 1980s are no longer produced because of financial problems (such as in Senegal and in Côte d'Ivoire). In fact, Islam increased its visibility in the media with the more regular and prominent broadcast of religious shows on the radio and the television;[11] the broad distribution of sermons on audio- and video-cassettes;[12] posters of clothing sporting the likeness of different preachers; a significant increase in the number of Islamic bookstores; and a new emphasis on clerics from around the world. All of these developments represented 'the circulation of religious knowledge within unregulated networks'.[13] The new element lay in the emergence of religious mass movements like the Moustarchidines in Senegal, and in the great increase in sermons delivered at large gatherings held at locations like stadiums. Protest marches became much more frequent, such as those held in reaction to world events like the Gulf War or the events of 11 September 2001, but also those organized in opposition to certain government measures like the eviction of residents from Zangouettin, a neighborhood in central Ouagadougou.

The Muslim had become both an activist for Islam and a missionary, roles which were reinforced in the 1990s when proselytism or *da'wa* was placed at the centre of a new strategy. The aim was for Islam 'to be everywhere at all times', 'to be present in, if not to dominate the public sphere', 'to present the message in such a way that it was accessible to all' and 'to enlarge Islamic space' so that the state would have no choice but to take notice. Many regulations adopted by Islamic associations underscored the importance of the *da'wa* and *wa'zi* (public study sessions).[14] In this context, mosques became important centers for political expression and were transformed into veritable complexes housing dispensaries, schools if not *madrasa*, and Arab literacy programs. Meanwhile, Islamic vacation destinations were established where children learned ablution and prayer while studying the Qur'an and the *hadith*.

Several factors help explain such a religious revival. The first set are internal and relate to the manner in which each society reacted to the failure of state policies, to various economic crises (the collapse of the coffee and cocoa markets in Côte d'Ivoire or the peanut crisis in Senegal, for example) and to student and social movements. The state was no longer able to satisfy the social and religious needs of the population. During the 1990s the process of democratization was 'a sign of normalization, that is the reflection of a sociological reality long hidden by an authoritarian power that could not deal with it without threatening its own survival'[15] in Niger and Mali. It generally tended to exacerbate identity-based demands and make them more politicized. These movements were made more visible by a new-found freedom of expression and by the expansion of television, radio and video, thanks to the arrival of inexpensive electronics imported from Asia. This opening of the airwaves also allowed for a wider broadcast of ideas and the circulation of translated texts and preachers. Meanwhile, the states in question withdrew from several sectors of the economy in favor of private interests, and fell even deeper into crisis following the devaluation of the CFA Franc in 1994 and the application of the Structural Adjustment Plans (SAP). The accelerated privatization of the economy and of education contributed to a new commodification of religion. A large part of the population was disappointed with the broken promises that had accompanied democratization and wanted to increase the credibility of Islam as a viable alternative in the public sphere.

This religious revival also reflected the fact that, since the 1980s, there had been greater diversity of Islamic activists and leaders. The new religious dynamics made room for the marginalized—the uneducated youth represented by the Association des Jeunes Musulmans de Côte d'Ivoire [Association of Young Muslims of Côte d'Ivoire]; socially disadvantaged women in Mali; readers of religious pamphlets written in Arabic, French or other national languages giving instructions on how to be a 'good Muslim',[16] the Arabic-speaking groups in Burkina Faso who were of 'low social status' and 'were second-class intellectuals'[17]—but did not do so exclusively. They were also the work of individuals who were conscious of the importance of speaking French for their commercial activities (the patrons of the *Yan-Izala* movement in Maradi, Niger)[18] and for relations with the state. Or they saw the importance of the Arab-French bilingualism, having been trained in both the Qur'anic and Arabic systems and their Western counterparts (*Adini Islam* sought to 'rehabilitate and make use of the Franco-Frabic upper managers';[19] the founders of the JIR;[20] Sidy Lamine Niasse, founder of *Wal Fadjri*,[21] as well as some pilgrims from Côte d'Ivoire were identified as 'a new set of Islamic clerics. (…) locally acknowledged as *ulamah*';[22] Al Hadj Idriss Koudouss Koné, president of the CNI, was trained at the École Nationale d'Administration Publique [National School of Public Administration] in Rabat;[23] in Niger, Cheikh Boureïma Abdou Daouda gave sermons in French and in Arabic).[24] This group created links with certain older Islamic activists (Cheikh Touré, founding president of the UCM in 1953, was known for his Islamic radicalism).[25] During the 1950s they had pursued their studies almost exclusively in North Africa or Egypt. But although Egypt remained a preferred destination, the location of their studies diversified between the 1970s and the 1990s to include Saudi Arabia, Sudan, Europe and the United States. These dynamics were also visible in francophone milieus: Latif Gueye;[26] the newspaper *Iqra* founded by intellectuals, university professors, engineers, physicians, professors from secondary schools and colleges who trained in Western schools; certain pilgrims from Côte d'Ivoire;[27] the founders of the AEMUD in Dakar; or the founders of the CERFI in Ouagadougou who targeted francophone civil servants. They could also be found within the Brotherhoods (those of Cheikh Touré, Latif Gueye of the *Tidjaniyya*, Sidy Lamine Niasse from the Niassènes family,[28] the ARCI founded by three grand *cheikhs* of the *Tidjaniyya* in Niger.[29] Finally, the world of business was also involved[30] (*Al-Falah*[31], the patrons of the *Yan-Izala* movement in Maradi).[32]

Meanwhile, bilingual and francophone citizens became active within the Islamic movement. Their strategies were more in line with trade globalization, neo-liberalism and modernity. Some prominent imams were able to manipulate the media with great success and learned how to capture the attention of uneducated followers while playing on the emotions of their audience.[33]

In parallel, world events accelerated the process of self-affirmation initiated by the Muslim communities under study. As Westerlund noted: 'Certainly the oil boom and its financial and psychological consequences has been an important factor. [...] It should be noted, furthermore, that the influence of foreign powers may also have a divisive and weakening effect on the Islamist movement'.[34] For example, in Niger during the 1980s and 1990s, there was an ongoing battle for influence between Libya and Saudi Arabia and between Kuwait and Iran.[35] The Islamic Revolution 'inspired an intensification of Islamic practice in many Muslim societies'[36] and was seen at the time as the beginning of a serious political project, although today this is no longer true.[37] By contrast, the Iran-Iraq War and the Gulf War are themes which highlight the fault lines within West-African Islamic movements.

## Discourse and Strategies: Continuity and Change

Criticism of secularism was a constant in discourse although it varied significantly from one country to the next. In Senegal, this debate was the focus of media attention throughout the 1980s. From its inception, the magazine *Djamra* attacked secularism much like the newspaper *Wal Fadjri*, up until the departure of its managing editor Latif Gueye in the mid-1980s. From the end of the 1980s, the strategy changed: a direct critique of the concept was abandoned in favor of a socio-cultural critique of the practice of secularism.

Three arguments were used against secularism. First, that such a principle had no place in a country where the majority of the population was Muslim. Second, they argued that it had been imported and imposed by French colonial power and continued to be the norm after independence and up to the present day. Finally, that it promoted the separation of religion and politics when, in fact, states used Islam to their own ends.

The critique of the foundations of the state and of its instrumentalist approach to Islam also evolved significantly from one decade to the next, with Senegal being the first country where the Islamic movement in francophone Africa turned its attention to politics. To begin with, there was the creation of the JIR, which broke away from the UCM because 'Islam wasn't being lived in its entirety' and because the association was increasingly becoming a mouthpiece for pro-government propaganda. Furthermore there was the secret creation of an Islamic party in 1979 by Ahmed Khalifa Niasse. This signaled an awakening on the part of Muslim political actors who wished to upset the political balance in their favor. Following this isolated success (Ahmed Khalifa Niasse went into exile after August 1979, and later re-emerged on the government side, going so far as to support Abdou Diouf during the 1993 elections) and given the state's ability to pursue a rather ambiguous Islamic policy (allowing the anti-secularism debate to carry so long as it did not threaten public order; increasing openness to the Arab world; banning the importation, distribution and sale of Salman Rushdie's *Satanic Verses* with a decree issued on 24 February 1989), the plan was to stay out of electoral politics and abstain from voting until the 1988 presidential elections. The reverse occurred in Burkina Faso and in Mali at the beginning of the 1980s. Muslim reformers, most of whom were Arabic-speaking, held that Sankara's revolutionary project corresponded to God's will, all the while believing that they had to go even further to establish a social order based on the Qur'an.[38] In Mali, Oumar S. Touré, the first director of the Centre pour la promotion de la langue Arabe [Centre for the Promotion of the Arabic Language], a fervent defender of the nationalization of the *madaris*, stood in opposition to his father, Saad Touré, founder of the first *madrasa* in Mali and kept his distance from the colonial administration and later the independent state.[39]

In 1988 a change occurred in Senegal; Islamic leaders did not call for the creation of a legally-recognized Islamic party but instead agreed to pressure existing political parties to take a stand on a society governed by Islamic values and institutions. In this vein, a first Islamic declaration was written during the JIR's fourth congress (September 1988). Later, a coalition of associations was formed to declare that Islam 'is a global religion, that it is both a spiritual and material vocation, and that consequently it embraces all aspects of the individual's life and that of humanity'. Nevertheless, support for this position was not unanimous: *Al Falah* did not participate in the initiative. In 1993, during the presidential elections, the Islamists entered the political arena by releasing a platform clearly listing their demands on matters social, political, economic and religious. They called on all candidates to take a position with regard to the platform and called on young voters to reject the street violence which had broken out following the announcement of the results of the 1988 presidential elections. A radicalization of religious life was notably evident in the speech given on 13 February 1993 by Moustapha Sy, the young Marabout manager of the *dahira Moustarchidatines*.[40]

During the 1990s, the battle against the state might appear to have moved underground. The fact that certain Islamic leaders were civil servants might suggest that their freedom of action was limited, but this was irrelevant. For their role as preachers came before all other considerations for this new generation of Muslims. 'The new Islamic intellectual could not be controlled by the state in his social being. Socially, he was not what he appeared, his profession did not define him'.[41] Regardless, the battle against state secularism was launched once again following the election of Abdoulaye Wade as president in 2000 and his initial decision to take the word 'secular' out of the constitution in January 2001. A Groupe d'initiative pour le référendum sur l'application de la loi Islamique [Working Group for the Referendum on the Application of Islamic Law] (GIPRALIS) coordinated by Mouhammad Niang was created to write a new constitution. In Niger, the AIN denounced 'the backward step in Islamic values' and criticized the secular foundations of the constitution adopted on 26 December 1992,[42] given that Muslims formed an overwhelming majority of the country's citizens.

In other countries too, Islam became a subject of national political debate in the context of the democratization process. During the Conférence nationale [National Convention] of August 1991 in Mali, there was a movement in opposition to the ban on religious political parties. One of the arguments used against the new constitution was: 'The Qur'an is our best constitution. Vote no on any other constitution!'[43] Indeed, a similar link had been established between the introduction of multi-party politics and the rise in the visibility of Islamic associations in Côte d'Ivoire,[44] and between the end of the long emergency regime of 1974–1987 and the religious revival in Niger. In Côte d'Ivoire, the Muslim associations, which had been discrete if not passive before December 1993 (death of Houphouët-Boigny), became involved in political debates. The mosques of the Lycée Technique d'Abdjan, of the Riviera II, of Aghien, and of the Riviera Golf: 'were recognized as vectors for the transmission of the political positions of the Muslim community. … Their policy positions dealt with the anti-Muslim measures, problems related to "ivoirité" and the question of the foreign nationals in the North. They openly accused the political authorities of wanting to destroy the energy of Islam and of making Muslims into second-class citizens'.[45] The electoral law of November 1994, which prevented foreigners from voting, and the constitution of 21 July 2000 were actively vilified and Al Hadj Idriss Koudouss moved to the forefront.[46] Also, the separation of religious and political matters was actively criticized by certain Islamic movements in Niger.[47]

The evolution of the positions taken in relation to the state, shows these movements needed the state.[48] They recognized that the state was incontrovertible and that it would be counterproductive to disregard it. However, the legitimacy of the state was sometimes questioned more directly, as when two associations in Niger raised the matter of introducing *Shari'a*. In 1999—the Organisation Islamique Nigérienne de Boubacar El Hadj Issa [Islamic Organization of Niger in Boubacar El Hadj Issa] and the Association pour la culture et l'éducation Islamique de Souleymane Imam Younous [Association for Islamic Culture and Education of Souleymane Imam Younous]. Or the state's legitimacy could be questioned in a less direct manner when the Qur'an was declared to be a central model, a guiding text which could overcome the economic, social and ideological failures that had plagued the African states since their independence. Some authors have argued that because of the limits placed on the democratic process (endemic corruption and nepotism, enduring economic crisis) there emerged 'outlet' strategies[49] that involved focusing on activities on the social front (such as donations of blood, clothing, food).

The entire Islamic movement was conscious of the fact that political Islam could emerge if only society as a whole perfectly understood and followed religious precepts. A complete transformation of the social landscape was an unavoidable prerequisite. This is why, throughout these two decades, and regardless of the group in question, certain issues were regularly alluded to in speeches: moral decline, the superficial practice of the faith and the Westernization of morals. Frequent calls were made for a return to traditional values and for moral reform: honesty, solidarity, and work; the closing of bars; the fight against prostitution, corruption, juvenile delinquency, and women's clothing considered indecent; mothers educating their children. In several countries, reforms to the Code of Family Law (Senegal, Mali, Burkina Faso and Niger) inspired stormy debates and virulent opposition campaigns. The document was even referred to as the 'Women's Code' to signify that it was anti-Islamic insofar as it supported monogamy and sought to reform relations between spouses with regard to inheritance. It was also considered imperialist because it supported Western concepts of family and gender relations. The fight against the reform of family law and against a ban on female circumcision was so virulent that in Mali the state backed down in 2002;[50] it is the same case in Niger.[51] In Senegal, the Comité Islamique pour la Réforme du Code de la Famille au Sénégal [Islamic Committee for the Reform of the Code of Family Law in Senegal] (CIRCOFS) was created with the participation of Al Falah, JIR, OAI and AEMUD. The committee denounced certain anti-Islamic elements of the text and proposed specific amendments to various articles according to the principles of the Qur'an.

Negative comments directed against women, blaming them for all sorts of deprivations and social problems (such as a lack of rain during winter), became increasingly common and normal as such messages were widely broadcast on radio and television during the 1990s. In Niger, a movement was formed to oppose the campaign for family planning and the prevention of AIDS, initiatives which were considered anti-Islamic.[52] Their next initiative was to unsuccessfully oppose the ratification of the Convention for the Elimination of all Forms of Discrimination against Women (CEDAW) in 1999, portraying it as an act of 'prostitution' as well as the holding of the Festival of African Fashion in Niamey in November 2000.[53] In Niger also, Islamist women contested the feminist vision of women's rights when the Quota Act[54] became effective on 28 February 2001.[55]

According to these groups, this also explains how the breakdown of society was caused by a poor understanding of Islam and of its fundamental principles by all Muslims. These groups rejected all belief in spirit possession, in ghosts, or in amulets. This is why they regularly denounced *dhikr* sessions (collective sessions for reciting payers) where there was a notable association made between the names of the founder of the Brotherhood, those of the subsequent Caliphs, and that of the Prophet Muhammed. According to them, the Brotherhoods bore a great share of the responsibility for the lack of unity within the community. By attacking the Brotherhoods, these groups placed themselves in a position to challenge the former's monopoly. Thus, they declared themselves to be the faithful and cautious interpreters of the texts that informed their beliefs. During the 1980s, criticism of the Brotherhoods was more muted in Senegal, a reflection of pragmatism within these groups. In order to reach a broader audience, efforts were made to cooperate with the Brotherhoods and evoked the founders of the Brotherhoods when preaching resistance to colonialism. The groups realized that it was difficult to directly attack the power of the Brotherhoods and socio-religious realities forced them to temper their discourse. At the same time, the Brotherhoods were conscious of the fact that the Islamic associations provided them with a means of reaching new social segments of the urban population, especially the youth. By contrast, in Niger, Salafi Islam remained

141

opposed to the Islamic Brotherhood of *tariqa Tidjaniyya*[56] as in Burkina Faso, where Arabic-speaking activists condemned 'the "ignorance" of the traditionalists (...) for claiming as legitimate the power to which they aspired'.[57]

Special treatment was given to international affairs and the situation of Muslims around the world. It is through these questions that the polymorphic nature of the discourse becomes apparent. In Niger, the newspaper *Iqra* analyzed the Qur'an and Sufi practices, attacked secularism, discussed Sayyid Qutb, condemned the *Satanic Verses*, called for moral reform (to be achieved by giving women a central role), and both stated and implied that it was allied with the authorities. In Senegal, the AEMUD followed in the footsteps of the JIR by translating excerpts from Sayyid Qutb's *Milestones on the Road*. Qutb was seen as the father of all dissenting Islamic movements of the 1970s. In Niger, 'the label "modernist Islam" referred just as much to radical Islamists as to the modernists Ibn Taymiyya, Mohamed Ben Abdelwahab, Hassane Al Banna, Sayyed Qutb, Abul A'la Maudud, Ahmed Deedat, Tariq Ramadan etc'.[58] It is the same in Senegal and in Burkina Faso.

Continuity emerged from the discourse during the 1980s and 1990s. Praise for the Iranian revolution was common in Islamic newspapers during the period insofar as the Ayatollah Khomeini personified the rejection of the West, was portrayed as a spiritual guide who helped make Islam a potent political force on the eve of the twentieth century, and acted as the leader who made possible a return to a more authentic version of Islam. From June to October 1984, *Wal Fadjri* published the *Manifeste de l'État Islamique* [Manifesto of the Islamic State] written by the Ayatollah Khomeini. In the same way, the rise of the Front Islamique du salut [Islamic Salvation Front] in Algeria in December 1991 was seen as part of a global 'awakening of the Islamic consciousness. Bin Laden also attracted attention for his defiance of the West to the point that youth opposed to evictions in the Zangouettin neighborhood formed a group with the same name. However these references did not necessarily indicate a total allegiance to the thinking of these leaders. Rather, they showed that West Africans were keen to listen to ideological debates across the *umma* and were impressed by the media profile these international leaders had achieved. Muslims in the region were also inspired by local and regional religious leaders and notably by the jihad carried on in West Africa during the nineteenth century.

But when diplomatic games and struggles for influence between Arab-Muslim countries took place, the *umma* was divided because of 'divergent interpretations of the facts'.[59] The reading of the Gulf War by the Islamic press in Senegal provides a good example. For *Jamra*, *Al-Falah*, the retreat of Iraqi troops from Kuwait was essential, Saddam Hussein was wrong to have invaded Kuwait, and the arrival of Western troops was the most acceptable solution. For the AEMUD, the monarchies of the Gulf were guilty of being on the same side as the West and Saddam Hussein was criticized for his 1991 invasion of Kuwait, despite his jihadist stances, because it has led to an enduring American presence in the region and near the sacred sites of Islam. For the JIR, the arrival of Western troops was unacceptable because they had come to defend Kuwait—not for humanitarian reasons but for strategic and economic ones. Following this watershed event, opposition to the United States was reinforced by the imprisonments at Guantanamo Bay in January 1992 and the invasion of Iraq in March 2003. And opposition to Israel was made definitive with the election of Ariel Sharon in February 2001, the subsequent construction of a protective wall in the West Bank, and Israel's assassination of Sheikh Ahmad Yassine (Hamas's spiritual leader) on 22 March 2004. Thus, international political developments having strong media impact and an 'ability to recruit'[60] were systematically analyzed by the West-African Islamic press.

In positioning themselves in relation to one another, the different Islamic associations continually called for a return to fundamental Islamic values through a return to the Qur'an and to the Sunna. Their calls for Muslim unity in order to create an exemplary community that would obey the Prophetic Message illustrates how they directly cast themselves as messengers of the Prophet, as guides and interpreters.[61] 'The pre-eminence of the Qur'an' was central to Islamic discourse.[62] Islam 'is not only a set of beliefs, it is an "all-encompassing order," a "total order," a *nizam*'.[63]

What changed in the 1990s was the increasingly central place given to cultural practice and a collective devotion to all aspects of

Islam. Prayer was both an act of consolidating one's individual faith and an act which reinforced the cohesion of the group.[64] Behaving like a 'good Muslim' as much through one's faith as one's behavior and style of dress were markers of identity and alternative or reformist postures, which came into conflict with 'the stereotype notion of "modernity" as "civilization" or "progress"'.[65] The *da'wa* also gained importance and became a central issue during the 1990s; this is why the control of the mosques became a major question. For example, the proliferation of mosques in Burkina Faso 'was the expression of internal crises, of rivalries between Islamic associations'.[66] Subsequently, the three main associations (CMBF, Mouvement Sunnite [Sunni Movement] and Association Islamique de la Tidjaniyya [Islamic Association of Tidjaniyya]) became more active because of the reorganization of urban space and the development of proselytism within the first two associations. The same situation developed in Côte d'Ivoire with the dynamic activities of the Conseil Supérieur des Imam [Superior Council of the Imams] (COSIM).[67] *Da'wa* caravans were used in the context of the proselytizing actions (AJMCI in Côte d'Ivoire and JIR in Senegal for instance).

In sum, the discourses of these groups considered the religious norm to be the only legitimate norm and progressively applied it to the world of politics. This 'globalized denunciation',[68] though sometimes radical, did not mean a constitution of a project for an Islamic state. Rather, it represented the cobbling together of ideological and cultural currents with a broad-based discourse which rejected the image of a 'black Islam' (a fixed image promoted by the colonial power) in favor of an Islam that was taking its place through a synthesis between its secular links with the rest of the Arab-Muslim world, its local characteristics and its internal dynamics. This new climate and these discourses illuminate the different logics of reconfiguration present within francophone West-African societies, where Muslims constituted a majority, while appreciating the ways in which this transformed individuals and the idea of citizenship.

## The Reconstitution of Muslim Communities or the Emergence of a 'Civil Religion' in Francophone West Africa

As early as the 1980s, Islam had become an instrument for conquering new spaces, a quest for an alternative frame of reference to be established in opposition to that imposed by the state since the time of independence. The control of spaces was focused on certain strategic locations for the construction of mosques, such as university campuses, residential headquarters or airports (unfinished Yoff mosque in Dakar, Cocody-Riviera II Al-Nûr mosque in Abidjan, Port-Bouet Bilal mosque in Abidjan for instance). During the 1990s, this phenomenon accelerated as part of a process of the deprivatization of religion,[69] insofar as the common strategy of all branches of Islam in West Africa was to systematically increase their presence in the public sphere (space for the exchange of conflicting ideas and discourse). Thus, Islam removed itself from the private sphere, while Muslims active in the different movements and associations discussed above increasingly defined themselves first and foremost as Muslim citizens before being a citizen of a particular country. Their Muslim identity informed all of their daily activities. In this way, these Muslim citizens demanded more and more from a 'civil religion', from an Islamic patriotism rooted in the *umma*.

This Islamic posture brought about a greater visibility of the faith during the 1990s while linking individual experience with collective experience. Within this context there can be observed a phenomenon of overvaluing piety through the abandonment of all family attachments in order to fully live one's faith, or by repeatedly making the pilgrimage to Mecca. Young pilgrims in Côte d'Ivoire:

claim a form of individuality, suggesting a modern self that lies between atomistic decision making and community obligations based on the universal notion of the *ummah*. Arabized selves correspond to claims for autonomous, emancipated subjects who seek to rework their belonging to alternative social worlds. The issue is to find new inscriptions within the collective order that blend individual and collective allegiances.[70]

This presentation of faith increasingly brought certain Muslims to target both symbolic and strategic spaces and also to contribute to the emerging new ways of being Muslim. It was firstly a matter of being present in mass gathering places, popular and recreational sites like stadiums (Mali and Côte d'Ivoire) in the same manner as a Pentecostal movement. It was also a matter of Islamicizing modernity by targeting sites associated with the West, with finance, or with capitalism—such as luxury hotels—in order to show how the Islamic movement had no borders and how it had a great capacity for attracting converts in the widest variety of milieus. Furthermore, it was a matter of putting one's Islamic identity in this context of de-privatizing religion. For example, it was in this manner that the youth of the Zangouettin neighborhood (Ouagadougou, Burkina Faso) targeted the street with their movement in opposition to the government's decision to evict the population of the neighborhood as part of the ZACA urban renewal project in 2001. They named their movement al-Qaeda in an attempt to attract the most media attention possible and also to highlight the differences between themselves and an older generation of Muslims which was more inclined to negotiate with the authorities.[71]

It was thus that access to state media also remained a central feature of the battle for increased legitimacy. In Niger:

in August 1995, the president of the ANASI appealed to the president of the Superior Council of Communication to tell him that the ORTN (Office of Radio Diffusion and Television of Niger) decision was deliberate and amounted to the exclusion of certain infra-state communities from air time—in particular, the Haoussa (the largest linguistic group).[72]

It was in this way that the state chose to co-opt certain preachers to control their capacity for influence. For example, in Mali, Haïdara, after having been marginalized and pushed aside by the state and excluded from official media:

very recently [...] has been admitted into a governmental committee on religious affairs. [...] Haidara's recent 'upgrade' in official status not only illustrates his successful 'reinvestment' of the symbolic capital he earned by his earlier criticism of institutional power but also demonstrates that religious and state authorities prefer to domesticate him through partial co-optation into the state apparatus, rather than letting him 'go loose' via audiocassettes and commercial radio stations.[73]

Once again, it is a question of knowing how to use the media in order to better publicize the religious message. It was in this way that certain preachers became veritable stars, 'formidable leaders of opinion'[74] who competed with the state; religious entrepreneurs from the moment they learned how to use the media in the manner of 'U.S. televangelist preachers',[75] marshaling behind them scores of followers; gaining fame beyond the borders of their own country; and widely broadcasting their speeches on audio-cassettes to which many faithful listened piously.[76] Around these preachers, a new logic of the legitimization and construction of authority was created. It was no longer only the acquisition of foreign knowledge that was essential but also talent as an orator and charisma. The fact that some of these people had been granted a nickname by the media attests to their fame, such as in the case of 'Wulibali Haidara (Haidara who speaks the undeniable truth)'.[77] Beside this example drawn from Mali, there were other well-known imams in the past or in the present: Cheikh Youssouf Hassane Diallo among francophones; Malam Chaïbou in Niger, a regional trader who created around himself a network of *Izala* traders; El-Hadj Samassi ('popular amongst the Muslim inhabitants of both the Riviera II and Riviera III neighborhoods');[78] Mohamed Seyni Gorgui Guèye, the founding imam of the mosque known as having 'fallen from heaven' in Dakar; Mbaye Niang, imam of the unfinished Yoff mosque in Dakar; El Hadj Aboubacar Sana, imam of the grand mosque managed by the CMBF in Ouagadougou; the late El Hadj Ouedraogo Sayouba of the grand Friday mosque managed by the Sunni Movement in the Zangouettin neighborhood in Ouagadougou; Imam Kanté of the AEMUD; Imam Niang at the Point E mosque in Dakar; and the preachers organized by the Ligue des Prédicateurs [League of Preachers] in Côte d'Ivoire at Abidjan. The lines were occasionally blurred when, in occupying the public sphere, these different varieties of Islam replicated the relationship existing between political leaders and the population, notably during the single-party period or between leaders of the Brotherhood and the *tullab*. In Mali, for example, during the gatherings where Haïdara spoke, the faithful wore boubous in his likeness, kissed his hands, and touched him as he passed.[79] These practices help to highlight new religious behaviors, as well as new forms of legitimacy and loyalty.

This Islamic mobilization, through the consumption of religious products, was facilitated and made more active. 'Because of their participatory and interactive formula, talk radio programs capture the moral imagination of listeners. The new, morally evaluating public they create and address illustrates that new forms of sociality emerge in and around practices of broadcast consumption'.[80] The modalities of the acquisition of religious knowledge were profoundly changed because the distribution of sermons on cassette removed the necessity of the presence of an intermediary. Each individual could customize their religious knowledge according to the quality of their listening, their comprehension of the content of the cassette, and the frequency with which they listened. This knowledge also mixed the preoccupations of each individual consumer of the cassette with those of the community as a whole because this medium could be accessed with friends, with neighbors, with members of an association, in the street, at the market, or during tea. Henceforth the cassette had several virtues: affordable, it was accessible to all; it was a pedagogical and proselytizing tool that was both accessible and banal, leading to a new sociability around religion and encouraging the emergence of a new social and cultural order, anchored in peoples' everyday lives. This commodification of the religious led to the emergence of competing preachers, which led to a new period of oratorical 'one-upmanship' during the 1990s. Moreover this commodification led to the constitution of 'a polycentric field of debate' and 'a marketplace of ideas'.[81]

Alongside this control of public space there developed a new freedom of speech which disrupted relations between elders and youth, between women and men, between society and the state. The generational conflict is often evoked because the emergence of a new generation of Muslims is understood as 'the objectification of Muslim consciousness' among many Muslims. For example, in Niger, a new generation of Muslims having completed the pilgrimage (the *alhazai*), activists from the *Izala* reform movement in Maradi, considered that 'Hausa society is too hierarchical, and consequently they challenge the power and authority of the elders. For example, they do not kneel in the presence of their father, mother, father-in-law, mother-in-law or any person who must be respected because of age or social status'.[82] The same observation was made in Zinder, with the emergence of young Muslim reformers who had studied in Arab countries. In Côte d'Ivoire, participation in radical movements reflected a desire to counter the power of the gerontocracy and against arranged marriages.[83] In Burkina Faso, young members of al-Qaeda stood opposed to the older generation, the latter belonging to a traditionalist branch of Islam and being ready to negotiate with the state. In Senegal, the JIR was created as a counterweight to the UCM, which had become a facilitator for the transmission of the Muslim politics of the authorities.

Nevertheless, other examples show how, beginning in the 1980s, the older generation worked together with youth on Islamic action. During the 1990s, with the central importance given to proselytism, bridges were established between youth and elders in the mosques. The power of the gerontocracy was renegotiated and remodeled. Neighborhood youth—known for their knowledge of the Qur'an— were called on by their elders to help spread the word about the Friday sermon in Dakar and in Ouagadougou.[84] It was also possible to observe a new way of managing relations between men and women within marriage. Three related elements needed to be present, namely active participation in neighborhood Islamic associations or in NGOs; accepting social codes or affirming the choice of following them; and the participation in the marriage market by choosing a spouse. In Mali, the success of the *madaris* shows the extent to which there was a strong desire to transmit religious knowledge, which assured a certain social status and made public speaking easier.

The distinction between associations friendly to the state and those who were not became less clear because of the liberalization of the airwaves. For example in Mali, the *ulama*'s radio aired more dissenting programs following the arrival of Arabic-speaking youth at the Bureau des ulama [Office of the *Ulama*] opposed to the methods of the AMUPI[85] and once the speeches of Haïdara appeared less virulent against the State. At the same time, a too-hegemonic state was pushed aside, rivaled, and could no longer control this brand of Islam which presented religion as the 'public norm'[86] and which widely spread its ideas via the 'small media'.[87]

In this context, a new relationship developed between civil society and the state.[88] In making this argument, this chapter contradicts the studies which argue that there was no civil society on the

African continent insofar as the state had annexed civil society. I concur with those authors who analyze the 'multiple methods of bypassing, avoiding and subverting by which society manages to erode the domination of the state'[89] and who consider 'civil society' as an 'intermediary space', 'an advanced space of society in the political field capable of detotalitarianizing the state', 'a site of interaction and negotiation between state and society'.[90] The battle against the proposed Code of Family Law in Mali provides a good example. It reveals how a part of civil society, within the neighborhood associations of Muslim women opposed to the reform, fought against the idea that the state would defend a notion of the nuclear family and would interfere in family relations, but also sought official recognition insofar as these women participated in the debate and took their place within the public sphere after having been marginalized by the regimes that had followed the fall of Moussa Traoré.[91] Ultimately, the picture was increasingly one of a civil society that was building regions of autonomy with the presence of charismatic religious leaders, anchored in the social fabric and having mastered modern technologies, with social groups which spoke publicly and did not hesitate to affirm their positions within tense political contexts (the question of 'ivoirité' in Côte d'Ivoire, for example).

The great increase in the number of Islamic organizations illustrates how the Islamic revival remains a vital force and how political Islam retains the capacity to gain ground and increase the number of its followers, especially among the young, women, and the educated. Political Islam, even if it does not yet represent a viable alternative and remains in the minority, is attractive 'not only because it offers modes of being and belonging, but also because it constructs new imaginations of the community and the individual'.[92] It also carries out a significant amount of social work by approaching a range of social groups, has become an important participant in local socio-political debates (on secularism, on family law), and remains connected to international affairs and geo-political issues.

Although in the minority and sometimes radical, if not intolerant for example, in (riots in Niger, skirmishes between members of *Al-Falah* and the followers of the tidjanes, campus violence between members of the JIR and the mourides in Dakar), political Islam is to a certain extent representative of a civil society which, by the opinions it expresses, is anchored within both the local and global contexts. Indeed, civil society manifests a clear attachment to the *umma* (whence the declarations of solidarity with the people of Palestine, Afghanistan and Iraq), an opposition to globalization, insofar as the latter is associated with the hegemonic policies of the United Sates, and to the impoverishment of the world's population. It also actively works toward a strong and united Islam which remains an important source of collective identity.

The rise of political Islam might suggest that certain countries are in the midst of difficult situations which might get worse in the medium term. Certain radical positions reveal the extent to which Muslim societies in francophone West Africa are torn by questions of identity or even communitarianism. But at the same time, these radical positions are sometimes also damaging to political Islam, serving to alienate either the general population (in Senegal, religious candidates were rejected by the population in the presidential elections of 2000) or the state itself (in Niger, the blocking of the adoption of the Code of Family Law was mostly a sign of the state's timidity to attack social conservatism). Political Islam has also lost battles such as that over the ratification of the Convention on the Elimination of All Forms of Discrimination against Women in Niger in August 1999, and over the revision of national constitutions which retained the principle of secularism.

Meanwhile, the leaders of political Islam need the State, despite their opposition to government policy. As a result, the question is whether political Islam will present itself as a new political alternative—as an alternative model of civilization. None of the movements discussed above, with only a few exceptions and despite their very critical discourses on the policies of their respective states, aimed to break away and seize power by force. They continued to respect the rules laid out by the existing political system, and did not advocate a withdrawal or exile (*hijra*) which could have led to the establishment of a different social model through violence. Nor did they advocate civil disobedience. Most of these movements sought to change society by reforming it from within. They sought to interpret reality and construct an alternative reality by contesting the status quo, but without inciting revolution. Very often their speeches were prefaced by recognition that the societies in question were not yet ready to live under a purely Islamic state, in order to explain that the introduction of *Shari'a* was not yet possible. In fact, by building bilingual Franco-Arabic schools and by organizing conferences on the foundations of Islam, they showed the extent to which they were reformers but not revolutionaries, ultimately showing little interest for the actual exercise of power.

Fundamentally, because of its heterogeneous nature, its moralizing speeches, and its capacity for using the media to capture the attention of the population, regardless of age or social status, political Islam has proven capable of bringing together collective imaginations, of anchoring religion at the center of debates, of making the divine an essential element of political life and life in general. Through its activism, this brand of Islam has redefined relations between generations, between men and women. It has unshackled religion by taking it out of the private sphere and placing it squarely in the public sphere. Because of all this, it provides a lens through which to view the major changes that have swept across the Muslim communities of francophone West Africa and civil societies more generally during the last twenty-five years.

# 7

# THE 'OTHER' POLITICAL ISLAM

## UNDERSTANDING SALAFI POLITICS

*Martijn de Koning*

In November 2007 the Dutch newspaper *De Telegraaf* published an article about the plans of Dutch radical anti-Islam politician Geert Wilders to release a 'provoking' film named *Fitna* about the Qur'an. This caused quite a stir in Dutch society. One of the voices in this debate was the Tawheed mosque, a Salafi mosque in Amsterdam.[1] The youth chapter of this mosque wrote an open letter to Dutch parliament claiming that Geert Wilders' right to freedom of speech was violating the right to freedom of religion for Muslims. The writers also stated that Wilders' 'offending' statements about Islam were detrimental to the integration of Muslims in society. They called upon the members of parliament to take the necessary steps to point out to Wilders the negative consequences of this film. The writers stated that this is the task of parliament since it is elected by the majority of the people and in a democracy the voice of the people is one of the most important constituent elements. The voice of minorities, so they wrote, should also be heard in order to have their interests defended in a respectful and acceptable manner.

Often the Salafi movement is seen as a cultural movement without a clear political program, which shies away from becoming involved in the political fray while the Islamist movement, in contrast, has politics at the heart of its ideology and aims to transform society into a 'true' Islamic society. The Salafi movement claims not to be involved in political negotiations with states and does not engage in the public sphere in defense of Muslim interests, let alone attempt to build an Islamic state.[2] Moreover, some currents in the Salafi movement claim to be interested in cultivating religious piety only, and have no political aims. Nevertheless in the Netherlands the very presence of the Salafi movement and its practices are experienced as a challenge to Dutch culture and political rule while at the same time the Dutch-Islam debate creates a platform on which its constituent networks are able (or even have to) engage with the Dutch state and in the public sphere. Moreover, several of these Dutch Salafi networks have been influenced by teachings of Salafi leaders who have created a mixture between Salafi thought and Islamist Muslim Brotherhood ideology. This chapter will go beyond the dichotomy between the cultural and the political. Rather than attempting to categorize this movement as cultural (or apolitical) or political, I argue that we need to identify and analyze the different types of politics this movement and its networks engages in, not only with regard to their involvement with other Muslims but also with the Dutch state. First the changing governance of religion and minorities in the Netherlands that provides the context for the emergence of the Salafi movement in the 1990s and after 2001, which will be outlined below. This will be followed by a discussion of the opposition between cultural and political movements and subsequently elaborate in more detail on an alternative framework of different types of politics: politics of lifestyles, distinction, and resistance that each of the networks engages in. This chapter will show that an analysis based upon different modalities of politics within the context of the shifting relations between the secular and the religious and the emergence of anti-Islam populism, can explain the changes within the Salafi movement and also exposes the political significance of the Salafi lifestyle, active non-engagement, and the intra-Muslim struggles over the representation of Muslims in the Netherlands.

*Religion in the Netherlands*[3]

Salafi politics do not occur in a vacuum but within a political and societal context that can be characterized as secular. Dutch secularism is mainly based upon the negotiations between the state and several Dutch denominations over several centuries. The question of how much difference can be allowed without compromising the need for social cohesion was always an important underlying principle in the conflicts between state and church. Kennedy and Valenta[4] are right in arguing that the Dutch state has played a major role in defining and sustaining religion in public life in negotiation with Christian civil society organizations (including churches) and we can add to this that the Christian civil organizations have had an important influence on Dutch secularism. The negotiations resulted in a series of compromises between churches and Christian political parties on the one hand and the state on the other. In the early twentieth century these compromises turned Dutch society into a pillarized society, which was divided into distinct and mutually antagonistic religious and ideological groups. Because of overarching cooperation at the elite level and by allowing each group as much autonomy as possible, a stable democracy was made possible.[5] Kennedy and Valenta[6] make clear that this not only allowed for a certain degree of autonomy but it also enabled the state to closely monitor and regulate what religious groups were doing and to set the parameters for their continuing participation in public life. The result was not a ban of religion from the public sphere but a politics of containment of religious differences by the state helping to define religious subcultures with their own organizations and elites and to understand their collective identities.[7]

After the loosening of ties to religious denominations by newspapers, labor unions, political parties, and so on, and the subsequent collapse of the pillarized system in the 1960s, debates concerning the position of religion in society have shifted towards the question of how to deal with (Christian) groups that do not acknowledge and accept the fundamental freedoms of a secular Dutch society. The way these challenges were regulated was seen as an affirmation of Dutch tolerance while the orthodox Christian groups were seen as remnants of a past that would gradually fade away in tandem with the ongoing secularization. More serious questions were raised during the 1990s when the issue of tolerance was linked to immigration and Muslims. An important difference between the discussions about the orthodox Christian Protestant groups and Muslims is that since the nineteenth century until now the Protestant groups acknowledge the Dutch nation-state as their moral community.[8] However, some politicians and opinion leaders question if the same is true of the Muslim community.[9] Moreover, although the institutionalization of Islam is partly based upon the remnants of the pillarization model, the Netherlands is broadly considered as a secular society and the rise of Islam in the public sphere is now considered by some to be a threat to secularism.[10]

The Rushdie Affair (1989), the public statements of Bolkestein, a political leader of the Dutch liberal party (VVD) who stated that Islam is incompatible with Western liberal values (1991), and the rise of populist politicians Fortuyn (between 1997 and 2002) and Wilders with a program of counter-Islamization, all signal a trend that the limits of religious and cultural difference and the conditions for social cohesion and integration are questioned by a broad political spectrum ranging from ultra-left to ultra-right, socialist and liberal parties, and religious parties.[11] Events such as the attacks of September 11 and the assassination of Theo van Gogh by Mohammed Bouyeri are drawn upon to explain what is wrong with Islam, or, conversely, what is wrong with the host countries of Muslim migrants. This does not necessarily mean that the state and political parties are trying to exclude Muslims and Islam but that they are trying to reform particular kinds of religious practices and beliefs in order to make them compatible with a liberal political rule and to (eventually) ban those religious practices and beliefs that are believed to be incompatible with the liberal political rule.[12]

Key themes in the debates on Islam are violence, fundamentalism, intolerance, hidden agendas, religious tensions and an orientation to the home countries in the Muslim world. In dealing with Muslims and Islam the state and/or local authorities usually support the Islamic institutionalization and integration of Muslims in society with a clear and sometimes outspoken preference for a so-called liberal Islam.[13] Those groups that are deemed incompatible with Dutch values are labeled as 'radicals' and in particular since the murder of van Gogh, the Dutch state has set up a policy in which several institutions such as the security and intelligence agency (AIVD) and municipalities work to ban radicalization among Muslims. Although there are major differences among Dutch political parties on what 'liberal' Islam actually is, all parties seem to accept that a fundamentalist Islam does not belong to the Dutch moral community. A party like Geert Wilders' Freedom Party is vehemently opposed to everything that appears to be leading to normalizing, recognizing, and institutionalizing Islam as part of the Dutch religious landscape, while others seem to agree that Islam needs to be reformed in order to fit in.[14] The Salafi movement in particular has become the focus of these counter-radicalization policies and, accordingly, particular practices that in the public debate are linked to Salafis have become controversial over the years: mainly the issues of the burqa and niqab, foreign imams, and imams who incite hatred and intolerance.

### The emergence of Salafi networks in the Netherlands

The Salafi movement aims to revitalize Islam based upon the life of the first Muslims and strives to live according to that idealized vision which its followers find more just and satisfying than the present.[15] It aims to cleanse Islam from so-called non-Islamic accretions, such as Sufism, Shi'a Islam, or local practices and doctrines, which have sullied a 'pure' Islam.[16] The only way to lead a pure and authentic life and to inherit paradise is to return to the period of the Prophet Muhammad and his companions and to emulate their lives. The sources of Islam, the Qur'an and the hadith, are seen as the written version of the authentic and pure Islam. All human action has to be derived from the sources of Islam in order for it to be legitimate, otherwise an act can be condemned as bid'a (innovation) or worse: in some cases such illegitimate acts may lead to kufr (disbelief). Moreover, since the Prophet Muhammad is considered to be an exemplary, perfect Muslim for all times, the Sunna, a close reading of the Qur'an and Hadith are essential sources with guidelines for leading the correct life and staying on the righteous path for any Muslim at any time. This applies to thought, behavior as well as appearance; and Salafi Muslims try to emulate the model of the Prophet and the first generations of Muslims as strictly as possible in all spheres of life.

The transnational Salafi movement consists of local and global branches and is characterized by a loosely coupled network structure as first described by Gerlach and Hine.[17] That is, non-hierarchical and characterized by a segmentary-like mobilization and fission and fusion of several sub-networks.[18] The different Salafi networks within the movement share the same doctrine of *tawhid* (the unity and Oneness of God) as Wiktorowicz[19] explains, but (contrary to Wiktorowicz's claim) do not agree on all aspects of this principle, such as what constitutes belief and unbelief and how to interpret particular attributes of Allah.[20] Furthermore, Salafi networks share the method of reading and interpreting the sources of Islam but differ on the details of worship and the manner of achieving their goals.[21]

During the 1990s and with increasing speed after '9/11', the different branches of Salafism in the Netherlands had developed into a social movement by building up their own mosques, websites, and informal networks used for resource mobilization and dissemination. Based upon the types of relations between and among networks (antagonistic or cooperative, national and transnational) and ideological similarities and differences we can distinguish between five main networks, each with its own internal divisions. First of all there are the Selefies (Salafi as pronounced in Dutch, Selefie being the label they give themselves), a quietist group that follows Sheikh Rabi' al-Madkhali.[22] One of the main preachers within this group is Abdelillah Boushta and also several native Dutch Muslims who have studied in Saudi Arabia. The second group consists of communities of several mosques in Amsterdam (Tawheed mosque, Imam Shershaby), The Hague (As Soennah mosque, Imam Fawaz Jneid), and Tilburg (ISOOK Foundation, Imam Ahmad Salam—in the south of the Netherlands). In 2001 they established the Foundation Islamic Committee for Ahl-u-Sunnah in the Netherlands.[23] Imam Fawaz Jneid and Imam Ahmad Salam are both of Syrian descent and have been implicated by the Dutch security services with the Syrian Muslim Brotherhood.

These connections, however, have remained largely unexplored. The Foundation is part of the Committee for Ahl-u-Sunnah in Europe with members in Spain, France, Germany, Belgium, and England with Adnane al-Aroor (also from Syria) as president. Both the national and European foundations seem to lead a rather dormant life but certainly on the national level these mosques often operate together. The third current is closely tied to the Ahl-u-Sunnah committee but is not a member of it: the Fourqaan mosque in the south of the Netherlands.[24] A Dutch Salafi leader who broke away from the Fourqaan mosque is Dutch convert Abdul-Jabbar van de Ven. He was a follower of some of the Sahwa sheikhs in Saudi Arabia who went on to establish his own (loose) network that can be seen as a fourth branch. In the past he was accused of being part of the fifth strand of the Salafi movement: the jihadi/takfiri[25] branch of Salafism in the Netherlands, although he seems to keep some distance now. In almost all instances this branch is directly or indirectly connected to the core of the old Hofstad network[26] (of which the assassin of van Gogh, Mohammed Bouyeri, and his friend Samir Azzouz are the most well-known members).

It is difficult to give reliable statistics on the number of Salafists in the Netherlands. According to a recent survey approximately 8 per cent of the Muslims in the Netherlands might be 'sensitive' to Salafism.[27] Based upon observations and interviews I estimate that the Madkhali Selefie network and the Ahl-u-Sunnah network attract just over half of the total Salafi population in lectures, conferences, and courses but participants of the latter group also visit other networks. The former Hofstad network was at the time very small; about thirty to forty members.

*Lifestyles, Distinction, and Resistance*

Political or Cultural Movement?

Before introducing an alternative framework, the issue of political versus cultural will be explored further. While the Islamist movement is often categorized as a political movement with a political program aimed at transforming society into an Islamic society, the Salafi movement is categorized as a cultural (or apolitical) movement satisfied with a minority status, with no clear political program, and focusing on identity politics; shying away from and criticizing the 'old' Islamist movement for engaging in party politics.[28]

This dichotomy between political and cultural is not typical for the discussion about Islamist and Salafi movements. Among theorists of social movements there has been a long-standing discussion about whether or not new social movements are political or cultural.[29] The 1960s movement in the West is in this debate seen as an example of a movement that successfully balanced the political with the cultural, while in the 1970s and 1980s some of these movements shifted to a predominantly cultural orientation in which questions of identity and identity politics became leading. The 'old' movements such as the labor movements in the nineteenth and twentieth century and the first feminist wave are seen as political movements while the 'new' social movements are seen as cultural movements in which attention to lifestyles and culture substituted any form of political action aimed at institutional power.[30] Several researchers, however, have questioned this dichotomy for neglecting the historical continuities between the old and the new movements and for not appreciating the cultural activities of 'old' social movements that took up issues such as work environments, women's status, community life and education.[31] The Islamist movement also engages in forms of a politics of lifestyles by emphasizing individual virtue and engaging in *da'wah*[32] as a means to reach their goals.[33]

Before explaining in depth why the dichotomy between 'cultural' and 'political' movements does not make sense in the case of the Salafi movement, a few words on the work of Wiktorowicz[34] are necessary since his distinction between purists, politicos and jihadis has become common property among researchers, policy-makers and politicians. According to Wiktorowicz[35] all Salafis share the same creed that provides principles and a method for applying religious beliefs to contemporary issues and problems. They are divided into three major factions by different interpretations about contemporary politics based upon different evaluations of contextual factors: the purists, the politicos (in particular the Sahwa movement) and the jihadis. The purists emphasize a focus on nonviolent *da'wah*, education, and purification of religious beliefs and practices. Contrary to the politicos they regard politics as a diversion or even innovation that leads people away from Islam. The politicos see politics as yet another field in which the Salafi creed has to be applied in order to safeguard justice and guarantee that the political rule is based upon the *Shari'a*. The jihadis claim that the current context calls for a (violent) revolution in order to counter the oppression of and injustice against Muslims.

Although this typology can be very useful, it cannot account for changes within and between the different branches and does not fully take into account that all of the Salafi networks engage in different types of politics that all constitute a challenge for the idea of the Netherlands as a secular society in which 'liberal' religious groups are incorporated and 'radical' groups are repressed. As is the case with the distinction between 'cultural' and 'political' movements, categorization of the Islamist movement as political and part of the Salafi movement as 'politicos' restricts the concept of the political to dealing with the state and engaging with party politics. In my opinion this view is too vague and too restrictive to encompass the full nature of political engagement.

It is too vague since it does not make a distinction between different forms of politics dealing with transforming state power and power relations. We can distinguish two types of politics that to a certain extent deal with these aspects: the politics of resistance (focused on a rejection of oppressive structures in society that keep particular groups in a powerless and alternate position) and the politics of distinction (based upon a rejection of an indiscriminate mainstream culture that does not allow much room for diversity).[36] The reasons for the Salafi movement to engage with these types of politics and its importance to them have developed over the years. According to many of the Salafi leaders I have spoken to and some whose lessons I followed in mosques and chat rooms, in the beginning of the 1990s emphasis in their engagement with Dutch society and Muslims in the Netherlands was based on the conviction that it was not allowed for Muslims to live in '*kafir*'-land.[37] Slowly but gradually they have changed this view due to increasing awareness that Muslims would not leave the Netherlands but would remain there. This realization made it necessary for Muslims, according to Salafi leaders, to re-organize themselves, to build up an infrastructure that would make it possible for Muslims to fulfill their religious obligations and to transfer their religious traditions to the following generations.

In their courses the Salafi networks, emphasize among other things, how individual Muslims can establish their position as Muslim citizens in the Netherlands by educating themselves not only in Islam but also by acquiring an education in general. Therefore in their political stance towards the Dutch state, Dutch society in general and other Muslims, many Salafi organizations aim to safeguard the right of Muslims to fulfill their religious obligations and the freedom of religion.

The concept of the political with regard to the dichotomy between the political and cultural is also too narrow since it does not fully appreciate a third type of politics that does not immediately concern influencing the Dutch state and/or power structures. Politics can be seen, as Eickelman and Piscatori[38] explain, as a competition over the meaning of symbols and language. Among others, Moors[39] provides examples of the 'symbolic salience' of family and gender (such as the dowry, women's dress, domestic relations) in the micro-politics of family relations (that only partly intersects with party and state politics) and the ways in which family ties and the family as an institution are employed in politics. I have discussed elsewhere the usefulness of this broader idea of politics in analyzing the negotiations of Muslim youth over the beliefs, practices and experiences that constitute their identity.[40] Many aspects of people's lifestyles such as veiling or praying do not by definition constitute political acts as such, but they become political acts when in those negotiations (with other Muslims or with non-Muslims) they are transformed into public symbols that are open to contestations from different sides. The negotiations of the interpretation of symbols in everyday life can be called politics of lifestyles.[41]

Together with the politics of distinction and the politics of resistance, the politics of lifestyles make up for a more nuanced approach of the different types of relations the Salafi movement has with its environment, which can be captured by using a distinction in cultural or political movement or by Wiktorowicz's approach. The remainder of this section will explore in more detail these types of politics of the Salafi networks in Dutch society; not as a typology where every movement should fit into one of these categories, but as a way to analyze how every Salafi network uses these different types of politics as a way to engage with other Muslims and with broader society.[42]

Politics of Lifestyles

All of the major currents of the Salafi networks in the Netherlands engage in some sort of politics of lifestyles aimed at providing Muslim youth with incentives for acquiring the right kind of knowledge and behavior. Many social movement researchers, in particular those focusing on political opportunity structures and resource mobilization have often neglected how culture, everyday life, identity-formation and daily routines are not only resources for social movements, but are also the focus of these movements.[43] As Brubaker notes, in the process of community-building it is not sufficient that people identify themselves as belonging to a particular social category (such as 'Muslim' or 'Dutch'); but people have to 'do things' with such categories—for example, excluding others, trying to monopolize or hinder access to scarce resources and so on.[44] One such thing is to educate insiders on what it means to belong to a particular kind of community, how they can recognize that community and how they can be recognized themselves as part of that community. Convincing and educating Muslims to share a common life and a common vision and practices that constitute a good life, is crucial for the establishment of a 'real' moral community.

An important part of the activities of the Salafi movement in the Netherlands is the idea of establishing a good, harmonious, and united community. For the Salafi movement the current community of Muslims (*umma*) finds itself in a moral crisis because of the neglect of the central principles of Islam. In order to establish this community all Dutch networks have their own circles for lectures, education and so on. In particular the first two networks are giving courses at several mosques on a regular basis. These courses involve basic instruction in *'aqidah* (doctrine), *fiqh* (Islamic law), and *sirah* (the biography of the prophet Muhammad). The Madkhali Selefies give courses in Arabic language and in the correct behavior of *Talib al 'Ilm* (the students of knowledge), the people who are being taught the Salafi *minhaj* (method) and *'aqidah* emphasizing good behavior, noble manners, and piety of the students. The material of the Institute for Training and Education (Ahl-u-Sunnah mosques) is based upon writings from An-Nawawi, Ibn Taymiyyah, Ibn Radjab, al-Albany, and Ibn 'Uthaymin. Abdul-Jabbar van de Ven, for example, has taught about avoiding *'nifaaq'*, or hypocrisy (meaning religious hypocrisy such as seemingly practicing Islam, while knowingly or unknowingly concealing ones disbelief).

Besides these activities aimed at providing the 'correct' Islamic knowledge Salafi networks have also established organizations outside the spheres of education. One example is the establishment of an alternative home care institution by the Madkhali Selefies, necessary, they say, according to them because the regular Dutch institutions do not take into account Islamic culture and religion.

As Tuğal[45] explains in the case of Turkish Islamists, in this case the Salafi networks try to reconfigure the everyday attitudes and practices of the participants by letting them focus on what matters in (their version of) Islam. The goal of this type of politics is to produce committed subjects with daily routines, attire, and (political) attitudes that differ from other Muslims and non-Muslims.[46] As such the Salafi networks reorganize the daily routines of their participants informed by (secular) education and labor and they denaturalize the discourse of integration as propagated by the Dutch state that is increasingly focused on compliance with Dutch (secular) standards, democracy (instead of God's law), and undivided loyalties (instead of the transnational loyalties of the Salafi movement) under the label of active citizenship.[47]

It is in particular the politics of lifestyles that attract many young Moroccan-Dutch Muslims and is closely connected to their daily lives. Since the end of the 1990s Muslim identity has become the most important identity for many of the Moroccan-Dutch youth (the most important ethnic group among the Salafi youth). The way young people construct their religious identity can best be described as a combination of a quest for 'one's true self' with the idea of an authentic core of Islam that is neither 'Moroccan' nor 'Dutch'.[48] In this search for a 'true' Islam the politics of lifestyles from the Salafi networks enables them to re-write their own life stories and to construct their sense of self as strong and self-confident people who find their purpose of life in Islam by connecting their own individual experiences with the larger narratives of Islam and the *umma*.[49] It also provides these young Muslims with feelings of belonging to a particular group—apparent by the fact that many of these young people address each other in terms of 'brothers' and 'sisters' thereby creating a feeling of kinship based upon a religious sentiment. For individual Salafi Muslims, it is not only politics of lifestyle but also their own activities on the internet that enable them to localize the global message of Salafi Islam. By appropriating this global message in to their own lives they are also able to identify themselves as people that are part of a global movement. This is a crucial part of the activities of the Salafi movement because it aims at transforming the very nature of the Muslim community and its social fabric as can be seen in the example of the life of one of the women in my research, Umm Salamah.[50]

Umm Salamah's involved in the Salafi movement (without a clear alignment to any of the branches) began after a turbulent period in her life. In 2004, after her return from a visit to Morocco, she started wearing the headscarf, and in 2006, when she became more interested in political issues and moved to the UK, she began to wear the niqab. The headscarf and later the niqab embody Umm Salamah's experiences and changes in worldview.[51]

Since the niqab is highly contested in Dutch society in general and in the Dutch-Moroccan community in particular (especially among first-generation Moroccan-Dutch Muslims), her niqab also articulated the sharp contrast with the Dutch fashion customs and the Islamic traditions of her Moroccan parents. Like many of the people in my research on young Muslims, she seeks an Islam that is neither 'Moroccan' nor 'Dutch' and her change in worldview was therefore not only a matter of inward experiences but also of outward appearances. Many of the Salafi networks tap into these feelings by giving lectures about female attire and spreading books about the 'correct' behavior of women. Other examples can be found on the Internet and in meetings where books are sold explaining the 'correct' Islamic lifestyle, electronic gadgets such as mobile phones that signal the times for prayer, lectures, and books concerning the 'Islamic' aspects of the relationship between men and women and how to be a Muslim in Western society. In practice, since Salafi Muslims have to function in the secular Dutch state and therefore have to adjust in a particular way, this does not necessarily go against participation in society with regard to education and labor, but it does re-arrange people's priorities; many Salafi Muslims (in particular in the Madkhali Selefie network) choose to interact with the broader society in a very minimal way.

The politics of lifestyles of the different Salafi networks are important to our understanding of young people's engagement with these Salafi networks and the goals of the Salafi movement. However, they do not always go uncontested: the everyday and the political are mixed and mutually reinforcing. During my research in a traditional Moroccan mosque in 2001 a new imam from the Madkhali Selefies gained enormous popularity among Moroccan-Dutch youth (in particular boys).[52] Although the board of the mosque appreciated him for gathering so many young people in the mosque, they were also very wary about his messages to these young people. This imam objected to women riding bikes, questioned the necessity for women to have a higher education, and abolished several traditions in the mosque which he deemed incompatible with 'true' Islam. This caused great controversy among older people who rejected his message about the 'correct' Islamic lifestyles as being unfit for youth in the Netherlands but in the eyes of young people this just meant that he was speaking 'the truth'.

Because the board of the mosque wanted to get rid of the imam and the young people supported him and wanted to have a say about the imam's resignation, the conflict escalated into a struggle about what the truth (Islam) actually is, who has the right to decide that and (in the words of Eickelman and Piscatori)[53] who controls the institutions (the mosque) that define and articulate particular values important to lifestyles. The politics of lifestyles therefore are developed as much in relation to secular Dutch society in general as to Muslims who do not (yet) comply with Salafi thought and practices.

Politics of Distinction

All of the Salafi currents engage in politics of distinction: activities aimed at rejecting what is perceived as an indiscriminate mainstream culture that does not allow much room for diversity. Whereas in the politics of lifestyles the emphasis is on the activities of the Salafi movement building a moral community and the indirect political significance of fragmented, disperse, and chaotic forms of everyday public presence Bayat[54] has labeled non-movements, the politics of distinction requires a more direct engagement with the state and/or wider society.

The Salafis of the Ahl-u-Sunnah committee, for example, use petitions and open letters to politicians and to newspapers as a means of contention. They have, for example, criticized Dutch politicians for trying to ban the burqa[55] from the public sphere, written an open letter to Dutch parliament after Geert Wilders announced his release for the film *Fitna*, and also have used their sermons to harshly condemn the 'anti-Islam campaigns' of people such as Wilders and Hirsi Ali[56] and in the past also Theo van Gogh.

I will focus here on the case of the burqa because it provides an interesting example of when and how the politics of lifestyle partially develop into the politics of distinction and it directs our attention to forms and styles of public presence, and how ethical, normative positions may also entail particular aesthetics and language.[57] It shows, for example, that politics of distinction entail a radically different kind of language than the politics of lifestyles; the Salafi movement is responding to the threat of a ban by appropriating their language to a secular public sphere.

In 2006 the populist-right wing politician Wilders and the then minister of integration Verdonk, stated that the burqa should be banned for security reasons. In order to provide for a safe environment people should be recognizable on the streets. Other reasons for this proposal were that the burqa is an 'inhuman' attire, degrading women and at odds with Dutch culture since, 'The Netherlands is not Iran or Saudi Arabia'.[58] Buitelaar[59] shows that values about female behavior and attire serve to maintain the integrity of the group. The proposal for banning the burqa can be seen as an attempt by (parts of) the state to control the criteria for inclusion and exclusion by controlling how women in Dutch society should dress. The one who controls women's bodies and sexuality controls the symbolic boundary marker between networks and therefore the group itself. In 2008 the Dutch government stated that 'face-coverings are considered misogynist and [...] to many these are a symbol of a fundamentalist Islam that does not suit Dutch soci-ety'.[60] Those women who wear the burqa are, accordingly, excluded from the Dutch moral community.

Although lessons about the right garment for women can be seen as politics of lifestyles, even if the Salafi networks claim that they are apolitical, the world around them is political and in particular focused on those Muslim lifestyles that are associated with radical-ism among Muslims, such as wearing a niqab or burqa. The Salafi commitment to minority status forces them to take positions when their lifestyles are threatened. The Ahl-u-Sunnah mosques have responded to the possible ban on the burqa in a very interesting way: by issuing a petition in which they adapt themselves to the secular performatives of the public sphere. This blurs the bounda-ries between religion and secularism and can be seen as a discursive assimilation that is necessary to gain ground and to be heard in the public domain.[61] The following is an excerpt of the petition:

> The announcement of a law prohibiting the burqas has not without reason caused unrest and concern among the Muslim community in the Nether-lands and outside. In a democratic constitutional state as the Netherlands, in which freedom and equality are central, a burqa ban will lead to major negative consequences, not only in judicial terms but also in the social field: negative consequences that will outweigh the intended effects.[62]

One could criticize this accommodation by the Salafis by stating that this is merely a cosmetic operation intended to mask itself as a moderate and compatible player in the arena of the public sphere. That may be the case but the underlying assumption that Salafi movement can do everything to 'sell' its message is equally questionable.

The proposal for banning the burqa means that movements such as Salafism are acquiring agency in relation to the state and in the public sphere. As Warner argues, entering the temporality of poli-tics and adapting to it may for many movements and publics mean to abandon hope of transforming the space of public life itself.[63]

This is one of the criticisms that the Madkhali Selefies have against the public appearances of the Ahl-u-Sunnah mosques. Another example can be found in Imam Ahmad Salam's (Ahl-u-Sunnah Foundation) refusal to shake hands with (female) minister Verdonk in a meeting. While many of the followers of the Ahl-u-Sunnah mosques thought this was a perfect demonstration of how Muslims should behave towards women (it would be disrespectful to shake hands), the Madkhali Selefies thought the Imam should not have been there in the first place since he was violating the separation between men and women.

Rather than qualifying the position of the Madkhali Selefies as apolitical (according to Wiktorowicz's classification) this position entails active non-engagement. The Dutch Madkhali Selefies have criticized the comments made by imams such as Fawaz about Dutch politicians as one of the spearheads in distinguishing themselves from other Salafi networks. According to the Madkhali Selefies Muslims should not interfere with politicians because their protest leads to adjustment of the community to the secular system and contaminates its doctrinal purity. This, in turn, leads the other Salafi networks to the conclusion that with their apolitical claim the Madkhali Selefies only serve the powers that be. Other Salafists who broke away from the Ahl-u-Sunnah mosques have also expressed such criticism.

The debates among Salafi Muslims become most clear when we look at the debates on the Internet.[64] Of particular importance in this regard is the release by the Madkhali Selefies in 2002 (and re-release in 2003) of the 'Black List with Names of Several Hizbies' denouncing several imams and preachers in Europe, including Dutch Salafists such as Ahmad Salam and Fawaz Jneid (both of the Ahl-u-Sunnah mosques) and Abdul-Jabbar van de Ven. They were called *Ahl al-Bid'a* (people of innovation, meaning here innovation and negative alteration of the 'true' Islam) and *'hizbies'*: people breaking away from the Salafi minhaj (according to the Madkhali Selefie understanding of it) but also used for those who engage with a 'Western' model of party politics and democracy, resulting in *hizbiyya* (partisanship) and a violation of the principle of *tawhid* (unity of God). According to them the principle of *tawhid* is violated because making laws is the prerogative of Allah only. Ruling by man-made laws is considered to be an act against the sovereignty of Allah.

After the release of the 'Black List', the Madkhali Selefie network grew significantly and they have used it to create a sense of belonging combined with a strong identity. Also the label they use for themselves (Selefie) is instrumental in this. The name Selefie is based upon Salafi as it is pronounced in Dutch. This is something they do with almost all Arabic terms, which appears not only to be an accommodation of these terms to the local context but also a way of distinguishing themselves from other Salafi networks in the Netherlands that denounce the use of the term, stating that it is not an obligation and that there is no proof found in the Islamic traditions to support such an appellation. The other Dutch Salafi networks do not call themselves Salafi but they do articulate that their teachings are in accordance with the Salafi *minhaj*.

## Politics of Resistance

The politics of resistance pertains to actions aiming at a transformation of the oppressive structures of surrounding society. While the politics of lifestyle are aimed at establishing and nurturing a strong Muslim community and the politics of distinction are aimed at rejecting pressure to assimilate in a climate that has become less tolerant towards (fundamentalist) expression of Islam, the politics of resistance entail an active attempt at changing the social and political institutions of a country that are seen as oppressive and unjust. Although in the past the Amsterdam Tawheed mosque has expressed a desire for making the Netherlands an Islamic society and some imams declared that Islamic laws apply before democratic laws, most of the activists aim to be pious Muslims in Dutch society, emphasizing the right for a religious identity (politics of distinction) and performing *da'wah* among other Muslims. With regards to the Netherlands there is no evidence that the Salafi movement engages in a politics of resistance in relation to the Dutch state.[65] There are a few significant exceptions to this: the stance of some Salafi networks towards international politics, the Hofstad Network, and (currently the most important exception) the verbal attacks on the national Muslim organizations.

The first important exception to this is constituted by an indirect challenge to the Dutch state. In the past, several imams of the Ahl-u-Sunnah foundation have criticized the US, Israel (Zionists), and UN declarations in which it is stated that all people are equal and declared ominously that 'Allah will deal with Bush, Sharon, and other enemies of Islam', while another imam praised a Palestinian suicide bomber. These criticisms do not directly target the Netherlands, but they do so indirectly since the Netherlands has committed itself to the UN and usually (although not uncritically) supports the US and Israel. The sermons are aimed at constructing a transnational consciousness in which events in, for example, the Palestinian areas, Iraq and Afghanistan take on a symbolic currency as an 'Islamic' issue by framing them as an attack against Islam and the Islamic *umma*. Since the publications of several of those sermons by the press and the increasing attention of the security and intelligence services, most of the Salafi leaders do not make those statements anymore during their sermons or other public appearances.

A second exception is constituted by the core of the jihadi Hofstad network with Mohammed Bouyeri and Samir Azzouz, who saw the Netherlands as part of the battleground of the struggle between 'good and evil', 'truth and falseness', 'light and darkness' and the murder on van Gogh as part of 'defending Islam' against politicians who were (in the view of the of the Hofstad network) out to destroy Islam. The Jihadi Salafis and in particular the Hofstad network have been heavily criticized by both the Madkhali Selefies and the Salafis of the Ahl-u-Sunnah committee. With regard to politics in the Middle East the Jihadi Salafis and the Ahl-u-Sunnah committee are more critical and have, to a certain extent, made political struggle part of their doctrine. Some of the Jihadi Salafis accuse religious and political leaders of being 'infidels', the Ahl-u-Sunnah committee are much more reluctant with regard to the practice of *takfir*. The Madkhali Selefies abstain from a politics of resistance, which again can be seen as an active non-engagement. According to the Madkhali Selefies it is forbidden to criticize leaders, let alone violently attack them and, as one of the preachers stated: 'it is better to have a bad Muslim leader than no Muslim leader'.

A third exception to the Salafi movement shunning from engaging in politics of resistance does not directly apply to the state but towards other Muslim organizations in the Netherlands. Salafi youth regard the regular umbrella organizations and local mosques as no longer legitimate since they do not address the problems of the youth and have 'sold out' to the Dutch state in order to get subsidized. While organizations such as the Federation of Islamic Organizations in the Netherlands (linked to the Muslim Brotherhood) become part of the institutionalized (and therefore subsidized) structures of the state as representatives of Muslims in the Netherlands, the Salafi networks try not to become involved in these representational structures. Becoming part of these structures would mean that they would (and have to) be playing by sets of rules that benefit existing power-holders and they would be much easier to co-opt through the normal channels of political representations and negotiation and therefore have to make compromises.[66] The necessity of making compromises would contaminate their message of 'true' Islam and therefore threaten their doctrinal purity. This is a widespread feeling not only among Salafi organizations and Salafi youth but also among Muslim youth in general.

The Salafi organizations usually do not participate in demonstrations because of their reluctance to take over the repertoires of contention that the Islamist movement or political parties use. Instead, they have tried to build up their position as a youth movement in order to take over the position as the only legitimate representatives of Islam in the Netherlands by using other means of contention such as websites, petitions, inflammatory sermons, and so on. For example, in a sermon a few weeks before the murder of van Gogh in 2004, Imam Fawaz (Ahl-u-Sunnah Foundation) cursed van Gogh and Hirsi Ali in very harsh ways. This caused great upheaval when the sermon was published, which mainly focused on the impolite, confrontational language and the fact that Mohammed Bouyeri was apparently present during this lecture. Less attention has been given to the largest section of the sermon in which the Imam stated:

Where are the Islamic institutions in the Netherlands? I'm told that Moroccans alone have more than 700 organizations just as the Turks and the Surinamese. Where are these organizations to defend the honour and belief of their Prophet? But the one who uses at the cost of this belief and religion, will not be able to stand up as one, in this time when we need it. People will not be able to do anything without asking their lawyer if that will lead to losing the subsidy. Or if that will have consequences for their residence permit. This type of people will not be supported by Muhammad and are not suited for that.[67]

Fawaz blames the dependency of Islamic institutions on state subsidies for their lack of reactions and calls for intellectual action, in the media and judiciary. He also calls for 'shock and awe' action, not directed against the Dutch people ('with whom we live together. With whom we live together well, thank God'), nor with the Dutch political parties that have showed no enmity towards Muslims, but against those who support Hirsi Ali. Although his verbal attack on Hirsi Ali violates the norms of the debate in the Dutch public sphere, his emphasis on intellectual, media and juridical action also show gradual accommodation of the Dutch political rule. In relation to the conventional Muslim organizations this is more than politics of lifestyles or politics of distinction, since the actions of Salafi networks are aimed at transforming the existing power structures within the Dutch Muslim communities and the ways in which they are organized as representatives for Dutch Muslims in relation to the state.

## Conclusion

Between the 1960s and 2011 the balance between the secular and the religious as well as the governance of ethnic minorities in the Netherlands has severely changed. This has resulted in greater pressure for Muslims to assimilate, and a situation in which Islam is often framed as hindering integration or as a threat to the security of Dutch secular society. The changing context of the secular and the religious in the 1990s was further altered by the Salafi movement in 2001. The Salafi movement is perceived as a fundamentalist movement that does not belong in Dutch society, particularly after the murder of Theo van Gogh in 2004, and has become the primary target of Dutch government and municipal counter-radicalization policies. Within this context and the shift made by the Salafi movement itself by focusing more on attempts to build a religious infrastructure in the Netherlands rather than urging Muslims to move to an Islamic country, it is inaccurate to think in terms of a dichotomy between political Islamic movements (the Islamists) and the cultural Islamic movements (the Salafi movement).

In particular, the appeal of the Ahl-u-Sunnah mosques to the right to freedom of religion and the right of a religious identity and establishing their own institutions (such as home care) by the Madkhali Selefies make clear that the Salafis aim to build up and defend their minority status in Dutch society instead of making Islam the ruling religion in Dutch society, contrary to the aims of the Islamist movement. It must be said, however, that Islamist networks in Europe in general do not aim at establishing an Islamic state within Europe, but their political program and sometimes their involvement in party politics (and their stance about engaging in party politics) constitutes a major difference with the Salafi movement. This important distinction, categorizing the Islamist movement as political and the Salafi movement as cultural, creates a dichotomy that is more blinding then revelatory. Trying to build up and protect a status as a minority group by definition means dealing with the state. The Salafists have constructed their movement much in the same way as in the past was done by Christian organizations during the time of the pillarization through the establishment of mosques and Islamic schools. Since the collapse of the pillarization system Dutch society is considered to be secular and the institutionalization of Islam (and Salafism in particular) is, therefore, seen as at odds with the secular political rule.

Although the emphasis of the Salafi movement is in general on remaining quietist with regard to affairs in wider Dutch society and to build up and protect the position of the Muslim minorities, they do engage in different forms of political participation. The lifestyle of Salafi preachers and the participants in the networks has a political significance in itself because of the controversy about, for example, the burqa in public debates, and because it involves competition with other Muslim groups over who defines and controls the symbols of Islam. The politics of lifestyles such as educating women about the correct 'Islamic' attire can easily turn into politics of distinction in the case of the proposal to ban the burqa and niqab or into politics of resistance when they criticize the lack of action among other Muslim organizations.

There is a continuous debate among Salafi networks about the boundaries between doctrinal purity, adjustment to, and protest against Dutch society or particular politicians. Whatever their stance, they are also caught in a secular political context in which the state, politicians and opinion leaders are targeting them as 'radicals'. They are therefore seen by definition as challenging the state and the secular political rule, which can make it necessary for them to take a political standpoint.

Singling out the Salafi movement as a radical movement in the Netherlands and the alignment between the state and the so-called liberal Muslim organizations has created a space in which the Salafi movement can engage in different kinds of politics and in which they can build up their position as the only legitimate representatives of a 'true' Islam that is unaffected by Dutch society or by the traditions of the parents of the Muslim youth. In establishing their own institutions, using petitions and websites as means of contention, they are re-appropriating Salafi creeds and methods into more secular discourses and practices for negotiating with the Dutch state and for expressing themselves in the public sphere. At the same time through this process of accommodation they also push their ideas about what constitutes 'true' Islam to the fore. The result of the intra-Salafist struggles and the counter-radicalization policies is that the Salafi movement is redefining the boundaries between adjustment and protest, and religion and politics as instilled by early European Christian and Islamist movements and the Dutch secular context. Moreover, since counter-radicalization policy is (among other things) aimed at affirming the democratic secular political rule in relation to Islam, the engagement of the Salafi networks with the Dutch state, their presence in the public sphere, and subsequent discursive assimilation, mean that the boundaries between religion and secularism in the Netherlands are also being challenged. Analyzing the different kinds of politics and their internal and external dimensions results in a more adequate framework which can better explain under which circumstances and how and why the different Salafi networks engage with the state, in the public sphere, and with other Muslim movements.

# PART III

# FROM REVOLUTION TO POP MUSIC

8

# VEILED ARTISTS IN EGYPT[1]

*Valentina Frate*

'One of the foremost tasks of the art has always been the creation of a demand which could be fully satisfied only later '[2]

Since 11 September 2001 the forms of religiosity that Muslims around the world could express have become sources of anxiety, especially for non-Muslims. And yet an increasing number of Muslims show an interest not only in speaking about Islam but in 'showing' their religion. Some of them are pressed to portray a positive image of themselves as Muslims. They are part of a general global trend. People are concerned about the image they present to others, which can be linked to collective representation (being young, Egyptian, modern or Muslim). We are living in a world where the role of images is dominant, and increasingly so with the spread of new technologies. Images accompanied by sounds, as with television, travel further and faster than speeches. In Egypt, as in much of the rest of the world, television remains the first, easiest and most common source of images. Television does not show the reality, but supplies images which we use to understand and create the world around us; it contributes to create a shared imaginary. Religion can also be approached as a complex symbolic system constituted by a set of images, experiences, feelings and practices shared by people. Television offers religion a very powerful way to go public, a way to escape marginalization in the private sphere[3] imposed by the secularist project, and to let the religious imaginary circulate in the aesthetic-expressive sphere. Conveying the image of what or who Muslims are today requires entering a specific symbolic order and exploring new horizons of representation.

As individuals and as a group, self-defined Muslims concerned with the problem of self-representation appear on our screens in a way that disturbs the usual discourses on Islam. They point not only to existing problems of representation of the Islamic difference in the media, but also to an increase in the audience exploring new aesthetics and introducing new points of view.

## *When Retired Veiled Artists Come Back on the Scene*

In the 1980s the Egyptian actress Shams al-Baroudi and her husband, also an actor, Hassan Youssef, were the first to quit their profession[4] in the name of Islam. This phenomenon, which concerns both the media and arts world, spread more visibly across the Egyptian arts in the 1990s when high profile artists such as Sohair Ramzi, Soheir al-Bably, Sahar Hamdi and Afaf Shoeib made the decision to cover their heads and bodies and stop working in the 'sinful' world of arts. Over twenty years, more than forty female artists have decided to wear the veil and retire, gaining press attention. Each time a new artist decides to put on the veil, the national and international press reports on it and thereby gives the artist a new and different type of popularity. Audiences immediately remember the name of these artists that they had almost forgotten. Following the Arabic definition, they have been labeled repentant, or *'al-fannanat al mu'tazilat'* (the retired female artists). That is, these artists have left their artistic careers in pursuit of a lifestyle change; the center of their new occupations is Islam and the family. Away from the spotlight some of these artists occupied new roles in Muslim charity organizations or NGOs, invested time and money in 'respectful' businesses[5] and attended religious classes.

Although such instances still occur, from 2002,[6] this stance has been challenged, with several veiled artists[7] returning to the artistic world after a hiatus from the screen and stage. New artists entering this world of redemption have no intention of giving up the artistic life but want only to take on acceptable roles which will allow them to perform without having to remove the veil. Common conditions are a refusal to participate in sexually explicit scenes or to act immoral characters. These artists profess to serve as models of religiosity and decency in the arts world and, no more repentant, reflect the birth of a new trend in the post-Islamist Egyptian stage. There is, according to this trend, no more conflict between Islam, art and 'proper'[8] entertainment. Leaving traditional Islamist activism and the old rigorous views about arts aside, these new veiled Muslim artists are more interested in showing Islam as a universally symbolic alternative to transform the arts and to improve the view of female artists' status and work. New discourses on art and Islam have apparently gained consensus: talent is God's gift and to deny it is to deny the mission God gave to the artist. 'God loves beauty' so art is a way to revitalize an intimate relation with God and to build the aesthetic of the new *umma*.[9] This way, post-Islamist actors enter the public arena with a new religious-aesthetic project.

Over the last few years former repentant stars such as Soheir el-Babli, Soheir Ramzi and Abir Sabri and even the actor Hassan Youssef have stepped back onto the screens, as television presenters or playing new pious characters. In May 2006, Hanan Turk, a famous young actress and dancer, shocked the media and declared her Islamic 'coming out'; this was not to be considered as a step towards retirement nor as in conflict with her professional work as an actress. Instead, she assured her audience that she was 'eager to explore the role of the veiled heroine'.[10]

Working for the entertainment industry has become Islamically respectful and even helpful in terms of the visibility[11] of the *umma*. The ethical-aesthetic choice, represented by the veil, aims not only to clean and 'Islamicize' television and cinema products but also to reflect a change in the construction of a modern neo-liberal Islam.

## *The Appearance of Veils On-screen*

In the Egyptian mass media the veil, which was normally reserved for the depiction of mothers, older women or radical fundamentalists on-screen, was considered a cloth representing a traditional past or rural origins such as in the case of the best-known, but now relatively rare, character of the *bint el-balad* in movies—a genuine and honest young woman from the countryside celebrating the Egyptian peasant class. The veil of the *bint el-balad* had vibrant colors, and hardly covered the hair; in contrast to the dress of the sophisticated women of the cities. Despite the fact that today the majority of Egyptian Muslim women wear the hijab, they are often overlooked by television and movie studios. The majority of female screen personalities and news presenters (anchor women) eschew the veil. From the 1990s until the present day the veil has become darker and thicker on screen, and new veiled characters, sometimes wearing the niqab, have been associated with terrorism and/or the influences of extremist religious group on society.

Cinema and television in Egypt have been considered important tools in influencing people's behavior, so the different ruling regimes have tried to maintain strong control over the cultural industry. Films and *musalsalat* (soap-operas) openly play a pedagogic role and Islam has always been a relatively marginal theme. Today the state controls the presence of the veil in its channels to the extent that it will openly prevent anchor women[12] from wearing the hijab. At the same time in the artistic world there is the awareness that wearing the veil and being an Islamist woman are different and television and cinema's writers are starting to change their approach to veiled characters. The colorful *hijab*, trivialized by its commercialization and glittering from the pages of magazines,[13] has lost some of its symbolic negative power and is becoming a sign of a positive public affirmation. In 2003 the actress Mona Zaki appeared in a very successful movie *Sahhar Al-Layali*,[14] playing a veiled middle-class married woman who loves her husband and, although she knows he is cheating on her, fights for her family and finally wins him back. Zaki is featured both with and without the veil according to the different scenes: at home she removes her veil so the veil is just an accessory of her character and not a personal behavioral choice. The movie was a success and received public acclaim and several awards outside Egypt. This veiled female character was not controversial because of her ability to tie religious to national identity and to maintain the symbolic status of the veil in the dynamics of the Egyptian national program.

When the new characters of veiled women emerged, the first veiled artists were declaring their intention to continue their professional careers. Willing to incarnate the Islamic awakening on the stage, the veiled artists challenge the tradition of female artists in Egypt and represent the symbolic, aesthetic bearers of a new utopian transnational Muslim project. Today the veiled artists have chosen to compete in the global market of cultural products re-imagining the Muslim woman. The time for 'retired' veiled women has passed; they are more concerned with creating new performances for the screen-mediated sphere[15] where real and fictional Muslim woman intersect and experience a common commitment to a new global Muslim community. Veiled artists have given the audience the power to replace in their imagination dark and negative images of veiled women with glittering, colorful and sophisticated images of veiled women.

According to the work of Karen Warren, since the end of the 1980s many Islamists have stopped consuming national cultural products.[16] This anti-consumer ethos was a response to a culture not considered to be Islamic and virtuous. It was probably the first way they found to complain about the negativity or lack of Islamic images on-screen. In front of this kind of audience, the first wave of repentant actresses has no alternative but to quit the stage. More recently these same actors seem to have stopped considering themselves to be martyrs whose image was denied or challenged by misinterpretation, and have instead begun occupy the screen with the intention of conveying constructive messages about Islam. This is because they were experiencing or developing neither popular nor traditional Islam, nor even that of terrorism, but a shifting Islam continuously adapting to the modernity of the believers' lives. Nowadays the veiled artists, instead of worrying about the Islamists' initial rejection of the cultural market, quitting in part due to martyr syndrome, are again spreading the pleasure of a consumption based on a new and more appealing image of Islam.

## Religion Will Be Televised[17] by Double Agents

A new type of veiled woman has appeared on television channels from the Gulf countries, especially in the religious programs of the

*Iqra'* channel, and in several adverts for other channels. The adverts portray a middle-class Muslim world symbolized by the beautiful veil of a smiling housewife, mothers or nice young women living a modern, sinless perfect life. When Tuchman and Kaplan use the concept of 'symbolic annihilation'[18] they consider that women appear less than men on the small screen and when they do so their roles are very limited or negative. They claim that the media often condemn or trivialize women's activities and experience. Many feminists also criticize the way women tend to be portrayed on television screen. Certainly television channels broadcasted in Arab countries over-emphasize the domestic roles of women. Being a housewife is the most common occupation for women in television adverts, even if one is wearing the veil.

These new veiled characters serve also to celebrate and promote the consumerist possibilities of veiled women and their families. The portrayal of women in these adverts does not depart significantly, except for the veil, from the portrayals of women already familiar to the audience. It appears obvious that these adverts are addressed to Muslims represented as new middle-class consumers rather than political activists. They confirm that the idea of the Islamist activist has been replaced by a modern self-identified Muslim devoted to her community, which promotes her religious diversity as well as her commitment to Western capitalist values such as free market consumerism and individualism. The difference is that consumption is solicited by and through the Islamic imagination of the Muslim audience. The Muslim middle class who could have a hard life in accepting and taking other television programs, which they consider to have a bad influence and to attack Islamic values, will probably buy products whose adverts mobilize some Islamic images, symbols or words. The veil solution coming from the satellite channels worked even to advertise beauty products for women. Hardly imaginable in the past, companies selling body products chose to add veiled women to their campaigns and to broadcast only material without explicit reference to seduction and nudity. For example, a shampoo advertisement in which hair does not feature, but only the smiling face of a modern veiled girl.

Thanks to their increasing presence on screen the image of veiled woman has been transformed into a symbolic site for circumscribing difference and 'Islamicate' (cultural) products.[19] By 'Islami-cate'[20] I mean the act of creating a positive and inspiring reference to Islam in the media. One may regard the characters of veiled women in the ads as not only intended to target new consumers, but also as the involuntary first step to setting the stage for the entrance of the 'veiled stars'. These veiled artists are not just ele-ments of the décor, they are uncomfortable intrusive protagonists who are trying to reassume control over their images, threatened by false ones. In order to respect both themselves and Islam, they have to change the rules of play. What is also highly controversial is that they perform as and are perceived to be double agents[21] who have infiltrated two separated worlds—the arts and Islam. They are double because they are not acting on an individualistic impulse; they simultaneously embody the first and the third narra-tive forms. They express their subjectivity but at the same time they freed themselves from the boundaries of the 'I' while speaking in the name of Islam and of the Muslim audience.

Islam is a source of subjectivity but also of a new aesthetic that is challenging the old imaginaries, transforming the arts and creat-ing new scenarios and characters. The self-adopted veil of the actress in fiction has added problematic realism to the female char-acters; it is not only a character portrayal, but these women are also genuinely veiled, alongside the majority of Muslim women in Egypt. Their veil has opened the production to new plots and gen-res, like the religious one. If these new productions are playing a role in enlarging the TV audience by co-opting the interests and the imagination of new viewers/consumers all over the world, the veiling of the actress's body has brought back a place for the sacred in a field (media) and a profession (artist) that was consid-ered highly profane.

### From the Screen to the Body

For a long time Egypt has been a pool of creativity and entertain-ment in the Arab world and its cultural industry still plays a dominant role. In TV drama production, Egypt monopolizes the market of the Arabic-speaking world and, through satellite televi-sion, is able also to reach a more distant market and exploit the

Arab presence in other continents. Egypt produces 100 TV serials and fifty drama specials a year,[22] but it is far from meeting the demand for the programs coming from Arab satellite channels. These channels have to fill their schedules by importing and dubbing foreign productions, such as talk shows, films, documentaries and even soap operas especially from Latin America and, more recently, from Turkey.

Television is still the main source of entertainment and information for Egyptians. Time spent watching television, alone or with family members or friends, is a moment of leisure, socialization or information. From audio, video tapes and CDs to cinema, television and computers, electronic media are playing the main role in organizing the leisure time of Egyptian people. Egyptian cinema has considerably decreased its production: in 2004, only twenty-four movies were produced while the average production in 1985 was seventy-eight films. Furthermore, the poor reputation of the cinema theatres and the crisis of the film industry have put Egyptians in front of their domestic screens. It is difficult to define precisely how these programs influence the lives of Egyptians. However, we can suppose that they have a significant part in defining their imagination and aspirations. Some programs are targeted at women specifically,[23] who spend a large part of their free-time watching television and who see there their values, habits or aspirations. Despite the fact that editors ask their audience about the program's content, each program reflects the editor's judgment of what the audience is interested in and what it wants to know about.

With the replacement of written culture with a visual one,[24] we can suppose that individuals who are not members of cultural or intellectual elites use broadcasted images to come to understand society and eventually transform themselves according to new visions, but this understanding is not a free and rational process. The main problem with a television entertainment product is that it is made by a flux of moving images that instead of appealing to one's reason, engages instead one's senses and desires and stimulates the imagination.

Veiled actresses on domestic screens have left the light of rational discourse and occupy the the domain of the collective psyche where images play a role stronger than words:

Television following the ways of film has adopted cinematographic edit-ing as the norm. [...] To edit a film or an image we have to cut it and piece it together to with other cuts. We edit images to a storyline in our minds adjusting them to fit the text. Film editing is a similar process, except that it is done outside our mind. In a manner of speaking, when we watch a film, it is our own mind that it is editing on the spot.[25]

Since the audience is not a passive recipient of images, only when it likes, loves or hates an actor, a character or a story, it means that an answer has been given to some audience's uncon-scious needs. The electricity has passed and the connection is made between the audience and its image of love or hate. In this coming and going of images between the actress and the audience, the audience's bodies are in the between. The bodies are receptive to what they are watching.[26] If Islam is what the images of the actresses represent for the viewer, the viewer will complete the storyline editing outside the television screen with new images of what Islam is. The nexus of internal and external images will affect the lifestyle of the audience. The viewer will start from the body to edit his own story about Islam. In this context the body as a medium of experience has become a sacred place. The body—both real and imagined—is a living project for a modern fluctuant sanc-tuary of Islam. These artists have discovered a modern holiness. They do not just perform piety in the same way as the participants in the brilliant work of Mahmood on womens' mosques move-ment[27] did, but they also sublimate their inner desire for salvation and holiness, becoming the modern saints of the screens. Not only the actresses but also each member of the audience can use a synaesthetic memory[28] of what they have experienced about this embodied Islam. This memory can be reactivated by the body in a vast range of activities. Therefore the audience will share with these actresses a common sensibility and the same imagination. Tied together in the name of God's beauty, the audience and artists are experiencing what Islam is and should be.

## The Veiled Artists' Challenge

Mona Abdel Ghany declared to *al-Ahram Weekly*[29] 'The main adjust-ment I've made to my life, for the most part, is in the intention', she said. 'In the past, everything I did was meant to bring me more fame and money; today, whatever I do is intended to please God'. Business and media are male dominated spheres that female artists are reorganizing under the banner of Islamic tradition. The veiled artists, using their veils, are managing a place of autonomy for themselves and marking a respectable place for women and Islam in the media. The veil provides an interesting example of mobilization of traditions. They are trying to re-activate a symbol of the Islamic tradition to influence the present state of the arts and to support the popular imagination through the spread of a regenerated Islamic sensibility. Islamic traditions, simultaneously real and imaginary, can be sources of cultural transformation and be mobilized in a struggle, investing in arts, towards a new society. The veil has also become the Islamic sign challenging the world of performing arts and the artists themselves and it raises the possibility of criticizing the process of modernization itself that took place on the Egyptian stage.

The veiled artists are new icons and they create anxiety in Egypt as a whole more than in the world of the artists who have been actively engaged in the country's cultural and political modernization. Therefore, few female artists look at veiled artists as breaking the libertarian and progressive definition of their profession, as supporting the backwardness of society and giving wrong representations of their social group and role. According to Nilüfer Göle, the veil is a voluntary adopted stigma. Hence, putting on the veil for an artist, compared to other symbolic actions, has a stronger impact in defining new relationships in the artistic world:

...the Islamic headscarf supplies information about the bearer, but is also subject to public perception. It communicates the individual and collective motivations of those who adopt it as much as the perceptions of those who reject it. The symbol of the headscarf makes sense as a language of relationships between those who assert their orientation toward values of Islam and those social classes that owe their status to normative values of modernity, such as equality and liberty.[30]

On screen veiled actresses have stimulated debate on what it is possible to imagine and perform in modern arts and media. In one of my first interviews in 2004 with a young Egyptian actress, she explained why being a veiled actress was almost unthinkable for her: 'Well, you know, I don't want to give a confused image of what I am. I think I will never accept to put the veil even if the role requires it ... I mean Egypt is a modern country and as you know the actresses have to show this'. Western popular culture and its system of representation first circulated in Egypt through imported movies and have partially been adopted and 'Egyptianized' by the Egyptian national cinema industry. Hence cinema has set standards for women, both in positive and negative characters, connecting them to an urban Westernized dominant culture. Female artists in Egypt were perceived and perceive themselves through their profession as the symbolic carriers of the modernization of society and the liberation of women. That is why Fatma Roushdi was able to entitle her biography *Kifahi fi al-masrah wa-l-sinima* ('My Struggle in Theatre and Cinema'). Similarly female characters in movies or in soap operas are constructed as embodying a pedagogical role to promote certain values according to different social projects. As Lila Abu Lughod has pointed out the role of television in Egypt and especially of melodramas, has been tied to the production of modern Egyptian citizens. Deploying nationalist and religious ideologies and focusing on the emotional reaction of the audience, the government and feminist script-writers have tried to make the audience, especially women, feel comfortable with modernity.[31]

The veiled actress does the same but she moves from the nationalist cultural project to the religious one and tries to embody the collective learning process of being a modern Muslim. By doing so she also (re)politicizes the arts and entertainment and transforms them in a symbolic battlefield. Veiled actresses are performing their Islamic femininity, which might stand in opposition to other models of femininity coming from inside and outside the Islamic tradition. They are not just other Muslim-born artists. The symbolic capital of the veil is now adopted based on the desire to show to the audience the difference of being a Muslim artist, comfortable with both Islam and modernity. They have new responsibilities because they embody a different social project and fight on the last frontier of Muslim agency: the aesthetic one.

## Modernizing Islam Through Arts

Veiled artists, for the first time in Egyptian history, have made their profession acceptable in an Islamic sense and opened Islam to the modernity of their professions. Moving from the secular tradition to the religious one, they have challenged some conceptions according to which women are not allowed to perform in public. Mona Abdel Ghany declared to the journalist:

I wanted, to brush away the widespread misconception that the female voice is *awra* (taboo). It is the way a woman uses her voice, not the voice itself, that is the issue. It is only forbidden for a woman to be too complaisant in her speech. It is the wording of a song that decides whether it is *haram* (forbidden).[32]

Veiled performers are challenging Islamic orthodoxy. They are asserting that the stage can be a suitable place for Muslim women and their profession can be respectable. Nilüfer Göle points out that 'Paradoxally, Islamist movements endow Muslims with a collective identity that works critically against both traditional subjugation of Muslim identity and mono-civilizational imposition of Western modernity'.[33] We also should remember that the female performer as we conceive of her is not a traditional figure either in the Egyptian artistic tradition or for Islam, and it arises from the encounter between Egyptian artists, theatre and cinema coming from Europe. Theatre arrived in Egypt in 1870 when Isma'il Pasha, who promoted cultural and intellectual development, invited some European artists, especially French and Italian companies, to perform in his palace and on the newly-built stages in Alexandria and Cairo. The Egyptian theatre author and director Ya'qoub Sannou'a (1839–1912) was the first and only person in this period to engage actresses in his company. The attempt resulted in a difficult experience:

[...] I had to put together a troupe of actresses. I was lucky enough to find two beautiful but poor girls who quickly learnt to read and play minor roles without too much difficulty. Their appearances on stage were met with vigorous, if hesitant, applause which encouraged the two girls to become real stars'.[34]

At that time only Christian and Jewish women were allowed to perform in front of an audience. For Muslim female artists to perform publicly, they had to refrain from showing any exterior sign of religiosity. The Muslim women who, discarding their veils, decided to become singers, dancers or actresses were emblematic of a new urban Westernized culture which would dominate the process of national construction. At the same time they were heavily criticized by religious scholars. Even today the performances are highly controversial[35] and censure or self-censure is quite common in Egyptian media. The government and traditional religious institutions support the moralization of the media and pursue a policy of 'cleaning up' cultural products. Censorship against modern decadence and the low moral standards of the television program is directed mainly at depictions of nude or dancing women. Veiled artists use this same rhetoric about the negative influence of Western mass media but still consider the media to be a powerful instrument in helping to spread Islamic values. They are also emancipating Islam from orthodox traditions. They have helped blur the boundary between the public and private spheres providing an example of modern Islamic lifestyles and encouraging women to seek a life outside the home, even in a profession that is rejected by traditional Islamic scholars.

## New Visual Supports for the Islamic Dream

Television plays a significant role in the lives of many Egyptians—whether in public or private, the television is switched on for several hours each day. Today in Egypt one is able to gain access to the same sorts of images and the same kinds of programs (music videos, talk shows and news) as in other parts of the world, with the only difference being the language. Lifestyles have crossed the national boundaries. The same genre of Western music can also be found in different cultural contexts (such as Arab hip hop, Indian rock). But the circulation of sounds and images appears easier when they are produced in the West. Egyptian stars who are by far the most famous in the Arabic-speaking world do not find the same recognition outside the Arab world. This is reserved, the world over, for American and European celebrities.

Muslims in Egypt, except for a few extremists, have never totally rejected technology and media but they have criticized its usage. As a consequence they have quickly shifted their preference to Saudi Arabian channels whose programming is regarded as less corrupted by the cultural imperialism of the West.[36] Competing with national or Western channels, these Saudi channels win viewers by offering an Islamic alternative that reinforces the new transnational identities of the audience. This Islamic focus allows these reluctant consumers to enjoy the media, the technology and the comforts of a modern lifestyle. Entertainment activities and products respect moral responsibility towards the well-being of the *umma*. Gradually this increasing need for more Islamic cultural products has pushed Muslim producers and artists to explore the field of arts. Instead of 'art for art's sake' Muslims should prefer 'art with a purpose' *(fen el-hadith)*.Listening to the sermons of new television preachers is part of the same process of transformation in leisure activities. The smiling and successful television preacher Amr Khaled gained celebrity for his programs which a mixed a message of divine love and individualism to support the viewers' faith and help them to find personal salvation. His religious talk shows have transformed satellite television into a pulpit.[37] He too, then, has participated in the construction of a new Islamic stage, which he shares with the veiled artists. For adherents these new television stars represent a novel and relaxed way of respecting their religiosity in an entertainment setting. The veiled artists are invited to Islamic salons[38] and to talk shows, not necessarily the religious ones, where they speak about their life experiences, their decisions to wear the veil and to move closer to God. They have a strong impact on the collective psyche of the audience. They encourage viewers to rediscover the power Islam can give to them. Having felt the need to distance themselves from Islam in the name of the profane duties of a profane profession, they say, they have decided to lift the mask and be themselves again. In this life-changing choice they offer examples of the individualization of the relationship with God. This experience of redemption responds to the believer's own need for salvation and reassures them, explaining that Islam is open to any kind of believer. The narrative of this conversion is frequently portrayed as emotionally powerful. The veiled artists cry or tell how they experienced altered states of consciousness and prophetic dreams.[39] The relationship with God, in short, is for them an intimate and unique experience.

They are unconsciously appealing for the audience to discover Islam again. As advertisers have known for a long time, television does not need to speak about the product itself, but it has to evoke a feeling or thought process in the viewer and then to link it to the product. These artists evoke synaesthetical images related to the sacred inner world of Islamic spirituality.

But there is also a secular material dimension to their experiences. They show how a person may better themselves by rediscovering Islam and regaining an imagined *umma*. Following the right models, the true examples of Islamic piety, the Islamic dream will be real. The *umma* will be as successful, beautiful, respectable and even happy as these actresses are. The screen has become a means of support of a modern religiosity and, in line with this, Islam has become a matter of taste and feeling. The veiled artists express their Islamic beliefs as a choice of personal freedom beyond the oppression of old institutions which are no longer able to impose their interpretations of Islam, and outside the media dominant national project which is no longer able to impose a strong Egyptian feeling. They give the power of the Islamic dream to the audience. The audience feels empathy before these new-born Muslim artists and hardly realizes that it is the relation with the screens and a neo-liberal mentality that is becoming stronger under the flag of the new Islamic dream.

## Choosing the Transnational Islamic Culture: Leisure, Market and Self-control

In post-Islamist Egypt, issues relating to belief, values and identity have become more important than the pursuit and achievement of political power. Women who want to publicly assert that they are Muslims do not have to be stronger than the Western enemy or abandon their modern lifestyle to express their submission to God. Having fun and enjoying the arts is no longer perceived as being in conflict with a religious attitude. The veiled actresses express these radical changes. In continuing their artistic careers the new-born Muslim artists began thinking about how to reform the media entertainment for the enjoyment of the Muslim audience. They are playing in a new *mise en scène* of their newly-acquired Muslim image. Islam is not only a religion but also a way of being and feeling, and religion is no more a utopia or a private matter, but a public transnational culture that is in large part visual, expressed in the movies people watch, the ways they dress or interact and perform their religiosity on a daily basis. The relation between the believer and religion has become stronger, beyond the traditional institutions. Islam has exited mosques and entered cafes, cinemas and beaches; the new spaces for living and promoting one's Islamicity. In other words, attention is drawn to the Islamic duty to meditate and exert an Islamic control on oneself in order to be a complete Muslim.[40] This idea relates to Foucault's concept of taking care of one's own self. Foucault states that the individualism of this culture is characterized by: 'The intensity of the relation to the self that is the forms by which we are summoned to consider ourselves as subject of knowledge and field of action, so to transform correct, purify, make your own salvation'.[41]

All over the world, television programs, parties, concerts, festivals and special Muslim celebrations are public occasions that are being reinvented and where new Muslim subjects, such as the veiled artist, can perform their religious roles. In modern societies, people want to participate in public gatherings which emphasize their emotional and material connection with others. Muslims are actors and spectators in the public spaces where they are celebrating themselves and their new Islamic culture. Watching television, going to cafes and cinema or to a concert, taking a walk in a park next to al-Ahzar, are moments of leisure that Muslims try to 'Islamicate'. They are transforming the practices of the former Westernized classes according to an Islamic ethos.[42] Islam cannot be understood in a nationalist perspective but has become a transnational phenomenon. The first festival of Muslim cinema,[43] where subject matter was not limited to Islam or Muslim culture but where no films with gratuitous violence, nudity or profanity were allowed, has been held in the USA. Since 2006 there is an annual festival in Abu Dhabi called 'el-mahabba awards' to encourage and evaluate artistic expressions of love for the Prophet Muhammad. The organizers wrote: 'It is our hope that this festival may be the start of a new love story between Muslims and their prophet. We hope to give the audience, Muslim or otherwise, enough energy and passion to search for the Prophet in their lives throughout the year'.[44]

In Paris, UOIF, a French Muslim organization, organizes an Annual Meeting for French Muslims. During the meeting, which lasts three to four days, Muslims from all over France gather to attend conferences, enjoy concerts and plays and to experience and take in what it means to be a French Muslim. Muslims consider these experiences as formative symbolic moments in their lives— many refer to this meeting as the 'mini-*hajj*' of the French Muslims. In the last few years, hundreds of festivals, gatherings and cultural events have been organized in the name of Islam all over the world.

However, in this new transnational Muslim culture, one also sees how the traditional religious events have changed. The pilgrimage (*hajj*) to Mecca or the month of Ramadan have been modernized and have been transformed into new leisure experiences for the socialization and the construction of modern Muslim subjects. According to Norbert Elias, leisure has the true function of contributing to temper the strong self-control of other activities.[45] Leisure activities have the function of allowing Muslims to forget to control their emotions in public and, with the support of others, learn the modern rules of the self-control and discipline. Moreover, leisure is a new way to perform a joyful respectful Muslimness, to show the difference compared to non-Muslims but even to those born Muslim. In this context veiled artists, who are often invited to participate in these festivals or celebrations of Islamicity, are contributing to expand the Islamic leisure market, particularly in relation to television products. During Ramadan, watching television is a key activity. The market of *musalsalat* during this month sees a growth in demand from all Muslim countries and the Egyptian *musalsal* producers try to meet the demand and to specialize in the religious genre of *musalsal*. Ramadan is the biggest television season. In 2006 it was marked by the return to the screen of the repentant artists, who proved particularly well-matched to the series airing during that month. They have performed in new television *musalsalat* that they consider respectable with good social values.[46] These proper *musalsalat* present what are supposed to be real social problems and then offering Islamic solutions rooted in individual effort and will-power to the good Muslims. The combination of morals and visual media join an emergent Islamic culture of leisure. The neo-liberal market is opening up for Islamic products. Salvation and self-realization through Islam are shown on-screen. The veiled artists represent a visual support for an Islamic culture of consumerism which has already spread in the globalized *umma*.

195

It remains to be seen if these artists most concerned with the problem of performing both as a Muslim and an artist will be able to create those forms of art that allow non-Muslim audiences to enter the Islamic imaginary, offering them appealing cultural products and representing a credible model of beauty for them too.

## Conclusion: An Islamic Renaissance

Our societies are facing serious problems ... We have no option but to engage actively in the media, the internet, the arts and entertainment. We cannot isolate ourselves anymore. We cannot pretend that these types of technologies do not exist. Yes indeed, the psychological divide between Islamists and the fields of arts and entertainment is great. However, we will be able to bridge it. In order to bring about our renaissance, development and prosperity, preserve our values, advance our causes, defend our rights, express positive images about us and spread our message, we have only one option. That option is to break the psychological barrier and overcome the mistakes made toward the fields of arts and entertainment.[47]

Writing on Islamonline.net, Nabil Shabeeb is worth quoting extensively for his impassioned call in the wake of September 11 to transform the fields of art and entertainment in a fundamental battle to keep Islam alive and give Muslims new perspectives. The veiled artists are working for what Shabeeb called the Muslims' Renaissance as part of an alternative cultural industry that can be labeled 'Islamic' and has grown up since the early 2000s. If we can categorize and make various lists of the different Islamic products produced by this industry a clear definition of who the Islamic artists behind this production are, is still difficult to determine. The veiled artists are certainly one part of a group who have entered the already existing Western-dominated aesthetic-expressive sphere that, according to Habermas' theory, occupies a central place.[48] The artist's is the first tool of expression of this new Islamic project and probably contains the 'divine' aesthetical message. Thanks to the previous social movements gender and racial differences of the artists may be accepted, but the Islamicity of the artist's body is problematic. These veiled artists have given the world's screens new living icons that are unconsciously setting new canons of beauty to compete with Western or nationalistic ones.

These veiled artists have first destroyed the 'universality' of Western images on screen and have shown how images and media are crucial sites of cultural and political negotiations in a globalized world. The veil for these controversial artists is a new call for Muslims in Egypt to push beyond the boundaries of national identity and to enter the modern globalized *umma*. They use the media and are limiting the use the media can make of them. In a sense beyond their individual choice of showing their 'Muslimness', they have agreed to become visual support for others' 'Muslimness'.

The principal aesthetic contribution of these veiled actresses is in reviving the sacredness of the body, which is possible only by hiding part of it according to the Islamic imaginary.[49] While in the European Renaissance the body was completely uncovered, naked and studied in all of its anatomy,[50] these artists are covering up again the same body. They are playing a role in the edification of a new body calling for secret beauty and unity. This new body is sacred because it shows God's remembrance, as the *dhikr* used by Sufis in their rituals. The female body of the veiled artist embodies doubly, because of the profession and in its femininity, the process of creation. Through the support of these new icons of Muslimness, of the new screen's saints, the members of the audience experience the invisible, the mystery of the process of creation and are called to change their point of view and to reconstitute a sacred space, where invisible, unspeakable and unconscious forces are working to create other possible worlds. Supported by the holiness of this body, post-Islamist Muslims will enter the globalized world without losing themselves, their privacy or their unity.

# 9

# HEAVY METAL MUSLIMS

## THE RISE OF A POST-ISLAMIST PUBLIC SPHERE

*Mark LeVine*

The contributions to this volume reveal the rich, complex and some-times distorted tapestry of contemporary Muslim belief and prac-tice. Yet most of the movements and discourses described thus far have at their core been political; they self-consciously identify, how-ever problematically, a religiously-grounded ideology with specific forms of political practice or goals. This chapter will extend the parameters of analysis in two directions: first, the political towards more culturally-grounded terrain; second, the religious to what ostensibly seems like secular identities and practices. In both cases I seek to expand the understanding of what can be described as the constitution of globalized Muslim public spheres, which during the last decade have taken a variety of forms, with an increasing num-ber of participants, which together call into question the boundaries of Islamism as envisioned by contemporary scholarship.

'I don't like heavy metal. Not because I think it's *haram* (forbid-den) but just because it's not my kind of music. But when we get together to pray, and pump our fists in the air and beat our chests, and chant very loudly, we're doing heavy metal too'. These words were spoken to me by Sheikh Anwar al-Ethari, a young Shi'i cleric from Sadr City, who's known by his community as 'the Elastic Sheikh' (al-sheikh al-lashuddudiyya) because he has a degree in sociology from Baghdad University as well as an advanced degree in theology from the al-Hawza seminary in Najaf, and is willing to use 'whatever works, whether it's Western or Islamically-sanctioned, if it will help my people'. Sheikh Anwar made this remark on a panel that brought him together with several young artists from the Arab world, among whom was a founder of the Moroccan heavy metal scene, Reda Zine.

Reda had just explained why, given Morocco's rich musical traditions, he decided to become a heavy metal musician: 'We play heavy metal because our lives *are* heavy metal. Can you think of a better soundtrack to life in poor and oppressive societies like ours?' Even as a scholar who has spent over a decade traveling across the Muslim world, the idea of heavy metal Islam was a great surprise.

Indeed, if you juxtapose the typical image of a metalhead and an Islamist the two don't seem like a natural fit—the long-haired, tattooed, t-shirt and ripped jeans wearing slacker facing off against the conservatively dressed, stern faced and bearded extremist who is contemptuous of anyone who disagrees with his seemingly atavistic interpretation of Islam. But as so often is the case, reality is much more complex than the stereotypical imaginings of both sides of the Muslim world's cultural divide.

In observing this (potential) crossing of the paths of aesthetic and political movements within contemporary Muslim societies, a new direction in the shape of religiously-grounded Muslim activism becomes apparent; one that moves beyond the traditional understanding of Islamism as being rooted in the push to establish (through political means or violence) an Islamic state, and with the failure of the project of 'political Islam', either to move towards political normalization with existing regimes and the nation-state framework more broadly, or to move towards a closed, conservative and largely transnational 'neo-fundamentalist' perspective.[1] On the one hand, this change is part of a larger secularization of politics in the region; yet the new landscape of religious activism as seen by its views on seemingly un-Islamic cultural practices and the reengagement of Islamist movements in political activism within the parameters of existing nation-states (rather than seeking either to take over or replace those states), reminds us of the need to move beyond the often simplistic notion of religion and politics as necessarily—or even optimally—two separate spheres of human activity.[2]

Finally, this discussion demonstrates the utility of exploring both 'Islamists' and fans of extreme music as equally viable counter-cultures whose presence has a 'spillover' effect in the larger social milieu by challenging both the politically and culturally dominant values of the larger society. Such counter-cultures create diverse yet cohesive communities that seek not merely to carve out autonomous spaces within society, but, when feasible, actively to transform it. At the same time, both movements constitute 'frontal engagements' with the problematic of modernity, and both pragmatically seek to make adequate use of available structures of opportunities and to mobilize available resources towards achieving greater independence of action and social acceptance. In short, as Taieb Belghazi writes of Moroccan Islamism, they are 'best understood as an engagement with the problematic of identity in a changing world',[3] but, crucially, unlike neo-fundamentalist Islam or 'post-traditional fundamentalist' Christianity, is not interested in constructing an alternative to modernity or using the state as a primary instrument of a larger cultural transformation.

Most important, however, is that both movements offer alternative ways of grappling with the nihilism that has, at least since Nietzsche, been considered the most dangerous effect of modernization and the loss of social meaning and grounding its emergence often produces. That is, more specifically to the region, the ongoing history of colonialism, authoritarianism, war, underdevelopment, and the lack of life chances that such a system produces.[4] In so doing, the personalities discussed in this chapter, in both the metal and Islamist 'scenes', represent more than just counter-movements or counter-cultures based primarily on deploying and defending closed, intolerant, hostile and sometimes violent identities—what the sociologist Manuel Castells terms 'resistance identities'. Instead, they represent, from what initially seems to be opposite sides of the social/political spectrum of most Muslim societies, some of the most powerful 'project identities'—that is, identities that are open to dialogue, more tolerant of divergence of opinion and envision a just future that does not rely on violence to be achieved.[5]

As more than one religious activist in the Arab world has explained, they have bigger problems to deal with today than policing the tastes of young Egyptians or Moroccans, especially when they are trying to become more legitimate in the eyes of their fellow citizens and cement a growing presence in the public spheres and civil societies of their countries, while at the same time fending off increasing government repression.

## When Religion Rocks: Defining the Boundaries of Religious Experience in a Globalized Context

One of the central debates in the study of Islam, and religion more broadly, is the relationship between religion and popular culture. By popular, or pop, culture, I do not mean popular religious practices, such as folk or Sufi Islam, which have long been the object of study by scholars. Rather, it is defined as cultural practices that are not ostensibly religious, and not considered part of the so-called 'high culture' of a country (as are classical Arabic music, calligraphy, Qur'anic recitation or poetry), and which therefore are often considered illegitimate in the eyes of the political, cultural or religious elites.

In the United States, scholars have in the last generation devoted increasing attention to studying the relationship between various forms of American Christianity and popular culture, be it novels (the [in]famous *End of Days* series of novels depicting Armageddon), or the genres of Christian rock, country or heavy metal that saw steady and increasing sales in the last two decades. Yet these cultural products, while clearly part of 'pop' culture, are not directly comparable to this study of Muslim popular cultures such as heavy metal or hip hop, because the former have specifically religious themes and are experienced as part of a larger, usually Evangelical cultural milieu (and also have received increasing corporate support), while for the most part the music and artists we will encounter here keep their distance from religious themes.

Indeed for Tillich,[6] what defines 'secularization' is not an absence of religion or faith, but instead an emptiness and materialistic perspective towards life which can no longer express ultimate concern. In the Muslim-majority world the problematic nature of secularism as an ideology is exacerbated by a persistent demonization by mainstream as well as conservative religious forces of anything that challenges its self-perception. Yet despite this process, I argue that heavy metal, and hip hop, can be understood as religious phenomena, even when practiced by secular musicians and fans, because they express the inherent need for identity, connection and—despite the often angry or depressing subject matter of metal or hip hop songs—hope, that are associated with traditional religion. Indeed, one only has to compare the physical movements and percussive rhythms of a traditional *Zar* ceremony to that of metalheads head-banging to their hard-driving music to understanding the similarities that allow these seemingly opposed phenomena to represent similar types of emotional and spiritual catharses.[7]

In his seminal writings on the relationship between religion and secularity, Talal Asad argues that:

...it is precisely in a secular state—which is supposed to be totally separated from religion—that it is essential for the state law to define, again and again, what genuine religion is, and where its boundaries should properly be... The phenomenon as a whole—that is the phenomenon of Islamism—as well as comparable religious movements elsewhere in the world ought to make us rethink the accepted narratives of triumphant secularism and liberal assumptions about what is politically and morally essential to modern life.[8]

By asking, for example, whether popular music can serve as a medium for religious experience, and concerts or other musical performances as a form of religious ritual, it is possible to develop more nuanced understandings of what we mean by categories such as 'religious experience' or 'ritual', how these relate to lived experience, and how this experience challenges established dichotomies that separate religious from supposedly secular spheres of life.

*Music in Islam: A Wide Spectrum of Beliefs and Practices*

More than most religions, Islam has a schizophrenic relationship to music. At its core, the Qur'an is a poetic work; although many Sunni authorities insist that it should never be 'sung', but rather merely 'recited' (*tajwid*), the myriad shifts in pitch and rhythm are—as Muslim proponents of the permissibility of music argue—clearly musical. Similarly, many Sunni and Shi'i religious authorities across the centuries have declared music to be *haram*, or forbidden, but there is nothing in the Qur'an prohibiting music.

Indeed, many supporters of music point to *Sura* 7:32, where God asks, '"Who prohibited the nice things God has created for His creatures, and the good provisions?" Say, "such provisions are to be enjoyed in this life by those who believe"', such as allowing music. Moreover, the *hadiths* that prohibit music, such as in the collection of Abu Dawud, or Bukhari, are not very convincing and are countered by other *hadiths* in Abu Muslim and Bukhari too, in which the Prophet clearly supports the performance of music, at least during feasts and as long as the music does not advocate or encourage unlawful activities.[9]

It is ultimately this latter caveat which Muslim critics of music focus on in their condemnations of the practice. As with Christian opponents of rock 'n' roll, they assume that the sensual, emotional and spiritual power of music divert attention away from worshipping God at all times and therefore lead to sin and even apostasy. Particularly if one is talking about young people performing styles of music, such as Death or Black metal, that are often labeled 'Satanic' in the West, it is not surprising that religious authorities—and governments trying to demonstrate their support for 'Islamic values'—would go after metalheads and others whose music and lyrics can seem obnoxious and even anti-social, at least for the uninitiated. Indeed, this sentiment led to a series of 'Satanic metal affairs' in the late 1990s and 2000s, in which metalheads and musicians in Egypt, Morocco, Lebanon and Iraq were arrested and in some cases convicted of being Satanists on the pretext of their love of heavy metal music.[10]

While there are some Middle Eastern metal or rock bands that do sing about decidedly un-Islamic subjects, the majority of artists I have encountered touch on topics such as war, lack of freedom, oppression and other themes common to extreme metal around the globe, which reflect issues most Muslims are dealing with. And they do so in a manner that either does not touch upon religion at all, or sympathizes with many of the issues being dealt with in the current generation of religiously-grounded activists.

The place of Middle Eastern heavy metal or other forms of extreme music within the framework of contemporary Islamic belief and practice is not unique. Within the genre of seemingly non-religious heavy metal, the British pioneering metal band, Black Sabbath, which is cited by almost every metal band in the region as their most important influence, featured strongly religious themes in their lyrics. Farther afield (at least aesthetically), the well-known southern country-rock band Drive-by Truckers have positioned themselves against the basic assumptions of Evangelical Christianity, offering instead a socially subversive 'redneck liberation theology' that is quite similar to the phenomenon of heavy metal in the Muslim world: both represent a 'a music of necessity', one that both challenges authority and affirms their lifestyle.[11] The simultaneous affirmation of life against, and at the same time challenging, perceived oppression share many similarities with the process of counter-identity formation practiced by Islamist movements that are crucial to combating the pervasive lack of faith in the future and attendant nihilism—or worse, the nihilistic utopianism underlying the ideologies and psychological appeal of groups like al-Qaeda—against which both groups struggle in the context of continued social, political, economic and international conflict.

Perhaps it is this new way of approaching the long-standing problem of nihilism—or at least hopelessness—that defines what Asaf Bayat and many other scholars term the 'post-Islamist' attitude, in which as both a condition and project, Islamists become more self-critical, willing to question their own assumptions and ideology, and to engage in dialogue with those who were once considered adversaries, if not infidels. Both metalheads and the younger generation of religiously-grounded activists are, to varying degrees following the Nietzschean vocation of 'cultural physician', whose goal is to heal, or at least ameliorate the symptoms of the disease of nihilism.[12]

The difference between the German philosopher and his contemporary counterparts in the Muslim world is that Nietzsche assumed that nihilism could only be cured by finding more resonant 'spiritual deceptions' that would energize the sick and decaying; for both the metalheads and the Islamists, the communities they have imagined and are trying to create must be grounded in a much more coherent and self-evident 'truth' that can challenge, and for activists, transform, the political and social status quo.[13]

## Dispatches From the New Islamist Undergrounds

My encounters with young religious activists and heavy metal musicians in the Middle East and North Africa have led me to question how the emergence of a new 'post-' Islamist social dynamic is experienced on the ground.[14] In almost all cases, what makes the people and situations I have encountered 'new', 'post-' or 'beyond' the traditional boundaries of what scholars describe as 'Islamism' (that is, religiously-grounded politics or social activism) is that they involve a redefinition of Islam and Muslim practice in which the bona fides of a particular action or belief from an orthodox Islamic legal or theological perspective is no longer the primary criterion for judging whether it is properly 'Islamic'.

Today, as Tariq Ramadan has declared, 'what is good for the world must be good for Islam, and what is bad for the world and its people can no longer be considered good for Islam'.[15] In other words, the participants in this study have situated Islam within a globalized, ecumenical context that sees the fate of Muslims strongly tied to the fate of the entire world.

One of the most powerful and important examples of the rise of post or new Islamism has emerged in Egypt, which since the late nineteenth century, is one of the chief centers of political Islam in the Arab world. For most of this period, Egyptian Islamism has been both quite conservative and in opposition to the Egyptian state. But beginning in the 1990s a new brand of Islamism emerged, what some Arab commentators have taken to calling 'air-conditioned Islam' that is, the consumer friendly, individualistic Islam of the rising, Western-educated bourgeoisie of Egypt and other Muslim countries.[16] This new, less scripturalist (but not Sufi) Islam, whose leading exponents include the likes of Egyptian television Imam Amr Khaled, focuses on issues such as increasing wealth and personal fulfillment as much (in many cases, more than) on veiling or other 'traditional' markers of Islamic morality. They are often simultaneously politically liberal and socially conservative, and began to coalesce more powerfully at the time that the Brotherhood decided to become fully engaged in the political process; a moment when ultra conservative and even violent forms of Islamism had become increasingly prominent, and against whom the Brotherhood and other members of the so-called *'wassatiyya'*, or moderate school, needed to define themselves.

This slow evolution achieved a milestone in 2005, when the Brotherhood won an unprecedented eighty-eight seats in the Egyptian Parliament. This victory, however, produced significant fear among more secular-minded Egyptians, and even more so among the political elite, who worried that the movement was poised to achieve a dangerous level of political and social power. Yet even as most Brotherhood parliamentarians displayed a high level of discipline, professionalism and relative moderation, the government rigged the next parliamentary vote, in 2010, to ensure fewer members were elected.

It is precisely the liberalization of the Brotherhood's modus operandi that made it a threat to the regime. This new ideology was on display, without air conditioning, on an unseasonably warm December day when I met Omar (not his real name), the Cairo Bureau Chief of the Brotherhood. Where in conversations a decade or even less in the past, faith and religious issues would often be the chief subject about which 'Islamists' wanted to talk, Omar was eager to talk about the political situation in Egypt and why the Brotherhood was the only group able to take on the system.

'There's no political life here', Omar began. 'The regime goes after everyone who tries to be political. The kids are scared; there's so much fear, censorship, and then self-censorship'. An increasingly popular alternative to direct political or social engagement is, of course, the internet. The problem for Omar was what young people find on the internet or other informal social networks:

They go on the internet, angry and frustrated, looking for an escape, and what do they find? Porn or bin Laden, or both. And those who don't go to extremes often become little more than 'negatively religious.' And Islam can't be just negative. You know, in the old days, before Qutb took over, Ikhwan members used to play *'oud*! We were cultured.

Omar further declared that as far as he was concerned, the Brotherhood had 'gone to Hell' in the 1960s when the movement became increasingly militant. 'It's really the Salafis' fault', he explained, referring to ultra-conservative, orthodox Muslims who base their

actions on what they believe to be the model of the earliest generation of Muslims (and which therefore includes jihad). This was the
first time I had heard an Islamist essentially blame everything on
Islamism, but Omar had not finished: 'And in some ways also al-
Azhar's for not correcting this tendency before it was too late'.

Such is the new or post-Islamism that one starts to become a bit
incredulous at the conversation; in this case a senior Muslim Brotherhood member attacking Salafis, al-Azhar and too much praying.
In a substantive departure from both the tenor and the substance
of over a decade of conversations with Islamic activists, not once
did Omar cite the Qur'an, *hadith* (the sayings of the Prophet
Muhammad that are the second source of Islamic law after the
Qur'an) or famous figures from Islamic history to back up his arguments. Instead, Omar explained: 'What we need to combat people
like them are more freedom of speech, more trained judges, more
human rights'.

The agenda laid out by Omar is in sympathy with that of the
Egyptian left, but Omar dismissed the Left with a wave:

First of all, the Left can't motivate most young people, even if its ideas are
good. More important, we are making up for the clear lack of bravery by
much of the Left... as there are some people, particularly secularists, who
argue that if the choice is between Islamists and dictatorship, they'll
choose dictatorship. Can you believe that?! But it's a false choice.

As important as the substance of Omar's remarks, is the opening
for dialogue with secular Egyptians that it represents. Indeed, such
dialogues are increasingly taking place, and in some cases, such as
within the structure of the umbrella organization Kefaya ('Enough'
in Arabic), which has spearheaded anti-government protests in the
last three years, secular and religious groups are working together
in an unprecedented manner. Making the situation more interesting is that many of the younger leaders of the Kefaya movement—
who are also among Egypt's most prominent bloggers, at the
forefront of creating the emerging public sphere—were and in
some cases remain metalheads, and count their youth spent in the
metal community as being among the factors that shaped their
activism later.[17]

But these developments have yet to convince Egypt's heavy
metal community—at least not the current generation, which is

only now recovering from the vicious attacks on it of the late 1990s 'Satanic metal affair' by government and religious forces—that it should be in dialogue with its generational cohorts across the cultural divide.[18] And so when al-Houbaidy, a young leader of the Muslim Brotherhood and one of the editors of its website, dropped by as I was sitting with several musicians from the metal scene, they immediately became quite uncomfortable and left soon thereafter, even though in many ways their backgrounds were quite similar to his. Indeed, one of them was, like al-Houbaidy, a twenty-five-year-old MBA graduate of the American University of Cairo and worked for an IT company.

As important, all shared the desire to create an alternative yet authentic identity to the one offered by the Mubarak regime and its local and international sponsors. 'But still', Ibrahim offered after they had left, 'they're being naïve. They should know that the movement is more diverse and less strictly hierarchical today. Women are more involved and young members have even started blogs, like 'ana ikhwan' [I'm a Muslim Brother] where they criticize the leadership'.

This younger generation has a radically different approach to politics than has traditionally existed among Islamists in the Muslim world, who have not been very interested in the rights of other oppressed groups in their societies, particularly those that do not follow their conservative views on religion and morality. Such an attitude puts him in direct confrontation with extremist versions of Islam, but also with the 'air-conditioned Islam' that is becoming so popular among the 'yuppie' Egyptians who today are among the Brotherhood's chief recruitment targets. As Ibrahim explains:

Air conditioned Islam is creating a shadow society, a culture of shadows. Take this new advertisement from the Gulf that's regularly on TV. It shows two kids playing on their Playstations when the call to prayer comes. They jump up and while they run to pray and their joysticks stay floating in the air until they come back and pick up right where they left off. What message is this supposed to send? Is this Islam? The Kuwaiti Ministry of Religion [which sponsored the TV spot] has become more secular than the communists!

Perhaps if officially sanctioned Islam is becoming secularized (in al-Houbaidy's view; and other Islamist activists have provided similar examples of this phenomenon), it is less surprising that underground musicians can feel more at home expressing a continuity between their music and religious sensibilities. Indeed, in Egypt their coexistence is epitomized by the teenage sons of the former Egyptian presidential candidate Ayman Nour, who as of spring 1998, remains jailed on what are generally accepted to be trumped up charges of election fraud.

Both in their late teens, Shady and Noor began to play metal in good measure to deal with their father's long and tortuous imprisonment by the Mubarak government (he suffered from several life-threatening ailments while in jail and was ultimately released in 2009 on medical grounds). As they explain it, their music, faith and activism come together thus: 'We listened to metal before our father's arrest, but it helps us deal with the anger since then, and to convert it to useful forms'. These included continuing to fight for their father's release, and being vocal about the abuses of the Mubarak government after that was achieved, while at the same trying to stretch the boundaries of Egyptian pop music.

Shady and Noor are also openly, though not conservatively, religious. Shady's Friday afternoon ritual is to go to *Jumu'a* prayer at the local mosque with his band and then rehearse for four hours. 'We go pray, and then play black metal', he said with a laugh, knowing how that probably sounded to a foreigner.[19] While not universally shared among metalheads, a growing number of musicians and fans are finding space inside their moral and aesthetic universe for rock and religion. Indeed, for many, the dividing line is increasingly hard to find. This becomes even more evident if you attend a metal show, which since late 2008 have again been allowed to take place inside Cairo more or less openly (although not without government/police harassment), and regularly features young hijab-wearing women headbanging beside their male peers, who in some cases stop in at the local mosque before attending a show.

It is also shared by other members of the Egyptian metal scene, including members of the all-female band Mascara (short for 'Massive Scar Era'), or the Oriental metal band Beyond East, both of whose members mix religious and musical devotion with no cognitive dissonance about their combination. As the lead singer of Mascara put it, 'I know why God put me on this earth; to create the first girl's band in the history of Egypt'. A similar dynamic is evident in all the other metal scenes I have come to know, from Morocco to Pakistan.

The question that remains to be answered, or even explored, is whether this still strange admixture heralds a larger cultural rapprochement between the secular and religious forces in Egypt, or whether the government will continue to succeed in dividing, and when necessary, playing, the two poles of Egyptian culture against each other in order to maintain its stranglehold on power.

## Elasticity As a New Islamist Ideal

Despite all the death and destruction he had seen, including that of his wife and numerous friends, Sheikh Anwar al-Ethari remains as committed as ever to working through non-violence and bridge-building to repair his country and build a new future. According to Sheikh Anwar, such an attitude is not unique, although it remains rarely reported in the media. Instead, it is common among the hundreds of his (mostly younger) colleagues who have combined secular and religious educations, and who draw both from Western and Muslim sources to solve the myriad problems facing their communities.

'I won't give up', he explains, 'I can't give up. If we believe in God we can say God is with us, not with terrorists; God is with peace, He's the biggest power in the universe. You can't say you're scared if you're Muslim because God said He will protect those fighting for justice or reward them if they die'. This sounds like the discourse of jihad, I suggested. 'Yes, but the good jihad! Even after my wife died, within a week I was rebuilding my area, cleaning my neighborhood of cluster bombs with my own hands, because if I didn't, the children would find and play with them. This is jihad'.

Sheikh Anwar's intellectual and theological 'elasticity' represents an important development among younger religious scholars—Sunni as well as Shi'i: a willingness to combine traditional religious training with so-called 'modern' or 'Western' educations. This is not the same thing as the well-established phenomenon of Islamist movements being founded by or populated with secular/Western educated middle-class members (such as, mostly, lawyers, scientists, engineers and doctors). In most cases they were lay people; the phenomenon discussed here specifically involves what could be termed 'religious professionals'—that is, scholars who have completed a significant course of advanced religious training and are qualified to hold official positions in the religious system (for example, as imams of mosques or *ulama*).

A Sunni parallel became apparent during a 2007 trip through Pakistan when I was invited to deliver several lectures at the International Islamic University in Islamabad, which since 1980 has been one of the most important centers of advanced religious study in the country. The University explicitly based its mandate on the 'Islamic awakening' in the 'postcolonial world'. The allusion to postcoloniality was not what was most interesting about the university. Instead, it was the task that the professors and graduate students had set before themselves. The former are designing and the latter pursuing an innovative curriculum that is combining 1,000 years of Islamic learning with the latest developments in American and European scholarship.

Most of my time was spent speaking with the PhD students in comparative religion. From their 'traditional' looking clothing and beards, one would imagine that they were closer in philosophy to the Taliban than to students of Pakistan's secular universities. But as is so often the case, appearances are deceiving. As soon as pleasantries had been exchanged, the students explained that they are all learning Hebrew, as well as biblical criticism and contemporary approaches to religious studies as part of their course work. They had little time or desire to engage in spirited critiques of the United States or the West; they were much more interested in discussing how to better integrate 'Western' and Islamic methodologies for studying history and religion, and more troubling, how to criticize the government 'without disappearing' into the dark hole of the Pakistani prison system for five or ten years, or worse.

This openness by a surprising number of young religious students is reflected in the powerful link between religion and music in Pakistan, particularly through Qawwali music, whose superstars like the late Nusrat Fatah Ali Khan have achieved world renown, and have influenced the creation of the genre of 'Sufi Rock' by platinum-selling artists such as Junoon, and today, groups like

Aaroh. For these artists there is no separation between religion and music; following in the Sufi tradition, both are viewed as key to healing society at large. Salman Ahmad, founder of Junoon (considered the 'U2 of Asia') has received death threats from extremists because of his activities, which include traveling to mosques in rural areas and singing verses from the Qur'an with the accompaniment of his guitar. For Ahmad, bridging the gap between musicians and mullahs is crucial to addressing the larger rifts in Pakistani society.[20]

Ahmad's good friend and former band mate, Junaid Jamshed, adds another dimension to this dynamic. Once the brightest star in Pakistani music, almost a decade ago Jamshed turned his back on music and became deeply religious (he also started a very successful clothing company). Yet while Jamshed firmly believes that music is in fact *haram*, he refuses to condemn his former colleagues and still supports their artistic efforts:

You can't try to impose your views on anyone. That's when power comes into the equation, and then oppression and resentment. People need to come to this realization themselves. Look, if I just tell society, 'Don't do this!' they will be flabbergasted. 'What the Hell is this guy talking about?' 'Who is he, a musician, to tell me music is *haram*,' etc. You must give them a better alternative. If I don't have a better alternative, I shouldn't tell them to stop or leave something... So I just try to offer my example and support everyone on their path.

Jamshed makes frequent *da'wa* tours around Pakistan, in which he travels around preaching his views of Islam to as many people as possible. These trips have brought him very close to the grass roots of Pakistani society, which led me to wrongly assume that he was quite pessimistic about the future of his country:

Yes, there's a lot of pain, suffering and poverty, but I'll tell you something, Mark, I'm optimistic. The other people you mention aren't optimistic because they don't have the answer. I do, and the answer is God. We just need to return to Him, and be willing to listen to others, and talk, and the rest will follow. And until then, Pakistan, the US, the whole world, will be disintegrating and disgruntled. It's that simple.

This attitude reflects the kind of 'project identity' that is at the core of the more progressive strand of the 'new' or 'post-' Islamist thinking—open, tolerant of different views, activist, and ultimately political, although often not as openly as the example of the Muslim Brotherhood would suggest. As Jamshed explains, 'If you preach too hard [that is, overtly political], people will refuse to listen. I'm an artist at the end of the day, and I have to think like one. If you want to tell people something this difficult you have to sugar coat it'. Of course, 'sugar-coated' is the last adjective most listeners would use to describe the kind of extreme metal Jamshed clearly believes is not Islamic, regardless of its intentions. But the attempt to use cultural expression to bring to light harder truths does reflect a similar sense of how to get people to confront basic problems in their society.

Given the high level of political violence in Pakistan, it is logical for someone like Jamshed to assume that the sugar of music might help the medicine of serious and likely painful political, economic and social reform 'go down' a little bit easier, or at least seem more acceptable. This view is not universally shared by Islamist activists; across the Muslim world, in Morocco, the main opposition movement, Adl wal-Ihsan (Justice and Spirituality Association, or JSA), also refrain from attacking artists on a regular basis, but the same cannot be said for the positions of the movement's leadership towards the government and even the monarchy. Like Egypt, Lebanon and Iran, Morocco has had its own 'Satanic metal affair', this one in 2003, when fourteen metal musicians and fans were arrested, tried and convicted of various crimes because of their devotion to the music. What makes Morocco unique, however, is that the metalheads fought back vigorously, waging a major campaign in the public sphere that brought thousands of supporters into the streets and international support, particularly from the French press.

In one of the few such victories anywhere in the Muslim world, the young metalheads won the battle, as all the verdicts were overturned, and within a couple of years the government and even the King himself were sponsoring heavy metal festivals with tens of thousands of fans, at which local and international bands performed. Even all-female metal bands have made their mark in Morocco (as have female rappers), most notably the group Mystik Moods, who became famous with their breakthrough performance at the 2005 Boulevard des Jeunes Musiciens festival in Casablanca.

Mystik Moods is perhaps the seminal all-girl metal group in the Muslim world, anticipating Egypt's Mascara by at least three years. The idea of an all-girl thrash metal band achieving a following in Morocco—indeed, becoming a favorite of the women of the royal family—is interesting in its own right. But the band's views on religion and music are equally telling. As one of the band's singers, Ritz, explained to me, 'Some people want to show off their religion, but you know what, not everyone. Look at my father, he prays *and* loves music too. In fact, he's doing the sound for the festival!' Indeed, all the band members have family members and friends who were 'traditionally' religious, and none of them were against their music.

For the band, their acceptance demonstrates, as Mystik Mood's other lead singer, Rita, put it, that 'in Morocco women have more opportunities because our regime is more liberal than in other Arab countries'. Bass player Kenza continued:

This country is always moving, on the way to developing. You know, they say that tradition and modernity are supposed to be contradictory, that if they become more globalized or Westernized young people automatically become more European and renounce their tradition. But this is a false idea of what religion and tradition are.

Perhaps, although nothing in the dress, language or attitudes of the members of Mystik Moods says that they incorporate Islam into their lives very much. As the band's guitarist, Anaïs, added: 'Young people are torn between two trends, two kinds of extremes. On the one side are young people who listen to everything Western, and on the other, they are only religious, they can't be open. But it's wrong to call them "traditional", because tradition is more temperate than this'. Ritz continued, 'You know, young people who like metal also are Muslims and pray'.[21]

At the same time, however, the whole band agreed that it was impossible to get along, or even have a conversation, with religious forces. In a clear dig at the Justice and Spirituality Association (JSA), an Islamist Sufi movement led by Nadia Yassine, she explained, 'The Islamists say, "Yeah, we want democracy and a republic", but what kind? Like Algeria and Iran?' Ultimately, Mystik Moods represent a very political moment in Morocco, but for the group's members the political is most definitely personal: the freedom to dress, act and play how they want.

As we have seen, the distrust by musicians of Islamists is a constant theme across the Muslim world. Yet in Morocco as in Egypt there are many parallels between the two forces. Indeed, the members of Mystik Moods are not the only mystical women in Morocco. Nadia Yassine, 'spokesperson' of the JSA, is the heir to the most important mystical movement in the country. Although not technically outlawed by the government, its members are constantly harassed and its publications largely banned. Indeed, Sheikh Yassine, her father, spent almost two decades under house arrest for writing an open letter to King Hassan II in 1974 calling on him to repent of his autocratic ways. A little over two decades later, his daughter Nadia was indicted by the government for treason for daring to suggest that a republic was perhaps a better form of government for Morocco than the monarchy.

Epitomizing the eclectic epistemological grounding of so many contemporary Islamist thinkers and activists, Yassine, a French teacher by training, is equally at home discussing French poetry, Continental philosophy, the works of Noam Chomsky and Howard Zinn, and the classic texts of *fiqh* and Sufi doctrine. It is not surprising that such a brew would lead the government has branded her a 'witch'—an appellation she's embraced, putting her in the company of Morocco's metalheads, whose music, however, she is not at all fond of.[22]

Yet however wide the cultural and aesthetic gulf between the two, neither the young metalheads nor the young Islamist activists are willing to 'suffer in silence' anymore, and both tend to be loud—the rockers and rappers with blasting music and searing lyrics, Nadia Yassine with her no holds barred attacks on Morocco's political system and her willingness to show up at court with her lips taped shut to demonstrate the government's desire to silence her. As she defiantly explains, 'Witches are witches because they think and act in different ways than other people. When people see a witch behaving differently, they get scared'.[23]

It is not just Yassine—father or daughter—whom the government is scared of, but it is also the JSA and its over two million strong supporters as well. The threat to the system is powerful enough so that the government regularly arrests members who gather in groups of larger than three. Yet the movement continues to hold regular meetings, and uses its strong web presence, which the government has never been able effectively to block in Morocco, to maintain its place as perhaps the most important oppositional force in the country.

Ultimately, while conversations with numerous members of the JSA reveal that most, young and older, are not metal or hip hop fans, neither do they spend any energy working against popular music either. This is, in fact, in sharp contrast to the country's officially tolerated Islamist party, the Justice and Development Party (JDP) that was active in the persecution of metalheads in the 2003 affair, and that continues to lash out at popular music and festivals. Like the Muslim Brotherhood, its Egyptian counterpart, however, the JSA has a lot more to worry about today than policing the musical tastes of young Moroccans.

Yet as in Egypt, in Morocco it seems as if many musicians are actually even less discriminating in their understanding of Moroccan Islamism than the average JSA member is about the differences between the various subgenres of extreme metal. 'That's the problem', one young woman at the meeting explained 'people have no idea what we're about, so [they] accuse us of all types of things or confuse us with other Islamist movements, like the Justice and Development Party, which plays the political game and has members in parliament, but who in fact was the group your friend was so angry at'. And the few times I have offered to set up meetings between metalheads and JSA members, it has always been the former, never the latter, who have told me to forget about it.

## Muhajababes in the Rubble

The debate over the permissibility of music in Islam continues, in mosques and newspapers, and competing *fatwas* issued on the Internet. Some religious scholars, however, have come to agree with Salman Ahmed that the debate over music epitomizes the need to bring greater openness to Islamic thought and practice. Sheikh Ibrahim al-Mardini of Beirut, is one such scholar. Although Sheikh al-Mardini has an advanced degree in theology, he works in a pharmacy to support his family. 'The Dar al-Ifta' [the official body responsible for issuing fatwas and approving Sunni imams] told me it would be better if I stayed away from mosques and madrasas', he said when explaining why he does not have a mosque at which to preach the *khutba*, or Friday prayer sermon, as do most religious scholars with his training.

For al-Mardini music clearly signifies a fault line between an Islam that is open to the world and tolerant, and one that is closed and negative. In his writings he argues that 'there is nothing in the Qur'an that says music should be prohibited. In fact, it can play a positive role in society as long as it's not insulting or offers views against Islam'. His most important work on the subject, titled *al-tibyan fi ahkam il-musiqi wa-l-alhan*,[24] explains that since there is little religious justification for most prohibitions on music, its censorship 'exists mostly to preserve regimes, not Muslim societies of some sort of Islamic personality'.

Sheikh al-Mardini believes that the complete opposition to music by conservatives indicates an even more serious threat to the public sphere in Lebanon. In a factionalist political environment in which a formally democratic system is trumped by the regular use of violence to silence anyone who wants to change the status quo, al-Mardini believes that music, and popular culture more broadly, is one of the few avenues for positively critiquing, and even transcending, the present situation.

Ultimately, for al-Mardini a music culture is necessary for people to develop themselves; any limitation on the arts will encourage the opposite of what a healthy religious system should call for. He believes that Muslims as individuals must make up their own minds about how to interpret religious law, not blindly follow the dictates of scholars. For him, when the Prophet Muhammad said to one of his Companions, 'You came with a very good ear', he meant an ear both for music and for wise political judgment; the two, ultimately, are hard to separate.

Music, according to al-Mardini, is a crucial part of the larger job of Muslims taking their religion and culture into their own hands. Al-Mardini believes that Muslims should engage in the process of returning to their original sources to learn what these sources have to say about music, rather than relying on what 'religious leaders' or 'learned men' dictate regarding these matters. Such a process has been occurring for over a century; if the downside of 'opening up the Gates of *Ijtihad*' is that Osama bin Laden (who has no religious training) can offer *fatwa*s, or religious degrees, justifying mass murder, the upside is that over one billion other Muslims are entering the public sphere and slowly taking the future of their societies into their own hands.

But the opening of the Muslim public sphere to people outside the religious and political establishment is both inevitable and crucial for the future of Islam, as it has been for Christianity and Judaism. In the same way that it allows seemingly marginal religious thinkers to reshape the contours of Islam, it allows musicians to claim a space in which a different vision of Lebanon can be articulated. As al-Mardini explained, 'Religion and cultural reform don't just come with other reforms, they're crucial to them. That's why it's better for all of them if everyone stays asleep, lazy and humiliated'.

This is also precisely why people like Moe Hamzeh, the lead singer of the Lebanese heavy rock group The Kordz, as well as Sheikh al-Mardini, and numerous other activists (including many of the more progressive people inside Hezbollah), need to be kept marginalized from the larger, national debates. Moe Hamzeh explains succinctly:

Power always wants the status quo, not reform… it's the role of culture to force those questions on their leaders, and it's the goal of leaders to stop these questions from being asked. And we're more important than ever because the gap between intellectuals and rest of society is growing, and benefits the *sulta*, [the powers running society], much. Society is lazy, system is lazy, music can't be lazy.[25]

*Conclusion: Forging the Weapon of the Future—Popular Culture and the Public Sphere in the MENA*

Not long before his death in 1997, the famed Nigerian musician Fela Kuti proclaimed that 'music is the weapon of the future'.[26] Having fought against the oppression and corruption of the Nigerian government for over two decades, Kuti knew very well that music or musicians could not change their societies alone. But he also understood that few attempts at large scale social and political change succeed unless they are grounded in popular culture, and where artists help shape the discourse of resistance and change.

From a very different starting point, Frankfurt School pioneer Theodor Adorno, argued that it was not politics, but art, and particularly music, through which a critical voice could posit an 'otherwise' to the 'present' and offer a different vision for the future.[27] For Adorno, it was the modern classical music of Schoenberg, Webern and Berg that had the power to illuminate the 'absurd, blindly violent element of the system' and reveal the 'truths behind reality's masks'.[28] Such illumination was at the core of the kind of 'immanent critique' practiced by the Frankfurt School and first elaborated by Hegel, who saw it as a 'pathway of doubt, or more precisely as the way of despair'.[29]

Today, extreme forms of rock, which in terms of dissonance and often atonality and sonic force are not only very much the descendants of the music Adorno held so dear, but are also among the most powerful locations for such an 'immanent critique' of society, balancing often brutal analysis with a refusal to succumb either to the violence and nihilism of their doppelgangers who profess extreme religious belief and praxis, or the uncritical consumerism of the majority of their peers. In so doing, they are not just musical performances, or more critically, performance art, but equally 'performance philosophy'. If the task of philosophy is to 'reliquify' 'congealed' ideological thought,[30] the force of the blast beats, guitar armies and brutal screams of the heavy metal performed and heard around the MENA have a similar power to liquefy, or at least shake up, their frozen political and social systems. As one of the founders of the Iranian metal scene put it to me, 'It's hard to understand how music about death can affirm life'. Similarly, Shady Nour explains, 'When I'm on the stage, I don't have any weapons, I only have my voice'.[31]

In truth, Nour and his musical comrades from Morocco to Pakistan have more than just their voices, guitars or drums. Their music, much of which constitutes an innovative blend of Euro-American metal and indigenous styles, instruments and sounds, can be understood not merely as a hybrid of cultures and genres, but in fact a kind of post-hybridity; a deeper hybridity that moves beyond the surface hybridities of more commercialized cultural and sonic intermixing that characterizes the more well-known and commodified forms of 'world music' (from which Middle Eastern heavy metal, and the genre more broadly, are largely excluded) and which tend to obscure the continuing imbalances in power involved in musical meetings of East and West.

Not only does the hybridity of the metal scenes in the Middle East not lose the centrality of imbalanced power that shape them—indeed, that is one of the most important generators of the music—but it is also precisely in the groups and scenes where critiques of power and its abuses are most present that the sonic hybridity is more innovative and revealing of new identities that transcend both East and West towards something more holistic and positive.[32] It is likely for this reason, among others, that Bruce Dickinson, lead singer of the group Iron Maiden (one of the most popular metal bands in the world with a huge fan base in the MENA) declared to me that the next Iron Maiden or Led Zeppelin might just as likely appear in Cairo or Karachi as in London or New York.[33]

Ultimately, the dynamics of the metal and larger extreme music scenes across the MENA reveal more than just the mutual embeddedness of art and politics, but equally point to the implicate relationship between the public sphere and popular culture. That is, how popular culture can serve as a crucial site for the performance of 'publicness' when the more formal locations, such as newspapers and other media, clubs and associations of civil society, are too heavily monitored or policed to allow for free expression and exchange of ideas, identities and visions by all classes of society.

This understanding of the public sphere and its relationship to popular culture, and to music in particular, challenges the model of the public sphere developed by Habermas, who largely ignored non-bourgeois, or 'plebian' publics while dismissing as episodic and 'ephemeral' the community and solidarity created by musical gatherings such as rock concerts. While feminists and subaltern historians have largely succeeded in demonstrating the problematic nature of his exclusion of women, workers or minorities from the public sphere on both empirical and normative grounds, few if any scholars have attempted to ensure that music and popular cultural scenes (so-called sub- or counter-cultures) also receive adequate attention by scholars of the public sphere.[34]

Similar to the role of the press within the larger public sphere in societies in the midst either of evolving into nation-states or turning against colonial rule, music today can play a dual role as simultaneously a 'popular' and 'public' text, and as a site of both 'buffering' between societies and governments and when necessary resistance of the former against the latter. Where traditional media are not free and pop music or culture more broadly coopted or overly commodified, music scenes can perform 'agenda-setting functions' vis-à-vis larger public discourses and, at least for their members, become 'leaders of public opinion', defenders of the 'people's cause' and even sound the 'revolutionary tones' against the sclerotic and oppressive existing order.[35]

To play this role, however, music and the metal scenes described in this chapter in particular, have to function as one location in a larger field of interaction between various sections of society—from religious to secular, bourgeois to working class, too old to rock 'n' roll, to too young fully to comprehend the political implications of their aesthetic choices. As societies across the MENA become increasingly frayed it is difficult to discern who can forge the kinds of relationships that would be necessary for such publics to force governments and economic elites to democratize. Moe Hamzeh, lead singer of the Kordz, put it this way:

When I was in college, I had many friends in Hizbullah. They'd tease me for being a rocker but we got along because we respected each other's views and gave each other space to express them and be who were were. But today more and more kids go to these new sectarian colleges and never meet Lebanese from outside their communities. How can they learn to trust, or even tolerate difference in such an environment?

For every Sheikh Anwar or Mardini and musician like Hamzeh Shady Nour, there are far more divisive figures that have even greater access to the public spheres within their societies and across the Arab/Muslim world. Ultimately, the answer to Hamzeh's question may well determine whether the rising generation of young people, not just in Lebanon, but across the MENA, can build a future that transcends the problems of the past, or whether instead the future will continue to repeat the past, with tragic results for the Muslim world and for the world at large.

10

# BEYOND ISLAMISM AT WORK

## CORPORATE ISLAM IN MALAYSIA

*Patricia Sloane-White*

In the mid-1990s, I attended a religious event in Kuala Lumpur, Malaysia; a *do'a*. Malay Muslims translate *do'a* as a supplication or prayer of thanks. This *do'a* occurred on a grand scale, held at the newly-built palatial house of a well-known Malay Muslim[1] entrepreneur. Many of Malaysia's most important Muslim political and corporate figures were invited, and so, too, was a well-known *ustaz*—a leader of a conservative *dakwah* or evangelical Muslim group with ties to the Islamic opposition party—and a band of his follower-students. Invitees had been informed that this *do'a* was an opportunity for the entrepreneur to publicly affirm and give thanks for his enormous good fortune. His fortune had indeed been bountiful. His honorific title of 'Dato' had recently been upgraded to 'Tan Sri'—in Malaysia this means he went from 'sir' to 'lord', a designation that can only be given by the sultan who rules as king.[2] Tan Sri Hassan, as he will be referred to in this chapter,[3] was also one of the most successful, philanthropic, and politically-connected corporate figures in this dynamic, Muslim-majority Southeast Asian nation. He had not long ago passed his fortieth year, entering a stage of life which for Muslims is an age for self reflection. As will be described further on in this chapter, he felt himself undergoing, in his words, a kind of 'spiritual transformation'.

The *d'oa* took place under enormous white tents in the garden of Tan Sri Hassan's enormous house. A stage with microphones was set up for the *ustaz*. Glittering chandeliers hung from the tent roof and guests were seated at tables cooled by electric fans that hummed overhead. At one end of the garden was a gazebo where hundreds of roses filled a Ming-style vase the size of a barrel, their sweet fragrance drifting into the crowd. BMWs, Mercedes and even a Bentley were being parked by attendants in the driveway. Servants laid enormous platters of food on long buffet tables. The *ustaz* led lengthy Qur'anic prayers, and later, during the feast, his band of followers, which was literally a band, sang verses to the beat of *kompang* drums, and performed *dikir barat*, a traditional Malay syncopation sometimes labeled 'Muslim rap'.[4] As they performed, Tan Sri Hassan wandered among the guests describing his gratitude to Allah for the gifts that had been bestowed upon him, weeping visibly as he spoke of his plans to now pass his blessings on to others.

For many years, I have followed this wealthy and highly positioned entrepreneur's personal, religious, and career trajectory,[5] but I begin this rendition with his transformative *do'a*. He had emerged in the early 1990s as one of the most successful and valorized of the Malay Muslim corporate leaders. Malaysia experienced extraordinary economic growth from the 1980s onward during the period known as the Mahathir era, the twenty-two years in power of Prime Minister Mahathir Mohamad (1981–2003); Tan Sri Hassan, like nearly all of the ascendant Malay Muslim corporate stars of that era, was a vigorous supporter of Mahathir and (although he denied its implications of corruption and cronyism) a direct recipient of massive political patronage from the ruling party.[6] In the early 1990s, entrepreneurs I knew like Tan Sri Hassan were the embodiment of Malaysia's dynamic economic and religious trajectory—who, as *bumiputeras*, were the ethnic recipients of ethnically-focused economic development programs like the New Economic Policy and the National Development Policy,[7] and as Muslims, participated in the enhanced spiritual observance that was transforming Malaysian Islam at the time. When I first met him in 1993, he was running a massive conglomerate linked to the ruling party, with direct access to the special tenders, licenses and subsidies provided to Malay Muslims alone. Today he remains a key player in Malaysia's economy, and, as will be described in this chapter, a key player in its vaunted Islamic economy as well.

The Mahathir era is known not only for its aggressive economic development policies targeted at uplifting the Malay Muslim ethnic group,[8] but also for its ever-escalating Islamization policies: the establishment and expansion of Islamic institutions, Islamic public culture, and the Islamic judiciary. Tan Sri Hassan, like many professional and urban Malay Muslims, had eagerly adopted a more Islamic lifestyle during the first decade of the Mahathir era, in which it was increasingly common to observe Malay Muslims actively participating in prayer groups and going to the mosque, going to *hajj*, adopting more pious dress and so on. It is conventional wisdom in scholarship on Malaysia to characterize Islamization in the Mahathir era (and since then, as the same ruling party remains in power) primarily as a consequence of political battles between the ruling ethnic/nationalist Malay party, the United Malays National Organization (UMNO) and the Islamist opposition party, Parti-al-Islam Se-Malaysia (PAS). Norani Othman describes UMNO as 'entangled with an unending "Islamist policy auction" in which, at any time, PAS can, and often does, "raise the stakes"'.[9] But Islamization or Islamism in the Mahathir era or since then among UMNO supporters and clients cannot be fully understood as mere Mahathirism, prime-ministerial polemic hyper-reactions to PAS's 'Islamist' politics. For in the telling of their own spiritual experiences and in the expression of their own pieties, many Malay Muslims I knew in the Mahathir era had deeply-held Islamist ideals and agendas of their own, even when they did not transfer their votes and political support to PAS.

My earlier research on capitalist lives among the group I have termed the economic 'virtuosi'—the most successful, valorized, and paradigmatic of the Malay Muslim entrepreneurs to emerge from Malaysia's period of rapid economic growth since the 1980s—had demonstrated their tendency to keep Islamism at arm's length while claiming to be newly, deeply, but most often privately pious. But at Tan Sri Hassan's VIP *do'a*, it appeared that something new was emerging in his religious experience. Just as it was every

Malay Muslim entrepreneur's dream in the mid-1990s to 'go public'—that is, to offer their privately held company shares in an IPO or 'initial public offering' on the KLSE or Kuala Lumpur Stock Exchange—now, too, was this corporate leader 'going public' with a new kind of piety, one that was corporate in orientation and, as I shall argue, was Islamism of its own discursive kind.

This chapter takes Tan Sri Hassan's 1996 'transformation' as a way to consider, via one prominent business man's endeavor, what are perhaps overlooked trends and dimensions of Islamism. Using three cases that explore Tan Sri Hassan's plans for reshaping corporate and capitalist life via Islam, the ways in which one Malay Muslim economic virtuoso sought to 'rebrand' Malaysian Islamism into a global corporate force will be highlighted in this chapter. While Tan Sri Hassan's point of view was perhaps novel in 1996, I will argue that it foreshadowed a key aspect of Malaysian Islam today, where the role of Islam both in everyday life and in institutional settings has been heightened not only as a consequence of the broadening of the reach of Islamic law and the Islamic bureaucracy,[10] but also by the impact of what I call 'corporate Islam'.

## Islam and Economy in Malaysia

In the 1980s and 1990s, Prime Minister Mahathir Mohamad promoted 'Islamic values' in governance and social policies. He expanded the reach and power of Islamic institutions, built Islamic universities and broadened the Islamic curriculum in schools. With Donald Trump-like exuberance, Mahathir strove to Islamize Malaysia's capitalist economy as well. He set up committees and organizations to ensure that no development policies in Malaysia would run counter to Islamic values,[11] held conferences on Islamic banking and Islamic financing in Malaysia, and sponsored the full emergence of its Islamic economy. By the mid-1990s, Malaysia was innovating in all sectors of Islamic finance, including Islamic insurance, an Islamic debt market offering the world's first *sukuk* or Islamic bonds, and Islamic leasing contracts known as *ijara*, until, for all practical purposes, Malaysia could claim to have a booming parallel Islamic financial system alongside its booming conventional one.[12] Mathathir wanted to make Malaysia the global center of the Islamic economy, tilting the balance of financial power away from the Arab world to its banks.[13]

In the mid-1990s, the Malay Muslim entrepreneurs I knew were increasingly well-positioned in UMNO political circles and financially secure. They saw vast spiritual meaning in the material world. As they bought houses in the new housing developments in and around Kuala Lumpur, imported foreign cars, ate in Western-style restaurants, and networked their computers and businesses to the Malaysian multimedia super-corridor, they described their good fortune as *barakah*—blessings from Allah—and their economic lives as contributing to *fard kifayah*, the collective social good of the *umma*. They made repeat pilgrimages to Mecca, increased their *zakat* contributions, refinanced interest-based loans with *halal* ones, dabbled in *sukuk* but invested the lion's share of their assets in *bumiputera* IPOs and government-linked companies listed on the Kuala Lumpur Stock Exchange, and discussed the Islamic merits of Malaysia's dynamic economic growth and the global vendibility of its Islamic financial sector. Malay Muslim entrepreneurs saw themselves as increasingly Islamic business people. This self-reflection was precisely what Tan Sri Hassan described as his 'religious transformation'. And now he intended to transform others.

I learned at Tan Sri Hassan's *do'a* that the *kurta*-and-*serban*-wearing *ustaz* and his band of followers were not merely there to lead the prayers and solemnize the occasion, but that Tan Sri had also been intensively studying with the *ustaz*. Before the prayers began, he described to me how he had recently left the major conglomerate of which he had been chief executive and was starting a new one, more deeply mindful of what he 'had to give back' in Allah's world to others. He was focusing now, he said, on what the *ustaz* could teach him about his duty to others in relation to his business and work life and in his role as a prominent industrialist.

Tan Sri Hassan had often made it clear in the past that he believed he could best discover his Islamic purpose through his individual and private economic actions led by ethical principles. Now he was imagining a more public and outward role for his Islam, to be realized best, he said, through his work. And then he invited me to visit his new offices, where he was now the chief executive of what he described as his new, Islamically-oriented corporation, where Islam 'determined everything'.

## Corporatizing Islam

Several days later, I visited his new company in Petaling Jaya, a burgeoning, modern township next to Kuala Lumpur within the massive conurbation called the Klang Valley, Malaysia's booming industrial corridor. He welcomed me into his office, at the very top of the building, which featured, at one end, a stone wall with orchids, small trees, and a tiny fountain. 'This is in honor of the Prophet's garden', he told me, referring to the description of the beauty of water and flowers as described in Qur'anic verses.[14] I had been in similarly 'Islamized' offices before in Malaysia; his former office at a huge UMNO-aligned conglomerate had not been one of them. He described how much more time he now allowed in his day for reflection and prayer. Motioning to me to sit, he told me about his new venture.

It was the financial arm of a charitable foundation, which he was intent to build into a highly profitable 'Islamic corporation'. It would, in the words of Tan Sri, 'do good and do well' on behalf of other Muslims and the nation at large by funding the 'good works' of the charity and working towards national development. It would support the needs of a new kind of society in Malaysia, where Islam benefitted Muslims and non-Muslims alike. So, too, was it like his previous conglomerate, an ascendant company at the very top-most reaches of the Malaysian political economy, funded by profits from projects that were directly or indirectly tied to the UNMO-led government's own development plans via the politi-cian whose interests it served. Its portfolio of national development projects was enormous—including bridges, power plants, shop-ping malls, five-star hotels, resorts, and housing projects on prime real estate on the Malaysian Peninsula. The foundation owned property in the top locations around the country, and through the work of the corporation, was primed, he said, to become one of the major developers of new communities and businesses, ventures as widespread as high-technology aviation manufacturing and food distribution, and residential properties that serviced everyone from low-cost populations to high-end tourists.

Tan Sri Hassan took a book from a shelf and laid it on the table in front of me. It was Edmund T. Gomez's *Political Business: Corpo-rate Involvement of Malaysian Political Parties*, a key text which explores the political-economic nexus in Malaysia, in which Tan Sri Hassan had been described as one of the major corporate beneficiaries of UMNO-based political patronage. 'I have been this in the past', he said, 'but I am not this now'. Referring to the early and mid-1990s as the 'get-Malays-rich-quick-era' in which he said he was focused on 'enriching myself, my family, and other Malays fast', he now saw a 'new era' of corporate change, in which 'Malays could work harmoniously and side by side with the other ethnic groups in Malaysia ... with the Chinese in China ... with Indians in India ... and, of course, with the West'. He said the era of 'privileging ethnic interests was coming to an end' with the new millennium,[15] but that a new era of Islamic-minded business was emerging. It could benefit not just the 'three ethnic groups in Malaysia', he believed, but could change the face and nature of modern capitalism everywhere. 'Islam holds the model for how we can do that', he insisted. 'And', he paused, 'perhaps you can help me'. With that, Tan Sri Hassan asked me to work for him. Thus was began my period of extraordinary access to this extraordinarily successful man and his exploration of Islamic capitalism.

## The Work of an Islamic Corporation

Complimenting what he called my anthropological 'sensitivity to Malay and Muslim culture' and business background (I had spent nearly a decade working on Wall Street, experience that was valued in Malaysia and allowed me, as I have described elsewhere to 'talk business' with men like Tan Sri Hassan),[16] he suggested that I could observe him, listen to his ideas, watch him develop this special new company that worked to fulfill the mission of a charitable Muslim foundation, and document some of the Islamic management philosophies that he was elaborating along the way. I could help him focus his thoughts as he outlined the key concepts for an Islamic management 'how-to' book that he intended to write when he retired. He suggested that I also help find worthy charitable and cultural projects to support with corporate funds, the way corporate philanthropists do in America. I could have a desk and a computer in his building.[17] Beyond that, he said, I could have access to his company to study any aspects of what he called its 'Islamic corporate culture' that I wanted.

I did not hesitate to accept his offer. Clerics and scholars in Malaysia were, at the time, sponsoring conferences and seminars at the International Islamic University Malaysia and writing voluminously about 'Islamic business culture',[18] but little research concerning the application of Islamic values and norms in everyday contemporary Malay Muslim business life had yet been conducted, and indeed, on-the-ground research on the role of Islamic teachings or practices in modern corporations is still relatively uncharted territory.[19]

For the next six months, I worked in Tan Sri Hassan's office, learning about the various business divisions and subsidiaries of the company as well as many of the projects and investments in its portfolio. Many of the people in the company were new, learning their jobs and exploring their role in the company's future. In this Islamically-oriented company were several key managers who were non-Muslims, a feature that was uncommon in many of the Malay-Muslim-owned companies I had studied in the past. The chief financial officer was an Indian; the office manager and a few other vital corporate employees were Chinese. There was also a handful of Muslim foreigners working in the company, including several Iraqi and Iranian engineers—for, as Tan Sri Hassan said, 'we must build bridges across the Muslim world'. But there were also several Western consultants under his employ, people like myself, who he believed added important perspectives of their own. He referred to himself as an equal among them, not a CEO who stood at the helm, but a 'facilitator', diminishing what he called the power of hierarchy in the organization and accentuating his eagerness to share his corporate role with other experts. More than once I heard him in deep conversation on the telephone with the *ustaz* who had led the *do'a*, discussing stories of the early Caliphs of Islam, whom he frequently described as 'delegators' not 'bosses', ever conscious of the perspectives of others.

As I learned about the jobs and responsibilities of the managers of the company's divisions, Tan Sri Hassan plotted them out for me into what he called an Islamically-ordered organizational chart, where each manager was considered an 'expert leader' who could speak on behalf of his group. And each manager I spoke to concurred with this characterization, describing the freedom and

openness of their jobs, where they were able to function independently to solve corporate problems and strategize solutions that
Tan Sri Hassan would welcome. Sometimes I was invited in with
these managers when they met with Tan Sri Hassan to explore new
areas for potential investment. Often they consulted with the *ustaz*
with whom Tan Sri Hassan was studying and other *Shari'a* experts
on the suitability of projects and financing. In their view, there
seemed to be no end to the possibilities for growth, both in terms
of the company's endeavors and in Tan Sri Hassan's vision of creating an ideal Islamic environment for a global capitalist future.

To better understand the nature and significance of what he and
his employees agreed was being sought after, innovated, and
achieved in this setting, I turn now to three episodes of Tan Sri
Hassan's Islamic corporate culture in action.

## Corporate Shura

Early one business day, I was summoned from my office to the
office of Tan Sri Hassan. He was staring out the window, where the
chimneys of Klang Valley's factories were visible just over the tree
tops, repeating over and again, 'How could this happen? What do
we do?' Several senior executives were standing nearby, grim-
faced and silent. His senior-most manager ushered me to a chair
and then described that the day before, there had been a physical
assault of a junior engineer who worked in another building. The
victim was a man named Abdullah. While the details were unclear,
the attacker was said to be the husband of a high-ranking female
project manager in the same office, a Muslim woman named Mariam. According to Mariam's secretary, who had been questioned
after the incident by co-workers, Abdullah had made sexually provocative comments to Mariam. Mariam apparently had summoned
her husband; he had beaten up Abdullah. Both parties had apparently filed police reports against the other.

'This is a crisis of the utmost seriousness', Tan Sri Hassan now
pronounced grimly. He was concerned about a scandal tainting the
reputation of a politically well-connected and, in his reckoning,
Islamically-structured corporation like his. He was deeply concerned that such a crisis, demonstrating volatile, threatening, and

explosive relationships among his employees, would be destructive to the atmosphere of openness, well-being, and warmth he believed characterized the Islamic corporate culture he was seeking to create.

Now Tan Sri Hassan described to the people in his office the concept of the *shura*, in which the Prophet Muhammad engaged in mutual consultation and discussion with others. A *shura* ideally includes people with different perspectives and different interests and is structured in such a way that everyone can participate openly and without fear of retribution or bias. Each member has an equal share of authority, he said, and each person's opinion counts as much as any other's. He was nominating four of the people in the room, he said, to an investigative *shura*. It would operate, he insisted, in an Islamic way, seeking to be objective, fair, and non-hierarchical. (As such, he explained, he would not be part of the *shura* but would follow our recommendations.)[20]

The *shura*, while it was to operate in a strictly Islamic way, was not comprized only of Muslims; indeed, only two of the four participants were to be Muslims. It was to include, Tan Sri Hassan said, the Muslim manager of both Mariam and Abdullah. Another member named to the *shura* was a Chinese woman, the office manager. The assistant manager of human resources, a Malay Muslim, was also to be in the group. I, too, would join the *shura*, in Tan Sri Hassan's words, as a consultant, anthropologist, and independent party 'sensitive to issues of Malay and Islamic corporate culture'. In this capacity, he asked me to remain loyal to what he called my local cultural experience, and not to overlay my 'Western and Wall Street perspective' on what I would learn in the investigation. On the day of the incident, none of us had been in the area where Mariam and Abdullah worked, another element in Tan Sri Hassan's perception that the *shura* would proceed with utmost fairness.

We must, he said, over the course of that day, interview every employee who had witnessed the incident. Then, we must interview Abdullah and lastly, Mariam. Our objective was to build, slowly and methodically, an understanding of the events that led to the physical assault of Abdullah and Mariam's claim of sexual harassment. While it was clear that there was, Tan Sri Hassan had pointed out, an act of physical harassment against Abdullah, it was unclear what had caused it. What had Abdullah done? Was there an act of sexual harassment? Another objective was to understand if one or both employees were guilty of professional misconduct. This was not merely an investigation to establish facts, he said, but one that would, as importantly, make personnel recommendations to him. And, he said, as upset as he was that something like this could happen at his company, he was also 'excited and challenged'. He described the events and the *shura* as a pivotal moment in the construction of an Islamic corporate culture, establishing how people should behave within and outside what Tan Sri Hassan had called its 'familial' bonds. It was, he said, the first time he could 'test' the Islamic values with which he was building the company.

The case of Mariam and Abdullah revealed much about how Islamic understandings concerning gender and appropriate interactions between the sexes shape workplace relations in Malaysia. The other members of the *shura* and I learnt much about the Islamic ideal of consensus. It was clear to us that the multi-ethnic, multi-religious composition of our group spoke to the valuing of divergent points of view that Tan Sri Hassan believed should characterize *shura*. We also understood and acted on the charge of collective responsibility we had been given, diligently conducting our interviews and investigation, and then discussing for hours the recommendations we ultimately would make. When the matter had been fully resolved, Tan Sri Hassan told me that an Islamically-oriented sexual harassment policy—as well as descriptions of *shura* as an ideal form of corporate decision-making—should be formalized as key aspects of Islamic management. He asked me to write up lengthy descriptions of these two milestones in the company's history, so that he could use them in his book.

## Zakat *and Islamic Philanthropy*

Tan Sri Hassan said that *zakat* is an investment, both in the sense that it would help determine his fate in the next world but also could provide a way to, as he often said, 'do good and do well' in this world. While *zakat*, he said, is well-understood as a Muslim's personal responsibility (and one which he met by funding *madrasas* and Muslim orphanages in Indonesia, Afghanistan and Palestine), he believed few Muslims thought about the greater charitable responsibility of the Islamic corporation beyond its basic *zakat* duties.[21] He and I spent many hours discussing his idea of philanthropy; he had read about and admired great American philanthropists like John D. Rockefeller, who funded and supported the growth of large-scale cultural and social institutions in America, and Bill Gates, who reached far beyond America to help the poor. He wondered why no Malay Muslim industrialists had yet funded universities, hospitals, research centers or museums, and envisioned a day in Malaysia when Muslim capitalists like him would become great sponsors of social and spiritual development and great givers of wealth. He believed in what he called 'Islamic philanthropy', corporate giving, in the corporation's name. He speculated that ethnic conflict could help to explain why there had been few Muslim philanthropists in Malaysia; *bumiputera* entrepreneurs wanted to keep their wealth from benefiting non-Muslims in Malaysia. He knew, too, that Allah provides more blessings for charity given secretly, which perhaps keeps Muslims from lending their names to foundations, but said that a new Muslim 'corporate consciousness' should emerge about corporate profits and *zakat*. To him, however, a key aspect of that consciousness was that Islamic philanthropy should promote well-being for all.

During the months that I spent in his company, I worked with him on two projects that he described as representing Islamic philanthropy. The first was a charitable organization for the multi-ethnic Malaysian poor that he was planning under the guidance of the *ustaz*. He wanted the foundation, which would be a division of his larger company, to be built around the twin concepts of *ihklas* (faith) and *kemajuan* (progress). While the foundation's faith would be that of Islam, it would also encourage faith in all forms; that is, it would be non-denominational in nature, giving assistance and succor to people in need, regardless of religion. He said that to be a true Muslim, you must give without bias, to support the needs of human beings. Therefore, 75 per cent of the charity provided would be reserved for Muslims; 25 per cent would be given purely on the basis of need, without regard for religion. That, he argued, represents 'progress' in Islam—that one acts purely on humanitarian impulses, not solely religious ones. The concept of multiethnic 'progress', sponsored under Islam's values, he said, also reflected the twenty-first-century goals of pan-Malaysian economic development, a theme that was increasingly reflected at the time in the speeches of Prime Minister Mahathir, despite the fact that throughout the 1990s, non-Muslims increasingly felt marginalized in Malaysia as a result of Mahathir's Islamization program.[22]

The second project met Tan Sri Hassan's definition of Islamic philanthropy 'Rockefeller-style'. He was investing in an arts project that would bring traditional Malay music, such as *dikir barat* (the traditional Malay 'rap' music that was performed at the *do'a*), as well as other forms of village music such as *ghazal*, *dodang sayang*, *joget*, *masri*, and *wayang kulit*, into performance halls, schools and community venues all over Malaysia. A concert hall had been built at the Petronas Towers to house the newly-formed Malaysian Philharmonic Orchestra (composed of Western classical musicians); Tan Sri Hassan wanted what he called 'Malay heritage music' to be promoted there as well. This project had deep significance, for it went beyond the goal of preserving for urban Malaysia what he called its 'rich cultural past'. In fact, all of the traditional Malay forms of singing, instrumentation and dancing had fallen under great scrutiny by PAS and other Islamist groups in the 1980s and early 1990s and had been declared 'anti-Islamic'. It was nearly impossible to see a performance of *wayang kulit* in Malaysia when I first arrived in the 1990s. *Joget*, which involved men and women dancing together, had similarly disappeared. When an old school friend and cultural impresario came to him with the idea to bring back these musical performances as 'heritage culture', Tan Sri Hassan was immediately interested in providing it with full corporate sponsorship. To him, the PAS position on Malay culture was part of the 'dark ages' that the Taliban, for example, wanted to create in the Muslim world. But a bold, confident Islamic culture, which was interested in art, music, beauty and progress, was the vision he had for Malaysia. Music and dance, he said, was part of Malay tradition, and it had been strongly influenced by Arab musical forms as well as Portuguese, Chinese and Indian styles; to him, its history represented the adaptability and strengths of Malaysia's Muslims. So, too, could it bring about Malaysia's harmonious future, for it would remind Malaysia's non-Muslims that they had also played a role in Malaysia's cultural history. He immediately issued a company check in the amount of one-quarter of a million *ringgit* (approximately £50,000) to his friend. This was, he said, just the kind of project he had been seeking for the company: the corporate sponsorship of 'heritage culture that could be enjoyed by everyone' under the tolerant banner of Islam. But so, too, was this corporate marketing: he envisioned this project could ultimately bring much profit to the company, and set his senior managers on a development plan to establish a publishing and music subsidiary so that books, CDs and DVDs could be produced and sold along the way. But profit was good, for it generated even more money for charity. He would meld *zakat* with business and profit into corporate *fard kifayah*; this kind of contribution to the collective good of the *umma* was his understanding of Islamic philanthropy.

## Communities and Corporations and the New Golden Age of Islam

Several times, Tan Sri Hassan welcomed me into meetings with the architects who were drawing up plans for the company's future headquarters. It was to be a family-oriented, multi-cultural corporate space, featuring a childcare and after-school tutoring center for employees' children; a nursing station for breastfeeding working mothers; a library and classroom, where everyone, Muslim and non-Muslim alike, could learn about Islam from prominent *ustaz*es; and a cafeteria serving healthy, low-fat *halal*-only food. Although a *surau* for Muslim-only prayer featured prominently in the design, there would also a small place for prayer or contemplation to which non-Muslims could retreat. The company would also support telecommuting; today's parents, he knew, needed more time at home and should have flexible schedules to accommodate family needs. While all of these modern ideas were refractions of the moral concerns of government leaders who decried the loss of family values as well as conservative *ulama* speaking on behalf of PAS, who increasingly sought to return working Malay women to their homes, Tan Sri Hassan had, in his design for company headquarters, a radical vision for what the Islamic firm could provide to the capitalist world. It allowed women to fulfill both modern and traditional roles; it imagined fathers who would take time off to care for children and parents; it was concerned with the education of young people and the broadened understanding (and practice) of Islam among Muslim employees and the broadening of Islamic understanding among employees of other religious backgrounds; it fed the soul, the spirit and the body. In one meeting with the architects, pointing to the small fountain in his office, he told the architects to build an 'Islamic garden' in the atrium of the building; here would be planted fragrant plants from Arab nations, Malaysian orchids and the hibiscus or *bunga raya* (the Malaysian 'national flower') alongside water features.

While the building was being planned, another Islamically-harmonious place was already in process. One of the current development projects of the company was a massive new residential and business community that was being built close to Malaysia's bridge to Singapore. Replete with all the elements of a developed society that appeared in speeches by politicians and Prime Minister Mahathir about a 'caring society',[23] it placed low-cost housing alongside higher-cost homes, and had parks and playgrounds. It also featured walking paths that wound through a small nature preserve; Islam, Tan Sri Hassan said, 'cares for the environment'.

Other communities like this one were in the investment portfolio of the company, and Tan Sri Hassan was committed to adding more and more elements of Islamic social welfare into their development. A project that was underway in the north of Malaysia had daycare centers for elderly people, where working men and women could confidently take their aged parents during the day. Another had local 'incubator' industries where entrepreneurial ventures of Malays, Indians, and Chinese working together could be fostered. While the actual Islamicity of any of these plans could have been drawn into question as merely generic 'good works', to him, they were the essence of bringing Islam into the everyday lives of all Malaysians. The image in his mind as he led the company's own progress as well as its residential and industrial development projects was, he said, 'a modern-day Medina', where Muslims and non-Muslims alike lived under the embrace of Islamic economic and social well-being. Via the corporation, Islam, he thought, could remake Malaysia.

*The Islamic Corporation's 'Balance Sheet'*

In July 1997, when I had been working in Tan Sri Hassan's company for several months, the currency of Thailand was dramatically devalued, setting off a chain reaction in parts of East and Southeast Asia that was to become known as the 'Asian Financial Crisis'. By year's end, the Kuala Lumpur Stock Exchange would lose almost half of its value. Although Tan Sri Hassan's company lost a great portion of the value of its assets, for many of its holdings were investments in the stock of KLSE-listed companies, it was still in better shape than many others. Calling together all of his senior managers, he described the crisis to them as an opportunity. We would see how an Islamic company could be managed in times of wealth and in times of scarcity. We would, he said, tighten our belts, cash out and withdraw from many of the more ambitious projects, retool and rethink, and use the time for planning and reflection. He understood that the Asian Financial Crisis was a test from Allah; it would weed out the weak Muslim capitalists and strengthen the talented ones. It would refocus Malaysia on a more reasonable path to wealth, rather than the no-holds-barred course it had been following.

He welcomed this change, for it would force him—and all of his employees—to better balance themselves. Using an analogy I had heard several times before from Malay Muslim business people, he referred to the life of a Muslim as a 'business', in which, on the Day of Judgement, Allah tallies up your 'profits' and 'losses' on the 'Book of Records', itself like a 'balance sheet'.[24] Unfortunate will be those with large losses and few profits. But even if the financial balance sheet of the company were diminished, Tan Sri Hassan said, the bigger spiritual profits that could be reaped by the employees of the corporation could still be realized. He vowed to lead the company wisely through this trying time, and encouraged all of us to work harder and show greater compassion for the less fortunate during the weeks and months ahead. With less to do, most of the employees and managers in the company focused on longer-term projects. Tan Sri Hassan was frequently called to meetings with government ministers and advisors to the Prime Minister. When I left the company several months later, no one had yet lost his or her job, but few employees had much to keep them busy.

While many Malay-Muslim owned companies became bankrupt in the next few years, Tan Sri Hassan's company survived, with massive government help. PAS—which believed that the economic crisis was a result of Mahathir-style governance—criticized the government bail-outs as one more example of UMNO-style corruption.[25] Tan Sri Hassan believed, however, that it was un-Islamic to let hundreds, maybe even thousands, of people become impoverished as a result of his company's bankruptcy. I turn now to Tan Sri Hassan's and Malaysia's story since then.

## *The End of the Mahathir Era*

Although it had been deeply affected by the Asian economic crisis of 1997 to 1998, Malaysia, unlike Indonesia and Thailand, did not ask for assistance from the International Monetary Fund. Sailing through the crisis on its own resources, Malaysia resumed progress on the path toward upward economic growth remarkably quickly and continued to present itself as Islam's most successful economic development story and the world's most accessible Islamic economy.[26]

Much more potentially destabilizing to Malaysia was the bizarre trial and sentencing on charges of sodomy and corruption of Prime Minister Mahathir's protégé, Deputy Prime Minister Anwar Ibrahim, which led to a strengthening of the Islamist party PAS. Anti-UMNO/pro-Islamist opposition forces grew in Malaysia, and the 1999 elections reflected the growing popularity of PAS. But PAS's ascendency was brief, as the events of September 2001 and the global 'War on Terror' provided Mahathir's government with greater incentives to crack down on Islamist parties.[27] Still, Mahathir, to fully counter any further empowerment of Malaysia's Islamist forces, stepped up UMNO's own Islamic commitments, declaring in 2002 that Malaysia was an 'Islamic state'.[28] When he stepped down in 2003, he named Deputy Prime Minister Abdullah Badawi—a trained religious scholar—as his successor.

Abdullah Badawi sought to help UMNO gain the Islamic moral high ground that Islamist opposition forces had been claiming. He told Malaysians that the image of global Islam was associated with violence and terrorism and needed to be rehabilitated. He announced 'Islam *Hadhari'*, or 'progressive Islam', as the way forward for Malaysia. Abdullah took the term '*hadhari*' from Ibn Khaldun, the fourteenth-century Muslim scholar. The term, he argued, expresses Islam's urbanity, plurality, progress, and civic interests. Abdullah's Malaysian '*hadhari*' emphasized hard work, tolerance, openness, and moderation and argued for the strong development of the Malaysian Islamic economy and a globally competitive Malay Muslim community where Malaysia's Muslim capitalists are 'ambassadors for moderate Islam', a claim that the Arab world could not make.[29] Tan Sri Hassan, whose corporate interests remained, under Abdullah as they were under Mahathir, intimately connected to mainstream UMNO politics, maintained a high profile as one of Malaysia's top Muslim capitalists embodying the values of Islam Hadhari. To him, its premises were built into his vision of Islamic corporate modernity; it was, he said, what had guided him all along.

### Malaysia as an Islamic (Producer) State

In late 2007, Malaysia's national carmaker, Proton, announced it was planning, along with partners in Iran and Turkey, the world's first 'Islamic car'. Perhaps nothing better represented the up-to-date Islamic economic modernity that Malaysia wanted to project to the Western and Muslim world than this car, which reportedly would include such features as a compass that orients the driver not north but to Mecca, a special box in which to store a Qur'an, and a compartment for a headscarf. And although it abandoned the Islamic car project in the post-2008 economic downturn, Malaysia has continued to fashion itself as a powerful magnet for the Islamic world's global consumer. The Central Bank of Malaysia, Bank Negara, celebrates its own enormous success in creating the world's 'most dynamic' Islamic economy, crafting Islamically-compliant financial products that wealthy investors in the Persian Gulf and global banks now seek out.[30] Malaysia sponsors the World Halal Forum, an annual event heralded as the world's largest convention bringing together producers and consumers in the global *halal* economy.[31] One need only visit Kuala Lumpur during June, July, and August, to understand the consumption-oriented role

Malaysia now plays in the Muslim world, when thousands of Muslim visitors from the Gulf descend on the city, filling its luxury hotels and massive shopping malls. Malaysia presents itself as the ultimate 'friendly' *halal* destination for global Muslims—welcoming, colorful, 'exotic', for Muslims seeking permissible pleasures in global modernity. Today, under yet another Prime Minister, Mohd. Najib bin Tun Haji Abdul Razak, Malaysia positions itself as the most 'corporate' of the Islamic nations. Providing the Muslim world with the most innovative and hyper-realized Islamic financial-services economy, vast resources for Islamic consumption, and Islamic ethics for multicultural business life, it seeks to demonstrate to the world that it is no less than the world's first Islamic producer state, orienting the compass of modern capitalism to its vision of the Islamic future.

So, too, has Islam fully penetrated the work lives and workplaces crafted by many contemporary economic virtuosi. Business men I speak to today in Malaysia's top Muslim-run corporations often participate in rigorous study groups that comb Islamic texts for connections between religion and economic life, and work closely with local scholars and *ustaze*s to understand the rules for commercial and organizational life contained within the Qur'an and *hadith*. Many are in frequent contact, sometimes even daily, with *Shari'a* advisors from local universities, not just for purposes of financial compliance at the corporate and product-development level, but for advice on all matters of business and management as well as on personal matters and self-management. *Shura* is today a term I now frequently hear in Malaysian corporate conference rooms.

When I last spoke with Tan Sri Hassan in 2008, I learned that his company continues to develop commercial and residential properties all over Peninsular Malaysia and many of these projects retain a commitment to the social and community-oriented goals that have long personally concerned him. The corporate headquarters has finally been built, on a somewhat smaller scale than he first envisioned and without some of the Islamic features he had planned, but the company does have a sexual harassment policy and a dress code for women based on the *Shari'a*, detailed in a *Shari'a* policy manual that lays out a set of Islamic corporate and 'human resources' rules, codes, procedures, and disciplines for employees. The Islamic workplace in his corporation is increasingly more Islamically-normative, and he expects employees, Muslim and non-Muslim alike, to exhibit the ethical values and moral principles laid out in the *Shari'a*. Tan Sri Hassan continues to develop the company's engagement in corporate philanthropy. While his Malay cultural heritage project fell victim to the economic downturn, more recently his name and company have funded an educational foundation, scholarships at Malaysia's Islamic University and a hospital. He has led his business into fully *Shari'*-compliant financing and, whether they are Muslim or not, all his employees' paychecks are deposited into an Islamic bank. He keeps several *Shari'a* advisors on retainer to advise him on all matters of business and personnel management. He believes that one day, Malaysia will put in place a fully Islamic economy guided by the rules and ethics of *Shari'a*, and that this will pave the way for Islamic principles that 'guide everything'. In 2008, as the American subprime lending crisis rocked the financial underpinnings of the global capitalist economy, his voice was increasingly confident: not only did Islam have an economic answer to the corruption and vast injustices of the Western market system, Malaysia had already put the solution in place.

*Beyond Islamism*

What, then, reflecting on the theme of this volume, is 'post-Islamist' about Tan Sri Hassan as he seeks to work out the Islamic culture of Malaysian economic life? What Tan Sri Hassan represents in the Malaysian case—and what is happening today in Malaysia among mainstream UMNO politicians and politically well-connected capitalists like Tan Sri Hassan, who increasingly follow the ministrations of *Shari'a* advisors and structure their corporations along what they perceive to be more Islamic lines—is, I would argue, the quintessential Malaysian post-Islamist project. Tan Sri Hassan takes us from the Islamism of the Islamic opposition party PAS to a place he perceives to be beyond politics. That is, Tan Sri Hassan does not postulate, as does PAS and political Islam, a vision of the Islamic state as the way forward for Malaysia; it pos-

tulates instead a vision of the ascendant Malaysian Islamic economy and the corporation. And in Malaysia, this is not mere
idealism. Malaysia's Islamic capitalists have arrived. One can read
all about them in the *Wall Street Journal*.[32]

Clifford Geertz, in his famous study of the failure of capitalism
to emerge among Muslims in Pare, Java (what he called 'Mojo-
kuto'), borrowed from Max Weber's study of Islam the premise
that Islam is too rigid, egalitarian, individualist, and doctrinaire to
allow capitalist firms to form. Geertz argued that the bazaar economy of Islamic trade—characterizing Islamic business since the
time of the Prophet himself—was too individuated and 'exclusiv-
istic'.[33] Men of Allah, Islamic traders, were too 'person-to-person,
higgling and haggling' in their mentality, which made them 'inadequate for the ... more collectively and systematically organized
world of the firm'.[34] As such, while Muslim entrepreneurs may
demonstrate Weber's ideal of the Protestant 'calling', the bazaar
economy hangs 'heavily over them'.[35] Geertz concurred with
Weber that the individualist character of Islam is so rigid that it
prevents the degree of economic advance required for the emergence of 'firms'. Indeed, to examine contemporary studies of
Islamic entrepreneurship—such as Filippo Osella's and Caroline
Osella's study of Kerala entrepreneurs and Jonah Blank's study of
Bohras[36]—one is struck by how much of the 'bazaar economy' continues to characterize Islamic business life. Elsewhere, Muslim
entrepreneurship and capitalism often takes the form of modernized and even globalized but still sole-proprietorship trade. But
what is notable about Tan Sri Hassan's practice of Islam in economic life beginning with his 1996 corporation, is that it is explicitly 'firm based'; it is institutionalized; it is corporate Islam. This is
what Malaysia itself has begun to master on a larger scale than
perhaps any other Muslim-majority nation.

In the retelling of his religious trajectory as was marked at his
*do'a*, Tan Sri Hassan believed he had found a new focus that went
far beyond spiritual introspection. Indeed, returning to Weber,
what Tan Sri Hassan's self-described 'spiritual transformation'
represented was a new bureaucratization and routinization of the
Islamic individual's entrepreneurial charisma into corporate
(Islamic) governance, what Weber referred to as the rational, mod-

ern capitalism which embeds our religious ideals into the demands of a modern, firm-based economy and the state that supports it.[37] Taken sequentially, the three projects I have presented from Tan Sri Hassan's Islamic corporation reflect the different domains of how, for him, Islamic practice and piety can be transformed into public corporate and institutionalized structures, an alternative vision and style of Islamism. In the episode of the *shura* set up to investigate the conflict between Abdullah and Mariam, Tan Sri Hassan envisioned a modern Islamic management culture within the corporation. Extending his understanding of the personal and individual obligations of *zakat* into a philosophy of corporate philanthropy, he postulated how the corporation could extend its reach into (and profit from) the larger community. Submerged in his plan for how corporations and newly-built communities could reflect larger social and economic values of Islamic life was a corporate contribution to a new 'golden age' of Islam, no less than a Medina-style modernity for Malaysia's Muslims and non-Muslims alike. Taken together, these projects presented the way in which the Islamically-oriented corporation could be the way of the future, building *fard kifayah*. But what characterized all of these ideals was an understanding that it was through the corporation that the best (and all of) Islam could be realized and broadened, for Muslims and non-Muslims alike.

And in that way, Tan Sri Hassan, like UMNO and PAS, presents a version of a world where Islam guides and structures everything, and becomes a global agent of change, all versions of Islamism. But unlike PAS, neither Tan Sri Hassan, nor the three successive Malaysian prime ministers he has served as a tycoon, has, beyond rhetoric, sought to refashion Malaysia into an Islamic state. Instead, for want of a better word, they 'rebrand' their version of Islamism into a corporate force. Like many of the Malay Muslim entrepreneurs and tycoons I have come to know in Malaysia in the new millennium, Tan Sri Hassan—who was inarguably the most impassioned and visionary of the business men I have met—today believes that Islamic capitalists in Malaysia can do everything. They can innovate in Islamic economics and remake the Malaysian nation via Islamic finance. They can be the world's most successful Islamic producers. They can create Islamic firms that employ (and instruct)

Muslims and non-Muslims alike. They can confidently engage with Western capitalism; they can also markedly improve upon it with their *Shari'a*-based ethics and virtues. Tan Sri Hassan believed that in Malaysia, a nation (and a world) fraught with ethnic, religious, political, and economic conflict, Islam in its corporate state could create a better life that could be shared by all. At his *do'a* in 1996, as he thanked Allah for his personal good fortune, he dreamt of a Malaysian wellbeing generated via an expanded corporate Islam; the last time I spoke to him, he hoped for its global domination.

# POSTFACE

## ISLAMISM IS DEAD, LONG LIVE ISLAMISM

*Frédéric Volpi*

*Where Were the Islamists During the 2011 Arab Spring?*

For all the media and policy talk of the dangers of political Islam throughout the 2000s, the 2011 Arab Spring was remarkable for the lack of leadership provided by Islamist movements throughout the region. From Libya to Yemen, from Egypt to Bahrain, Islamists were certainly not leading from the front, if they were leading at all. That the 'Islamist threat' invoked by most of the authoritarian regimes of the Middle East and North Africa (MENA) did not materialize in the way policy makers said it would is in itself no great surprise. Most ruling elites in the region had chosen to exaggerate this threat after 9/11 in order to receive (or keep receiving) military, political and financial rewards from the leading advocates of the 'War on Terror' (WOT). The United States and other lesser proponents of the WOT had already convinced themselves of the reality of a global Islamist threat and only needed positive reinforcement from their MENA partners to keep believing in this depiction of the world, no matter how flawed it might have been.[1]

The popular uprising that lead to the failure of several authoritarian regimes in the region in 2011 made plain what was already evident to many: that the Islamist threat depicted in the WOT narratives did not meaningfully reflect the dynamics of Islamism in these polities. Yet, at the same time, any detailed account of these momentous protest movements and of their aftermath in the MENA would remark that if Islamists were not involved in the way it was feared, they remained nonetheless present and active in multiple roles. Whilst there was hardly any Islamic dimension to Tunisia's democratic revolution, it is hard to miss the role played by Islamic actors in the new multiparty system of the country.[2] Whilst the Egyptian Muslim Brotherhood might only have joined the revolutionary bandwagon once the popular uprising was already in full swing, its social and political networks did contribute to the resilience of the protest movement in the country.[3] And whilst the Libyan Islamic Fighting Group did not single-handedly topple the Qadhafi regime by waging 'jihad', it did nonetheless visibly contribute to organize the armed struggle against the Qadhafi's forces. Politically, socially, militarily—as well as culturally, economically, legally, spiritually, etc.—the Islamists have been involved in the recent wave of successful (and unsuccessful) popular uprisings in the region. They remain significant participants in multiple aspects of life in these polities; be they political actors strategically toning down their political ambitions (Nahda, the Muslim Brotherhood), or the multitude of sub-, trans-, and supra-national actors spontaneously occupying parts of a civil sphere which were previously controlled by an autocratic state administration.

## Of the Usefulness of Grand Narratives on Islamism

To understand why Islamists may not be where we expect them to be, or why they may not behave in the way we supposed they would, we have to critically assess the grand narratives on Islamism that have been dominant over the decades. In effect, we have to ask ourselves why it is that we constructed a picture of political Islam with such characteristics and implications in the first place.[4] Looking back at the main portrayals of Islamism in the last few decades, four representations are readily identifiable. In the 1960s and 1970s, when politics in the developing world was seen through the prism of modernization and secularization theories, Islamism was deemed to be a case of political backwardness, and religiously framed ideas and ideals were thought to be destined for the dust-bin of history. The 1980s saw these representations turned on their head after the Iranian Islamic revolution, and for most of the decade Islamism was perceived as a potentially revolutionary movement that could topple secularizing regimes throughout the Muslim world. In the 1990s, this Islamist model was once more revised in the light of an Algerian scenario that illustrated how Islamism could gain power by operating as a political party during a process of democratic transition. In the 2000s, after the al-Qaeda attacks on the United States on 11 September 2001, portrayals of Islamism were once again revised to emphasize the prominent role played by violent transnational Islamist networks in the international system.

Although all these descriptions of the phenomenon of Islamism contained some very relevant insights, each perspective was undermined by its own success as conceptual shorthand for the entire phenomenon.[5] Traditional religious authorities, revolutionary movements, political parties, transnational jihadi networks, etc. are all possible embodiments of Islamism (alongside many other manifestations of the drive to make Islam more relevant to contemporary societies). They are not, however, exclusive forms of Islamic activism and any apparent dominance of one type of activism over another is at best temporary and limited to specific socio-historical contexts. As a response to (and a part of) modernity, Islamism has always been, is, and will most probably remain a multifarious phenomenon. It is neither here nor there in particular, but it continuously permeates a multiplicity of activities (political, social, religious, etc.). To emphasize the importance of a particular type of movement, activity or idea for the internal dynamics of Islamism or for its interactions with other, non-Islamic actors can be useful in explaining and understanding specific events and processes. Yet at the same time these conceptual and analytical choices ensure that other dimensions of Islamism remain outside mainstream debates and narratives. It is the evolution of those under-investigated aspects of Islamism that time and time again undermine the dominant representation of the phenomenon.[6]

## Accounting for the Multiplicity of Islamism

To talk about new and old forms of Islamism is not only to investigate the rise and fall of different trends and movements in historical terms, but it is also to consider two types of dynamics intrinsic and extrinsic to Islamism. To consider meaningfully the evolution of Islamism we have to investigate first the internal evolution of the phenomenon—i.e. what Islamism means for those who are interested in giving Islam a greater place in their life, individually and collectively.[7] The dynamics of resistance and of hegemony within and between Islamist movements articulate themselves around what Islamism is an answer to and/or an aspiration for. The changing fortunes of various Islamist trends are in part a reflection of the changing function that Islamism has for its advocates and its supporters. Socio-historical changes (underpinned in recent decades by factors like urbanization, new media, consumerism, globalization, etc.) make different forms of Islamism more or less relevant to greater or fewer numbers of people in different historical junctures and/or geographical locations. What could once be viewed as a good articulation of Islamic ideas and practices may then lose some its relevance (e.g. traditional Ulema), while interpretations that were thought to be outdated may regain some pertinence (e.g. various Sufi traditions); and all the while new and hybrid modes of being a 'good Muslim' emerge and spread out in the community. These internal dynamics and their accompanying narratives provide crucial insights into understanding past and present trends, as well as highlighting some possible futures for Islamism.[8]

Second, to appreciate the multiplicity of Islamism, we also have to investigate and understand the changing landscape of the external readings of the Islamist phenomenon—i.e. what Islamism means for actors not interested in having Islam play a more important role in society. Over the decades, multiple domestic and international actors have depicted and acted upon Islamist phenomena in order to advance their own agenda, and they provided accounts of Islamism that suited their own worldviews and interests.[9] What Islamism 'is' also depends on the kind of questions that are being asked about it—i.e. the conceptual and analytical frameworks that scholars (and the media, policy makers, the public, etc.) use to make sense of it. Over time, as the interests of the people doing the questioning changed, as conceptual and analytical frameworks went in and out of fashion, depictions of Islamism also changed as a result. Daniel Lerner's suggestion that Muslim societies faced a choice between 'Mecca or mechanization' is now deemed to be more indicative of the assumptions about modernization and secularization that were commonly made in the 1950s than of the prospects for Muslim polities.[10] No doubt in the near future, the security-minded analyses of Islamism that dominated the debate during the period of the 'War on Terror' will be looked at in the same critical light, and lessons learnt about mindset of the international community at the turn of the century. This evolution of the narratives about Islamism is not caused solely by a changing Islamist phenomenon but also by a change of analytical and conceptual lenses used to frame political Islam. As time goes by, external readings of Islamism are simply not asking the same questions and/or expecting the same answers of the phenomenon. The changing multiplicity of Islamism is therefore generated, at least in part, by the changing multiplicity of external actors considering what political Islam means for them.

## Where Will Islamism Go Next?

Future articulations of Islamism will remain shaped by what is being asked of Islamism, by whom and for what purpose. The prevailing political and socio-economic trends at the beginning of the twenty-first century makes it very likely that two main contexts will be salient in the short to medium term for the articulation of Islamism. In crude geopolitical terms we could outline two main clusters of Islamism, in the 'West' and in the 'East'. Any detailed account of the 'West' would evidently have to go beyond a mere geopolitical construct and consider processes of secularization, consumerism, globalization, etc. that originated in the 'West' but that have become embedded in (parts of) non-western societies, as well as becoming hybridized in the process. As for the 'East', the issue is not simply that of the (problematic) involvement of Islamism in the institutional governance of Muslim majority countries, but also the global articulation of transnational forms of Islamic

251

religiosity across the ummah, not least in Muslim-minority contexts.[11] The 'West' and the 'East' correspond also to two approaches to the Islamist phenomenon, one external using the western political tradition to question and understand Islamism, the other internal, using Islamic resources to question and understand both Muslim societies and 'western' modernity. These two conceptual perspectives are of course like their geopolitical relatives, only crude approximations of what remain irremediably interconnected and hybrid worldviews.

In the global 'West' the main tensions (and opportunities) revolve around the inclusion of Islamist subjectivities in a framework defined by liberal notions of politics and of the public sphere. From a western perspective, this accommodation is often seen as a one-way process, with 'universal' relevance in the context of globalized modernity. From socio-economic integration to the now pervasive issue of securitization, the evolution of different strands of Islamism will be framed and judged in relation to these opportunities for inclusion in this modernity. In the 'East', for the foreseeable future, the issue of the involvement of Islamist into the frameworks of governance of Muslim-majority countries will remain a defining characteristic of Islamism domestically and internationally. From the perspective of the Islamic tradition, this involvement will generate ever greater efforts at re-conceptualizing Islamic ideals and practices to make them ever more relevant and useful for globalized forms of modernity.[12]

The heritage of al-Qaeda and the WOT will still bear heavily on the external perceptions of Islamism for some time to come. Whilst violent transnational jihadism may become less and less consequential as the years go by, the fear that it generated in governing circles will remain very well alive for many years to come. The choices of the US government in May 2011 to kill Osama Bin Laden rather than to make him prisoner, and to make his body disappear at sea rather than to bury it, are indicative of the Islamist fear factor that has been introduced in even the highest policy-making circles. WOT narratives may no longer be dominant after 2011 but whichever master narrative about political Islam will mark the coming decade, it will be constrained by the memories of this period.

As multifarious Islamic actors are gearing up to have a greater influence in the democratizing the polities of (at the time of writing) Tunisia, Egypt and Libya, the international community remains most concerned by the implications of this involvement for 'Security'. For the citizens of those polities, by contrast, the institutionalization and the everyday articulation of Islamism will be framed according to more pragmatic social, economic, political and religious criteria. It will then be up to specific Islamic movements to show the relevance of political Islam to their fellow citizens and coreligionists, and to provide durably the kind of practical solutions to the problems that these polities will face. Whether these local experiments with political action can produce more useful representations and embodiments of Islamism remains to be seen; but at the very least, the 2011 Arab Spring has created opportunities for the emergence of a public sphere that were simply not there before. Will these new contexts herald a new trend toward post-Islamism? Undoubtedly if by this it is meant a new articulation of political Islam that supersedes older ways of being and acting as an Islamist—for political parties this could be for example an evolution similar to that of the AKP in Turkey. But post-Islamism could also mean a more substantive reformulation of the phenomenon in the post-modern context. In this perspective, Post-Islamism would recast itself as a phenomenon without a master narrative that could encapsulate the ethos and telos of the movement. Whether we now enter post-Islamism or Post-Islamism will be for future generations to adjudicate.

# NOTES

## INTRODUCTION

1. Here the terms 'political Islam' and 'Islamism' will be used interchangeably to refer to the ideological project that integrates Islam as a means for political action, mobilization and identification.
2. For a discussion of the emergence of Islamism in the early twentieth century and its gradual evolution through the 1970s, see Olivier Roy, *The Failure of Political Islam*, London: I.B. Tauris, 1994.
3. This characterization of political Islam as linked only to opposition and violence has been challenged by a number of scholars. For an example of this critique, see Saba Mahmood, 'Islam and Fundamentalisms', *Middle East Report* no. 191, November-December 1994, pp. 29–30; or Quintan Wiktorowicz, *Islamic Activism: A Social Movement Theory Approach*, Bloomington: Indiana University Press, 2004. Richard Martin and Abbas Barzegar, eds, *Islamism. Contested Perspectives on Political Islam* (Stanford: Stanford University Press, 2010).
4. The construct of Islamism as contemporary Nazism is promoted by politicians, essayists and novelists more than scholars; for instance, President George W. Bush used the term in a speech to the 88th Annual American Legion National Convention (29 August 2006); Christopher Hitchens defended the term in his article, 'Defending *Islamofascism*: It's a valid term. Here's why', *Slate*, 22 October 2007 .
5. Amel Boubekeur, 'Algeria's Protests in the Shadow of Tunisia,' *Foreign Policy*, 17 January 2011.
6. For one of the seminal works employing the term 'political Islam', see Joel Beinin and Joe Stork (eds), *Political Islam: Essays from 'Middle East Report'*, Berkeley: University of California Press, 1997.
7. 'Islamism' is a movement that historically originated in the Muslim world. Today it encompasses a set of tendencies whose common trait is 'the political and militant use of religion'. This definition quotes Henri Laurens, *L'Orient Arabe: Arabisme et Islamisme de 1798 à 1945*, Paris:

Armand Colin, 2000, who is also quoted by Mounia Bennani-Chraïbi and Olivier Fillieule in *Résistance et protestations dans les sociétés musulmanes*, Paris: Presse de Sciences Po, 2003.

8. For more information on the ideological underpinnings of political Islam, see Nazih N. M. Ayubi, *Political Islam: Religion and Politics in the Arab World*, New York: Routledge, 1991. See also, Joel Beinin and Joe Stork, 'Introduction: On the Modernity, Historical Specificity, and International Context of Political Islam', in Joel Beinin and Joe Stork (eds), *Political Islam*.

9. Bernard Rougier, 'L'Islamisme Face Au Retour De L'Islam?' *Vingtième Siècle. Revue d'histoire*, vol. 82, April-June 2004, pp. 103–118.

10. For more on the growth of political Islam in the 1970s, see Joel Beinin, 'Political Islam and the New Global Economy: The Political Economy of Islamist Social Movements in Egypt and Turkey', (Paper prepared for the conference on French and US Approaches to Understanding Islam, France-Stanford Center for Interdisciplinary Studies, September 2004).

11. The Algerian example best illustrates these various phases. See Amel Boubekeur, 'The Future of Algerian Islamist Parties', *The Maghreb Center Journal*, Issue 1, Spring-Summer 2010.

12. The phenomenon of de-territorialization is related to the concept of transnationalism, broadly defined as a 'coordination of resources, information, technology and sites of social power across national borders for political, cultural, economic purposes'. The mode of action of transnationalism is de-territorialized. That is, transnational nationalism creates new expressions of belonging and political engagement as well as a 'de-territorialized' understanding 'nation'. For Islam, the rhetoric of the *ummah*, or worldwide unified Muslim community, is reinterpreted in such a way that reframes all national diversity as one imagined 'political' community, getting away from its religious definition. See Riva Kastoryano, 'The Reach of Transnationalism', *SSRC* http://essays.ssrc.org/sept11/essays/kastoryano.htm.

13. For an in-depth explanation of the concept of 'neo-fundamentalism', see Olivier Roy, 'Neo-Fundamentalism', *SSRC* http://essays.ssrc.org/sept11/essays/roy.htm.

14. The term Salafism is used in this chapter to denote its 'Wahhabi' trend. On the various uses of Salafism by various groups including political Salafism and jihadi Salafism, see Amel Boubekeur, 'Salafism and Radical Politics in Postconflict Algeria', *Carnegie Papers*, Washington, DC: Carnegie Endowment for International Peace, 2008; and John L. Esposito, *What Everyone Needs to Know about Islam*, Oxford: Oxford University Press, 2002.

15. Salafi groups are anti-*hizb*, or against forming political parties for organization and mobilization.

16. On the historical path and current dynamics of Wahhabism, see Madawi Al-Rasheed, *Contesting the Saudi State: Islamic Voices from a New Generation*, Cambridge: Cambridge University Press, 2007.

17. For works on Islamism and post-Islamism, see, among others, Dale Eickelman and James Piscatori, *Muslim Politics*, Princeton, NJ: Princeton University Press, 1996; Joel Beinin and Joe Stork (eds), *Political Islam*; Mohammed Hafez, *Why Muslims Rebel*, Boulder, CO: Lynne Rienner, 2003; Quintan Wiktorowicz, (ed.), *Islamic Activism*. Scholars have advanced a number of theories to describe the phenomenon of post-Islamism. See Olivier Roy, *L'échec de l'Islam politique*, Paris: Seuil, 1992 and Roy, *L'Islam mondialisé*, Paris: Seuil, 2004; Gilles Kepel, *Jihad, expansion et déclin de l'Islamisme*, Paris: Gallimard, 2000; Patrick Haënni, *L'Islam de marché*, Paris: Seuil, 2005; François Burgat, *L'Islamisme à l'heure d'al-Qaida*, Paris: La Découverte, 2005; and Alain Rousillon, 'Dans l'attente du post-Islamisme', *La vie des idées*, November 2005, http://www.repid.com/spip.php?rubrique113. One may also find debates on the validity of the concepts of Islamism and post-Islamism in Olivier Roy and Patrick Haënni (eds), 'A la recherché du monde musulman', special issue, *Esprit* 277, August 2001, pp. 116–38.

18. See Jean Marcou, this volume.

19. 'Post-Islamism' designates the historical inheritor of Islamism after the failure of the latter with regard to the Islamization of the political field and the State. See Olivier Roy and Patrick Haënni, 'Le post-Islamisme', *Revue des mondes musulmans et de la Méditerranée*, nos. 85–86, Aix-en-Provence: Edisud, 1999. For Asef Bayat, the creator of the term, 'post-Islamism' is characterized by 'rights instead of duties, plurality in place of a singular authoritative voice, historicity rather than fixed scriptures, and the future instead of the past', see Bayat, 'What Is Post-Islamism?', *ISIM Newsletter*, no. 16, Autumn 2005, p. 5.

20. See Asef Bayat, *Making Islam Democratic: Social Movements and the Post-Islamist Turn*, Stanford: Stanford University Press, 2007.

21. For an approach to the link between the new spirit of politically engaged Islam and the historical ideology of Islamism, see Amel Boubekeur, this volume.

22. For example, see Ermin Sinanovic, 'Post-Islamism: The Failure of Islamic Activism?', Review of *Globalized Islam: The Search for a New Ummah* in *International Studies Review*, vol. 7, 2005, pp. 433–436.

23. Asef Bayat, 'Islam and Democracy: What is the Real Question?', *ISIM Paper 8*, Amsterdam University Press, 2007.

24. Grace Davie, 'New Approaches in the Sociology of Religion: A Western Perspective', *Social Compass*, vol. 51, no. 1, 2004, pp. 76–77.
25. Nilüfer Göle, 'Islam in Public: New Visibilities and New Imaginaries', *Public Culture*, vol. 14, no. 1, Winter 2002, pp. 173–190.
26. See Mohamed Mosaad Abdel Aziz, this volume.
27. For more on the notion of Islamic culture, see Amel Boubekeur, 'L'Islam est-il soluble dans le Mecca Cola? Marché de la culture Islamique et nouveaux supports de religiosité en Occident', *Maghreb Machrek*, vol. 183, Spring 2005, pp. 12–13.
28. See Amel Boubekeur, 'Post-Islamist Culture: A New Form of Mobilization?', *History of Religions*, vol. 47, no. 1, 2007, pp. 75–94. Another example is the Society of the Islamic Spectacle, which organizes numerous festivals of Islamic songs in Europe where, for example, Yusuf Islam (Cat Stevens) or Sami Yusuf, one of the UK's leading modern *nasheed* artists, perform 'Islamic songs' in English.
29. For example, see the works of Abd al Malik, a French Muslim rapper who converted to Sufi Islam in his twenties, and who is now one of the most popular rap artists in France. He is also the author of *Qu'Allah bénisse la France!*, Paris: Albin Michel, 2004.
30. See Mark Levine, this volume.
31. See Valentina Frate, this volume.
32. See Patricia Sloane, this volume.
33. See Muriel Gomez, this volume.
34. Martijn de Koning, this volume.
35. Roel Meijer, this volume.
36. Davie, 'New Approaches', p. 82.
37. Ulrich Beck, 'The Cosmopolitan Society and its Enemies', *Theory, Culture & Society*, vol. 19, nos 1–2, pp. 17–44.
38. Olivier Roy, *La sainte ignorance. Le temps de la religion sans culture*, Paris: Seuil, 2008.
39. Terence Ball and Richard Dagger, *Political Ideologies and the Democratic Ideal*, Indiana: Addison-Wesley, 2001.

## 1. IS 'ISLAMISM' A NEO-ORIENTALIST PLOT?

1. The most articulate and exhaustive criticisms can be found in the articles by Gilles Roussillon, and François Burgat in the French journal *Esprit*, (August-September 2011); see also, Frédéric Volpi, *Political Islam Observed*, London: Hurst, 2010, which excellently exposes and summarizes the various critiques of the concept of 'Islamism'. The reader will find quotations from many of the scholars involved in the debate, which is why this chapter will not explore these criticisms in depth.

2. Volpi, *Political Islam Observed*, p. 9.

3. See, for instance, Talal Asad's critique of Clifford Geertz: Asad dismisses Geertz's analysis precisely because he used a Western concept of religion; Talal Asad, *Formations of the Secular: Christianity, Islam, Modernity*, Palo Alto, CA: Stanford University Press, 2003.

4. As a Frenchman, I am appalled by the use of the 'tool-box' in 'French Theory' to disconnect an abstruse academic debate from the reality of the field. Derrida and Foucault's texts were far more open and complex; something was clearly lost in translation (subtlety?).


2. THE PROBLEM OF THE POLITICAL IN ISLAMIST MOVEMENTS

1. Islamism is the name usually given to political Islam, which strives for the establishment of a modern caliphate based on Islamic law, the *Shari'a*.

2. Antony Black sums up the political vacuum left after the death of the Prophet succinctly: 'It was assumed, after Muhammad's death, that someone must succeed him in his role as Leader (Imam) of the community, as his Deputy (Caliph). Apart from that, there is almost nothing about political leadership or state structures [in the Qur'an and hadith]'. Cited in *The History of Islamic Political Thought: From Prophet to the Present*, Edinburgh: Edinburgh University Press, p. 14.

3. Daphna Ephrat, *A Learned Society in a Period of Transition: The Sunni 'Ulama of Eleventh-Century Baghdad*, New York: SUNY Press, 2000.

4. Olivier Roy, *The Failure of Political Islam*, London: I.B. Tauris, 1992, p. 10, 21 and 29.

5. Ibid., p. 27.

6. Ibid., p. 45.

7. For the history of *hisba*, see Michael Cook, *Forbidding Wrong in Islam*, Cambridge: Cambridge University Press, 2003. For the application of this practice in its activist form see Meijer, 'Commanding Good and Forbidding Wrong as a Form of Social Action: The Case of the Jama'a al-Islamiyya', in Roel Meijer (ed.), *Global Salafism: Islam's New Religious Movement*, London: Hurst, 2009, pp. 189–220.

8. Madawi al-Rasheed, *Contesting the Saudi State: Islamic Voices from a New Generation*, Cambridge: Cambridge University Press, 2007.

9. The term 'jihad' should be translated as 'religious war' as opposed to 'holy war'.

10. The word *hizb* means party and *hizbiyya* means accepting party politics or the pluralism of opinions.

11. Besides Olivier Roy, Gudrun Krämer and Amr Hamzawy have written the most important books on the subject: Gudrun Krämer, *Gottes Staat*

*als Republik: Reflexionen zeitgenössischer Muslime zu Islam, Menschenrechten und Demokratie*, Baden-Baden: Nomos Verlagsgesellschaft, 1999; Amr Hamzawy, *Zeitgenössische politisches Denken in der arabischen Welt: Kontinuität und Wandel*, Hamburg: Schriften der Deutschen Orient-Instituts, 2005. In fact, Gudrun Krämer wrote one of the first articles on the subject more than ten years ago, 'Islamists Notions of Democracy', in Joel Benin and Joe Stork (eds), *Political Islam: Essays from Middle East Report*, Berkeley: University of California Press, 1997, pp. 71–82. For an anthropological analysis of the relationship between Islam and politics, see Dale F. Eickelman and James Piscatori, *Muslim Politics*, Princeton: Princeton University Press, 1996, and Salwa Ismail, *Rethinking Islamist Politics: Culture, the States and Islamism*, London: I.B. Tauris, 2006.

12. Richard Mitchell, *The Society of the Muslim Brothers*, 2nd edn, Oxford: Oxford University Press, 1993, p. 14.

13. Ibid., pp. 14 and 218–20.

14. Ibid., pp. 16–19 and 39–42.

15. Ibid., pp. 55–79.

16. Joel Gordon, *Nasser's Blessed Movement: Egypt's Free Officers and the July Revolution*, Oxford: Oxford University Press, 1992, p. 183.

17. Johannes Reissner, *Ideologie und Politik der Muslimbruder Syriens. Von den Wahlen 1947 bis zum Verbot undetr Adib as-Shishakli 1952*, Freiburg: Klaus Schwarz Verlag, 1980.

18. Uriel Dann, *King Hussein and the Challenge of Arab Radicalism: Jordan, 1955–1967*, Oxford: Oxford University Press, 1989, pp. 60–1.

19. Hani al-Hurani et al. (eds), *al-Harakat wa-l-Tanzimat al-Islamiyya fi-l-Urdun* [Islamic Movements and Organisations in Jordan], Amman: Dar Sindbad li-l-Nashr, 1997.

20. Beverley Milton-Edwards, *Islamic Politics in Palestine*, London: I.B. Tauris, 1996, pp. 61 and 123–9.

21. *Fitna*, or internal strife in the *umma* (Muslim community) is, in classical theory, regarded as a major sin and is condemned. Unsurprisingly the term is used by Salafis to warn against political activism in any form, whether it is peaceful or violent.

22. Diya Rashwan, *Muslim Brotherhood in Egypt* (no date). www.ikhwan-web.com [Last accessed: May 2007].

23. Sayyid Qutb, *Milestones*, Damascus: Dar al-Ilm, no date, p. 11.

24. Ibid., pp. 57–8.

25. For the ideas of Sayyid Qutb (1906–66), see Gilles Kepel, *The Prophet and the Pharaoh: Muslim Extremism in Egypt*, London: Saqi Books, 1985, pp. 36–58; Leonard Binder, 'The Religious Aesthetics of Sayyid Qutb: A Non-Scriptural Fundamentalism', in Binder (ed.), *Islamic Liberalism:*

*A Critique of Development Ideologies,* Chicago: The University of Chicago Press, 1988, pp. 170–205; Roxanne L. Euben, *Enemy in the Mirror: Islamic Fundamentalism and the Limits of Modern Rationalism. A work of Comparative Political Theory,* Princeton: Princeton University Press, 1999, pp. 49–92.

26. Gilles Kepel, *The Prophet and the Pharaoh,* pp. 61–64; Barbara Zollner, *The Muslim Brotherhood: Hasan al-Hudaybi and Ideology,* Abington: Routledge, 2009.

27. For the apolitical character of Salafism as a means of sanctioning the state, see Madawi Al-Rasheed, *Contesting the Saudi State,* pp. 22–58. For the thought of Juhayman al-Utaybi, see Thomas Hegghammer and Stephane Lacroix, 'Rejectionist Islamism in Saudi Arabia: The Story of Juhayman al-'Utaybi Revisited', *International Journal of Middle East Studies,* vol. 39, no. 1, 2007, pp. 103–122.

28. Quintan Wiktorowicz, *The Management of Islamic Activism: Salafis, the Muslim Brotherhood, and State Power in Jordan,* New York: SUNY Press, 2001, pp. 111–146.

29. Fawaz A. Gerges, *The Far Enemy: Why Jihad Went Global,* Cambridge: Cambridge University Press, 2005.

30. For more on the Jama'at al-Islamiyya and the connection with hisba, see Meijer, 'Commanding Good and Forbidding Wrong as a Form of Social Action', pp. 189–220.

31. Hisham Mubarak, *al-Irhabiyyun qadimun! Dirasa muqarana bayn mawqif al-Ikhwan al-Muslimin wa Jama'at al-Jihad min qadiyat al-'unf, 1928–1994* ['The Terrorists Are Coming: A Comparative Study of the Views of the Muslim Brotherhood and the Jihad Society on the Issue of Violence, 1928–1994'], Cairo: Kitab al-Mahrusa, 1995, pp. 158–170.

32. For the disagreement on the use of violence with the Muslim Brotherhood, see: Muntasar al-Zayyat, *al-Jama'at al-Islamiyya: Ruy'a min al-dakhil* ['The Jama'at al-Islamiyya: A View from Within'], Cairo: Dar Misr al-Mahrusa, 2005, pp. 71 and 90; 'Abd al-Rahim 'Ali, *Muqamara al-Kubra: Mubadara waqf al-'unf bayn rihan al-hukuma wa-l-Jama'at al-Islamiyya* ['The Great Gamble: The Initiative to End Violence between the Hostages of the Government and the Gama'at al-Islamiyya'], Cairo: Markaz al-Mahrusa li-l-Nashr, 2002, p. 141. Mubarak, *al-Irhabiyyun qadimun!,* p. 139.

33. Zayyat, *al-Jama'at al-Islamiyya,* p. 73, and Mubarak, *al-Irhabiyyun qadimun!* pp. 159 and 164.

34. Zayyat, *al-Jama'at al-Islamiyya,* p. 73, 104 and 215; and Mubarak, *al-Irhabiyyun qadimun!* p. 162. For an analysis of the classic texts, see Michael Cook, *Forbidding Wrong in Islam,* Cambridge: Cambridge University Press, 2003.

35. Zayyat, *al-Jama'at al-Islamiyya*, p. 83.

36. Ibid., p. 91.

37. Ibid., pp. 143–5.

38. For the translation of the 'Abd al-Salam Faraj's tract, see Johannes J.G. Jansen, *The Neglected Duty: The Creed of Sadat's Assassins and Islamic Resurgence in the Middle East*, New York: Macmillan, 1986, pp. 159–234.

39. Zayyat, *al-Jama'at al-Islamiyya*, p. 183.

40. Ibid., pp. 179–89. It is fair to mention that strong doubts about the feasibility of the assassination attempt had arisen among the leaders of the Jihad Organisation, especially the military members, such as 'Abbud Zomr.

41. Ali, *Muqamara al-Kubra*, pp. 144–5.

42. *Mithaq al-'Amal al-Islami* [Charter of Islamic Action]. The Charter is an internal document, 194 pages long in handwriting, issued in 1985, and photocopied for distribution. It is written by the three leaders who were at that time in prison, convicted for the assassination of president Sadat, Muhammad Isam Darbala, 'Asim 'Abd al-Majid, Najih Ibrahim. A shorter version is *Min nahnu wa madha nuridu* [Who are We and What it is We Want], which is fifty pages long and also handwritten and is meant as an introduction for new recruits to the movement. Copies of the two documents are at the International Institute for Social History in Amsterdam.

43. *Mawqif al-haraka al-islamiyya min al-'amal al-hizbi fi Misr* [The View of the Islamic Movement on Party Politics in Egypt], is partly re-published in Rif'at Sayyid Ahmad, *al-Nabi al-Musallah: Rafidun* [The Prophet Armed: The Rejectionists], Part I, London: Riad El-Rayyes Books, 1991, pp. 273–82.

44. *Hatmiya al-muwajaha* [The Confrontation is Inevitable] was published in 1987 and has been republished by 'Abd al-Rahim 'Ali in his *al-Mukhatira fi safqa al-hukuma wa-jama'at al-'unf* [The Danger of the Deal between the Government and the Society of Violence], Cairo: Mirit li-l-Nashr wa-l-Ma'lumat, 2000, pp. 252–94.

45. *Taqrir khatir: Li-man kana lahu qalb aw ulqi al-sam'* [An Important State-ment: For Whom Had a Heart or Has Received the Inauguration], is sixty-one pages long and handwritten, probably in 1990, after the increasing tensions with the authorities.

46. *Mithaq al-'Amal al-Islami*, p. 83.

47. Khalid al-Birri, *al-Dunya ajmal min al-janna: Sira usuli Misri*, Beirut: Dar al-Nahhar li-l-Nashr, 2001. The book has been translated into French, *La terre est plus belle qua le paradis*, Paris: J.C. Lattès, 2002.

48. Patrick Haenni, *L'ordre des caïds: Conjurer la dissidence urbaine au Caire*, Paris: Karthala, 2005.

49. Communiqué of Khalid Ibrahim, photocopy at the International Institute for Social History in Amsterdam.

50. The series is called *Silsila tashih al-mafahim* [Series of the Correction of Concepts]. The first deals with general concepts and is called *Mubadara waqf al-'unf: Ru'ya waq'iyya wa nazra shari'iyya* [The Initiative for the Ending of Violence. Realism and Legal Theory], written by Usama Ibrahim Hafiz and 'Asim 'Abd al-Majid. The second is entitled *Hurma al-ghuluw fi-l-din wa takfir al-muslimin* [Forbidding of Extremism in Religion and the Excommunication of Muslims], written by Najih Ibrahim 'Abdallah and 'Ali Muhammad 'Ali Sharif. The third is entitled, *al-Nashr wa-l-tabayyun fi tashih mafahim al-muhtasibin* [Advise and Clarification in the Correction of the Concepts of the Overseers], written by 'Ali Muhammad 'Ali Sharif and Usama Ibrahim Hafiz. The fourth is entitled *Taslit al-adwa' ala ma waq'a fi-l-jihad min ikhta'* [Clarification of Mistakes in Waging the Jihad], written by Hamdi 'Abd al-Rahman al-'Azim and Najih Ibrahim 'Abdallah. The Series was published by Maktaba al-Turath al-Islami in Cairo in 2002.

51. *Tafjirat al-Riyad: al-Ahkam wa-l-athar* [Explosions in Riyad: Legal Opinions and (Political) Effects], Cairo: Matktaba al-Turath al-Islami, 2003. It is a collective book written by the nine original leaders called the 'historical leadership'.

52. *Nahr al-Dhikriyya: al-Muraja'at al-fiqhiyyat li-l-Jama'at al-Islamiyya* [The River of Memories: Legal Revisionism of the Jama'a al-Islamiyya], Cairo: Maktaba al-Turath al-Islami, 2003.

53. *Mubadara waqf al-'unf: Ru'ya waq'iyya wa nazra shari'iyya*, pp. 36–48.

54. Ibid., p. 49 and *Tafjirat fi Riyad*, pp. 37–48.

55. *Taslit al-adwa' ala ma waq'a fi-l-jihad min ikhta'*, p. 4.

56. Ibid., p. 13. See also *Mubadara waqf al-'unf*, p. 39.

57. Ibid., p. 38. *Nahr al-Dhikriyyat*, p. 42.

58. *Nahr al-Dhikriyyat*, p. 44.

59. *Tafjirat fi Riyad*, p. 21–2.

60. *Nahr al-Dhikriyyat*, pp. 121–2.

61. *Tafjirat fi Riyad*, pp. 37–45.

62. Ibid., p. 162.

63. *Hisba* is an interesting principle that can be used for empowering the believer and can therefore be used as a starting point for evolving a theory of civil rights and the duties of the citizen and his/her relationship with the state.

64. See Roel Meijer, 'Yusuf al-'Uyairi, and the Making of a Revolutionary Salafi Praxis', *Die Welt des Islams*, vol. 47, nos 3–4, 2007, pp. 422–59.

65. The websites include www.tawhed.ws and www.ozoo,tk. Recently his works have been translated into English and even into Dutch.

66. *Tawajud al-Amrika fi al-Jazira al-'Arabiyya: Haqiqa wa-ahdaf* [The Presence of America on the Arabian Peninsula: Truth and Goals] (no date).

67. *al-Mizan li-haraka Taliban* [The Taliban Movement in the Balance] (no date).

68. *Hal intaharat Hawwa am istashhadat? Bahth mutawwal fi hukm al-'amaliyyat al-ishtishhadiyya* [Has Eve Committed Suicide or Has She Martyred Herself? Elaborate Study on Martyrdom Operations] (no date). *'Amaliya "al-Masrah fi Moscow": Madha rabh minha al-mujahidun wa madha khasaru?* [The 'Moscow Theatre' operation: What is the Benefit of it for the Mujahidun and what did They Lose?] (no date).

69. *Ma hakadha al-'adl ya fadila al-shaykh! Difa'an 'an Jama'a Abi Sayyaf al-Filbiniyya* [This is Not Justice, Oh Honoured Shaykh: In Defence of the Society of Abu Sayyaf of the Philippines] (no date).

70. *al-'Iraq wa-l-Jazira al-'Arabiyya* [Iraq and the Arabian Peninsula], (no date) and *Silsilat al-harb al-salabiyya 'ala al-Iraq* [The Series of the Crusader War], 2003.

71. See his work on the American presence in the Arabian Peninsula, *Tawajud al-Amrika fi al-Jazira al-'Arabiyya* (no date)

72. See for instance his work on the Taliban, *al-Mizan li-haraka Taliban*, a movement that is often condemned by Saudi Salafi sheikhs for *bid'a*, innovation.

73. See his critique of the Saudi Sahwa shaykh Salman al-'Awda, *Munasahat Salman al-'Awda* [Advise to Salman al-Awda] (no date), p. 6.

74. See especially his works on jihad, *Thawabit 'ala darb al-jihad* [Principles of Jihad] (no date); and *Hukm al-jihad wa-anwa'ihi* [The Pronouncement of Jihad and its Forms] (no date).

75. *al-'Iraq wa-l-Jazira al-'Arabiyya*, p. 5.

76. The concept is based on the *hadith* that in Islam there are seventy-three sects, of which only one will be saved. It is synonymous with *al-firqa al-najiya* (the saved sect), explained in the section on quietist Salafism further on.

77. See *Hal intaharat Hawwa am istashhadat?* p. 5.

78. See Roel Meijer '"The Cycle of Contention" and the Limits of Terrorism in Saudi Arabia' in Paul Aarts and Gerd Nonneman (eds), *Saudi Arabia in the Balance: Political Economy, Society, Foreign Affairs*, London: Hurst, 2005, pp. 271–311; and Thomas Hegghammer, 'Terrorist Recruitment and Radicalisation in Saudi Arabia', *Middle East Policy*, vol. 13, no. 4, 2006, pp. 39–60. Hegghammer argues that most of the members of the groups in Saudi Arabia were not attracted to such *jihadi* grand strategies and ideological radicalism of its leaders.

79. See Uyairi's fascinating war diary, *Silsilat al-harb al-salabiyya 'ala al-Iraq*.

80. For a full analysis of the AMS between 2003 and 2005, see Meijer, 'Muslim Politics under Occupation. The Association of Muslim Scholars and the Politics of Resistance in Iraq', *Arab Studies Journal*, vols 13/14, nos 1 and 2, 2005, pp. 93–112.

81. Interview with Harith al-Dhari by the TV station al-Arabiyya, broadcast on 11 December, 2005, and published on the AMS website.

82. *al-Sharq al-Awsat*, 6 October 2004.

83. Interview with Harith al-Dhari by al-Arabiyya, 11 December 2005.

84. www.swissinfo.org, 29 April 2005.

85. Interview with 'Abd al-Salam al-Kubaysi in *al-Sabil*, 7 October 2003, www.assabeel.info.

86. Interview Harith al-Dari by Al Arabiyya, 11 December 2005.

87. See Roel Meijer, 'Sunni Factions and the Political Process', in Markus Bouillon et al. (eds), *Iraq: Preventing a New Generation of Conflict*, Boulder: Lynne Rienner, 2007, pp. 89–108.

88. He wrote a series of twenty articles on the topic, of which the first ten were published in the Jordanian newspaper *al-Sabil*. They were published as *Min al-fiqh al-muqawama wa-l-jihad* [On the Jurisprudence of Resistance and Jihad], Amman: Al-Sabil, 2005. I bought the booklet at the Amman Marriott where it was sold in the lobby.

89. Transcript of the program of *Al-Jazeera, al-Shari'a wa-l-Hayat* [Islamic Law and Daily Life] in which Muhammad Ayyash al-Kubaysi participated, broadcast on 28 December 2004.

90. See for comparisons with Hamas: Beverley Milton-Edwards, *Islamic Politics in Palestine*.

91. *Min fiqh al-muqawama wa-l-jihad*. Part 11, 'Mujahidun am du'a?', www.iraq-amsi.org, 4 May 2005.

92. *Min fiqh al-Muqawama wa-l-jihad*, Part 3, 'al-Muqawama wa-'aqida tawhid', originally published in *al-Sabil*, 1 March 2005.

93. Interview with Harith al-Dhari by the TV station al-Arabiyya, 11 December 2005.

94. *Bayan* (no. 18) *hawl ahdath fi-l-mudun al-'Iraqiyya*, 15 February 2004, on the website of the AMS, www.iraq-amsi.org, [Last accessed: March 2004].

95. *Min fiqh al-muqawama wa-l-jihad*, Part 4, 'al-Muqawama…al-ihtilal… wa-harb al-mustalahat', originally published in *al-Sabil*, 29 March, 2005.

96. *Bayan* (no. 18) *hawl ahdath fi-l-mudun al-'Iraqiyya*, 15 February 2004.

97. See, for example, *Bayan* (no. 21) *hawl al-'itida' 'ala al-Rawda al-Kazimiyya*, 28 February 2004, www.iraq-amsi.org, [Last accessed: 21 March 2004].

98. *Min fiqh al-muqawama wa-l-jihad*, Part 12, 'al-Muqawama wa-l-waraqa al-ta'ifiyya', www.iraq-amsi.org, 11 May 2005, [Last accessed: June 2005].

99. *Al-Jazeera* debate, 28 December, 2004.

100. See Meijer, 'Sunni Factions and the Political Process'.

101. Cited in Hesham Al-Awadi, *In Pursuit of Legitimacy: The Muslim Brothers and Mubarak, 1982–2000*, London: I.B Tauris, 2004, p. 16.

102. Ibid., p. 57.

103. For a more detailed analysis of the ambiguity in Tilmisani's political thinking, see Meijer 'The Muslim Brotherhood and the Political: An Exercise in Ambiguity', in Roel Meijer and Edwin Bakker (eds), *The Muslim Brotherhood in Europe: Burdens of the Past, Challenges of the Future*, London: Hurst, 2011 (forthcoming).

104. Ibid., p. 82 and 116. Also Amr Hamzawy and Nathan J. Brown, 'Can Egypt's Troubled Elections Produce a More Democratic Future?', *Policy Outlook*, Carnegie Endowment for International Peace, December 2005, p. 7. Mona El-Ghorbashi, 'The Metamorphosis of the Egyptian Muslim Brothers', *International Journal of Middle East Studies*, vol. 37, 2005, pp. 378 and 380.

105. Al-Awadi, *In Pursuit of Legitimacy*, p. 93.

106. Ibid., p. 84.

107. El-Ghorbashy, 'The Metamorphosis', p. 379.

108. Ibid., p. 383.

109. Ibid., pp. 384–5.

110. Ibid., p. 389.

111. Noha Attar, 'The Muslim Brotherhood's Success in the Legislative Elections in Egypt 2005: Reasons and Implications', *EuroMeSCo*, October 2006, p. 16.

112. Ibid., p. 24.

113. Amr Hamzawy and Nathan Brown, 'Can Egypt's Troubled Elections', p. 6; and Barbara Kerr, 'The Egyptian Brotherhood—a Normal Conservative Party?', p. 3.

114. Attar, *The Muslim Brotherhood's Success*, p. 21.

115. Nathan J. Brown, Amr Hamzawy and Marina Ottaway, 'Islamist Movements and the Democratic Process in the Arab World: Exploring Grey Zones', *Carnegie Papers*, no. 67, March 2006.

116. Bruce K. Rutherford, 'What Do Egypt's Islamist Want? Moderate Islam and the Rise of Islamic Constitutionalism', *Middle East Journal*, vol. 60, no. 4, 2006, pp. 726–31.

117. Attar, *The Muslim Brotherhood's Success*, p. 24.

118. For the most comprehensive account of Salafism, see Roel Meijer

(ed.), *Global Salafism: Islam's New Religious Movement*, London: Hurst, 2009.

119. The term Salafism derives from the pious forefathers, *al-salaf al-salih*, which includes the first three generations of Muslims the *sahaba* or the companions of the Prophet, the subsequent generation of followers (*tabi'un*) and the next generation ('the followers of the followers' or *atba' al-tabi'in*), the last of whom died around 810. They form the sources of the *hadith*, the sayings of the Prophet.

120. Theoretically, the concept of *tawhid* (the Oneness of God, or strict monotheism) is egalitarian and also the principle of *ijtihad*, individual interpretation of the sources of Islam, the Qur'an and *hadith*, is basically democratic. Apolitical or quietist Salafism, however, has become a current that has strong hierarchical overtones as all issues must be referred to the *ulama*, for they alone have the necessary religious knowledge (*'ilm*) to give the right answers.

121. Abdu al-Salam bin Salim bin Rajaa'as-Sihaymee, *The ideology of Terrorism and Violence in the Kingdom of Saudi Arabia: Its Origins: The Reasons for its Spread and Solution*, Abridged version of *Fikr al-irhab wa-l-unf fi-l-Mamlaka al-'Arabiyya al-Sa'udiyya: Masdaruhu, asbab intisharuhu ilaj* (Transl. by AbdulHaq for SalafiManhaj, 2007), Cairo: Dar al-Manhaj, 1426/2005, p. 54.

122. Noorhaidi Hasan, 'Ambivalent Doctrines and Conflicts in the Salafi Movement in Indonesia', in Roel Meijer (ed.), *Global Salafism*, pp. 169–188.

123. 'This negation means that many questions must be avoided, especially those that are connected to obstinacy, evoking strife, and debate of what is valueless (*batil*), as well as excessive in demanding questions that cannot be answered.' Cited in *Mudhakkira al-hadith al-nabawi fi-l-'aqida wa-l-ittiba'i* [Memoirs of the *hadith* of the Prophet in the *'aqida* and followers] Cairo: Dar al-Manhaj, 1424/2004. Originally published in 1406/1985, p. 36.

124. My account of quietist Salafism is mainly based on an analysis of Rabi' bin Hadi al-Madkhali's work and those close to him. Although he is one of the most strident and most polemical of the older generation Salafi sheikhs, his campaigns against 'deviants' have been endorsed by the three great founders of modern Salafism, Nasir al-Din al-Albani (d. 1999), Salih Fawzan bin Fawzan, and 'Abd al-'Aziz bin Baz (d. 1999), the former Mufti of Saudi Arabia, who have bestowed upon him the title of *jarh wa-l-ta'dil al-'asr* (the person who has the right to wound and determine what is correct [of *hadith*] of the age), a classical term that gives someone the right to evaluate

*hadith*, but in the modern political context denotes the right to make the distinction between who is a friend and who is an enemy.

125. Anwar 'Abdallah, *al-'Ulama' wa-l-'arsh: Thani'yya al-sulta fi-l-Sa'udiyya* [The Ulama and the Throne: The Second Power in Saudi Arabia], 3rd edn, Paris: Maktabat al-Sharq, 2004.

126. Quintan Wiktowicz, 'Anatomy of the Salafi Movement', *Studies in Conflict & Terrorism*, vol. 29, no. 3, April-May 2006, pp. 207–39.

127. In a recent Salafi book against terrorism the *hadith* (saying of the Prophet) on the doctrine of *wali al-amr* was reproduced: 'There will come leaders who will not follow my guidance and not follow my Sunnah. There will be among them men who will have hearts of devils in the bodies of humans.' He (the Companion of the Prophet) asked 'What shall I do, O Messenger of Allah, if I reach that?' He replied, 'You should hear and obey the ruler even if he flogs your back and takes your wealth, then still hear (*sam'*) and obey (*ta'a*).' For this quote see *'The Brothers of the Devils': Islamic Condemnation of Terrorists, Hijackers & Suicide Bombers* (Transl. by SalafiPublications.com and published in Birmingham in October 2001), 2nd edn published in May 2003, p. 22. Incidentally the doctrine of 'hearing and obeying' is also the principle that rules the relationship between leader and followers in the Muslim Brotherhood and has only recently been contested.

128. Typical of the Salafi attitude towards politics is the pronouncement of imam al-Barbahaaree (Barbahiri): 'If you find a man making supplication (*nasiha*) against the ruler, know that he is a person of innovation. If you find a person making supplication for the ruler to be upright, know that he is a person of the Sunnah, if Allah wills.' Quoted in *'The Brothers of the Devils'*, p. 22.

129. Sulayman bin 'Abdallah bin Hamud Aba al-Khayl, *Mawqif al-Mamlaka al-'Arabiyya al-Sa'udiyya min al-irhab:Dirasa shar'iyya 'ilmiyya watha'iqiyya* [The Position of the Kingdom of Saudi Arabia towards Terrorism: An Academic Legal Study Based on Documents] Riyad: Maktab al-Malik Fahd al-Wataniyya athna'al-Nashr, 2003, p. 10.

130. *Saudi Arabia's Permanent Council of Senior Scholars on Terrorism & Related Issues* (no date), pp. 7–8. www.answering-extremism.com [Last accessed: 10 February 2009].

131. Rabi' bin Hadi al-Madkhali, *Nasiha ila al-umma al-Jaza'iriyya sha'ban wa-hukuma* [Advice to the Algerian Nation, Its Population and Government], 14/1/1422 HA, 2001, p. 2.

132. *Bayan marahil fitna Abi al-Hasan* [Communiqué on the Phases of Dissension of Abu al-Hasan] www.alathary.net/vb2/showpost.php?p= 2607&postcount=1, December 2003, accessed 10 February 2009, p. 4.

133. 'Aqil bin 'Abd al-Rahman bin Muhammad al-'Aqil, *al-Irhab afat al-'asr: Madha qala 'anhu al-'ulama wa-l-mashayikh w-l-mufakkirun wa-l-tarbiyyun wa-bi-madha wa wafuhu* [Terrorism, the Bane of the Century: What Do the 'Ulama,the Shaykhs, the Thinkers and the Pedagogues Say on the Issue and How Do They Analyse It], Riyad: Maktaba Fahd al-Wataniyya Athna'al-Nashr, 1st edn, 1425/2004, p. 12.

134. Muhammad bin 'Umar bin Salim Bazmul, *Takfir wa-dawabituhu* [Excommunication and its Principles] Cairo: Dar al-Tawhid wa-l-Sunna, 1428/2007, pp. 8–9.

135. Rabi' bin Hadi al-Madkhali, *al-Bahth 'ala al-muwadda wa-l-i'tilaf wa-l-tahdhir min al-firqa wa-l-ikhtilaf.* www.rebee.net/show_des.aspx@pid=3&d=263. 12/21/1429/2007, p. 13. Downloaded 22 January 2009.

136. Salafism is not only opposed to political Islam, but it is also opposed to all forms of Islam that do not comply with its restricted version of Islam: Sufism, Shi'ism, and most schools of law except Hanbalism.

137. Bernard Haykel, 'On the Nature of Salafi Thought and Action', in Roel Meijer (ed.), *Global Salafism: Islam's New Religious Movement*, London: Hurst, 2009, pp. 33–57.

138. For a more elaborate analysis of the ambiguity of Salafism, see Meijer, 'Salafism: Doctrine and Practice', in Khaled Hroub (ed), *Political Islam: Context versus Ideology*, London: Saqi Books, 2010.

139. For an interesting analysis of this skilful maneuvering of Muqbil bin Hadi al-Wadi'i, see Laurent Bonnefoy, 'How Transnational is Salafism in Yemen?' in Meijer (ed.), *Global Salafism*, pp. 321–41. This model seems to apply to all the countries in the Middle East where Salafism is active and is used by the state against its political Islamist adversaries.

140. See Christopher Boucek, 'Extremist Re-education and Rehabilitation in Saudi Arabia," in Tore BJØRGO and John Horgan, *Leaving Terrorism Behind: Individual and Collective Disengagement*, New York: Routledge, 2009, pp. 212–223.

141. There exists a whole library on the Salafi campaign against extremism. Some of the most salient publications are reprinted in work mentioned in note 126, *The Position of the Kingdom of Saudi Arabia towards Terrorism*. Needless to say, the Salafi concept of extremism differs from the liberal concept of this phenomenon. Its roots and solutions in these works are not typically sought in socio-economic or political causes but in religious 'deviation' and bringing people back to the straight path. Salafis themselves argue that the campaign against extremism is inherent in Salafism itself and has been waged since the rise of the *khawarij* in the first century *hijra* and against later medieval innovations, such as Mu'tazilism.

142. See the refutation of Rabi' bin Hadi al-Madkhali of 'Abd al-Kahliq's accusation that Saudi Wahhabi *ulama* are irrelevant to the modern world because they do not deal with reality in his, *Jama'a wahida la Jama'at: Wa-sirat wahid la 'asharat* [One Group not Many Groups. One Life of the Prophet not Ten], 5th edn, 1423/2002 (1st edn 1995).

143. Sayyid Qutb is a favorite target of Salafi sheikhs. Someone like Rabi' bin Hadi al-Madkhali has written five books against Qutb, the most famous one, *Adwa'a islamiyya 'ala 'aqida Sayyid Qutb wa fikruhu* [Islamic Light Cast on the Creed of Sayyid Qutb and his Thought], 1413/1982.

144. Zayd bin Muhammad bin Hadi al-Madkhali, *al-Irhab wa-atharuhu 'ala al-afrad wa-l-umam* [Terrorism and Its Influences on Individuals and Nations], 2nd edn, United Arab Emirates: Maktabat al-Furqan, 1417/1996, 1420/1999.

145. See, for instance, http://www.salafipublications.com/sps/downloads/pdf/NDV090003.pdf

146. See, for instance, http://www.salafitalk.net/st/viewmessages.cfm?Forum=23&Topic=947. Putting the Fitnah of Abu-Fitan al-Ma'ribee into Perspective. Rabi' bin Hadi al-Madkhali is also the most prominent critique of Abu Hasan, see his, *al-Tankil bi-ma fi al-jaj Abi al-Hasan al-ma'rabi min al-abatil*, United Arab Emirates: Maktaba al-Furqan, 1424/2003.

147. *Nasiha al-shaykh Rabi ' li-l-salafiyyin fi Firansa.* www.rabee.net/show_des.aspx?pid=3&id=103 (no date), pp. 1–2. Downloaded 21 January 2009.

148. as-Sihaymee, *The ideology of Terrorism and Violence in the Kingdom of Saudi Arabia*, p. 63.

149. Ibid., pp. 65–66.

150. Zayd bin Muhammad bin Hadi al-Madkhali, *al-Irhab wa-atharuhu*, p. 82.

151. as-Sihaymee, *The ideology of Terrorism and Violence in the Kingdom of Saudi Arabia*, p. 74.

152. Rabi' bin Hadi al-Madkhali, *Jama'a wahida la Jama'at: Wa-sirat wahid la 'asharat* [One Group not Many Groups. One Life of the Prophet not Ten], Maktabat al-Furqan, United Arab Emirates, 1423/2002 (1st edn 1995), p. 88.

153. Ibid., p. 68.

154. Ibid., pp. 58, 97.

155. Ibid., p. 75.

156. See especially Hans Gunther Lobmeyer, *Opposition und Widerstand in Syrien*, Hamburg: Deutsches Orient Institut, 1995.

157. "al-Bayanuni yaftihu mu'tamar Lundun li-hiwar ikhwan suriya

yu'aduna li-mashru'mithaq watani," [Bayanuni Opens the London Conference to Prepare the Debate on the National Charter]," *Al-Jazeera Net*, 28 July 2002.

158. *Jama'a al-Ikhwan al-Muslimin fi Suriya 'ala Masharif al-Alfiya al-Thalitha li-l-Milad Tajarib … wa Tatall'at*, [The Society of the Muslim Brothers in Syria on the Eve of the 21st Century. Experiences and Aims], www.ikhwan-muslimoon-syria.org/01ikhwansyria/tajarub.htm [Last accessed: in March 2005].

159. "al-Bayanuni yaftihu mu'tamar Lundun li-hiwar ikhwan suriya yu'aduna li-mashru'mithaq watani," *Al-Jazeera Net*, 28 July 2002.

160. *al-Mithaq al-Sharaf al-Watani fi Suriya*, 2001, www.ikhwan-muslimoon-syria.org/04malaffat_nasharat/mithak2.htm. Accessed in March 2005. It was signed on 25 August 2002. The original charter was issued in May 2002.

161. *al-Mashru' al-Siyasi li-Suriya al-Mustaqbal*. 2004, available on the Brotherhood's website.

162. *Mashru'*, p. 8.

163. Ibid., p. 9.

164. Ibid., pp. 8–9.

165. Ibid., p. 14.

166. Ibid., p. 12.

167. Ibid., p. 23.

168. Ibid., p. 18.

169. Ibid., p. 10.

170. Ibid., pp. 15–16.

171. Ibid., p. 11.

172. Emphasis added.

173. Ibid., p. 13.

174. Ibid., p. 15.

175. Ibid., p. 10.

176. Ibid., p. 23.

177. Ibid., p. 23

178. Ibid., p. 24

179. *al-Mithaq al-Sharaf al-Watani*, p. 1.

180. Ibid., p. 2.

181. *Mashru'*, p. 11.

182. Ibid., p. 22.

183. Ibid., p. 21; and *al-Mithaq*, p. 2.

184. Aside from the numerous attacks of Ayman al-Zawahiri on the Muslim Brotherhood, whether in the form of the Egyptian or Palestinian (Hamas) form, the most closely reasoned attacks have been written by Abu Basir al-Tartusi. See his attack on Egyptian revisionism,

*Mubadara al-Jama'at al-Islamiyya al-Misriyya. 'I'tiraf bi-l-khita' am inhi-yar wa-suqut* [The Egyptian Jama'a al-Islamiyya: Acknowledgement of their Mistakes or Their Annihilation and Fall], and of the Syrian Muslim Brotherhood, *Wa la-na kilmat nazra shar'iyya li-Mithaq al-Sharaf al-Watani alladhi tarahahu al-Ikhwan al-Muslimun al-Suriyyun* [Our Theoretical Analysis of the Noble National Charter on the Basis of the Shar'iyya], and of the Association of Muslim Scholars (AMS), *Hay'at 'Ulama al-Muslimin fi mizan al-Tawhid wa-l-jihad* [The Association of Muslim Scholars in the light (balance) of Unity of God and Jihad]. All of them were published on the site www.tawhed.ws [Last accessed: April 2004].

185. See Gilles Kepel's chapters on the Society of Muslims, *The Prophet and the Pharaoh*, pp. 70–102.

## 3. TURKEY: BETWEEN POST-ISLAMISM AND POST-KEMALISM

1. See Nilüfer Göle, 'La revendication démocratique de l'islam', in S. Yerasimos (ed.), *Les Turcs*, Paris: Autrement, 1994, pp. 132–3.

2. On the history of the democratization process in Turkey, see Ergun Özbudun, *Turkish Politics: Challenge to Democratic Consolidation*, London and Boulder: Lynne Rienner Publishers, 2000.

3. Turkish abbreviation of Adalet ve Kalkınma Partisi, Justice and Development Party.

4. On this concept, see Jean Marcou, 'Islamisme et post-islamisme en Turquie', *Revue Internationale de Politique Comparée*, vol. 11, N° 4, 2004, especially pp. 600–08.

5. DSP, Turkish abbreviation of Demokrat Sol Partisi, Left Democratic Party: a small group seeing itself as to the left of the CHP, founded by Bülent Ecevit in the 1980s.

6. MHP, Turkish abbreviation of Milliyetçi Hareket Partisi, Party of the Nationalist Movement, a far-right nationalist party founded by General Turkeş. It was a partner in the government of Bülent Ecevit (1999–2001).

7. CHP, Turkish abbreviation of Cumurhuriyet Halk Partisi, Republican People's Party, formerly the Kemalist single party.

8. DYP, Turkish abbreviation of Doğru Yol Partisi, True Path Party, the party of ex-President Suleiman Demirel et Mrs Tansu Çiller (Prime Minister 1993–96). This party sees itself as the heir to Adnan Menderes' Democratic Party which was in power in the 1950s.

9. See interview with Ruşen Çakır (journalist with *Vatan*) by Jean Marcou, Istanbul, December 2002.

10. Saadet Partisi, Turkish abbreviation for Happiness Party, created by Necmettin Erbakan after the dissolution of the Fazilet Partisi (see above).

11. See Jean Marcou, 'Islamisme et post-islamisme en Turquie', 2004, especially pp. 589ff.

12. Under the 1982 Constitution, in its initial draft which appeared in the 1961 Constitution, the NSC had very extensive powers, enabling it to issue orders to the government when it believed that the foundations of the state were under threat. On the NSC cf. Ergun Özbudun, *Türk Anayasa Hukuku*, Ankara: Yetkinyayınları, 2005, especially pp. 49–56.

13. Fazilet Partisi, Virtue Party, created in 1998 by Necmettin Erbakan after the dissolution of Refah.

14. Very significant, in this respect, is a letter written by Zülfü Livanelito Deniz Baykal after the defeat of the CHP in the parliamentary elections of 2007. The famous singer revealed, notably, that Deniz Baykal, leader of the CHP, had facilitated Recep Tayyip Erdoğan's rise to become head of government in 2003, thinking that in any case Erdoğan would not last 'more than two months as prime minister'.

15. YÖK, Turkish abbreviation for Yüksek Ögretim Kurulu, the Supreme Council for Higher Education, set up by the miliitary after the 1980 coup d'état to place Turkey's universities—where large-scale political agitation had developed in the 1960s and 70s—under their control.

16. *Laikçi*, an expression referring here to supporters of traditional secularism in Turkey.

17. On the Turkish political regime, see Jean-Paul Burdy and Jean Marcou, *La Turquie à l'heure de l'Europe*, Grenoble: PUG, 2008.

18. See the very long article 104 of the Constitution.

19. Notably, Ahmet Necdet Sezer had been President of the Constitutional Court, before his election as President of the Republic.

20. Çankaya is the presidential palace in Ankara.

21. This expression describing the army in France dated from the Third Republic, and referred to the military's obligation to refrain from all political activity and comment.

22. A distinguished constitutional expert, former Rector of the University of Galatasaray.

23. While Article 102 of the 1982 Constitution did stipulate a two thirds quorum (367 out of 550 members) for election of the President of the Republic in the first or second round, it did not specify at all that 367 deputies must be physically present in the chamber for the vote to take place. But that was in fact the reading adopted by the Constitutional Court—in the wake of the YÖK chairman's interpretation—

273

when it annulled the first round of the presidential election on 1 May 2007 (see below).

24. Türk Sanayicileri ve İşadamları Derneği (Association of Turkish Industrialists and Businessmen).

25. This body had played a role of some importance in causing the fall of Erbakan in the 'post-modern coup d'état' in 1997. In 2007, having rather retreated at the beginning of the crisis, the TÜSIAD chair-woman, Mrs Arzuhan Doğan Yalçındağ, then expressed—before the closing date for candidacies—her conviction 'that Recep Tayyip Erdoğan will have the sense not to stand.'

26. A Turkish transcription of the English word *meeting*, in this case, how-ever, meaning 'demonstration' or 'public gathering'.

27. In Ankara, on 14 April 2007, more than a million people demonstrated in support of secularism, on the approaches to the Atatürk mauso-leum. Parades of similar size took place afterwards at Istanbul (29 April 2007) and Izmir (13 May 2007). These demonstrations, strongly backed by Kemalist organizations, succeeded in mobilizing a portion of the urban middle classes, especially a strong contingent of young woman, opposed to Tayyip Erdoğan's candidacy.

28. Parliamentary elections were still scheduled normally for the begin-ning of November 2007.

29. In addition Mrs Gül, who had been expelled from the University of Ankara because of her headgear, brought an action against Turkey before the European Court of Human Rights in 1998; she eventually withdrew her action when her husband joined the government.

30. DTP, Turkish abbreviation for Demokratik Toplum Partisi, Party for a Democratic Society. This party was dissolved in December 2009 by the Constitutional Court, but re-established under the name of the BDP (Baris ve Demokrasi Partisi, Party for Peace and Democracy).

31. *Laikçi* and *dinci* are the usual terms in Turkey for 'secularists' and 'people of religious feeling'.

32. This atmosphere of consensus was well reflected in the colloquium organized by the Union of Turkish Bar Associations in Ankara in Janu-ary 2001: cf. *Uluslararası Anayasa Hukuku Kurultayı*, Ankara: Türkiye Barolar Birliği Yayın, 2001.

33. This revision, adopted by referendum on 21 October 2007, altered the term of each parliament (reduced to four years) and the president's term of office (reduced to five years), and provided for election of the president by popular vote from then on.

34. This was thirty years to the day after the 1980 coup d'état.

35. Parliamentary elections, November 2002; local elections, March 2004; parliamentary elections, July 2007; referendum, October 2007; local elections, March 2009; referendum, September 2010.

36. cf. Ali Bayramoğlu, *28 Subat, bir mudahalenin güncesi*, Istanbul: Birey Yayıncılık, 2001. See also the lecture by Ahmet Insel at the Institut Français d'Etudes Anatoliennes, 'L'armée est-elle encore un acteur politique en Turquie' (8 April 2010), available on the l'IFEA website: http://www.ifea-istanbul.net/website_2/

37. A grenade attack in 2005 on a bookshop belonging to a former Kurdish activist, by Turkish soldiers in civilian dress. The attack caused a scandal and exposed methods used by the army in its fight against the Kurdish rebellion. See Guillaume Perrier, *Le Monde*, 13 August 2009.

38. A plan drawn up by some soldiers, exposed in 2008, to assassinate prominent non-Muslim persons so as to create a situation of chaos.

39. A plan drawn up by military personnel close to the general staff, revealed by the daily *Taraf* in June 2009. The aim was said to be to discredit the government and Fethullah Gülen's religious movement.

40. A plot hatched by some generals after the AKP's coming to power in 2003, and revealed by *Taraf* in January 2010. It was said to involve numerous operations aimed at destabilizing the country (attacks on important mosques in Istanbul or museums, arranging of air traffic incidents with Greece, etc.).

41. *Taraf*, whose motto is *Düşünmek taraf olmaktır* ('to think is to take up a position'), was started in November 2007 by the novelist Ahmet Altan, and has specialized in revealing military plots and officially taboo matters. It has a print run of 60,000; its enemies allege that it is financed by Fethullah Gülen's religious organization, which has never been proved.

42. Several revelations in *Taraf* have also shown how the army, having been informed by satellite or drone aircraft intelligence about preparations for PKK attacks, allegedly refrained from taking any counter measures, so that deaths of Turkish national servicemen could increase public hostility against the Kurds.

43. YAŞ: Yüksek Asker Şura, the Supreme Military Council, the body which manages the careers of the military and makes appointments to the supreme command of the armed forces.

44. A Turkish holding company operating not only in the media sector but also in the energy, industrial, financial, insurance and tourism sectors. It is the owner, notably, of dailies such as *Posta, Milliyet, Hürriyet, Radikal* and *Vatan*, and television channels such as Star TV, Kanal D and CCN Türk.

45. A pro-government newspaper, which is currently the leading Turkish daily in terms of circulation, with more than 800,000 copies daily.

46. Hanefi Avci, *Haliç'te Yasayan Simonlar*, Angora Kitaplar, 2010.

47. cf. Jean Marcou, 'La Turquie, puissance régionale au Moyen-Orient' in

Bertrand Badie and Dominique Vidal, *La fin d'un monde unique*, Paris: La Découverte, 2010, p. 267.

## 4. THE NEW TREND OF THE MUSLIM BROTHERHOOD IN EGYPT

1. The use of political Islam implies recognition of the controversial thesis of secularization. The heart of secularization does not lie in the confinement of religion to the private sphere and separating it from politics and state business. It lies in the possibility of differentiating Islam into political, social, spiritual, economic, etc. domains.

2. Eric Davis, 'Ideology, Social Class and Islamic Radicalism in Modern Egypt' in Said Amir Arjomand (ed.), *From Nationalism to Revolutionary Islam*, Albany: State University of New York Press, 1984, pp. 134–138.

3. Ibid., pp. 134–140.

4. Ibid., p. 137.

5. Ibid., p. 138.

6. Ibid., p. 139.

7. Ziad Munson, 'Islamic Mobilization: Social Movement Theory and the Egyptian Muslim Brotherhood', *The Sociological Quarterly*, vol. 42, no. 4, 2001, pp. 487–510.

8. The detention of twenty-nine MBG members, most of whom are wealthy businessmen, and whom the General Prosecutor prohibited from acting on their money, resulted, according to analysts such as Magdy Mehanna in *al-Masri al-Youm*, issue 968, 6 February 2007, in a 2.54 decrease in the index of the Egyptian stock market. Mehanna in this article referred to the size of MBG members' economic activity as 20 billion Egyptian Pounds.

9. Bryan S. Turner, 'Class, Generation and Islamism: Towards a global sociology of political Islam', *British Journal of Sociology*, vol. 54, no. 1, (March 2003), pp. 139–147.

10. Michaelle L. Browers, 'The Secular Bias in Ideology Studies and the case of Islamism', *Journal of Political Ideologies*, vol. 10, no. 1, (February 2005), pp. 75–93.

11. Asef Bayat, 'Islamism and Social Movement Theory', *Third World Quarterly*, vol. 26, no. 6, 2005, pp. 891–908.

12. Gregory Starrett, *Putting Islam to work: Education, Politics and Religious Transformation in Egypt*, CA: University of California Press, 1998.

13. Jakob Skovgaard-Petersen, *Defining Islam for the Egyptian State: Muftis and Fatwas of Dār al-Iftā*, Leiden: Koninklijke Brill, 1997, p. 29.

14. Jakob Skovgaard-Petersen, *Defining Islam for the Egyptian State: Muftis and Fatwas of Dār al-Iftā*, Leiden: Koninklijke Brill, 1997, p. 28.

15. Arthur Goldschmidt Jr., *Modern Egypt: The Formation of a Nation State*, New York: Westview Press, 1988, p. 29.

16. Edward W. Said, *Orientalism*, New York: Vintage Books, 1994, p. 65.

17. Arthur Goldschmidt Jr., *Modern Egypt*, p. 27.

18. Ibid.

19. Enid Hill, 'Norms and Distributive Processes in Egypt's New Regime of Capitalist Accumulation', in Eberhard Kienle (ed.), *Politics from Above, Politics from Below: The Middle East in the Age of Economic Reform*, London: Saqi, 2003, p. 82.

20. Pauline Marie Rosenau, *Post-Modernism and the Social Sciences: Insights, Inroads and Intrusions*, Princeton: Princeton University Press, 1992, p. 77.

21. The founders of IOL nevertheless refuse any explicit or implicit relationship with the Group. Some of them had left the Group before joining IOL; others left it after joining IOL. There are those who have maintained their relationship with the Group. In every case, however, they categorically refuse to accept that IOL is linked to the MBG. IOL has also maintained a critical tone with the MBG, sometimes in spite of frequent appeal from the Group to stop it.

22. Zygmunt Bauman, *In Search of Politics*, Palo Alto: Stanford University Press, 1999, p. 125.

23. Zygmunt Bauman, *Postmodernity and its Discontents*, New York: New York University Press, 1997, pp. 134–135.

24. Fredric Jameson, 'The Cultural Logic of Late Capitalism', in Fredric Jameson (ed.), *Postmodernity, or the Cultural Logic of Late Capitalism*, Durham, NC: Duke University Press, 1991, pp. 1–54.

25. Ibid.

26. Mike Featherstone, *Consumer Culture and Postmodernism*, London: SAGE Publications, 1991, p. 84.

27. Ibid.

28. Kenneth Thompson, 'Social Pluralism and Postmodernity', in Stuart Hall et al. (eds), *Modernity: An Introduction to Modern Societies*, The Open University, 1995, pp. 580–1.

29. Eberhard Kienle, 'Domestic Economic Liberalization: Controlled Market-Building in Contemporary Egypt' in Eberhard Kienle (ed.), *Politics from Above, Politics from Below*, p. 148.

30. Nazih N. Ayubi, *The State and Public Policies in Egypt since Sadat* (Political Studies of the Middle East Series, No. 29), Reading: Ithaca Press, 1991, p. 225.

31. Ibid., p. 226

32. Ibid.

33. James B. Mayfield, *Local Government in Egypt: Structure, Process and the*

*Challenges of Reform,* Cairo: The American University in Cairo Press, 1996, pp. 8–9.

34. Robert Springborg, *Mubarak's Egypt: Fragmentation of the Political Order,* New York: Westview Press, 1989, pp. 124–125.

35. See, for instance, Diaa Rashwan, 'Muslim Brothers in Egypt: Distinctions of Generations and Attitudes', *Al-Iqtisadiya e-newspaper,* 5177 (14 December 2007), http://www.aleqt.com/article.php?do=show&id=764 [Last accessed: 14 December 2007].

36. http://www.ikhwanonline.com/Article.asp?ArtID=30042&SecID=0 [Last accessed: 15 December 2007].

37. Ibid.

38. Alan Richards and John Waterbury, *A Political Economy of the Middle East,* NewYork: Westview Press, 2008, pp. 250–251.

39. Marc Lynch, 'Young Brothers in Cyberspace', *Middle East Report,* 245 (Winter 2007), http://merip.org/mer/mer245/lynch.html#_edn2 [Last accessed: 15 December 2007].

40. http://www.egyptwindow.net/modules.php?name=News&file=article&sid=7335 [Last accessed: 15 December 2007.

## 5. REINVENTING POLITICAL ISLAM: THE DISENGAGEMENT OF EUROPEAN ISLAMISTS

1. Islamism is not a homogeneous phenomenon, its actors differ according to time and place, and the modes of action that it proposes have evolved over the years. It has passed from the goal of inventing modernity for the Muslim world that was autonomous to that of the West at the beginning of the twentieth century, to the aim of establishing an Islamic state in the 1970s, to more recently promoting leadership of a competitive Islamic identity in line with Western capitalist standards. However it is possible to isolate certain elements of Islamist ideologies through ages and spaces. Islamism has always been concerned with the internal goal of reappropriating the 'authentic Islam' of the golden age of the Prophet, in response to what is seen as common Muslims abandoning their Islamic identity. In voluntarily seeking to differentiate themselves from 'classical' Muslims who belong to traditional Muslim societies, and for whom the inheritance of Islam is lived passively, the promoters of this current are engaged in actively reclaiming the precedence of Islamic principles within social and political systems. From the outset Islamism has had an external and reflexive objective: asking Muslims to assert themselves vis à vis the West. Historically, it is in the wake of the downfall of the Caliphate of the Ottoman Empire in 1924 that Islamism was conceived as an alternative ideology to rethink the

*umma*, the Islamic community that was lost and whose 'authentic' identity was threatened by colonial processes. The same conception was used when opposing Islamism to new ideologies that were arising in the Muslim world such as communism or nationalism. The political identity of Islamism throughout the twentieth century thus aimed to renew the framework of Muslims' life, in view of responding to the challenges of Western 'modernity' often understood as a Western domination of Muslim populations. The means employed were those of political and social activism and aimed to impose new 'Islamic' norms concentrated, among other things on questions of identity, on the relation to Western modernity and the place of women, the relation between religion and the State, or on the questioning of the economic, political and intellectual imperialism of the West. This chapter will analyze the history of Islamism in Europe that is more specifically linked to the movement of the Muslim Brotherhood. It is necessary to understand how, in this region, methods of mobilization and participation inspired by Islamism have been successively re-thought by different generations of activists in light of their specific histories and the causes that they aim to defend.

2. On the complexities of the mutual influences between Europe and Islam, see Nilüfer Göle, *Interpénétrations. L'Islam et l'Europe*, Paris: Galaade, 2005.

3. Albert Bastenier and Felice Dassetto, *Immigration et espace public. La controverse de l'intégration*, Paris: CIEMI/L'Harmattan, 1993.

4. Stefano Allievi, 'How the Immigrant has become Muslim. Public Debates on Islam in Europe', *Revue Européenne des Migrations Internationales*, vol. 21, no. 2, 2005, pp. 135–163.

5. The term 'Islamic' is used in this chapter to refer to individuals strictly determining their actions and identity in relation to Islam.

6. Amel Boubekeur, 'Political Islam in Europe: A changing landscape' in Amel Boubekeur and Michael Emerson (eds), *European Islam: The challenges for public policy and society*, CEPS/Open Society Institute, 2007.

7. Juan Jose Escobar Stemmann, 'Middle East Salafism's Influence and The Radicalization of Muslim Communities in Europe', *Meria Journal*, vol. 10, no. 3, September 2006.

8. Post-Islamism designated the historical framework that is the successor of Islamism, following the failure of the latter principally as concerns the Islamization of the political domain of the state in the Muslim world. Following the failure of Islamism, principally due to the Islamization of the political domain of the state in the Muslim world, Post-Islamism considers the historical framework of Islamism. For academic

references on the concepts of Islamism, political Islam, neo-fundamentalism or post-Islamism see the Introduction to this volume.

9. Jean-Noël Ferrié, *Le Régime de la civilité. Public et réislamislamisation en Egypte*, Paris: CNRS, 2004, p. 15.

10. Jocelyne Cesari, *When Islam and Democracy Meet: Muslims in Europe And in the United States*, New York: Palgrave MacMillan, 2006.

11. In francophone Europe, Islamic preachers, such as Tariq Ramadan and Hassan Iquioussen, who were born in Europe or arrived at a young age and were inheritors of the original Islamist codes, embody this diffused re-Islamization. Despite the restricted number of members in their immediate circle of activists, the identification that they generate among young Muslims structures a large part of the process of re-Islamization, without the preachers having to directly supervise the process.

12. Romain Garbaye, *Getting Into Local Power: The Politics of Ethnic Minorities in British and French Cities*, Oxford: Blackwell Publishing, 2005.

13. Amel Boubekeur, 'Islam and Women's rights: Empowerment of a new Islamic Elite, *New Voices, New Perspectives Program*, UN—INSTRAW, March 2006.

14. John Bowen, *Why the French Don't Like Headscarves: Islam, the State, and Public Space*, Princeton: Princeton University Press, 2007.

15. These actors play essential roles in the Islamist philosophy of the Muslim Brotherhood. Sayyid Qutb (1906–1966), an Egyptian intellectual, conceptualised the revolutionary, and even violent, use of Islam in contemporary politics. Hassan al-Banna (1906–1949), also Egyptian, is the founder of the movement of the Muslim Brotherhood. Yusuf al-Qaradawi (1925–) is a theologian and president of the European Council for Fatwa and Research (ECFR).

16. For an analysis of these relations, see Amel Boubekeur, *La voile de la mariée. Jeunes musulmanes, voile et projet matrimonial en France*, Paris: l'Harmattan, 2004.

17. For a more in-depth exploration of the arts in the process of re-Islamization and the renewal of the committed Islamic spirit, see Amel Boubekeur, 'Post-Islamist culture: A new form of Mobilization?' *History of Religion*, vol. 47, no. 1, 2007.

18. This term is taken from Khadija Mohsen-Finan, 'La mise en avant d'une citoyenneté croyant: le cas de Tariq Ramadan', in Rémy Leveau, Catherine Withol de Wenden and Khadija Mohsen-Finan (eds), *De la Citoyenneté locale*, Paris: Ifri, 2003.

19. Jytte Klausen, *The Islamic Challenge: Politics and Religion in Western Europe*, Oxford: Oxford University Press, 2005.

20. Clifford Geertz, *Islam Observed, Religious Development in Morocco and*

*Indonesia,* Yale University Press, 1968, p. 85. The exact quote refers to Islam, this author has replaced it with Islamist re-Islamization.

21. 'Notabilization' occurs through the institutionalization of a certain number of Islamist activists within State representative councils of Muslims in Europe.

22. Moreover the feeling of being locked into an activist career for life explains the following statement from one of our interviewees: 'It's always the same: what do you think about polygamy, lapidation, Iran? OK! Being Muslim isn't our job!'

23. Armando Salvatore, *The Public Sphere: Liberal Modernity, Catholicism, Islam,* New York: Palgrave Macmillan, 2007.

24. Tariq Modood, *Multicultural Politics: Racism, Ethnicity and Muslims in Britain,* Minneapolis: University of Minnesota Press, 2005.

25. Olivier Roy, *Secularism Confronts Islam,* New York: Columbia University Press, 2007.

26. Jørgen S. Nielsen, *Towards a European Islam: Migration, Minorities and Citzenship,* London: Macmillan, 1999.

27. Amel Boubekeur, 'Time to Deradicalise? The European Roots of Muslim Radicalisation', *The International Spectator,* vol. XLIII, no. 3, July–September 2008.

28. In the Sufi tradition, the *murshid* designates the spiritual guide of the brotherhood. For the Muslim Brotherhood, this function was institutionalized as the general guide of the organization.

29. See Amel Boubekeur, 'Cool and Competitive. New Muslim Culture in the West', *ISIM Newsletter,* no. 16, Autumn 2005.

30. An Algerian philosopher (1905–1973) who was involved with reformist Islam, he was one of the principal sources of inspiration for Algerian Islamism. According to Bennabi 'Colonizability' represents the state of decadence (of Islamic thought) which made the colonization of Muslim peoples possible.

31. John Holloway, *Change the World Without Taking Power, The Meaning of Revolution Today,* London: Pluto Press, 2002.

## 6. POLITICAL ISLAM IN WEST AFRICA FROM THE 1980s TO THE PRESENT

1. The posture of crossing one's hands on the chest after each prostration of the ritual prayer was adopted in a context of a struggle for power in the mosques of French Sudan, see Paul Triaud, 'Le mouvement réformiste en Afrique de l'Ouest dans les années 1950', *Mémoires du CERMAA,* vol. 1, 1979, pp. 195–212; and Lansiné Kaba, *The Wahhabiyya: Islamic reform and politics in French West Africa,* Evanston: Northwestern Uni-

versity Press, 1974. On the other hand, the administration identified them as reformers.

2. Fédération des Associations Islamiques Sénégalaises [Federation of Islamic Senegalese Associations] (FAIS) on 6 October 1962 in Senegal, the Communauté Musulmane de la Haute-Volta [Muslim Community of Upper-Voltam in 1962 (renamed Communauté Musulmane du Burkina Faso in 1973), Association Islamique du Niger [Islamic Association of Niger] (AIN) formed on 15 August 1974 on the initiative of Lieutenant-Colonel Seyni Kountché in power. This association 'up until 1992, [...] not only had a monopoly on granting official authorization to give the waazi (sermon to the marabouts), but also the power to control the activities of each marabout', see Olivier Meunier, *Dynamique de l'enseignement Islamique au Niger*, Paris: L'Harmattan, 1997, p. 172. Also the Association Malienne pour l'Unité et le Progrès de l'Islam [Malian Association for the Unity and Progress of Islam] (AMUPI) in 1980.

3. In Mali, 'there were in 1974 about ten (Islamic) radio programmes [...]. I can state that in 1975, the Islamic programmes were perfected and perfectly integrated into the regular radio programs' and 'from July 1987, the listings included, as with the radio, regular, special and one-time programmes as well as religious songs', Biritou Sanankoua and Louis Brenner, (eds), *L'enseignement Islamique au Mali*, Bamako: Jamana, 1991, pp. 134–135). The same author discusses the success of the special program *'Rencontre avec les ulama'* [Meet the *Ulama*].

4. For Niger, see Abdoulaye Niandou Souley and Gado Alzouma, 'Islamic Renewal in Niger: from Monolith to Plurality', *Social Compass*, vol. 43, no. 2, 1996, p. 254.

5. See Muriel Gomez-Perez, *L'Islam politique au sud du Sahara. Identités, discours et enjeux*, Paris: Karthala, 2005; and Muriel Gomez-Perez, 'Généalogie de l'Islam réformiste au Sénégal des années 50 à nos jours: figures, savoirs et réseaux', in Laurent Fourchard, André Mary and René Otayek (eds), *Entreprises religieuses transnationales en Afrique de l'Ouest*, Paris: Karthala, 2005, pp. 193–222.

6. See Muriel Gomez-Perez, 'The Association des Étudiants Musulmans de l'Université de Dakar (AEMUD): Between the Local and the Global. An analysis of Discourse', *Africa today*, vol. 54, issue 3, Spring 2008, pp. 95–117.

7. See Christian Coulon, *Les musulmans et le pouvoir en Afrique noire*, Paris: Karthala, 1983, pp. 171–172.

8. On Senegal, see the works of Erin Augis: 'Jambaar or Jumbax-out? How Sunnite Women negotiate power and belief in Othodox Islamic Femininity', in Mamadou Diouf and Mara Leichtman (eds), *New perspectives*

on *Islam in Senegal: Conversion, Migration, Wealth, Power and Femininity*, London: Palgrave, Macmillan, 2009, pp. 210–233; idem., 'Les jeunes femmes Sunnites et la liberalization économique Dakar', *Afrique Contemporaine*, vol. 231, 2009, pp. 79–98; idem., 'Dakar's Sunnite Women: the Politics of Person', Muriel Gomez-Perez, (ed.), *L'Islam politique au sud du Sahara*, pp. 309–326; idem., *Dakar's Sunnite Women: The Politics of Person*, PhD Dissertation, Department of Sociology, University of Chicago, 2002. On Côte d'Ivoire, see Marie-Nathalie LeBlanc, '*Imaniya* and Young Muslim Women in Côte d'Ivoire', *Anthropologica*, vol. 49, 2007, pp. 35–50; and idem., 'Fashion and the politics of identity: Versioning Womanhood and Muslimhood in the face of tradition and Modernity', *Africa*, vol. 70, no. 3, 2000a, pp. 443–481. On Niger, see, for example, Ousseina Alidou and Hussana Alidou, 'Women, Religion and the discourses of legal ideology in Niger Republic', *Africa today*, vol. 54, issue 3, Spring 2008, pp. 21–36; and Masquelier, *Women and Islamic revival in a West African town*, Bloomington: Indiana University Press, 2009.

9. Between 1991 and 2000, fifty Islamic associations were officially recognized in Niger; see Souley Hassane, 'Les nouvelles élites Islamiques du Niger et du Nigeria du Nord. Itinéraires et prédications fondatrices (1950–2003)', in Fourchard, Mary and René Otayek (eds), *Entreprises religieuses et transnationales en Afrique de l'Ouest*, p. 141. Among the most typical examples were the Association pour la diffusion de l'islam au Niger [Association for the Dissemination of Islam in Niger] (Adini-Islam), the Association pour le rayonnement de la Culture islamique [Association for the Spread of Islamic Culture] (ARCI), Association Nigérienne pour l'Appel à la Solidarité Islamique [Niger Association of the Call for Islamic Solidarity] (ANAUSI).

10. The Conseil National Islamique [National Islamic Council] was created in 1993; the Conseil Supérieur des imams de Côte d'Ivoire [Côte d'Ivoire Superior Council of Imams] was created in 1988, received its agreement in 1991, it was the same for the Ligue Islamique des prédicateurs de Côte d'Ivoire [Islamic League of Preachers of Côte d'Ivoire]. The Association des jeunes Musulmans de Côte d'Ivoire [Association of Young Muslims of Côte d'Ivoire] was created in 1992, the *Conseil National Islamique* [National Islamic Council] (CNI) in 1993 and the Association des Femmes Musulmanes de Côte d'Ivoire [Association of Muslim Women of Côte d'Ivoire] (AFMCI) in 1994. See also Marie Miran, *Islam, histoire et modernité en Côte d'Ivoire*, Paris: Karthala, 2006, Marie-Nathalie LeBlanc, 'Proclaiming Individual Piety: Pilgrims and religious Renewal in Côte d'Ivoire', in Vered Amit and Noel Dyck (eds), *Claiming Individuality: The cultural Politics of Distinct*, London:

Pluto Press, 2006, pp. 173–200; and, Mathias Savadogo, 'L'intervention des associations musulmanes dans le champ politique en Côte d'Ivoire depuis 1990', in Muriel Gomez-Perez (ed.), *L'Islam politique au Sud du Sahara*, pp. 583–600.

11. In the case of Niger, the ANAFI hosted radio programmes (Radio R et M, Radio anfani) for a francophone audience (Hassane, 'Les nouvelles élites Islamiques du Niger', p. 141). In the case of Mali, since 1994 preachers appeared as often on television as they did on *Radio Islamique* (Benjamin Soares, 'Islam in Mali in the Neoliberal Era', *African Affairs*, 105/418, 2005, p. 80). In the case of Senegal, Côte d'Ivoire and Burkina Faso, see Muriel Gomez-Perez, Marie-Nathalie LeBlanc and Mathias Savadogo, 'Young Men and Islam in the 1990s: Rethinking an Intergenerational Perspective', *Journal of Religion in Africa*, vol. 39, no. 2, 2009, pp. 186–218.

12. However, it is important to note that in Mali, from the mid-1980s, Haïdara distributed his sermons on audio and video cassette. See Dorothea Schulz, 'Political Factions, ideological Fictions: The controversy Over Family Law reform in Democratic Mali', *Islamic Law and society*, vol. 10, no. 1, 2003, pp. 132–164.

13. Olivier Roy, 'Le post-Islamisme', *Revue des mondes musulmans et de la Méditerranée*, vols 85–86, 1999, p. 23.

14. Abdoulaye Sounaye, '*Izala* au Niger: une alternative de communauté religieuse', in Laurent Fourchard, Odile Goerg and Muriel Gomez-Perez, (eds), *Lieux de sociabilité urbaine en Afrique*, Paris: L'Harmattan, 2009a, pp. 481–500; idem., 'Islam, Etat et Société: à la recherche d'une éthique publique', in Benjamin Soares and René Otayek (eds), *Islam, Etat et Société en Afrique*, Paris: Karthala, 2009b, pp. 327–352; Miran, *Islam, histoire et modernité*; Hassane, 'Les nouvelles élites Islamiques du Niger'; Robert Glew, 'Islamic Associations in Niger', *Islam et Sociétés au sud du Sahara*, vol. 10, November 1996, pp. 187–204.

15. Niandou Souley and Alzouma, 'Islamic Renewal in Niger', p. 255.

16. Dorothea Schulz, 'Charisma and Brotherhood revisited: Mass-mediated forms of spirituality in Urban Mali', *Journal of Religion in Africa*, vol. 33, no. 2, 2003, pp. 146–171.

17. René Otayek, 'L'affirmation élitaire des arabisants au Burkina Faso. Enjeux et contradictions', in René Otayek (ed.), *Le radicalisme Islamique au sud du Sahara. Da'wa, arabisation et critique de l'Occident*, Paris: Karthala, 1993, p. 241.

18. Meunier, *Dynamique de l'enseignement*, p. 197.

19. Ibid., p. 174.

20. Trained at the Franco-Arabic Falilou MBacké College in Dakar, as well as foreign schools. See Muriel Gomez-Perez, 'Une histoire des associa-

tions Islamiques sénégalaises', Saint-Louis, Dakar, Thiès: Itinéraires, stratégies et prises de parole (1930–1993), thèse de doctorat *nouveau régime*, Université Paris 7-Denis Diderot, 2 tomes, 1997, p. 637 and Gomez-Perez, 'Généalogie de l'Islam réformiste au Sénégal'.

21. He became known among the pro-Arab activists during the third convention of the Union nationale des étudiants en langue Arabe [National Union of Arab-Speaking Students] in 1971. He served as president of the organization at the time. He defended the status of Arab-speaking students and especially fought for the autonomy of his organization vis-à-vis the central powers. Government officials cancelled his stipend. In 1975, he was permitted to continue his studies. Registered at the Faculty of Law and Islamic Legislation in *Al-Azhar*, he became president of the Union of Senegalese Students in Cairo. In 1979, having returned to Dakar, he supported his brother in the latter's project of creating an Islamic political party. See Gomez-Perez, 'Une histoire des associations Islamiques sénégalaises'; and Gomez-Perez, 'L'Islamisme à Dakar: d'un contrôle social total à une culture du pouvoir?', *Afrika Spectrum*, vol. 29, 1994, pp. 79–98.

22. LeBlanc, 'Proclaiming Individual Piety', op. cit., pp. 178–181.

23. Savadogo, 'L'intervention des associations musulmanes', p. 590.

24. Hassane, 'Les nouvelles élites Islamiques du Niger', p. 379.

25. Gomez-Perez, 'L'Islamisme à Dakar'; Roman Loimeier, 'Cheikh Touré. Du réformisme à l'Islamisme, un musulman sénégalais dans le siècle', *Islam et sociétés au sud du Sahara*, vol. 8, November 1994, pp. 55–66. Beginning in 1977, Cheikh Touré published several magazines: *La loi islamique du travail* [Islamic Labour Law], *Le code de la famille musulmane* [Islamic Code of Family Law], *L'Etat islamique, ses spécificités et ses caractéristiques* [The Islamic State, its Specificities and Characteristics], *L'Islam au Sénégal, le vrai et le faux* [Islam in Senegal, the Truth and the Falsehoods].

26. Founder of *Jamra*, son of Abbas Gueye, former union activist and former member of the French National Assembly, trained as a journalist, former Marxist-Leninist activist. See (Gomez-Perez, 'L'Islamisme à Dakar').

27. LeBlanc, 'Proclaiming Individual Piety'.

28. A branch of the tidiane brotherhood, established in the Kaolack region of Senegal.

29. Meunier, O., *Dynamique de l'enseignement*, p. 172.

30. This group was already well represented in the 1950s, see Kaba, *The Wahhabiyya*.

31. See Gomez-Perez, 'Généalogie de l'Islam réformiste au Sénégal'; and Gomez-Perez, 'Une histoire des associations Islamiques sénégalaises'.

32. These were 'small businessmen gone bankrupt because of […] the economic crisis […] since the end of the 1980s', Meunier, *Dynamique de l'enseignement*, pp. 197–198.

33. Dorothea Schulz, 'Charisma and Brotherhood revisited: Mass-mediated forms of spirituality in Urban Mali', *Journal of Religion in Africa*, vol. 33, no. 2, 2003, pp. 146–171.

34. See David Westerlund, 'Reaction and Action: Accounting for the rise of Islamism', in David Westerlund and Eva Evers Rosander (eds), *African Islam and Islam in Africa: Encounters between Sufis and Islamists*, Ohio: Ohio University Press, 1997, pp. 308–333.

35. Abdoulaye Niandou Souley, 'Les 'licenciés du Caire' et l'État du Niger', in René Otayek (ed.), *Le radicalisme Islamique au sud du Sahara. Da'wa, arabisation et critique de l'Occident*, Paris: Karthala, 1993, pp. 213–252.

36. John L. Esposito, *Islam: The Straight Path*, New York: Oxford University Press, 1988.

37. Gomez-Perez, 'The Association des Étudiants Musulmans'; and Gomez-Perez, 'Généalogie de l'Islam réformiste au Sénégal'.

38. Otayek, 'Une relecture Islamique du projet révolutionnaire de Thomas Sankara', Jean-François Bayart (ed.), *Religion et modernité politique en Afrique noire*, Paris: Karthala, 1993, pp. 101–127.

39. Louis Brenner, 'Constructing Muslim Identities in Mali', Louis Brenner (ed.), *Muslim identity and social change in sub-saharan Africa*, Indianapolis: Indiana University Press, 1993, pp. 59–77.

40. Fabienne Samson, *Les Marabouts de l'Islam politique. Le Dahiratoul Moustarchidina Wal Moustarchitady, un mouvement néo-confrérique sénégalais*, Paris: Karthala, 2005.

41. Olivier Roy, *L'échec de l'Islam politique*, Paris: Seuil, 1992, p. 124.

42. See *Le Manifeste pour la réhabilitation de l'Islam au Niger [Manifesto for the Restoration of Islam in Niger]*

43. Brenner, 'Constructing Muslim Identities in Mali', p. 190.

44. Miran, *Islam, histoire et modernité*; Savadogo, 'L'intervention des associations musulmanes'.

45. Savadogo, 'L'intervention des associations musulmanes', p. 595.

46. Ibid.; Daouda Gary-Tounkara, 'La communauté musulmane et la conquête de l'égalité politique dans la Côte d'Ivoire de l'ivoirité (1993–2000)', in Muriel Gomez-Perez (ed.), *L'Islam politique au sud du Sahara: Identités, discours et enjeux*, Paris: Karthala, 2005, pp. 601–620.

47. Sounaye, 'Islam, Etat et Société'; and Sounaye, 'Les politiques de l'Islam', 2005.

48. Sounaye, 'Islam, Etat et Société'; idem., Sounaye, 'Les politiques de l'Islam'; Gomez-Perez, *L'Islam politique au sud du Sahara*; Gomez-Perez,

'Généalogie de l'Islam réformiste au Sénégal'; Roman Loimeier, 'L'Islam ne se vend plus: The Islamic reform Movement and the State in Senegal', *Journal of religion in Africa*, vol. XXX, no. 2, 2000, pp. 168–190.

49. Hassane,'Les nouvelles élites Islamiques du Niger'.

50. Soares, 'Islam in Mali in the Neoliberal Era'; Schulz, 'Political Factions, ideological Fictions: The controversy Over Family Law reform in Democratic Mali', *Islamic Law and society*, vol. 10, no. 1, 2003a, pp. 132–164.

51. Abdouramane Idrissa, 'Modèle Islamique et modèle occidental: le conflit des élites au Niger', in Gomez-Perez (ed.), *L'Islam politique au sud du Sahara. Identités, discours, enjeux*, Paris: Karthala, 2005, pp. 345–372; and Sounaye, 'Les politiques de l'Islam'.

52. Sounaye, 'Les politiques de l'Islam'.

53. Idrissa, 'Modèle Islamique et modèle occidental'.

54. The Quota Act ensures women's greater participation in electoral positions and government posts.

55. See Alidou and Alidou, 'Women, Religion and the discourses of legal ideology in Niger Republic'.

56. Hassane, 'Les nouvelles élites Islamiques du Niger'.

57. Otayek, 'L'affirmation élitaire des arabisants au Burkina Faso', p. 243.

58. Hassane, 'Les nouvelles élites Islamiques du Niger'.

59. John L. Esposito, 'Political Islam and Gulf security', in John L. Esposito, *Political Islam: Revolution, Radicalism, or reform?*, London: Lynne Rienner Publishers, 1997, pp. 53–74.

60. Yves Goussault, 'Les frontières contestées du politique et du religieux dans le tiers Monde', *Tiers Monde*, July-September, no. 123, 1990, p. 493.

61. Gomez-Perez, 'Généalogie de l'Islam réformiste au Sénégal'.

62. Gomez-Perez, 'The Association des Étudiants Musulmans'; and Gomez-Perez, *L'Islam politique au sud du Sahara*.

63. Roy, *L'échec de l'Islam politique*, pp. 60–61.

64. Marie-Nathalie LeBlanc and Muriel Gomez-Perez, 'Jeunes musulmans et citoyenneté culturelle: retour sur des expériences de recherche en Afrique de l'Ouest francophone', *Sociologie et Société*, 2007.

65. Eva Evers Rosander, 'The Islamization of "Tradition" and "Modernity"', in Westerlund and Rosander (eds), *African Islam and Islam in Africa*, p. 11.

66. Assimi Kouanda, 'La lutte pour l'occupation et le contrôle des espaces réservés aux cultes à Ouagadougou', René Otayek, Filiga-Michel Sawadogo and Jean-Pierre Guingané (eds), *Le Burkina entre révolution et démocratie (1983–1993)*, Paris: Karthala, 1996, p. 94.

67. Miran, *Islam, histoire et modernité.*

68. Alain Roussillon, 'L'Occident dans l'imaginaire des hommes et des femmes du Machreq et du Maghreb', in *Revue Vingtième siècle*, 'Islam et politique en Méditerranée au 20ème siècle', April/June, no. 82, 2004, p. 78.

69. Chris Hann, 'Problems with the (de)privatization of religion', *Anthropology Today*, vol. 16, no. 6, 2000, pp. 14–20; and José Casanova, *Public Religions in the Modern World*, Chicago: University of Chicago Press, 1994.

70. Marie-Nathalie LeBlanc, 'Proclaiming Individual Piety', p. 193.

71. See Louis Audet-Gosselin and Muriel Gomez-Perez, 'L'opposition au projet ZACA à Ouagadougou (2001–2003): feu de paille ou mutations profondes de l'islam burkinabè?', *Revue canadienne des Études africaines*, forthcoming; Gomez-Perez, LeBlanc and Savadogo, 'Young Men and Islam in the 1990s'; LeBlanc and Gomez-Perez, 'Jeunes musulmans et citoyenneté culturelle'.

72. Niandou Souley, 'Les 'licenciés du Caire', p. 258.

73. Dorothea Schulz, 'Promises of (im)mediate salvation: Islam, broadcast media, and the remaking of religious experience in Mali', *American Ethnologist*, vol. 33, no. 2, 2006, p. 215.

74. Hassane, 'Les nouvelles élites Islamiques du Niger', p. 373.

75. Schulz, 'Promises of (im)mediate salvation', p. 215.

76. 'The Chérif Madani (Haidara) visited Bobo-Dioulasso four times (1992, 1995, 2001 and 2004). The followers were almost exclusively as businessmen and farmers, but there were also workers, civil servants and even soldiers present. […] The strength of the movement resided with the youth […]. This was why the speeches recorded on audiocassette were listened to alongside the music of Alpha Blondy, Fakoly-Dja, Black-So-Man during teas', Djigui Traoré, 'Islam et politique à Bobo-Dioulasso de 1940 à 2002', in Gomez-Perez, M. (ed.), *L'Islam politique au sud du Sahara. Identités, discours, enjeux*, p. 439.

77. Schulz, 'Promises of (im)mediate salvation' op. cit., p. 215

78. Marie-Nathalie LeBlanc, 'The production on Islamic identities through knowledge claims in Bouaké, Côte d'Ivoire', *African Affairs*, vol. 98. 1999, p. 506.

79. Benjamin Soares, 'Islam and Public Piety in Mali', in Armando Salvatore and Dale Eickelman, *Public Islam and the Common Good*, Leiden: Brill, 2004, pp. 205–226.

80. Schulz, 'Charisma and Brotherhood revisited', p. 152.

81. Dorothea Schulz, 'Morality, Community, Publicness: Shifting Terms of Public Debate In Mali', in Birgit Meyer and Annelies Moors (eds),

*Religion, Media and the Public Sphere*, Indianapolis: Indiana University Press, 2006, p. 144.

82. Emmanuel Grégoire, 'Islam and The Identity of Merchants in Maradai (Niger)', in Brenner, *Muslim identity and social Change in Sub-Saharan Africa*, pp. 107 and 112.

83. LeBlanc, 'The production on Islamic identities'; and '*Imaniya* and Young Muslim Women'.

84. Gomez-Perez and LeBlanc, *L'Afrique d'une génération à l'autre*, Paris: Karthala, forthcoming; Muriel Gomez-Perez, 'Autour de mosquées à Ouagadougou et à Dakar: lieux de sociabilité et reconfiguration des communautés musulmanes', in Fourchard, Goerg, and Gomez-Perez, (eds), *Lieux de sociabilité urbaine en Afrique*, pp. 405–433; and Gomez-Perez, LeBlanc and Savadogo, 'Young Men and Islam in the 1990s'.

85. Schulz, 'Promises of (im)mediate salvation'.

86. Armando Salvatore, 'Staging Virtue: The Disembodiment of Self-Correctness and the Making of Islam as a Public Norm.' in Georg Stauth (ed.), *Islam: Motor or Challenge of Modernity*, Hamburg: LIT, 1998, pp. 87–120.

87. Annabelle Sreberny-Mohammadi and Ali Mohammadi, *Small Media, Big Revolution: Communication, Culture and the Iranian Revolution*, Minneapolis: University of Minnesota Press, 1994.

88. John L. Comaroff and Jean Comaroff (eds), *Civil Society and the Political Imagination in Postcolonial Africa: Critical perspectives*, Chicago: University of Chicago Press, 1999.

89. Jean-François Bayart, 'Civil Society in Africa', in Patrick Chabal, (ed.), *Political Domination in Africa: Reflections on the Limits of Power*, Cambridge: Cambridge University Press, 1986, pp. 109–125; Otayek, Identité et démocratie dans un monde global, p. 123.

90. François Constantin and Christina Coulon, 'Religion et démocratie. Introduction à une problématique africaine', in François Constantin, and Christian Coulon (eds), *Religion et transition démocratique en Afrique*, Paris: Karthala, 1997, p. 19.

91. Schulz, 'Charisma and Brotherhood revisited'.

92. Mamadou Diouf, 'Engaging Postcolonial Cultures: African Youth and Public Space', *African Studies Review*, vol. 46, no. 1, September, 2003, pp. 1–12.

## 7. THE 'OTHER' POLITICAL ISLAM: UNDERSTANDING SALAFI POLITICS

1. The Salafi movement constitutes a strict and puritanical branch of Islam trying to 'purify' the Islamic creed and its religious applications of all

forms of historical, cultural influences, and other influences that are deemed un-Islamic. In their attempt to 'purify' Islam they try to follow the example of the Prophet Muhammad and *al-salaf al-salih* (the first generation of Muslims). This chapter refers to Islamism as those ideologies and political movements, such as the Egyptian and Syrian Muslim Brotherhood, that draw upon Islamic symbols and traditions to articulate a particular political agenda usually criticizing Western political and cultural influence on the Middle East and engaging with the challenges resulting from the fall of the Ottoman Empire, colonization, and modernity. See Guilain Denoeux, 'The Forgotten Swamp: Navigating Political Islam', *Middle East Policy*, vol. 9, no. 2, 2002, pp. 16–17.

2. Ibid., pp. 56–81.

3. This paragraph is largely based upon Martijn de Koning, 'Understanding Dutch Islam: Exploring the Relationship of Muslims with the State and the Public Sphere in the Netherlands', in Haideh Moghissi and Halleh Ghorashi (eds), *Muslim Diaspora in the West Negotiating Gender, Home and Belonging*, Burlington: Ashgate Publishing, 2010, pp. 181–197.

4. James C. Kennedy and Markha Valenta, 'Religious Pluralism and the Dutch state: Reflections on the future of article 23', in W.B.H.J. Van de Donk et al. (eds), *Geloven in het publieke domein. Verkenningen van een dubbele transformatie*, Amsterdam: Amsterdam University Press, 2006, pp. 337–353.

5. Arend Lijphart, *The Politics of Accommodation: Pluralism and democracy in The Netherlands*, Berkeley: University of California Press, 1968.

6. Kennedy and Valenta, 'Religious Pluralism and the Dutch state', p. 340.

7. See Peter Rooden, *Religieuze regimes: Over godsdienst en maatschappij in Nederland 1570–1990*, Amsterdam: Bert Bakker, 1996; Kennedy and Valenta, 'Religious Pluralism and the Dutch state'.

8. Rooden, *Religieuze regimes*, pp. 29–31.

9. Martijn de Koning, 'Understanding Dutch Islam'; Martijn de Koning and Roel Meijer, 'Going All the Way: Politicization and Radicalization of the Hofstad Network in the Netherlands', in Assaad E. Azzi et al. (eds), *Identity and Participation in Culturally Diverse Societies: A Multidisciplinary Perspective*, Oxford: Wiley-Blackwell, 2011, pp. 220–239.

10. See José Casanova, 'Religion, European Secular Identities, and European Integration', *Eurozine.com* (2004), http://www.eurozine.com.

11. Alfons Fermin, *Nederlandse politieke partijen over minderhedenbeleid 1977–1995*, Amsterdam: Thesis Publishers, 1997, p. 247.

12. Saba Mahmood, 'Secularism, Hermeneutics, and Empire: The Politics

of Islamic Reformation', *Public Culture*, vol. 18, no. 2, 2006, p. 328 and n. 11.

13. Marcel Maussen, *Constructing Mosques: The governance of Islam in France and the Netherlands*, Amsterdam: Amsterdam School for Social Science Research (ASSR), 2009, PhD thesis.

14. Martijn de Koning, 'Understanding Dutch Islam'.

15. This definition is inspired by Charles Price, Donald Nonini and Erich Fox Tree, 'Grounded Utopian Movements: Subjects of Neglect', *Anthropological Quarterly*, vol. 81, no. 1, 2008, pp. 127–159.

16. Roel Meijer, 'Introduction: Genealogies of Salafism', in Roel Meijer (ed.), *Global Salafism: Islam's New Religious Movement*, London: Hurst, 2009, pp. 1–32.

17. L.P. Gerlach and V.H. Hine, *People, Power, Change: Movements of Social Transformation*, Indianapolis: Bobbs-Merrill, 1970.

18. Price et al., 'Grounded Utopian Movements', p. 146.

19. Quintan Wiktorowicz, 'Anatomy of the Salafi Movement', *Studies in Conflict and Terrorism*, vol. 29, 2006, pp. 207–239.

20. See Joas Wagemakers, 'A Purist Jihadi-Salafi: The Ideology of Abu Muhammad al-Maqdisi', *British Journal of Middle Eastern Studies* vol. 36, no. 2, 2009, pp. 281–297.

21. Joas Wagemakers, *A Quietist Jihadi-Salafi: The Ideology and Influence of Abu Muhammad al-Maqdisi*, Nijmegen: Radboud University Nijmegen, 2010.

22. Al-Madkhali is a Saudi Salafi leader who preaches unconditional surrender to the religious and political authorities in Saudi Arabia, condemning the Sahwa scholars. The Saudi authorities stimulated the al-Madkhali current as a reaction against the growing support for the Sahwa movement who became more vocal in their criticisms during the 1990s.

23. Meaning the group who follows the Sunna of the Prophet Muhammad. A term that actually applies to Sunni Muslims in general (Salafism is a Sunni current) but is used in this case in the sense that these groups are the only legitimate followers of the Sunna).

24. Imam Ahmad Salam was based here until he established his own foundation in Tilburg after an internal conflict.

25. *Takfir* is declaring someone, previously considered Muslim, an unbeliever or *kafir*.

26. The Hofstad network is the network of jihadi Salafists such as Mohammed Bouyeri (the murderer of film director and writer Theo van Gogh who made the film *Submission I* together with Ayaan Hirsi Ali). Samir Azzouz first came into the picture after he tried to reach Chechnya in order to fight with the jihadis against the Russians. In 2004 he was

arrested for planning an attack on Schiphol Airport; a charge of which he was initially acquitted but later (recently) convicted and sentenced to six years. In 2006 he was again sentenced to eight years imprisonment for planning a terrorist attack (the so-called Piranha-case). Fore on the Hofstad Network see Lorenzo Vidino, 'The Hofstad Group: The New Face of Terrorist Networks in Europe', *Studies in Conflict & Terrorism*, vol. 30, no. 7, 2007, pp. 579–592; de Koning and Meijer, 'Going All the Way'.

27. Ineke Roex, Sjef van Stipout and Jean Tillie, *Salafisme in Nederland; aard, omvang en dreiging*, Amsterdam: IMES, 2010).

28. Guilain Denoeux, 'The Forgotten Swamp'.

29. Steven. M. Buechler, 'New Social Movement Theories', *The Sociological Quarterly*, vol. 36, no. 3, 1995, pp. 451–453.

30. Ibid.

31. Marc Edelman, 'Social Movements: Changing Paradigms and Forms of Politics', *Annual Review of Anthropology*, vol. 30. 2001, pp. 296–297.

32. Proselytizing by 'inviting' people to Islam.

33. Meijer, this volume; Cihan Tuğal, 'Transforming everyday life: Islamism and social movement theory', *Theoretical Sociology*, vol. 38, 2009, pp. 423–458.

34. Wiktorowicz, 'Anatomy of the Salafi Movement'.

35. Ibid., pp. 207–208.

36. Mary Bucholtz, 'Youth and cultural practice', *Annual Review of Anthropology*, vol. 31, 2002, pp. 525–552.

37. *Kafir* means 'infidel'.

38. Dale Eickelman and James Piscatori, *Muslim Politics*, Princeton: Princeton University Press, 1996, pp. 5–16.

39. Annelies Moors, *'Muslim cultural politics': What's Islam got to do with it?*, Amsterdam: Vossiuspers UvA, 2004, p. 7.

40. Martijn de Koning, *Zoeken naar een 'zuivere' islam. Geloofsbeleving en identiteitsvorming van jonge Marokkaans-Nederlandse moslims*, Amsterdam: Bert Bakker, 2008.

41. As Melucci has argued, people's involvement in collective action is tied to their capacity to define an identity. See Alberto Melucci, 'Getting Involved: Identity and Mobilization in Social Movements', *International Social Movement Research: From Structure to Action*, vol. 1, 1988, p. 100. Moreover, Giddens shows that the reflexive project of people and their self-actualization and identity formation inevitably have political dimensions, strongly related to the connection between personal and global survival in late modernity. He proposes the term 'life politics' to capture this political dimension. Since most of the discussions among Muslim youth in my research are related to lifestyle or

more precise lifestyles, I will use the term politics of lifestyles. See Anthony Giddens, *Modernity and Self-Identity: Self and Society in the Late Modern Age*, Stanford, CA: Stanford University Press, 1991; see also Buechler, 'New Social Movement Theories'.

42. For a different approach, see Thomas Hegghammer, 'Jihadi Salafis or Revolutionaries: On Religion and Politics in the Study of Islamist Militancy', in Roel Meijer (ed.), *Global Salafism*, pp. 244–266.

43. Tuğal, 'Transforming everyday life'.

44. Rogers Brubaker, 'Ethnicity without groups', *Archives Européennes de Sociologie*, vol. XLIII, no. 2, 2002, pp. 163–189.

45. Tuğal, 'Transforming everyday life'.

46. Ibid., p. 452.

47. Willem Schinkel, 'The Virtualization of Citizenship', *Critical Sociology*, vol. 36, no. 2, 2010, pp. 265–283; de Koning, 'Understanding Dutch Islam'.

48. Martijn de Koning, 'Changing Worldviews and Friendship: An Exploration of the Life Stories of Two Female Salafists in the Netherlands', in Roel Meijer (ed), *Global Salafism*, pp. 372–392.

49. Ibid.

50. Umm Salamah is a pseudonym to protect her identity. She has changed her Moroccan name into a name that 'sounds' more Islamic and that begins with Umm, meaning mother. For Umm Salamah her idea of becoming a pious Muslim woman was combined with her idea of motherhood as the way to achieve that ideal. For a more extensive analysis of her life story, see Martijn de Koning, 'Changing Worldviews and Friendship'.

51. A headscarf covers the head and bosom while a niqab covers the whole body including the face except for the eyes.

52. de Koning, *Zoeken naar een 'zuivere' islam*.

53. Eickelman and Piscatori, *Muslim Politics*, p. 9.

54. Asef Bayat, *Life as Politics: How Ordinary People Change the Middle East*, Stanford: Stanford University Press, 2009; see also Magnus Marsden, *Living Islam: Muslim religious experience in Pakistan's North West Frontier*, Cambridge: Cambridge University Press, 2005.

55. It is not always clear if politicians mean a burqa (which covers the whole body, including the eyes) or niqab. In the discussions in parliament and in the media they refer to it as burqa.

56. Hirsi Ali is a member of the VVD, a conservative-liberal party and one of the most vocal critics of Islam and (radical) Muslims stating that Islam is incompatible with democracy and renowned for her accusation that the Prophet Muhammad is a 'paedophile' according to 'contemporary Western standards'. Together with film director van Gogh

she has made the film *Submission I.* Hirsi Ali was threatened numerous times with an attack on her life and lived in hiding several weeks after the murder of van Gogh. Currently she works in the US for the conservative think tank American Enterprise Institute.

57. See Annelies Moors, '"Islamic Fashion" in Europe: Religious conviction, aesthetic style, and creative consumption', *Encounters*, vol. 1, no. 1, 2009, pp. 175–201; Charles Hirschkind, *The Ethical Soundscape: Cassette Sermons and Counterpublics*, New York: Columbia University Press, 2006; Valérie Amiraux and Gerdien Jonker, 'Introduction: Talking about visibility, actors, politics, forms of engagement', in Valérie Amiraux and Gerdien Jonker (eds), *Politics of visibility. Young Muslims in European Public Spaces*, Bielefeld: Transcript, 2006, pp. 9–21.

58. http://www.geertwilders.nl/index.php?option=com_content&task=view&id=285&Itemid=103.

59. Marjo Buitelaar, 'Negotiating the rules of chaste behaviour: re-interpretations of the symbolic complex of virginity by young women of Moroccan descent in the Netherlands', *Ethnic and Racial Studies*, vol. 25, no. 3, 2002, p. 466.

60. de Koning, 'Understanding Dutch Islam'; Annelies Moors, 'The Dutch and the face-veil: The politics of discomfort', *Social Anthropology*, vol. 17, no. 4, 2009, pp. 393–408.

61. Nancy Fraser, 'Rethinking the Public Sphere: A Contribution to the Critique of Actually Existing Democracy', *Social Text*, vol. 25, 1990, p. 69; Michael Warner, 'Public and Counterpublics', *Public Culture*, vol. 14, no. 1, 2002, p. 89.

62. Niqaab.org—author translation [No longer available online].

63. Warner, 'Public and Counterpublics', p. 89.

64. Martijn de Koning, *Identity in Transition: Connecting Online and Offline Internet Practices of Moroccan-Dutch Muslim Youth*, London Metropolitan University—Institute for the Study of European Transformations (ISET), 2008, http://www.londonmet.ac.uk/londonmet/library/c52116_3.pdf.

65. de Koning and Meijer, 'Going All the Way'.

66. Buechler, 'New Social Movement Theories', p. 452.

67. http://forums.ansaar.nl/vraag-antwoord/43701-sheikh-fawaz-jneid.html

8. VEILED ARTISTS IN EGYPT

1. Dedicated to the memory of Alain Roussillon, Director of the CEDES in Cairo, who encouraged this research.

2. Walter Benjamin, 'The Work of Art in the Age of Mechanical Reproduc-

tion', in Walter Benjamin (ed.), *Illuminations*, 2007, New York: Shocken books.

3. José Casanova, *Public religions in the modern world*, Chicago: University of Chicago press, 1994.

4. Radi Saadia, 'De la toile au voile: les actrices égyptiennes voilées et l'islamisme', *Monde Arabe—Maghreb Machrek*, no. 151, January-March 1996, pp. 13–18.

5. Besides working with Islamic Relief in 2007 Hanan Turk coined the new concept of a café beauty center in Cairo, called 'Saboya', with special treatments for veiled women.

6. This was the year in which Mona Abdel-Ghany was the first Egyptian performer to keep her veil on while performing.

7. In Arabic *fannanat al-mohajabat* are the veiled artists. This definition is commonly used and accepted by audiences and journalists and has replaced the previous definitions.

8. In this context 'proper' means that these actresses do not act in scenes with nudity, kisses and immoral behavior.

9. Olivier Roy, *Globalised Islam: The search for a new ummah*, London: Hurst, 2004.

10. Ruz el-Yussef, 15 May 2006.

11. Nilüfer Göle, 'Islam in Public: New Visibilities and New Imaginaries', *Public Culture*, vol. 14, no. 1, 2002, pp. 173–190.

12. For instance, the famous cases of two Egyptian anchor women, Hala el-Malky and Ghada el-Tawil.

13. *Hijab fashion* is one of the first magazines to appear in Cairo.

14. Hanan Turk, not yet veiled, also appeared in this film.

15. These veiled actresses illustrate the fragmentation of the public sphere and the power of the media in television in creating such dichotomies.

16. Karen Werner, '"Coming close to God" through the Media: A phenomenology of the media practices of Islamist women in Egypt' in Kai Hafez (ed.), *Mass Media, Politics, and Society in the Middle East*, Cresskill, NJ: Hampton Press.

17. Inspired by the song by Gil Scot-Heron 'The revolution will not be televised'.

18. Gaye Tuchman and Arlene Kaplan Daniels, *Heart and Home: images of women in mass media*, Oxford: Oxford University Press, 1978.

19. In 2007 a song and video by singer Hasem el-Hajj represent one of last attempt to Islamicate the world of songs. The song title, *'ithajibit, bravo aleyky'*, translates as 'You have don the hijab, good on you'.

20. Mukul Keshavan, 'Urdu, Awadh and the Tawaif: the islamicate roots of Hindi cinema', in Zoya Hasan, (ed.), *Forging Identities*, New Delhi: Kali, 1994. According to Mukul Keshavan the term 'Islamicate' would

refer not directly to the religion, but instead to the social and cultural complex history associated with Islam and the Muslim.

21. According to similar rumors that spread throughout Egypt, when an artist decides to wear the hijab or niqab she is considered to be an 'agent' from the Gulf. That is, she would have allegedly been paid to infiltrate the artistic world in Egypt with an agenda: to promote extremist Islam among artists.

22. Said Sadek, 'Cairo as Global/regional cultural capital?' in Diane Singerman and Paul Amar (eds), *Cairo Cosmopolitan: Politics, culture and urban space in the new globalised Middle East*, Cairo: American University in Cairo Press, 2006.

23. Note that approximately 50 per cent of women in Egypt are illiterate.

24. The works of Marshall McLuhan and his student Derrick de Kerckhove have inspired this chapter.

25. Derrick De Kerckhove and Christopher Dewdney (eds), *The skin of culture: Investigating the new electronic reality*, London: Kogan Page, 1998, p. 16.

26. An individual's physical reaction to images or movie scenes that one dislikes illustrates this; for instance, closing one's eyes or placing hands over eyes.

27. Saba Mahmood, *Politics of Piety*, Princeton: Princeton University Press, 2005.

28. Charles Hirschkind has conducted in-depth studies about the sensory experience recorded in the body and the synaesthesia in relation to the popular media in Egypt. See Charles Hirschkind, *The Ethical Soundscape: Cassette Sermons and Islamic Counterpublics*, New York: Columbia University Press, 2006.

29. *Al-ahram weekly*, 7–13 November 2002.

30. Nilüfer Göle, 'The voluntary adoption of Islamic stigma symbols', *Social Research: An International Quarterly of Social Sciences*, vol. 70, num. 3, 2003, pp. 809–828.

31. Lila Abu-Lughod, *Dramas of Nationhood*, Chicago: University of Chicago Press, 2005.

32. http://weekly.ahram.org.eg/2002/611/profile.htm

33. Nilüfer Göle, 'Snapshots of Islamic Modernities', DAEDALUS, vol. 129, no. 1, 2000, pp. 91–117.

34. Extract of a speech delivered by Sannou'a in Paris, 1903 [editor's translation].

35. For instance, the film *Girls* was shown at the 2007 Egyptian Film Festival, depicting the lives of four young Cairene women including their sexual experiences, which prompted criticism and accusations that the film had portrayed an immoral example for girls in Egypt.

36. Karen Werner, '"Coming close to God"'.

37. Patrick Haenni, *L'islam de marché, l'autre révolution conservatrice*, Paris: Seuil, 2005.

38. Samia Serageldin, 'The Islamic Salon', in Miriam Cooke and Bruce B. Lawrence (eds), *Muslims Networks from Hajj to Hip Hop*, NC: University of North Carolina Press, 2005.

39. *Ru'ya* (vision), is normally the good dream. Dreaming occupies a special position in Islam: believing in true dreams is considered to be part of a general belief in Allah.

40. Complete in the sense that all human activities, even leisure activities, are blessed.

41. Translated from French; Michel Foucault, *Histoire de la sexualité* III, Paris: Gallimard, 1994 pp. 60–94.

42. Amel Boubekeur, 'Cool and Competitive Muslim culture in the West', *ISIM Review*, no. 16, Autumn 2005.

43. www.muslimfilmfestival.org

44. The Egyptian veiled artist Hanan Turk has been invited to participate in these events since the first edition, see http://www.mahabba.tv/site/index.php?option=com_content&task=view&id=20&Itemid=39&lang=en.

45. Norbert Elias and Eric Dunning, *Sport et civilisation*, Paris: Fayard, 1994.

46. The actress Soheir Al-Babli, appeared in *Qalb Habiba* (Habiba's Heart) broadcasted in Kuwait, Sudan and on the satellite channels, *Dream* and *Baghdadéya*. Soheir Ramzi returned to the screen with *Habib al-roh* (The Dearest Love), broadcasted in satellite television in Syria, Algeria, Yemen and Dubai. Sabrin played in *Kashkoul li kol muwaten* (Notebook for Every Citizen) . Hanane Turk has played wearing the veil for the first time during Ramadan, in the *musalsal Awlad al-shaware'a* (Street Kids). Abir Sabri has chosen to play in the *musalsal Asaab qarar* (The Most Difficult Decision) and Mona Abdel-Ghani for the third year in a row preferred an historical drama: *'Ala bab Masr* (At Egypt's Door).

47. http://www.islamonline.net/iol-english/dowalia/art-3–2–2000/art2.asp, accessed 2006 but since removed.

48. Jurgen Habermas speaks of aesthetic-expressive rationality in his article 'Modernity an incomplete project' in Hal Foster (ed.), *Postmodern culture*, London: Pluto press, 1985.

49. Greeks, Romans, Hindus, Jews and Christians have used veils to link themselves to God, saints, divinities or in general sacred spaces and objects.

50. Artists studied anatomy by cutting up bodies and studying each of them separately as in the famous Da Vinci sketches.

## 9. HEAVY METAL MUSLIMS: THE RISE OF A POST-ISLAMIST PUBLIC SPHERE

1. See Olivier Roy, *Globalized Islam: The Search for a New Ummah*, London: Hurst, 2004, Chs. 1–2.

2. Ibid., pp. 80–84.

3. Taieb Belghazi, 'The Politics of Identity in the Context of Moroccan Islamic Movements', paper delivered at the Workshop on Socio-Religious Movements and the Transformation of Political Community: Israel, Palestine and Beyond, UC Irvine, October 2002.

4. For a fascinating discussion of how Nietzsche's concept of nihilism applies to the Muslim world, see Roy Jackson, *Nietzsche and Islam*, London: Routledge, 2007.

5. Manuel Castells, *The Power of Identity*, New York: Blackwell, 1996; Philip Sutton and Stephen Vertigans, *Resurgent Islam: A Sociological Approach*, London: Polity Press, 2005, pp. 90–100.

6. Donald Mackenzie Brown, (ed.), *Ultimate Concern—Tillich in Dialogue*, New York: Harper & Row, 1965.

7. Herbert London, *Closing the Circle: A Cultural History of the Rock Revolution*, Chicago: Nelson-Hall, 1984.

8. 'Interview with Talal Asad', *Asia Source*, Asiasource.org, 16 December 2002.

9. The interpretation of some Qur'anic verses, such as al-Isra' (*sura* 17) and an-Najm (53) as prohibiting music broadly have also been discredited by many scholars, including leading figures such as Yusuf al-Qaradawi, and in the classical period, Ibn al-'Arabi, and the commentators on the great law collections of Ibn Hazm, Malik, Ibn Hanbal, and Ash-Shafi'i.

10. This is discussed in-depth in Mark LeVine, *Heavy Metal Islam: Rock, Resistance and the Struggle for the Soul of Islam*, New York: Random House, 2008.

11. See Wilfred Mellers, *Twilight of the Gods: The Music of the Beatles*, New York: Schirmer, 1975.

12. See Daniel Ahern, *Nietzsche as Cultural Physician*, University Park, PA: Pennsylvania State Press, 1995.

13. Asef Bayat, 'The Coming Post-Islamist Society', *Critique: Critical Middle East Studies*, no. 9, Fall 1996, pp. 43–52; Asef Bayat, 'What is Post-Islamism?, *ISIM Newsletter*, no. 16, Autumn 2005; Daniel Ahern, *Nietzsche as Cultural Physician*, University Park, PA: Pennsylvania State UP, 1995.

14. Asef Bayat, *Making Islam Democratic: Social Movements and the Post-Islamist Turn*, Palo Alto: Stanford University Press, 2007.

15. Tariq Ramadan, quoted in LeVine, 2003

16. Patrick Haenni and Husam Tammam, 'Egypt's Air-Conditioned Islam', *Le Monde Diplomatique*, September 2003.

17. Among the figures who came out of the metal scene are bloggers Alaa Abdel Fatah and Hossam el-Hamalawy, the latter of whom is also one of the leaders of Kefaya.

18. The 'Satanic metal affair' saw the arrest of well over 100 young musicians and fans in 1997. The Grand Mufti of Egypt called for the death penalty for those arrested if they did not repent from their evil and un-Islamic ways.

19. Interview with author, December 2006.

20. Interview with author, September 2007.

21. Interviews with band members, Casablanca, June 2006 and in subsequent email conversations.

22. In her book *Full Sails Ahead*, she declares that rock and hip hop can 'give vent to the distress in the face of a shattered world', yet in the end they remain 'crude' and 'devoid of meaning', composed most notably of 'groupies and spaced-out fans' who together represent the grand dismantling of the modern world. 'Rap is a succession of desperate yelps; rock, hysteria; Hard Rock, insanity.' Quoting Proust, she laments that 'music can no longer be a means of communication among souls' (Nadia Yassine, *Full Sails Ahead*, New Britain, PA: Justice and Spirituality Publishing, 2006).

23. Nadia Yassine, '"The King and the Witch"', 13 July 2005 blog entry at http://www.nadiayassine.net/en/page/print/10836.htm.

24. Ibrahim al-Mardini, *al-tibyan fi ahkam il-musiqi wa-l-alhan*, Beirut: Dâr al-nohmania, 2001. In it he argues that explains that, 'there is no Qur'anic text banning music', and that seventy of the eighty sayings of the Prophet Muhammad traditionally used to prove music unlawful are considered legally 'weak or very weak' (and so not binding on Muslims).

25. Interviews with author, Beirut, Winter 2006–Spring 2007.

26. Fela Kuti, *Music is the Weapon of the Future*, Xworks Records, 1998.

27. Theodor Adorno, *Essays on Music*, (Introduction, Commentary, and Notes by Richard Leppert, New translations by Susan Gillespie), Berkeley: University of California Press, 2002.

28. Ibid., pp. 96–7, 158.

29. GWF Hegel, *Phenomenology Of Sprit*, Oxford: Oxford University Press, 1977 [1807], section 78.

30. Theodor Adorno, *Negative Dialectics*, New York: Continuum, 1983, p. 97.

31. Interviews, Tehran, April 2007; Cairo, December 2008.

32. Spivak, as discussed by John Hutnyk, 'Adorno at Womad: South Asian crossovers and the limits of hybridity talk', *Postcolonial Studies*, vol. 1, no. 3, 1998, pp. 401–26. See LeVine, *Heavy Metal Islam*, conclusion; Jan Pieterse, *Globalization and Culture: Global Melange*, Chicago: Rowman and Littlefield, 2009.

33. Interview with author, May 2008, Irvine, CA.

34. Jurgen Habermas, *Between Facts and Norms: Contributions to a Discourse Theory of Law and Democracy*, Cambridge: Polity Press, 1996, p. 273. For a critique of Habermas's position here see Armando Salvatore and Mark LeVine, *Religion, Social Practices and Contested Hegemonies: Reconstructing the Public Sphere in Muslim Majority Societies*, NY: Palgrave, 2005; and LeVine, *Heavy Metal Islam*.

35. Mark LeVine, 'The Palestinian Press in Mandatory Jaffa: Advertising, Nationalism and the Public Sphere', in Rebecca Stein and Ted Swedenburg (eds), *Palestine, Israel, and the Politics of Popular Culture*, Raleigh-Durham, NC: Duke University Press, 2005, pp. 51–76. For the role of the press in the emerging discourses of nationalism, see Benedict Anderson, *Imagined Communities: Reflections on the Origin and Spread of Nationalism*, London: Verso, 1991, p. 35. See Aida Ali Najjar, 'The Arabic Press and Nationalism in Palestine, 1920–1948', PhD Dissertation, Syracuse University, 1975, p. 62. Also see Stuart Hall, 'Popular Culture and the State', in Tony Bennett, Colin Mercer and Janet Woollacott, (eds), *Popular Culture and Social Relations*, Milton Keynes, UK: Open University Press, 1986, pp. 22–49, 32.

## 10. BEYOND ISLAMISM AT WORK: CORPORATE ISLAM IN MALAYSIA

1. All Malays are, by constitutional definition, Muslims. However, there are Muslims in Malaysia who are not Malay. Malays and a few other ethnic groups in Malaysia are eligible for special affirmative action policies (and are referred to as *bumiputera*, 'sons of the soil', while Malaysian Chinese and Indians are ineligible for such benefits. The Malay Muslims are politically and demographically dominant in Malaysia, making up around 60 per cent of the population. The term 'Malay Muslims' is used in this chapter to emphasize the overlap between ethnicity, nationalism and religion that is characteristic of Malaysian 'Malayness'. For a discussion of 'Malayness', see Anthony Milner, *The Malays*, Oxford: Wiley-Blackwell, 2008.

2. One of nine sultans (each representing a Malaysian state) rotates for a period of five years as king or constitutional sovereign of Malaysia.

Titles such as 'Dato' and 'Tan Sri' are bestowed in recognition of outstanding public service.

3. This name is a pseudonym; some biographical details have been altered to maintain anonymity. The ethnographic field research upon which this chapter is based was conducted between 1996 and 1998; multiple field visits from 2007–2010 have supplemented the research.

4. See Mark LeVine, this volume.

5. Tan Sri Hassan is referred to as Dato Hassan in Patricia Sloane, *Islam, Modernity and Entrepreneurship among the Malays*, Basingstoke: Palgrave, 1999.

6. See, for example, Edmund Terence Gomez, *Political Business: Corporate Involvement of Malaysian Political Parties*, Queensland: Centre for South-East Asian Studies, 1994.

7. In 1970 many Malaysians were poor, with official estimates at 49.3 per cent in peninsular Malaysia. Malay poverty was estimated at 74 per cent of that segment. Ethnic and class-based resentment against the Malaysian Chinese, perceived to have monopolized the modern economy in post-Independence Malaysia, erupted into riots in 1969. Proposed as multi-ethnic policy aimed at overall poverty reduction, social restructuring, and the creation of what the government called 'national unity' among Malaysia's Malay, Chinese, and Indian citizenry, the Malay-led government put in place the New Economic Policy from 1970 to 1990. It was a highly interventionist state-led economic and affirmative-action program directed at creating a capitalist class among the Malay Muslim ethnic group. In 1990 the National Development Policy was put in place to extend its initiatives for an indefinite period.

8. For a study of the social and cultural effects of economic development in Malaysia, see Abdul Rahman Embong, *State-led Modernization and the New Middle Class in Malaysia*, Basingstoke: Palgrave, 2002.

9. Norani Othman, 'Religion, citizenship rights and gender justice', in Norani Othman, Mavis C. Puthucheary and Clive Kessler (eds), *Sharing the Nation: Faith, Difference, Power and the State 50 Years After Merdeka*, Petaling Jaya, Malaysia: Strategic Information and Research Development Center, 2008. See also Joseph C. Liow, *Piety and Politics: Islamism in Contemporary Malaysia*, (Religion and Global Politics Series), Oxford: Oxford University Press, 2009.

10. See Liow, *Piety and Politics*.

11. Mohamed Aslam Haneef, 'Islam and economic development in Malaysia—a reappraisal', *Journal of Islamic Studies*, vol. 12, no. 3, 2001, pp. 269–90; Rodney Wilson, 'Islam and Malaysia's economic development', *Journal of Islamic Studies*, vol. 9, no. 2, 1998, pp. 259–76; see also Khadijah Md. Khalid, 'Voting for change? Islam and personalized

politics in the 2004 general elections', in Edmund Terence Gomez (ed.), *Politics in Malaysia: The Malay Dimension*, London: Routledge, 2007.

12. Wilson, 'Islam and Malaysia's economic development', p. 281.

13. See Judith Nagata, 'Religious correctness and the place of Islam in Malaysia's economic politics' in Timothy Brook and Hy Van Luong (eds), *Culture and Economy: The Shaping of Capitalism in Eastern Asia*, Ann Arbor: University of Michigan Press.

14. J.E. Campo, *The Other Sides of Paradise: Explorations into the Religious Meanings of Domestic Spaces in Islam*, Columbia, SC: University of South Carolina Press, 1991.

15. In 2010, the persistence of preferential *bumiputera* rights remained hotly contested.

16. Sloane, *Islam, Modernity and Entrepreneurship*.

17. For an example of another anthropologist who worked in the corporations he was studying see Roger L. Janelli, *Making Capitalism: The Social and Cultural Construction of a South Korean Conglomerate*, Stanford: Stanford University Press, 1993. Much more common are ethnographies of anthropologists working alongside factory laborers, for example, Ching Kwan Lee, *Gender and the South China Miracle*, Berkeley: University of California Press, 1998.

18. Publications of the Institute of Islamic Understanding (IKIM), set up under Prime Minister Mahathir Mohamad, best reflected this genre in Malaysia; see, for example, Syed Othman al-Habshi and Nik Mustapha Nik Hassan (eds), *Quality and Productivity*, Kuala Lumpur: IKIM, 1995. Tan Sri Hassan attended talks and seminars at IKIM in 1997 and 1998.

19. For an example of an ethnography of Islamic corporate training in Indonesia, see Daromir Rudnyckyj, 'Spiritual economies: Islam and neoliberalism in contemporary Indonesia', *Cultural Anthropology*, vol. 24, no. 1, 2009, pp. 104–141. For examples of Muslim capitalists and their ideas, see Filippo Osella and Caroline Osella, 'Muslim entrepreneurs in public life between India and the Gulf: Making good and doing good', *Journal of the Royal Anthropological Institute*, vol. 15, no. 1, 2009, pp. S202–S221, and Bjorn Olav Utvik, *The Pious Road to Development*, London: Hurst, 2006; Jonah Blank, *Mullahs on the Mainframe: Islam and Modernity among the Daudi Bohras*, Chicago: University of Chicago Press, 2001.

20. For a description of the way in which a *shura* is understood in business settings, see al-Habshi and Hassan (eds), *Quality and Productivity*, p. 31.

21. Today, publicly-listed Malaysian companies are required under

Malaysian securities law to engage in what is called 'Corporate Social Responsibility' or 'CSR'. In recent visits to Malaysia, I have found practice of 'Islamic CSR'—a concept I first heard described by Tan Sri Hassan—is now commonplace.

22. See Othman, 'Religion, citizenship rights and gender justice'.
23. See Mahathir Mohamad, 'Towards a developed and industrialized society: Understanding the concept, implications and challenges of Vision 2020', Speech reprinted in Ahmad Sarji Abdul Hamid (ed.), *Malaysia's Vision 2020*, Kuala Lumpur: Pelanduk, 1993.
24. A detailed explanation of this concept appears in Nik Mohamed Affandi bin Nik Yusoff, *Islam and Wealth*, Kuala Lumpur: Pelanduk, 2002, pp. 10–11.
25. Khalid, 'Voting for Change', pp. 140–41.
26. Yaroslav Trofimov, 'Borrowed ideas: Malaysia transforms rules for finance under Islam', *Wall Street Journal*, 4 April 2007.
27. See Johan Fischer, 'Boycott or buycott? Malay middle-class consumption post-9/11', *Ethnos*, vol. 72, no. 1, 2007, pp. 29–50.
28. Speaking to lawmakers in the Malaysian parliament in 2002, Mahathir announced that "Malaysia was not only an Islamic state, but a model Islamic state" (see Patricia A. Martinez, 'The Islamic state or the state of Islam in Malaysia', *Contemporary Southeast Asia*, vol. 23, no. 3, 2001, pp. 474–503.
29. Terence Chong, 'Malay capitalists: Ambassadors for moderate Islam', *The Straits Times* (Singapore), 27 September 2004. See also Trofimov, 'Borrowed Ideas'. For a discussion of Badawi's theory, see Syed Al-Tawfik Al-Attas and Ng Tieh Chuan, *Abdullah Ahmad Badawi, Revivalist of an Intellectual Tradition*, Kuala Lumpur: Pelanduk, 2005.
30. Bank Negara Malaysia, *Epicentre: The MIFC eNewsletter*, November 2010.
31. See www.worldhalalforum.org.
32. See, for example, a recent interview with a top Malaysian Muslim CEO, Tor Ching Li, 'The interview: Managing in Asia: *MALAYSIA'S* CIMB Sets Sights Far, Wide' *Wall Street Journal*, 23 June 2008.
33. Clifford Geertz, 'Religious belief and economic behavior in a central Javanese town', *Economic Development and Cultural Change*, vol. 4, no. 2, 1956, pp. 134–58.
34. Clifford Geertz, *Peddlers and Princes: Social Development and Economic Change in Two Indonesian Towns*, Chicago: University of Chicago Press, 1963, p. 139.
35. Ibid.
36. Osella and Osella, 'Muslim entrepreneurs'; Blank, *Mullahs on the Mainframe*.

37. Max Weber, 'Bureaucracy', in H. H. Gerth and C. Wright Mills (eds), *From Max Weber: Essays in Sociology*, London: Routledge & Kegan Paul, 1948.

POSTFACE: ISLAMISM IS DEAD, LONG LIVE ISLAMISM

1. See Mahmood Mamdani, *Good Muslim, Bad Muslim: America, the Cold War, and the Roots of Terror*, New York: Three Leaves Press, 2005.
2. Graham Usher, 'The Reawakening of Nahda in Tunisia', *MERIP*, 30 April 2011.
3. Joshua Stacher, 'Egypt Without Mubarak', *MERIP*, 7 April 2011
4. See Frédéric Volpi, *Political Islam Observed: Disciplinary Perspectives*, New York: Columbia University Press, 2010.
5. A good illustration of this trend is Olivier Roy, *The Failure of Political Islam*, trans. Carol Volk, Cambridge, MA: Harvard University Press, 1994. See also Roy's own assessment of this predicament in this volume.
6. In relation to secularism/secularity for example see, Talal Asad, *Formations of the Secular: Christianity, Islam, Modernity*, Stanford: Stanford University Press, 2003.
7. As illustrated in this volume, these explorations cover everything from self-help Islamic manuals to scholarly theological debates, from online jihadi propaganda to Sufi discourses, from the views of classically trained Ulema to those of popular TV preachers.
8. See for example in connection to the emergence of a 'western' Muslim constituency, Tariq Ramadan, *Western Muslims and the Future of Islam*, Oxford: Oxford University Press, 2004.
9. In this respect, many of the narrative about contemporary Islamism can be seen as a reformulation of older Orientalist perspectives.
10. Daniel Lerner, *The Passing of Traditional Society: Modernizing the Middle East*, New York: Free Press, 1958.
11. See Robert W. Hefner (ed.), *Remaking Muslim Politics: Pluralism, Contestation, Democratization*, Princeton: Princeton University Press, 2004.
12. For a tentative combination of these two perspectives see, Abdullahi Ahmed An-Na'im, *Islam and the Secular State: Negotiating the Future of Sharia*, Cambridge: Harvard University Press, 2008.

# BIBLIOGRAPHY

Aba al-Khayl, Sulayman bin 'Abdallah bin Hamud, *Mawqif al-Mamlaka al-'Arabiyya al-Sa'udiyya min al-irhab: Dirasa shar'iyya 'ilmiyya watha'iqiyya* [The Position of the Kingdom of Saudi Arabia towards Terrorism: An Academic Legal Study Based on Documents], Riyad: Makatab al-Malik Fahd al-Wataniyya Athna'al-Nashr, 2003.

'Abdallah, A., *al-'Ulama' wa-l-'arsh: Thani'yya al-sulta fi-l-Sa'udiyya* [The Ulama and the Throne: The Second Power in Saudi Arabia], 3rd edn, Paris: Maktabat al-Sharq, 2004.

'Abdallah, N. I. and A. M. 'Ali Sharif, *Hurma al-ghuluw fi-l-din wa takfir al-muslimin* [*Forbidding of Extremism in Religion and the Excommunication of Muslims*], Cairo: Maktaba al-Turath al-Islami, 2002.

Abuznaid, S., 'Islam and Management: What Can Be Learned?', *Thunderbird International Business Review*, vol. 48, no. 1, 2006, pp. 125–39.

Alidou, O., *Engaging Modernity: Muslim Women and the Politics of Agency*, Madison: University of Wisconsin Press, 2009.

Alidou, O. and H. Alidou, 'Women, Religion and the discourses of legal ideology in Niger Republic', *Africa today*, vol. 54, issue 3, Spring 2008, pp. 21–36.

Amiraux, V., and G. Jonker, 'Introduction: Talking about visibility, actors, politics, forms of engagement', in V. Amiraux and G. Jonker (eds), *Politics of visibility: Young Muslims in European Public Spaces*, Bielefeld: Transcript, 2006, pp. 9–21.

al-'Aqil, 'Aqil bin 'Abd al-Rahman bin Muhammad, *al-Irhab afat al-'asr: Madha qala 'anhu al-'ulama wa-l-mashayikh wa-l-mufakkirun wa-l-tarbiyyun wa-bi-madha wa wafuhu* [Terrorism, the Bane of the Century: What Do the 'Ulama and the Shaykhs and the Thinkers and the Pedagogues Say on the Issue and How Do They Analyse It], 1st edn, Riyad: Maktaba Fahd al-Wataniyya Athna'al-Nashr, 1425/2004.

al-Attas, Syed Al-Tawfik, and Ng Tieh Chuan, *Abdullah Ahmad Badawi, Revivalist of an Intellectual Tradition*, Kuala Lumpur: Pelanduk, 2005.

al-Awadi, H., *In Pursuit of Legitimacy: The Muslim Brothers and Mubarak, 1982–2000*, London: Tauris Academic Studies, 2004.

al-'Azim, Hamdi 'Abd al-Rahman and 'Abdallah, Najih Ibrahim, *Taslit al-adwa' 'ala ma waq'a fi-l-jihad min ikhta'* [*Clarification of Mistakes in Waging the Jihad*], Cairo: Maktaba al-Turath al-Islami, 2002.

Al-Habshi, Syed Othman and Nik Mustapha Nik Hassan (eds), *Quality and Productivity*, Kuala Lumpur: IKIM, 1995.

'Ali, 'Abd al-Rahim, *al-Mukhatira fi safqa al-hukuma wa-jama'at al-'unf* [The Danger of the Deal between the Government and the Society of Violence], Cairo: Mirit li-l-Nashr wa-l-Ma'lumat, 2000.

———, *Muqamara al-Kubra: Mubadara waqf al-'unf bayn rihan al-hukuma wa-l-Jama'at al-Islamiyya* [The Great Gamble: The Initiative to End Violence between the Hostages of the Government and the Gama'at al-Islamiyya], Cairo: Markaz al-Mahrusa li-l-Nashr, 2002.

Attar, N., 'The Muslim Brotherhood's Success in the Legislative Elections in Egypt 2005: Reasons and Implications', *EuroMeSCo*, October 2006.

Audet-Gosselin, L. and M. Gomez-Perez, 'L'opposition au projet ZACA à Ouagadougou (2001–2003): feu de paille ou mutations profondes de l'Islam burkinabè?', *Revue canadienne des Études africaines*, forthcoming.

Augis, E., 'Jambaar or Jumbax-out? How Sunnite Women negotiate power and belief in Othodox Islamic Femininity', in M. Diouf and M. Leichtman (eds), *New perspectives on Islam in Senegal: Conversion, Migration, Wealth, Power and Femininity*, London: Palgrave Macmillan, 2009, pp. 210–233.

———, 'Les jeunes femmes Sunnites et la liberalization économique Dakar', *Afrique Contemporaine*, Special issue edited by J.-L. Triaud and L. Villalón, 'Économie morale et mutations de l'Islam', vol. 231, 2009, pp. 79–98.

———, 'Dakar's Sunnite Women: the Politics of Person', in M. Gomez-Perez (ed.), *L'Islam politique au sud du Sahara. Identités, discours et enjeux*, Paris: Karthala, 2005, pp. 309–326.

———, *Dakar's Sunnite Women: The Politics of Person*, PhD Dissertation, Department of Sociology, University of Chicago, Chicago, Illinois, 2002.

Bayart, J-F., 'Civil Society in Africa', in P. Chabal (ed.), *Political Domination in Africa: Reflections on the Limits of Power*, Cambridge: Cambridge University Press, 1986, pp. 109–125.

Bayat, A., *Life As Politics: How Ordinary People Change the Middle East*, Stanford: Stanford University Press, 2009.

Bazmul, Muhammad bin 'Umar bin Salim, *Takfir wa-dawabituhu* [Excommunication and its Principles], Cairo: Dar al-Tawhid wa-l-Sunna, 1428/2007.

Blank, J., *Mullahs on the Mainframe: Islam and Modernity among the Daudi Bohras*, Chicago: University of Chicago Press, 2001.

Bank Negara Malaysia, *Epicentre: The MIFC eNewsletter*, November 2010.

Binder, Leonard, *Islamic Liberalism: A Critique of Development Ideologies*, Chicago: The University of Chicago Press, 1988.

al-Birri, K., *al-Dunya ajmal min al-janna: Sira usuli Misri* [The World is Better than Paradise: Life of an Egyptian Fundamentalist], Beirut: Dar al-Nahhar li-l-Nash,. 2001.

Black, A., *The History of Islamic Political Thought: From Prophet to the Present*, Edinburgh: Edinburgh University Press, 2001.

Bonnefoy, L., 'How Transnational is Salafism in Yemen?' in R. Meijer (ed.), *Global Salafism: Islam's New Religious Movement*, London: Hurst, 2009, pp. 321–41.

Boucek, C., 'Extremist Re-education and Rehabilitation in Saudi Arabia', in T. Bjorgo and J. Horgan (eds), *Leaving Terrorism Behind: Individual and Collective Disengagement*, New York: Routledge, 2009, pp. 212–223.

Brenner, L., *Controlling Knowledge: Religion, Power and Schooling in a West African Muslim Society*, Indianapolis: Indiana University Press, 2001.

Brown, N. J., A. Hamzawy, and M. Ottaway, 'Islamist Movements and the Democratic Process in the Arab World: Exploring the Grey Zones', *Carnegie Papers*, no. 67, March 2006.

———, 'Constructing Muslim Identities in Mali', in L. Brenner (ed.), *Muslim identity and social change in sub-saharan Africa*, Indianapolis: Indiana University Press, 1993, pp. 59–77.

Brubaker, R., 'Ethnicity without groups', *Archives Européennes de Sociologie*, vol. XLIII, no. 2, 2002, pp. 163–189.

Bucholtz, M., 'Youth and cultural practice', *Annual Review of Anthropology*, vol. 31, 2002, pp. 525–552.

Buechler, S. M., 'New Social Movement Theories', *The Sociological Quarterly*, vol. 36, no. 3, 1995, pp. 441–464.

Buitelaar, M., 'Negotiating the rules of chaste behaviour: Re-interpretations of the symbolic complex of virginity by young women of Moroccan descent in the Netherlands', *Ethnic and Racial Studies*, vol. 25, no. 3, 2002, pp. 462–489.

Calvès, A. and, R. Marcoux 'Entre individualisme et communautarisme: les sociétés africaines en mutation', vol. XXXIX, no. 2, 2007, pp. 39–59 (2008 online version accessed).

Campo, J.E., *The Other Sides of Paradise: Explorations into the Religious Meanings of Domestic Spaces in Islam*, Columbia, SC: University of South Carolina Press, 1991.

Casanova, J., *Public Religions in the Modern World*, Chicago: University of Chicago Press, 1994.

———, 'Religion, European Secular Identities, and European Integration', *Eurozine.com* (2004), http://www.eurozine.com.

Cissé, I., 'Le wahhabisme au Burkina Faso: dynamique interne d'un movement Islamique réformiste', *Cahiers du CERLESHS*, tome XXIV, no. 22, juillet 2009, pp. 1–33.

———, 'Les associations de la révolution d'août 1983 à la IVe République', in *Cahiers du CERLESHS*, publication de l'université de Ouagadougou, no. 28, 2007, pp. 51–77.

Comaroff, J., *Civil Society and the Political Imagination in Postcolonial Africa: Critical perspectives*, Chicago: University of Chicago Press, 1999.

Comaroff, J. and J. Comaroff (eds), *Modernity and its Malcontents: Ritual and power in Postcolonial Africa*, University of Chicago Press, 1993.

Cooper, B., 'The Anatomy of a Riot: The Social Imagery, Single Women, and Religious Violence in Niger', *Canadian Journal of African Studies*, vol. XXXVII, nos 2–3, 2003, pp. 467–512.

Constantin, F. and C. Coulon, 'Religion et démocratie. Introduction à une problématique africaine', in Constantin, F. and C. Coulon, (eds), *Religion et transition démocratique en Afrique*, Paris: Karthala, 1997, pp. 9–24.

Coulon, C., *Les musulmans et le pouvoir en Afrique noire*, Paris: Karthala, 1983.

Chong, T., 'Malay capitalists: ambassadors for moderate Islam', *The Straits Times* (Singapore), 27 September 2004.

Cook, M., *Forbidding Wrong in Islam*, Cambridge: Cambridge University Press, 2003.

Cruise O'Brien, D., *Symbolic Confrontations: Muslims imagining the State in Africa*, London: Hurst, 2003.

Dann, U., *King Hussein and the Challenge of Arab Radicalism: Jordan, 1955–1967*, Oxford: Oxford University Press, 1989.

Denoeux, G., 'The Forgotten Swamp: Navigating Political Islam', *Middle East Policy*, vol. 9, no. 2, 2002, pp. 56–81.

Diouf, M., 'Engaging Postcolonial Cultures: African Youth and Public Space', *African Studies Review*, vol. 46, no. 1, September, 2003, pp. 1–12.

Edelman, M., 'Social Movements: Changing Paradigms and Forms of Politics', *Annual Review of Anthropology*, vol. 30, 2001, pp. 285–317.

Eickelman D. and J. Anderson, (eds), *New Media in the Muslim World: The Emerging Public Sphere*, Indianapolis: Indiana University Press, 2003.

Eickelman, D. and J. Piscatori, *Muslim Politics*, Princeton: Princeton University Press, 1996.

Eickelman, D. F. and J. Piscatori, *Muslim Politics*, Princeton: Princeton University Press, 1996.

――――, *Muslim Politics*, Princeton: Princeton University Press, 1996.

Ellis, S. and G. Ter Haar, 'Religion and Politics in Sub-Saharan Africa', *The Journal of Modern African Studies*, vol. XXXVI, no. 2, 1998, pp. 175–201.

Ephrat, D., *A Learned Society in a Period of Transition: The Sunni 'Ulama of Eleventh-Century Baghdad*, New York: SUNY Press, 2000.

Embong, A. R., *State-led Modernization and the New Middle Class in Malaysia*, Basingstoke: Palgrave, 2002.

Esposito, J. L., 'Political Islam and Gulf security', in J. L. Esposito, *Political Islam: Revolution, Radicalism, or reform?*, London: Lynne Rienner Publishers, 1997, pp. 53–74.

――――, *The Iranian Revolution: Its Global Impact*, Miami: Florida International University Press, 1990.

――――, *Islam: The Straight Path*, New York: Oxford University Press, 1988.

Euben, R. L., *Enemy in the Mirror. Islamic Fundamentalism and the Limits of Modern Rationalism: A work of Comparative Political Theory*, Princeton: Princeton University Press, 1999.

Fatton, R., 'Africa in the Age of Democratization: The Civic Limitations of Civil Society', *African Studies Review*, vol. 38, no. 2, 1995, pp. 67–100.

Fermin, A., *Nederlandse politieke partijen over minderhedenbeleid 1977–1995*, Amsterdam: Thesis Publishers, 1997.

Fischer, Johan, 'Boycott or buycott? Malay middle-class consumption post-9/11', *Ethnos*, vol. 72, no. 1, 2007, pp. 29–50.

Fraser, Nancy, 'Rethinking the Public Sphere: A Contribution to the Critique of Actually Existing Democracy', *Social Text*, vol. 25, 1990, pp. 56–80.

Gary-Tounkara, D., 'La communauté musulmane et la conquête de l'égalité politique dans la Côte d'Ivoire de l'ivoirité (1993–2000)', in M. Gomez-Perez (ed.), *L'Islam politique au sud du Sahara: Identités, discours et enjeux*, Paris: Karthala, 2005, pp. 601–620.

Geertz, C., 'Religious belief and economic behavior in a central Javanese town', *Economic Development and Cultural Change*, vol. 4, no. 2, 1956, pp. 134–58.

――――, *Peddlers and Princes: Social Development and Economic Change in Two Indonesian Towns*, Chicago: University of Chicago Press, 1963.

Gerges, F. A., *The Far Enemy: Why Jihad Went Global*, Cambridge: Cambridge University Press, 2005.

Gerlach, L.P., and V.H. Hine, *People, Power, Change: Movements of Social Transformation*, Indianapolis: Bobbs-Merill, 1970.

Giddens, A., *Modernity and Self-Identity: Self and Society in the Late Modern Age*, Stanford, CA: Stanford University Press, 1991.

Glew, R., 'A discourse-centered approach toward understanding Muslim identities in Zinder, Niger', *Islam et Sociétés au sud du Sahara*, vols 14–15, 2000–2001, pp. 99–119.

———, 'Islamic Associations in Niger', *Islam et Sociétés au sud du Sahara*, vol. 10, November 1996, pp. 187–204.

El-Ghorbashi, M., 'The Metamorphosis of the Egyptian Muslim Brothers', *International Journal of Middle East Studies*, vol. 37, no. 3, 2005, pp. 373–395.

Göle, N., 'Islam in Public: New Visibilities and New Imaginaries', *Public Culture*, vol. 14, no. 1, 2002, pp. 173–190.

Gomez-Perez, M., 'Autour de mosquées à Ouagadougou et à Dakar: lieux de sociabilité et reconfiguration des communautés musulmanes', in L. Fourchard, O. Goerg, and M. Gomez-Perez, (eds), *Lieux de sociabilité urbaine en Afrique*, Paris: L'Harmattan, 2009, pp. 405–433.

———, 'The Association des Étudiants Musulmans de l'Université de Dakar (AEMUD). Between the Local and the Global. An analysis of Discourse', *Africa today*, vol. 54, issue 3, Spring 2008, pp. 95–117.

———, *L'Islam politique au sud du Sahara. Identités, discours et enjeux*, Paris: Karthala, 2005.

———, 'Généalogie de l'Islam réformiste au Sénégal des années 50 à nos jours: figures, savoirs et réseaux', in L. Fourchard, A. Mary and R. Otayek (eds), *Entreprises religieuses transnationales en Afrique de l'Ouest*, Paris: Karthala, 2005, pp. 193–222.

———, (1997), 'Une histoire des associations Islamiques sénégalaises', Saint-Louis, Dakar, Thiès: Itinéraires, stratégies et prises de parole (1930–1993), thèse de doctorat nouveau régime, Université Paris 7-Denis Diderot, 2 tomes, 1997, p. 637.

———, 'L'Islamisme à Dakar: d'un contrôle social total à une culture du pouvoir?', *Afrika Spectrum*, vol. 29, 1994, pp. 79–98.

———, 'L'affaire des "Versets sataniques" au Sénégal. Dossier de presse', *Islam et sociétés au sud du Sahara*, vol. 4, November, 1990, pp. 173–177.

———, M. N. LeBlanc and M. Savadogo, 'Young Men and Islam in the 1990s: Rethinking an Intergenerational Perspective', *Journal of Religion in Africa*, vol. 39, no. 2, 2009, pp. 186–218.

Gomez, E. T., *Political Business: Corporate Involvement of Malaysian Political Parties*, Queensland: Centre for South-East Asian Studies, 1994.

Gomez-Perez, M. and M. N. LeBlanc, *L'Afrique d'une génération à l'autre*, Paris: Karthala, forthcoming.

Gordon, J., *Nasser's Blessed Movement: Egypt's Free Officers and the July Revolution*, Oxford: Oxford University Press, 1992.

Goussault, Y., 'Les frontières contestées du politique et du religieux dans le tiers Monde', *Tiers Monde*, July-September, no. 123, 1990, pp. 485–497.

Grégoire, E., 'Islam and The Identity of Merchants in Maradai (Niger)', Brenner, L., *Muslim identity and social Change in Sub-Saharan Africa*, Indianapolis: Indiana university Press, 1993, pp. 106–115.

Habermas, J., *The Structural Transformation of the Public Sphere*, Cambridge: MIT Press, 1989.

Haenni, Patrick, *L'ordre des caïds: Conjurer la dissidence urbaine au Caire*, Paris: Karthala, 2005.

Hegghammer, T., 'Terrorist Recruitment and Radicalisation in Saudi Arabia', *Middle East Policy*, vol. 13, no. 4, 2006, pp. 39–60.

———, 'Jihadi Salafis or Revolutionaries: On Religion and Politics in the Study of Islamist Militancy', in R. Meijer (ed.), *Global Salafism: Islam's New Religious Movement*, London: Hurst, 2009, 244–266.

Hafiz, Usama Ibrahim and 'Asim 'Abd al-Majid, *Mubadara waqf al-'unf: Ru'ya waq'iyya wa nazra shari'iyya* [*The Initiative for the Ending of Violence. Realism and Legal Theory*], Cairo: Maktaba al-Turath al-Islami, 2002.

Hamzawy, A., *Zeitgenössische politisches Denken in der arabischen Welt: Kontinuität und Wandel*, Hamburg: Schriften der Deutschen Orient-Instituts, 2005.

Hamzawy, A., and N. J. Brown, 'Can Egypt's Troubled Elections Produce a More Democratic Future?' *Policy Outlook*, Carnegie Endowment for International Peace, December 2005.

Haneef, M. A., 'Islam and economic development in Malaysia—a reappraisal', *Journal of Islamic Studies*, vol. 12, no. 3, 2001, pp. 269–90.

Hann, C., 'Problems with the (de)privatization of religion', *Anthropology Today*, vol. 16, no. 6, 2000, pp. 14–20.

Harbeson, J. et al., *Civil Society and the State in Africa*, London: Lynne Rienner Publishers, 1994.

Hassane, S., 'Les nouvelles élites Islamiques du Niger et du Nigeria du Nord. Itinéraires et prédications fondatrices (1950–2003)', L. Fourchard, A. Mary, and R. Otayek, (eds), *Entreprises religieuses et transnationales en Afrique de l'Ouest*, Paris: Karthala, 2005, pp. 373–394.

Haynes, J., *Religion and Politics in Africa*, Nairobi: East African Educational publishers Ltd., 1996.

Hefner, R., *Remaking Muslim Politics: Pluralism, Contestation, Democratization*, Princeton: Princeton University Press, 2005.

Hirschkind, C., 'Civic Virtue and Religious Reason: An Islamic Counterpublic', *Cultural Anthropology*, vol. 16, no. 1, 2001, pp. 3–34.

———, *The Ethical Soundscape: Cassette Sermons and Counterpublics*, New York: Columbia University Press, 2006.

al-Hurani, Hani, et al. (eds), *al-Harakat wa-l-Tanzimat al-Islamiyya fi al-Urdun* [Islamic Movements and Organisations in Jordan], Amman: Dar Sindbad li-l-Nashr, 1997.

Idrissa, A., 'Modèle Islamique et modèle occidental: le conflit des élites au Niger', M. Gomez-Perez (ed.), *L'Islam politique au sud du Sahara. Identités, discours, enjeux*, Paris: Karthala, 2005, pp. 345–372.

Isam Darbala, Muhammad, 'Asim 'Abd al-Majid, Najih Ibrahim, *Mithaq al-'Amal al-Islami* [Charter of Islamic Action], handwritten copy at the International Institute of Social History, Amsterdam, 1985.

Ismail, S., *Rethinking Islamist Politics: Culture, the States and Islamism*, London: I.B. Tauris, 2006.

Janelli, R. L., *Making Capitalism: The Social and Cultural Construction of a South Korean Conglomerate*, Stanford: Stanford University Press, 1993.

Jansen, J.G., *The Neglected Duty. The Creed of Sadat's Assassins and Islamic Resurgence in the Middle East*, New York: Macmillan Publishing Company, 1986.

Kaba, L., *The Wahhabiyya: Islamic reform and politics in French West Africa*, Evanston: Northwestern University Press, 1974.

Kasfir, N., 'Civil Society, the State and Democracy in Africa', *The Journal of Commonwealth and Comparative Politics*, vol. 36, no. 2, 1998, pp. 123–149.

Kennedy, J. C., and M. Valenta, 'Religious Pluralism and the Dutch state: Reflections on the future of article 23', in eds W.B.H.J. Van de Donk, A.P. Jonkers, G.J. Kronjee, and R.J.J.M. Plum (eds), *Geloven in het publieke domein. Verkenningen van een dubbele transformatie*, Amsterdam: Amsterdam University Press, 2006, pp. 337–353.

Kepel, G., *The Prophet and the Pharaoh: Muslim Extremism in Egypt*, London: Saqi Books, 1985.

Khalid, K. M., 'Voting for change? Islam and personalised politics in the 2004 general elections', in Edmund Terence Gomez (ed.), *Politics in Malaysia: The Malay Dimension*, London: Routledge, 2007.

de Koning, Martijn, *Identity in Transition: Connecting Online and Offline Internet Practices of Moroccan-Dutch Muslim Youth*, London Metropolitan University—Institute for the Study of European Transformations (ISET), 2008, http://www.londonmet.ac.uk/londonmet/library/c52116_3.pdf.

———, *Zoeken naar een 'zuivere' islam. Geloofsbeleving en identiteitsvorming van jonge Marokkaans-Nederlandse moslims*, Amsterdam: Bert Bakker, 2008.

———, 'Changing Worldviews and Friendship: An Exploration of the Life Stories of Two Female Salafists in the Netherlands', in R. Meijer (ed.), *Global Salafism: Islam's New Religious Movement*, London: Hurst, 2009, pp. 372–392.

———, 'Understanding Dutch Islam: Exploring the Relationship of Muslims with the State and the Public Sphere in the Netherlands', in H. Moghissi and H. Ghorashi (eds), *Muslim Diaspora in the West Negotiating Gender, Home and Belonging*, Burlington: Ashgate Publishing, 2010, pp. 181–197.

de Koning, M., and R. Meijer, 'Going All the Way: Politicization and Radicalization of the Hofstad Network in the Netherlands', in Assaad E. Azzi, Xenia Chryssochoou, Bernd Klandermans, and Bernd Simon (eds), *Identity and Participation in Culturally Diverse Societies: A Multidisciplinary Perspective*, Oxford: Wiley-Blackwell, 2011, pp. 220–239.

Kouanda, A., 'La lutte pour l'occupation et le contrôle des espaces réservés aux cultes à Ouagadougou', Otayek, R., F. Sawadogo, and J-P. Guingané, (ed.), *Le Burkina entre révolution et démocratie (1983–1993)*, Paris: Karthala, 1996, pp. 91–99.

Krämer, Gudrun, *Gottes Staat als Republik. Reflexionen zeitgenössischer Muslime zu Islam, Menschenrechten und Demokratie*, Baden-Baden: Nomos Verlagsgesellschaft, 1999.

———, 'Islamists Notions of Democracy', in Joel Benin and Joe Stork (eds), *Political Islam: Essays from Middle East Report*, Berkeley: University of California Press, 1997, pp. 71–82.

Lacroix, S., and T. Hegghammer, 'Rejectionist Islamism in Saudi Arabia: The Story of Juhayman al-'Utaybi Revisisted', *International Journal of Middle East Studies*, vol. 39, no. 1, 2007, pp. 103–122.

Launay, R., 'The Electronic Media and Islam among the Dyula of Northern Côte d'Ivoire', *Africa*, vol. 67, no. 3, 1997, pp. 441–453.

LeBlanc, M. N., 'Nouveaux regards sur la vie des jeunes musulmanes en Côte d'Ivoire: dynamiques de sociabilité chez les jeunes arabisantes au tournant du XXIème siècle', in L. Fourchard, O. Goerg, and M. Gomez-Perez, (eds), *Lieux de sociabilité urbaine en Afrique*, Paris: L'Harmattan, 2009, pp. 435–459.

———, '*Imaniya* and Young Muslim Women in Côte d'Ivoire', *Anthropologica*, vol. 49, 2007, pp. 35–50.

———, 'Proclaiming Individual Piety: Pilgrims and religious Renewal in Côte d'Ivoire', in A. Vered and N. Dyck, (eds), *Claiming Individuality: The cultural Politics of Distinct*, London: Pluto Press, 2006, pp. 173–200.

————, 'Hadj et changements identitaires: les jeunes musulmans d'Abidjan et de Bouaké, en Côte d'Ivoire, dans les années 1990', in M. Gomez-Perez (ed.), *L'Islam politique au sud du Sahara: Identités, discours, enjeux,* Paris: Karthala, 2005, pp. 131–157.

————, 'Between Ethnicity, Religion and Citizenship: Young Muslims in Côte d'Ivoire', in C. Coquery-Vidrobvitch et al. (eds), *Etre étranger et migrant en Afrique du XXème siècle,* vol. 1, Paris: L'Harmattan, 2003, pp. 233–258.

————, 'Fashion and the politics of identity: Versioning Womanhood and Muslimhood in the face of tradition and Modernity', *Africa,* vol. 70, no. 3, 2000, pp. 443–481.

————, 'The production on Islamic identities through knowledge claims in Bouaké, Côte d'Ivoire', *African Affairs,* vol. 98. 1999, pp. 485–508.

LeBlanc, M. N. and M. Gomez-Perez, 'Jeunes musulmans et citoyenneté culturelle: retour sur des expériences de recherche en Afrique de l'Ouest francophone', *Sociologie et Société,* 2007, Special Issue.

Lee, C. K., *Gender and the South China Miracle,* Berkeley: University of California Press, 1998.

Lijphart, A., *The Politics of Accommodation: Pluralism and Democracy in The Netherlands,* Berkeley: University of California Press, 1968.

Liow, J. C., *Piety and Politics: Islamism in Contemporary Malaysia,* (Religion and Global Politics Series), Oxford: Oxford University Press, 2009.

Lobmeyer, H. G., *Opposition und Widerstand in Syrien,* Hamburg: Deutsches Orient Institut, 1995.

Loimeier, R., '"Political Islam" in Contemporary Senegal', in M. Bröning, and H. Weiss, *Politisher Islam in West Afrika. Eine Bestandsaufnahme,* LIT, 2006, pp. 190–219.

————, 'L'Islam ne se vend plus: The Islamic reform Movement and the State in Senegal', *Journal of Religion in Africa,* vol. XXX, no. 2, 2000, pp. 168–190.

————, 'Cheikh Touré. Du réformisme à l'Islamisme, un musulman sénégalais dans le siècle', *Islam et sociétés au sud du Sahara,* vol. 8, November 1994, pp. 55–66.

al-Madkhali, Rabi'bin Hadi, *Adwa'a islamiyya 'ala 'aqida Sayyid Qutb wa fikruhu* [Islamic Light Thrown on the Creed of Sayyid Qutb and his Thought], 1413/1982.

————, *Jama'a wahida la Jama'at: Wa-sirat wahid la 'asharat* [One Group not Many Groups. One Life of the Prophet not Ten], 5th edn, United Arab Emirates: Maktabat al-Furqan, 1423/2002 (1st edn in 1995).

————, *Nasiha ila al-umma al-Jaza'iriyya sha'ban wa-hukuma* [Advice to the Algerian Nation, Its People and Its Government], 1422/2001.

————, *al-Tankil bi-ma fi al-jaj Abi al-Hasan al-ma'rabi min al-abatil*, United Arab Emirates: Maktaba al-Furqan, 1424/2003.

————, *Mudhakkira al-hadith al-nabawi fi-l-'aqida wa-l-ittiba'i* [Memoirs of the *hadith* of the Prophet in the *'aqida* and the followers], Cairo: Dar al-Manhaj, 1424/2004.

————, *Nasiha al-shaykh Rabi' li-l-salafiyyin fi Firansa*, www.rabee.net/show_des.aspx?pid=3&id=103 (no date), pp. 1–2.

al-Madkhali, Zayd bin Muhammad bin Hadi, *al-Irhab wa-atharuhu 'ala al-afrad wa-l-umam* [Terrorism and Its Influences on Individuals and Nations], United Arab Emirates: Maktabat al-Furqan,1420/2000.

Mahmood, S., 'Secularism, Hermeneutics, and Empire: The Politics of Islamic Reformation'. *Public Culture* 18, 2 (2006): 323–347.

Marsden, M., *Living Islam: Muslim Religious Experience in Pakistan's North West Frontier*, Cambridge: Cambridge University Press, 2005.

Martinez, P. A., 'The Islamic state or the state of Islam in Malaysia', *Contemporary Southeast Asia*, vol. 23, no. 3, 2001, pp. 474–503.

Masquelier, A., *Women and Islamic revival in a West African Town*, Bloomington: Indiana University Press, 2009.

————, 'Negotiating Futures: Islam, Youth, and the State in Niger', in B. F. Soares and R. Otayek, (eds), *Islam and Muslim politics in Africa*, New York: Palgrave Macmillan, 2007, pp. 243–262.

————, 'Debating Muslims, Disputed Practices: Struggles for the Realization of an Alternative Moral Order in Niger', in J. L. Comaroff and J. Comaroff (eds), *Civil Society and the Political Imagination in Africa*, Chicago: University of Chicago Press, 1999, pp. 219–250.

————, 'Identity, alterity and ambiguity in a Nigerien community: Competing definitions of "true" Islam', in R. Werbner and R. Ranger, *Postcolonial Identities in Africa*, London: Zed Books, 1996, pp. 222–244.

Maussen, M., *Constructing Mosques: The Governance of Islam in France and the Netherlands*, Amsterdam: Amsterdam School for Social Science Research (ASSR), PhD thesis, 2009.

Meijer, R., '"The Cycle of Contention" and the Limits of Terrorism in Saudi Arabia', in P. Aarts and G. Nonneman (eds), *Saudi Arabia in the Balance: Political Economy, Society, Foreign Affairs*, London: Hurst, 2005, pp. 271–311.

————, 'Muslim Politics under Occupation: The Association of Muslim Scholars and the Politics of Resistance in Iraq', *Arab Studies Journal*, vols 13–14, nos 2–1, 2005, pp. 93–112.

————, 'Sunni Factions and the Political Process', in M. Bouillon et al. (eds), *Iraq: Preventing a New Generation of Conflict*, Boulder: Lynne Rienner, 2007, pp. 89–108.

———, 'Yusuf al-'Uyairi, and the Making of a Revolutionary Salafi Praxis', *Die Welt des Islams*, vol 47, nos 3–4, 2007, pp. 422–59.

———, 'Introduction', in R. Meijer (ed.), *Global Salafism: Islam's New Religious Movement*, London: Hurst, 2009, pp. 1–32.

———, 'Commanding Good and Forbidding Wrong as a Form of Social Action: The Case of the Jama'a al-Islamiyya', in R. Meijer (ed.), *Global Salafism: Islam's New Religious Movement*, London: Hurst, 2009, pp. 189–220.

———, 'Naar een politieke islam', in Sipco Vellenga, et al. (eds), *Mist in de polder: Zicht op ontwikkeling omtrent de islam in Nederland*, Amsterdam: Aksant, 2009, pp. 31–46.

———, 'Salafism: Doctrine and Practice', in K. Hroub (ed.), *Political Islam: Context versus Ideology*, London: Saqi Books, 2010, pp. 37–60.

———, 'The Muslim Brotherhood and the Political: An Exercise in Ambiguity', in R. Meijer and E. Bakker (eds), *The Muslim Brotherhood in Europe: Burdens of the Past, Challenges of the Future*, London: Hurst, 2011 (forthcoming).

Melucci, A., 'Getting Involved: Identity and Mobilization in Social Movements', *International Social Movement Research: From Structure to Action*, vol. 1, 1988, pp. 329–348.

Meunier, O., *Dynamique de l'enseignement Islamique au Niger*, Paris: L'Harmattan, 1997.

Meijer, Roel, 'Introduction: Genealogies of Salafism', in Roel Meijer (ed.), *Global Salafism: Islam's New Religious Movement*, London: Hurst, 2009, pp. 1–32.

Meyer, B. and A. Moors, *Religion, Media and the Public Sphere*, Indianapolis: Indiana University Press, 2006.

Milner, Anthony, *The Malays*, Oxford: Wiley-Blackwell, 2008.

Milton-Edwards, B., *Islamic Politics in Palestine*, London: I.B. Tauris, 1996.

Miran, M., *Islam, histoire et modernité en Côte d'Ivoire*, Paris: Karthala, 2006.

———, 'Vers un nouveau prosélytisme Islamique en Côte d'Ivoire: une révolution discrète', *Autrepart*, vol. 16, 2000, pp. 139–160.

Mitchell, R., *The Society of the Muslim Brothers*, 2nd edn, Oxford: Oxford University Press, 1993.

Mohamad, M., 'Towards a developed and industrialized society: understanding the concept, implications and challenges of Vision 2020', Speech reprinted in Ahmad Sarji Abdul Hamid (ed.), *Malaysia's Vision 2020*, Kuala Lumpur: Pelanduk, 1993.

Moors, A., *'Muslim cultural politics': What's Islam got to do with it?* Amsterdam: Vossiuspers UvA, 2004.

———, '"Islamic Fashion" in Europe: Religious conviction, aesthetic style, and creative consumption', *Encounters*, vol. 1, no. 1, 2009, pp. 175–201.

————, 'The Dutch and the face-veil: The politics of discomfort', *Social Anthropology*, vol. 17, no. 4, 2009, pp. 393–408.

Mubarak, Hisham, *al-Irhabiyyun qadimun! Dirasa muqarana bayn mawqif al-Ikhwan al-Muslimin wa Jama'at al-Jihad min qadiya al-'unf, 1928–1994* [The Terrorists Are Coming. A Comparative Study of the Views of the Muslim Brotherhood and the Jihad Society on the Issue of Violence, 1928–1994], Cairo: Kitab al-Mahrusa, 1995.

Nagata, J., 'Religious correctness and the place of Islam in Malaysia's economic politics', in Timothy and Hy Van Luong (eds), *Culture and Economy: The Shaping of Capitalism in Eastern Asia*, Brook, Ann Arbor: University of Michigan Press.

Niandou Souley, A. and G. Alzouma, 'Islamic Renewal in Niger: from Monolith to Plurality', *Social Compass*, vol. 43, no. 2, 1996, pp. 249–265.

Niandou Souley, A.S., 'Les 'licenciés du Caire' et l'État du Niger', R. Otayek, (ed.), *Le radicalisme Islamique au sud du Sahara. Da'wa, arabisation et critique de l'Occident*, Paris: Karthala, 1993, pp. 213–252.

Noorhaidi, H., 'Ambivalent Doctrines and Conflicts in the Salafi Movement in Indonesia', in R. Meijer (ed.) *Global Salafism: Islam's New Religious Movement*, London: Hurst, 2009, pp. 169–188.

Osella, F. and C. Osella, 'Muslim entrepreneurs in public life between India and the Gulf: making good and doing good', *Journal of the Royal Anthropological Institute*, vol. 15, no. 1, 2009, pp. S202–S221.

Otayek, R., *Identité et démocratie dans un monde global*, Paris: Presse de Science Po, 2000.

————, 'L'Islam et la révolution au Burkina Faso: mobilisation politique et reconstruction identitaire', *Social Compass*, vol. 43, no. 2, 1996, pp. 233–247.

————, 'Une relecture Islamique du projet révolutionnaire de Thomas Sankara', in Bayart, J-F. (ed.), *Religion et modernité politique en Afrique noire*, Paris: Karthala, 1993, pp. 101–127.

————, 'L'affirmation élitaire des arabisants au Burkina Faso. Enjeux et contradictions', in Otayek, R., (ed.), *Le radicalisme Islamique au sud du Sahara. Da'wa, arabisation et critique de l'Occident*, Paris: Karthala, 1993, pp. 229–252.

Othman, N., 'Religion, citizenship rights and gender justice', in N. Othman, M. C. Puthucheary and C. Kessler (eds), *Sharing the Nation. Faith, Difference, Power and the State 50 Years After Merdeka*, Petaling Jaya, Malaysia: Strategic Information and Research Development Center, 2008.

Piga, A., 'Neo-traditionalist Islamic associations and the Islamist press in contemporary Senegal', in Biershenk, T. and G. Stauth (eds), *Yearbook of the Sociology of Islam*, vol. 4, Hamburg: LIT, 2002, pp. 47–68.

Price, C., D. Nonini, and E. F. Tree, 'Grounded Utopian Movements: Subjects of Neglect', *Anthropological Quarterly*, vol. 81, no. 1, 2008, pp. 127–159.

Qutb, Sayyid, *Milestones*, Damascus: Dar al-Ilm, no date.

bin Rajaa'as-Sihaymee, Abdu al-Salam bin Salim, *The Ideology of Terrorism and Violence in the Kingdom of Saudi Arabia: Its Origins. The Reasons for its Spread and Solution* (transl. by AbdulHaq IT for SalafiManhaj, 2007).

al-Rasheed, M., *Contesting the Saudi State: Islamic Voices from a New Generation*, Cambridge: Cambridge University Press, 2007.

Rashwan, D., *Muslim Brotherhood in Egypt* (no date), www.ikhwanweb. com [Last accessed: May 2007].

Reissner, J., *Ideologie und Politik der Muslimbruder Syriens. Von den Wahlen 1947 bis zum Verbot undetr Adib as-Shishakli 1952*, Freiburg: Klaus Schwarz Verlag, 1980.

Rosander, E.E. 1997, 'The Islamization of "Tradition" and "Modernity"', in D. Westerlund and E. E. Rosander (eds), *African Islam and Islam in Africa*, London: Hurst, pp. 1–27.

Roy, Olivier, *The Failure of Political Islam*, London: I.B. Tauris, 1992.

———, 'Le post-Islamisme', *Revue des mondes musulmans et de la Méditerranée*, vols 85–86, 1999, pp. 11–30.

———, 'Le néo-fondamentalisme Islamique ou l'imaginaire de l'oumah', *Esprit*, April 1996, pp. 80–107.

———, *L'échec de l'Islam politique*, Paris: Seuil, 1992.

———, 'De l'Islam révolutionnaire au néofondamentalisme', *Esprit*, July-August 1990, pp. 5–14.

Rooden, P., *Religieuze regimes: Over godsdienst en maatschappij in Nederland 1570–1990*, Amsterdam: Bert Bakker, 1996.

Roussillon, A., 'L'Occident dans l'imaginaire des hommes et des femmes du Machreq et du Maghreb', in *Revue Vingtième siècle*, 'Islam et politique en Méditerranée au 20ème siècle', April/June, no. 82, 2004, pp. 69–79.

Rudnyckyj, D., 'Spiritual economies: Islam and neoliberalism in contemporary Indonesia', *Cultural Anthropology*, vol. 24, no. 1, 2009, pp. 104–141.

Rutherford, B. K., 'What Do Egypt's Islamist Want? Moderate Islam and the Rise of Islamic Constitutionalism', *Middle East Journal*, vol. 60, no. 4, 2006, pp. 707–31.

Salafi Publications *'The Brothers of the Devils': Islamic Condemnation of Terrorists, Hijakers & Suicide Bombers*, Birmingham: Salafi Publications, 2003.

Salvatore, A., 'Staging Virtue: The Disembodiment of Self-Correctness and the Making of Islam as a Public Norm'. in G. Stauth (ed.), *Islam: Motor or Challenge of Modernity*, Hamburg: LIT, 1998, pp. 87–120.

Samson, F., 'Islam, Protest, and Citizen Mobilization: New Sufi Movements', in M. Diouf and M. Leichtman (eds), *New Perspectives on Islam in Senegal: Conversion, Migration, Wealth, Power and Femininity*, London: Palgrave, 2009, pp. 257–272.

———, *Les Marabouts de l'Islam politique. Le Dahiratoul Moustarchidina Wal Moustarchitady, un mouvement néo-confrérique sénégalais*, Paris: Karthala, 2005.

Sanankoua, B. and L. Brenner (eds), *L'enseignement Islamique au Mali*, Jamana: Bamako, 1991.

Savadogo, M., 'L'intervention des associations musulmanes dans le champ politique en Côte d'Ivoire depuis 1990', M. Gomez-Perez (ed.), *L'Islam politique au Sud du Sahara: identités, discours et enjeux*, Paris: Karthala, 2005, pp. 583–600.

Schinkel, W., 'The Virtualization of Citizenship', *Critical Sociology*, vol. 36, no. 2, 2010, pp. 265–283.

Schulz, D., '(Re)Turning to Proper Muslim Practice: Renewal and Women's Conflicting Assertions of Sunni Identity in Urban Mali', *Africa today*, vol. 54, issue 4, Summer 2008, pp. 21–43.

———, 'Morality, Community, Publicness: Shifting Terms of Public Debate In Mali', in B. Meyer and A. Moors (eds), *Religion, Media and the Public Sphere*, Indianapolis: Indiana university Press, 2006, pp. 132–151.

———, 'Promises of (im)mediate salvation: Islam, broadcast media, and the remaking of religious experience in Mali', *American Ethnologist*, vol. 33, no. 2, 2006, pp. 210–229.

———, 'Political Factions, Ideological Fictions: The controversy over Family Law reform in Democratic Mali', *Islamic Law and society*, vol. 10, no. 1, 2003, pp. 132–164.

———, 'Charisma and Brotherhood revisited: Mass-mediated forms of spirituality in Urban Mali', *Journal of Religion in Africa*, vol. 33, no. 2, 2003, pp. 146–171.

———, *Islam and the Prayer Economy, History and Authority in a Malian Town*, London: Edinburg University Press, 2005.

———, 'Islam in Mali in the Neoliberal Era', *African Affairs*, 105/418, 2005, pp. 77–95.

———, 'Islam and Public Piety in Mali', in A. Salvatore and D. F. Eickelman, *Public Islam and the Common Good*, Leiden: Brill, 2004, pp. 205–226.

Sharif, 'Ali Muhammad 'Ali, and Usama Ibrahim Hafiz, *al-Nashr wa-l-tabayyun fi tashih mafahim al-muhtasibin* [*Advise and Clarification in the Correction of the Concepts of the Overseers*], Cairo: Maktaba al-Turath al-Islami, 2002.

Sloane, P., *Islam, Modernity and Entrepreneurship Among the Malays*, Basingstoke: Palgrave, 1999.

Soares, B. and R. Otayek (eds), *Islam and Muslim Politics in Africa*, New York: Palgrave Macmillan, 2007.

Sounaye, A., 'Izala au Niger: une alternative de communauté religieuse', in L. Fourchard, O. Goerg and M. Gomez-Perez (eds), *Lieux de sociabilité urbaine en Afrique*, Paris: L'Harmattan, 2009, pp. 481–500.

———, 'Islam, Etat et Société: à la recherche d'une éthique publique', in O. Otayek and B. Soares (eds), *Islam, Etat et Société en Afrique*, Paris: Karthala, 2009, pp. 327–352.

———, 'Les politiques de l'Islam dans l'ère de la démocratisation de 1991 à 2002', in M. Gomez-Perez (ed.)., *L'Islam politique au sud du Sahara. Identités, discours et enjeux*, Paris: Karthala, 2005, pp. 503–525.

Sreberny-Mohammadi, A. and A. Mohammadi, *Small Media, Big Revolution: Communication, Culture and the Iranian Revolution*, Minneapolis: University of Minnesota Press, 1994.

Syrian Muslim Brotherhood, *Jama'a al-Ikhwan al-Muslimin fi Suriya 'ala Masharif al-Alfiya al-Thalitha li-l-Milad. Tajarib wa Tatall'at*, [The Society of the Muslim Brothers in Syria on the Eve of the 21st Century. Experiences and Aims], 2000, www.ikhwan-muslimoon-syria.org/01ikhwan-syria/tajarub.htm.

———, *al-Mithaq al-Sharaf al-Watani fi Suriya* [The Noble National Charter in Syria], 2001, www.ikhwan-muslimoon-syria.org/04malaffat_nasharat/mithak2.htm.

———, *al-Mashru' al-Siyasi li-Suriya al-Mustaqbal* [The Political Project for Syria], 2004, www.ikhwan-muslimoon-syria.org.

al-Tartusi, Abu Basir, *Mubadara al-Jama'at al-Islamiyya al-Misriyya: 'I'tiraf bi-l-khita' am inhiyar wa-suqut* [The Egyptian Jama'a al-Islamiyya: Acknowledgement of their Mistakes or Their Annihilation and Fall], www.tawhed.ws (no date).

———, *Wa la-na kilmat nazra shar'iyya li-Mithaq al-Sharaf al-Watani alladhi tarahahu al-Ikhwan al-Muslimun al-Suriyyun* [Our Theoretical Analysis of the Noble National Charter on the Basis of the Shar'iyya], www.tawhed.ws (no date).

———, *Hay'at 'Ulama al-Muslimin fi mizan al-tawhid wa-l-jihad* [The Association of Muslim Scholars in the light (balance) of Unity of God and Jihad], www.tawhed.ws (no date).

Tor Ching Li, 'The interview: Managing in Asia: *MALAYSIA'S* CIMB Sets Sights Far, Wide', *Wall Street Journal*, 23 June 2008.

Traoré, B., 'Islam et politique à Bobo-Dioulasso de 1940 à 2002', in M. Gomez-Perez (ed.), *L'Islam politique au sud du Sahara. Identités, discours, enjeux*, Paris: Karthala, 2005, pp. 417–447.

Triaud, J.-L., 'Le mouvement réformiste en Afrique de l'Ouest dans les années 1950', *Mémoires du CERMAA*, vol. 1, 1979, pp. 195–212.

Trofimov, Y., 'Borrowed Ideas: Malaysia transforms rules for finance under Islam', *Wall Street Journal*, 4 April 2007.

Tuğal, C., 'Transforming everyday life: Islamism and social movement theory', *Theoretical Sociology*, vol. 38, 2009, pp. 423–458.

Utvik, B. O., *The Pious Road to Development. Islamist Economics in Egypt*, London: Hurst, 2006.

al-'Uyairi, Y., *Tawajud al-Amrika fi al-Jazira al-'Arabiyya: Haqiqa wa-ahdaf* [The Presence of America on the Arabian Peninsula: Truth and Goals] (no date).

———, *al-Mizans li-haraka Taliban* [The Taliban Movement in the Balance] (no date).

———, *Hal intaharat Hawwa am istashhadat? Bahth mutawwal fi hukm al-'amaliyyat al-ishtishhadiyya* [Has Eve Committed Suicide or Has She Martyred Herself? Elaborate Study on Martyrdom Operations] (no date).

———, *'Amaliya "al-Masrah fi Moscow": Madha rabh minha al-mujahidun wa madha khasaru?* [The 'Moscow Theatre' operation: What is the Benefit of it for the Mujahidun and what did They Lose?] (no date).

———, *Ma hakadha al-'adl ya fadila al-shaykh! Difa'an 'an Jama'a Abi Sayyaf al-Filbiniyya* [This is Not Justice, Oh Honoured Shaykh. In Defence of the Society of Abu Sayyaf of the Philippines] (no date).

———, *al-'Iraq wa-l-Jazira al-'Arabiyya* [Iraq and the Arabian Peninsula] (no date).

———, *Silsilat al-harb al-salabiyya 'ala al-Iraq* [The Series of the Crusader War] 2003.

———, *Munasahat Salman al-'Awda* [Advise to Salman al-'Awda] (no date).

———, *Thawabit 'ala darb al-jihad* [Principles of Jihad] (no date).

———, *Hukm al-jihad wa-anwa'ihi* [The pronouncement of Jihad and its Forms] (no date).

Vidino, L., 'The Hofstad Group: The New Face of Terrorist Networks in Europe', *Studies in Conflict & Terrorism*, vol. 30, no. 7, 2007, pp. 579–592.

Villalon, L., 'The Moral and the Political in African Democratization: The *Code de la famille* in Niger's Troubled Transition', *Democratization*, vol. III, no. 2, 1996, pp. 41–68.

———, 'Generational Changes, Political Stagnation and the evolving Dynamics of religion and Politics in Senegal', *Africa today*, Summer/ Autumn, vol. 46, nos 3–4, 1999, pp. 129–147.

———, 'ASR Focus: Islamism in West Africa: Senegal', *African Studies Review*, vol. 47, no. 2, September 2004, pp. 61–71.

Wagemakers, J., 'A Purist Jihadi-Salafi: The Ideology of Abu Muhammad al-Maqdisi', *British Journal of Middle Eastern Studies*, vol. 36, no. 2, 2009, pp. 281–297.

———, *A Quietist Jihadi-Salafi: The Ideology and Influence of Abu Muhammad al-Maqdisi*, Nijmegen: Radboud University Nijmegen, 2010.

Warner, M., 'Public and Counterpublics', *Public Culture*, vol. 14, no. 1, 2002, 97–114.

Weber, M., 'Bureaucracy', in H.H. Gerth and C. Wright Mills (eds), *From Max Weber: Essays in Sociology*, London: Routledge & Kegan Paul, 1948.

Westerlund, D., 'Reaction and Action: Accounting for the rise of Islamism', in D. Westerlund and E. E. Rosander (eds), *African Islam and Islam in Africa: Encounters between Sufis and Islamists*, Ohio: Ohio University Press, 1997, pp. 308–333.

Wiktorowicz, Q., *The Management of Islamic Activism. Salafis, the Muslim Brotherhood, and State Power in Jordan*, New York: SUNY Press, 2001.

Wilson, Rodney, 'Islam and Malaysia's economic development', *Journal of Islamic Studies*, vol. 9, no. 2, 1998, pp. 259–76.

———, 'Anatomy of the Salafi Movement', *Studies in Conflict and Terrorism*, vol. 29, 2006, pp. 207–239.

Young, C., 'In Search of Civil Society', in Harbeson, J. et al., (eds), *Civil Society and the State in Africa*, London: Lynne Rienner Publishers, 1994, pp. 33–50.

Yusoff, Nik Mohamed Affandi bin Nik, *Islam and Wealth*, Kuala Lumpur: Pelanduk, 2002, pp. 10–11.

# INDEX